Other People's Colleges

OTHER PEOPLE'S COLLEGES

THE ORIGINS OF AMERICAN HIGHER EDUCATION REFORM

Ethan W. Ris

The University of Chicago Press

Chicago and London

The University of Chicago Press, Chicago 60637

The University of Chicago Press, Ltd., London

© 2022 by The University of Chicago

Published 2022

Printed in the United States of America

31 30 29 28 27 26 25 24 23 22   1 2 3 4 5

ISBN-13: 978-0-226-82019-4 (cloth)
ISBN-13: 978-0-226-82022-4 (paper)
ISBN-13: 978-0-226-82023-1 (e-book)
DOI: https://doi.org/10.7208/chicago/9780226820231.001.0001

The University of Chicago Press gratefully acknowledges the generous support of the University of Nevada, Reno, toward the publication of this book.

Library of Congress Cataloging-in-Publication Data

Names: Ris, Ethan W., author.
Title: Other people's colleges : the origins of American higher education reform / Ethan W. Ris.
Other titles: Origins of American higher education reform
Description: Chicago ; London : The University of Chicago Press, 2022. | Includes bibliographical references and index.
Identifiers: LCCN 2021054637 | ISBN 9780226820194 (cloth) | ISBN 9780226820224 (paperback) | ISBN 9780226820231 (ebook)
Subjects: LCSH: Education, Higher—United States—History—20th century. | Educational change—United States—History—20th century.
Classification: LCC LA227.1 .R57 2022 | DDC 378.7309/04—dc23/ eng/20211106
LC record available at https://lccn.loc.gov/2021054637

♾ This paper meets the requirements of ANSI/NISO Z39.48-1992 (Permanence of Paper).

For Liana

CONTENTS

INTRODUCTION

In recent years, "higher education policy" has been synonymous with "higher education reform." A consensus unites business, government, foundations, and political sentiment from across the spectrum: American colleges and universities must change. To earn the right to survive, they must become more efficient, more accountable, and more useful to both students and society.

We have been here before. In the early twentieth century, a powerful cohort of elite reformers operating under the mantle of philanthropy worked in sync to transform American higher education. They called for sweeping changes in the sector and raised existential questions about its sustainability. And while they fell short of their goals, they left indelible marks on the sector.

Because of these reformers, we can speak of an American *system* of higher education, and we can recognize core components of that system that they introduced: the community college, the flagship university, extension services, and much more. We can also recognize ideas that the reformers brought into the system: that higher education must be efficient and practical, that it must be accountable to the public interest (expressed through government and foundations), that funding can be sought from sources other than students and alumni, and that colleges and universities exist within a self-evident status hierarchy that helps organize American society.

But that's not all. We can also speak of infrastructure and ideas that emerged out of a broad *resistance* to the reformers. That resistance came from a coalition of academics, religious leaders, journalists, politicians, and advocates for marginalized communities, and from hundreds of low-status higher education institutions that felt threatened by top-down reform. They established protective interinstitutional associations and the accreditation process, and they preserved the universal liberal arts curriculum. They also enshrined ideas like academic freedom, institutional autonomy, and the distinctive openness of American higher education—

the notion that any student can aspire to earn a bachelor's degree and that any institution can aspire to elite status.

In this book, I examine all of these effects and many more. I also offer an in-depth view of the people who led the charge for reform, the organizations they formed to pursue it, the people who opposed them, and the schools that served as the objects of both a fierce disputation and, eventually, a new consensus about the role of higher education in American society.

The policies and initiatives I analyze here came from outside of the campus bubble. Many scholars have recognized that contestation has been a key shaper of educational institutions; here, I argue emphatically for the importance of *external* contestation in the formative years of American higher education. And by that adjective, I mean not just external to individual campuses but external to the larger community of colleges and universities. My intervention is to show that long before the modern era, the sea of institutional influences on higher education—the sector's "organizational field"—included external actors like foundations, the business community, and the state.[1] Campus politics matter, but external ideas and programs, often tied to money or status, have been the primary drivers of reform.

The ideas and programs, as well as the money and status, came primarily from two philanthropic foundations that typically show up as side notes in the historiography of higher education. However, their significance is enormous. The wealthiest and most influential capitalists in history endowed them with the modern-day equivalent of billions of dollars; they received the blessings of the federal government; the leaders of the nation's most elite universities oversaw them; and a groundswell of enmity and resistance rose up against them. And more: these were the first true foundations in history. They established not only the idea that the nonprofit sector could have an agenda for higher education but that it could have an agenda about *anything*.

The fact that the initiatives these foundations pushed did not work out as planned does not make them any less important. Their failure, despite tremendous wealth and power, is important in and of itself. To that end, this book offers two core contributions. The first is the surprising history of how a tight-knit group of reformers precipitated so much of what we take for granted about higher education today. The second is an implicit message of faith to people and institutions today who fear external topdown reform as a novel existential threat. Yes, it poses a challenge, but it is not new, and it is not unyielding. This type of reform has been a part of American higher education for more than a century, and colleges and universities have long since found ways to live with it, assimilate it, divert it, and subvert it.

The Narrative

What follows plays out over a three-part chronological arc, comprising an early period in which ideas about higher education reform were emerging (1890–1905); a pivotal "crucible of reform" when the foundations were established and had their greatest effect (1905–1915); and an extended period in which the initiatives launched in the previous decade were either beaten back or assimilated into a new consensus that emerged among the reformers and their many detractors (1915–1936). The three sections of the book only tenuously follow the timeline, however; sections one and two focus on the reformers' ideas and efforts up through 1920 while section three focuses on the resistance to reform that emerged around 1908.

The events that drive this book's narrative depended on four contingent conditions that were in place before 1890, only one of which had direct implications for education. The first was the accumulation and disbursement of Gilded Age wealth. The reformers were bankrolled by the Carnegie and Rockefeller fortunes: unprecedented accumulations of private money that demanded to be spent on something beyond personal luxury.[2] The second and third contingencies were the rise of two bodies of ideas that appealed to the nouveau riche: a nationwide obsession with industrialization, especially expressed through the emerging field of engineering, and a movement to reshape society along supposedly scientific lines—a project commonly described as "social Darwinism."[3]

These circumstances and interests created a classic "solution in search of a problem."[4] Rich people had newly found money, and they wanted to use it to apply engineering logic to social issues. That solution would eventually find many problems, but the first one it settled on emerged out of the fourth contingency: the success of the nineteenth-century common school movement, followed by the success of the high school movement, which created a swell of educated young people, including women, immigrants, and minoritized racial and ethnic communities.[5] These new entrants wanted to go to college, and hundreds of colleges across the land were eager to give them that chance. But the reformers had different ideas.

On that note, the battles I describe in this book were waged over the second part of that dyad: institutions, not students. The big foundations sought to cull the herd of American colleges, to limit their revenue and ambitions, and to curb their degree offerings. Those restrictions, of course, would necessarily constrain the opportunities available to students, especially new entrants. But the reformers never dwelled on this fact. In return, when resistance emerged at the end of the crucible of reform, it came in defense of institutions, especially low-status ones. These colleges, of course, served low-status students, but again, students were rarely the object of resistance.

Targeting institutions let the reformers seem less heartless and more businesslike, which suited their origins and their conception of the world. This is the theme of my book's first section, two chapters that document the *ethos of reform.*

I open with an overview of the reformist cohort, who were influenced both by the business orientation of their benefactors and by the logic of engineering, which was itself informing American business. Because of this, I call the reformers the "academic engineers."[6] Borrowing the language and ethos of engineering, these individuals were united in their desire to reshape the landscape of American colleges and universities into a coherent system governed by efficiency and tended by "expert" managers (i.e., themselves). Their mechanisms to do so were two philanthropic foundations explicitly set up for higher education reform and backed by money derived from engineering-dependent businesses: the General Education Board (GEB), endowed by John D. Rockefeller, and the Carnegie Foundation for the Advancement of Teaching (CFAT), endowed by Andrew Carnegie.

Those philanthropists never went to college. The academic engineers who ran their foundations typically did, but those administrators also positioned themselves as external to American higher education. We can often spot the academic engineers by their self-styled "outsider" status, pointing to their humble origins on the periphery of nineteenth-century American society or, conversely, to their experience in Europe, especially graduate study in German universities. Their externality was further cemented by their use of the foundations as devices for top-down control. Even though many of the academic engineers were the presidents of elite universities, when they met together as the GEB or the CFAT board, they were not making decisions for their exclusive club but rather for the hundreds of lower-status schools without seats at the table. Furthermore, others had no formal connections to higher education. Like Carnegie and Rockefeller, they were purportedly disinterested reformers who chose to focus their energy on changing colleges. In addition to framing the cohort, in the first chapter I explain the origins of the two intertwined foundations and offer portraits of some exemplary academic engineers.

The second chapter examines the overarching goals of the academic engineers' reform project: establishing normative and coercive control over colleges and universities and using that control to reduce their numbers and maximize efficiency. Their ideas came directly from the prevailing economic theory of the turn of the twentieth century, which maintained that market-based competition was wasteful and potentially ruinous. The answer, both in business and in the foundations' plans for higher education, was systemization and centralized control. The reformers' strategies toward these goals included picking winners and losers among colleges, encouraging consolidation between neighboring institutions, and creating a new institution called the "junior college" (today's community college) to serve as a consolation prize for "loser" schools. They also fought against existing systems of control, especially the religious denominations that had oversight over most private colleges at the turn of the century.

The book's next section comprises three chapters on the *program of reform*. Here, I show how the academic engineers tried to shape a system by promoting and demoting colleges, how they boosted sub-baccalaureate institutions in the name of "practical" postsecondary education for the masses, and how they tried to limit the educational prospects of women, religious and ethnic minorities, and people of color.

In the first of these chapters, I focus on the academic engineers' efforts to build systemic hierarchies, which they viewed as mechanisms to cement efficiency and noncompetition between colleges and universities. A hallmark of these imagined hierarchies was the limitation of university status, and even baccalaureate status, to the top tiers of an institutional pyramid. The first half of the chapter examines national or regional-level reform projects in the name of this idea, including the use of the federal bureaucracy or a proposed National University to exert top-down control from Washington. The second half turns to case studies of four states— Mississippi, Ohio, California, and Iowa—in which the reformers and their allies attempted to establish formal institutional hierarchies, with varying degrees of failure.

The fourth chapter continues the theme of limiting access to the more esteemed parts of higher education (especially the bachelor's degree) but turns away from the academic engineers' efforts to delimit existing institutions. My focus here is the reformers' promotion of new types of "practical" postsecondary schooling. I analyze several of these new or newly embraced forms: normal schools, land-grant colleges, junior colleges, university extension divisions, and technical schools. All of these owed a debt to highly visible ideas in adult education, including manual training and the Chautauqua movement, as well as to the translation of the harsher implications of social Darwinism into the less threatening assertion that not all students are "college material."

In the fifth chapter, I show how that assertion was a real threat after all, especially when it was applied to marginalized students. I explain how the academic engineering agenda played out for women, religious minorities, African Americans, and Appalachians. In each case, the reformers sought to exclude the bulk of students from these groups from accessing mainstream higher education and instead tried to redirect them to sub-baccalaureate schools. This chapter marks the narrative's turning point by showing how members of those marginalized groups pushed back on the reformers and began to gain the privileges that had been denied to them because of their backgrounds and identities.

That shift leads into the book's final section, three chapters that present an account of the *decline of reform*. Here, I explain the wave of resistance that rose up against the academic engineers, the creation of organizations designed to claw away power from the foundations, and the surprising consensus about the form and function of higher education that emerged by the 1930s.

The sixth chapter explains the widespread hostility to academic engineering that first became apparent in 1908. It came from many sectors: religious leaders, proponents of local control, professors, journalists, defenders of liberal arts colleges, defenders of Black colleges, and students (especially students at Black colleges). This pushback was disorganized but highly visible, and it effectively raised public scrutiny of the reformers and set the stage for their fall from power and prominence.

In the seventh chapter, I show how informal resistance became organized defiance around 1915. A number of organizations formed almost simultaneously, each of them seeking either to directly challenge the academic engineers or to claw back authority from them. These included the Association of American Colleges; the American Association of University Professors; groups of normal schools, women's colleges, Black colleges, and junior colleges; and regional accreditation bodies. None of these groups brought down the reformers, but they forced them to make concessions, give up programs, and come to the table of compromise (which in part took the form of a new umbrella association: the American Council on Education).

The book's final chapter describes the end of academic engineering, which sustained some direct blows at the end of the crucible of reform but did not truly leave the scene until the end of a long fade in the '20s and early '30s. I explain what happened to the GEB and the CFAT as well as to the various types of colleges they sought to repress. I also describe the novel consensus that emerged out of the battles of the previous decades: that social efficiency and liberal learning could be bedfellows and that a liberal education at an autonomous institution was the ideal locus for crafting economically productive, democratic citizens. This new consensus came with a new ethos. Instead of efficiency, higher education in the decades following 1936 would be organized around "uplift": the idea that going to college could improve people and that therefore it was wrong to limit anyone's ambition—either the ambition of a student to earn a bachelor's degree or the ambition of a postsecondary institution to *offer* bachelor's degrees.

Four Conversations

With this book, I hope to contribute to four bodies of literature. The first is the most obvious: the history of American higher education. Many of the events and individuals I discuss will be familiar to my fellow historians. Certainly the decades around the turn of the twentieth century have been described as pivotal by many of the seminal books in the field.[7] But I am telling a different version of the story. Much has been written about how William Rainey Harper shaped the University of Chicago, how Nicholas Murray Butler shaped Columbia, and how Woodrow Wilson shaped Princeton. Those stories are important, but they do not reflect the external contestation at the heart of my argument. I am much more interested in Harper's involvement with Kalamazoo College, Butler's with Seth Low Junior College, Wilson's with Berea College, and in the GEB's and the CFAT's involvement with hundreds of other lower-tier institutions. This book is also not about what John Thelin calls the "reform contingents [who] were comparable to teams of termites, each working industriously beneath the surface of campus life to topple the dominant structures."[8] My focus is external reform, specifically *top-down* reform. While I detail many bottom-up efforts that emanated from students, professors, and the leaders of low-status institutions, they are examples of people trying to preserve or grow their institutions, not fundamentally transform them.

Furthermore, much of the historiography of American higher education is predominantly the history of Chicago, Columbia, Princeton, and other elite universities. There is no doubt that these places are enormously important, but as Philo Hutcheson argues, paring the study of American higher education to "the mission and structure of the research university is using Occam's razor far too quickly."[9] This book centers on non-elite institutions including technical schools, teachers colleges, land-grant institutions, historically Black colleges, community colleges, and low-tier liberal arts colleges.[10] These schools, and the regional public universities that evolved from some of them, educate the vast majority of today's college students. The history of higher education is, largely, their history.[11]

I am also intervening by suppressing the sagas of specific colleges and universities and instead pursuing what Thelin calls the "horizontal history" of higher education.[12] There are many case studies of individual institutions in this book, but my focus is always on how they responded to the incentives and pressures placed upon them by external actors that operated on a national scale. In taking a broad view of higher education's organizational field, I am also building on David Levine's examination of the growth of college-going before World War II. Levine also offers an analysis of non-elite colleges and universities and how they interacted with the rapidly changing American economy and society. However, Levine focuses on informal processes of stratification, whereas this book is about formal efforts to control institutions and create a policy-based stratification. Also, Levine starts the story in 1915, based on a mistaken claim that prior to then "public attention was rarely focused on the colleges" and that higher education did not "play a prominent role in the development of American society" until World War I.[13] While their undergraduate enrollments were still very modest by today's standards, I will show in this book just how much attention and prominence colleges and universities commanded before the war.

The big foundations were the ones driving that attention, but in the historiography of higher education they have often been treated as a curiosity that had little effect; recent surveys typically give them just a few pages of notice.[14] And yet, a look at the archives of just about any American college or university from the early twentieth century, especially between 1905 and 1915, will reveal a flurry of activity related to the foundations.[15] In the case of elite institutions, the activity is there typically because their leaders sat on the CFAT or GEB boards or at least were working in sync with them. In the case of low-status institutions, the activity is about jockeying for money or recognition from the foundations or about pushing back on their agenda.

Why so little notice for the foundations? History, supposedly, is written by the winners, and the academic engineers were not winners. Despite their eye-popping wealth and prominence, the bulk of their reforms did not work as intended, and many were abandoned by the 1920s. Most historians have instead focused on more successful reforms in the areas of graduate and professional education as well as on the rapid development of the research function in American universities.[16] Two important books do deal directly with the foundations, although neither attempts to cover as much territory as I am attempting here. Ellen Lagemann's *Private Power for the Public Good* is a close examination of the CFAT, commissioned by the foundation itself.[17] While it is very objective and even critical, it deals with the CFAT largely in isolation and not as part of a national movement; Lagemann barely mentions the GEB, for example, despite its obvious alignment with the book's subject. Clyde Barrow's *Universities and the Capitalist State* (1990) examines both foundations and analyzes their national-level reform agenda but does so from a hypercritical Marxist standpoint and focuses on reforms that targeted the professoriate, a theme that is only tangential to my narrative.[18]

My focus on the foundations lends this book to a second scholarly conversation: the study of philanthropy. One of the major findings of this project is the extent to which higher education reform was integral to the formal organization of the philanthropic foundation itself.[19] At the heart of my story are two entities that were the very first examples of the classic twentieth-century foundation, with a permanent endowment, central offices in New York, and full-time executives and program officers who oversaw a wide variety of grants and initiatives across the entire nation. (Both also held congressional charters, which makes them particularly distinctive.) This origin story is little noted by scholars who study philanthropy, even historically, who tend to focus on the larger foundations established in the next decade: the Carnegie Corporation and the Rockefeller Foundation.[20]

The fact that the first true foundations were not dedicated to eradicating disease, poverty, or warfare but rather to advancing higher education reform is certainly a surprise. But it helps us understand this novel type of organization as rooted in complex social action rather than simple generosity.[21] It also provides a historical basis for the modern critique of private philanthropy as ideological and elite-friendly rather than unqualifiedly benevolent.[22] The immense controversy and pushback that the academic engineers inspired also set the stage for a century of debates over who gets to direct civil society, how to balance the demands and promises of the "third sector" (i.e., the nonprofit sphere) with the market and the state, and how to balance all three with the interests of the nonsector: the people.

My examination of that balancing act also speaks to a third field, focused on historical political analysis. Commonly termed "American political development," this line of inquiry often focuses on the early twentieth century as an era in which various forms of governance, both state and nonstate, were created or transformed in the United States. The field goes beyond studying the basic interactions of these institutions with society, to what Karen Orren and Stephen Skowronek call "intercurrence," in which "several different sets of rules and norms are likely to be operating simultaneously."[23]

This type of analysis is useful in studying the development of higher education, as historically minded sociologists have pointed out.[24] American colleges and universities and their would-be reformers were enmeshed in multiple overlapping political arenas in the early twentieth century. One of these was the most visible arena of all: electoral politics. The best example of this was the astonishing rise of Woodrow Wilson. History books list "governor of New Jersey" as his prior occupation before the presidency, but he was in that position for less than a year before he launched his bid for the White House. Instead, his national prominence came from his presidency of Princeton and his reputation as a passionate, if unsuccessful, higher education reformer.[25] Equally astonishingly, the vice-presidential nominee on the Republican ticket opposing Wilson in 1912 was Nicholas Murray Butler, the sitting president of Columbia University. Until a few months prior, the two men had served together on the CFAT board.

But my narrative's connection to American political development goes well beyond the ballot box. Historians have recently started approaching both K–12 education[26] and higher education[27] as integral components of nation-building in the United States, showing how the sectors served simultaneously as instruments of the layered American state and as shapers of that state. This book reflects Padgett and Ansell's concept of "robust action," centering the role of powerful elites in brokering alliances and shaping the form of social and political institutions.[28] The philanthropists and the academic engineers they enabled recognized higher education as a potential fulcrum for lifting the nation's economy and society into the modern, rational ideal they envisioned for the new century, and they threw their wealth and energy into its reform.[29] Some of that reform was meant to be prosecuted by official state actors, like the federal Bureau of Education, but when those actors fell short, the foundations (blessed by Congress and operating on a national scale) stepped in. Additionally, as an extension of the nation-building idea, higher education served as a point of international comparison. The reformers I study constantly invoked a race (first friendly, then hostile) with Germany in which educational efforts were central. Some of the largest exhibits in the US pavilion at the 1904 World's Fair were focused on colleges and universities, in a proud display of their critical importance in the coming "American century."[30] In short, the individuals and organizations at the heart of my story were not just reckoning with the form and function of higher education; they were reckoning with the form and function of the United States. And they were absolutely aware of this fact.

The final scholarly conversation to which I hope to contribute is about higher education once again—not just its history but also its essential nature. While many of their reforms failed, the ideas and debates that the academic engineers launched did not die in 1936. I do not make many explicit comparisons to contemporary phenomena here, but today's discourse about the form and function of higher education certainly has many echoes of the discourse that I describe in this book. It also can be mapped onto other periods of history, especially the 1960s, when a new interest in systemic reorganization swept over the sector.

As such, this book fits into a contemporary body of work that interrogates higher education reform from a variety of angles. Some of this literature explicitly advocates reform, citing inefficiencies and shortcomings in student outcomes, institutional and systemic organization, costs to students and taxpayers, and benefits to society.[31] Other authors celebrate the status quo and criticize the notion that American higher education needs reform in terms of either structure[32] or curriculum.[33] A third category contends that the reform has already happened, with deleterious results.[34] As a historical study, this book does not fit into any of these categories, and it certainly does not take a normative stance. Instead, it serves as a corrective to the idea that the elite impulse to reform American higher education is a new one. One hundred years ago, similar camps engaged in a similar set of debates. This does not mean that the current moment is any less of an opportunity, or any less of a threat, than its participants believe it to be. But my demonstration of the academic engineers' many failures and the novel consensus that replaced their vision by the 1930s should be instructive.

Top-down design is not destiny. Design matters, and so does power, but they are not irrepressible. The American higher education system, wildly successful and maddeningly disappointing at the same time, is not the direct product of anyone's design or anyone's power. It is not the product of organic development, either. It is the product of contests and compromises, attacks and counterattacks, ideas and exigencies.

PART ONE

The Ethos of Reform

1: THE ACADEMIC ENGINEERS

Although it is not an intellectual history, this is a book about ideas. The reformers at the heart of the narrative were brimming with them. The ideas did not originate on college campuses. They were in wide circulation in the turn-of-the-century United States, and they were applied to many contexts, not just higher education. Throughout the book, and especially at chapter beginnings, I will describe impactful ideas from many sources—economics, politics, constitutional law, social science, race relations—that informed higher education reform as well as counter-reform.

The academic engineers worked hard to make those ideas their own. In their quest to fundamentally restructure the higher education sector, they borrowed the ideas and then conducted surveys, wrote detailed reports, drew elaborate graphs, and created detailed statistical tables to back them up. This was not neutral research; they knew the answers before they started.

Then, they published those answers constantly, in every available format: through the academic journals that were then becoming the gold standard for knowledge dissemination and in books, white papers, and highbrow periodicals like *The Atlantic*, *The Outlook*, and *The North American Review*. Although they also used their considerable wealth and influence to actively pursue programmatic reform, they spent much of their time practicing pragmatism: feeding back to the world the ideas that they had borrowed, gussied up with data, and applied to higher education. Conveniently, this aids the historian's task in understanding the reformers' theory of action; the academic engineers were not shy with their ideas.

A warning: at many times in this book, I will take unfair shortcuts. One is the suggestion that all of the academic engineers shared the same ideas. That was never true; they often disagreed with each other and sometimes even worked at cross-purposes. But they did share an *ethos*. As I will show in this chapter and the next, that ethos had three parts. First, they believed that American higher education represented a problem to be solved. Second, they thought the solution to that problem would come from outsiders—people who were not loyal to the status quo and brought a novel perspective to the situation. Third, they thought that core concepts from the newly emerging field of engineering were the best ways to measure and improve higher education, first among them efficiency and systemization.

I will also take the related unfair shortcut of referring to the academic engineers as a unified cohort. This was also not true. Even though their most prominent members sat on either the GEB or the CFAT board or both, others operated only in loose connection to the big foundations, or even on their own. Most drifted in and out of the movement throughout the period under study here, although all were active at some point during the crucible of reform from 1905 to 1915. Still, the reformers functioned as what Upton Sinclair, one of their most prominent critics, called an "interlocking directorate."[1] They sat on boards and daises together, traveled and socialized together, supported each other's causes and wrote each other's biographies. They did not share a mind, but they shared an agenda as well as the communicational and organizational tools to carry it out.

IDENTIFYING THE ACADEMIC ENGINEERS

The reformers were critics, first and foremost. The first two decades of the twentieth century were marked by what Michael McGerr succinctly calls "a fierce discontent" about the disorganized nature of American society.[2] While it is hard for us to understand the discontent of people who were generally very privileged (to say nothing of their ludicrously wealthy benefactors), their focus on higher education is a clue to their goals.

Progressive Era reform, a broad movement, was a top-down effort to bring order to the United States. The reformers' goal, McGerr argues, was "to remake the nation's feuding, polyglot population in their own middle class image."[3] In one sense, the reformers in this book saw educational institutions as instruments in that remaking; schools could do the work of socializing students and equipping them for a new era of national life. But they also saw *the institutions themselves* as a "feuding, polyglot population." The academic engineers believed that higher education had an important role to play in nation-building, but first the nation's hundreds of heterogeneous colleges and universities had to get their act together.

We can find versions of this discontent in many Progressive Era reform efforts, especially elsewhere in the education sector. Historians have long since identified a distinct cohort of reformers active in K–12 education in the early twentieth century, most memorably described by David Tyack as the "administrative progressives."[4] Tyack's analysis builds on Raymond Callahan's, which explains how the United States' emerging "business society" demanded that public schools be administered with the same type of efficiency-minded management that was becoming de rigueur in the corporate world.[5] Callahan's analysis is mostly confined to the curriculum and internal dynamics of schools, whereas Tyack focuses his attention on administration: the consolidation and centralization of school districts and the installation of ostensibly expert and nonpartisan administrators and school boards. David Labaree picks up on this difference, arguing that administrative progressivism was "a movement aimed at the formal structure of schooling and not at the instructional core."[6] That description also applies to the academic engineers, who rarely bothered with details like instruction.

While Tyack is clear about the detrimental effects of the administrative progressives' reforms, especially the relegation of students from impoverished or minority communities to a second-class form of schooling, he took care to point out that these individuals saw themselves as making positive, forward-looking changes. Their touchpoint was the world of American business, which was, of course, a tremendous success story at the turn of the twentieth century. They railed about "accountability" and "wished to emulate the process of decision-making used by men of the board of directors of a modern business corporation." Tyack describes them as an "interlocking directorate" of "liberal industrialists" and "civic-minded elites" who were willing to spend their own money to build schools, conduct research, and sponsor political efforts to fulfill their vision of reform.[7] Again, the description closely matches the academic engineers.

There are other parallels between the two groups, and some individuals were clearly members of both.[8] But there was a key difference in their agendas, beyond their interest in different educational levels. The K–12 reformers almost exclusively focused on local or state-level efforts. The higher education reformers dreamed of national-level reform. Commensurately, the ideas and the ethos that undergirded the academic engineers' efforts were grander in scope and more passionately invoked.

So, how do we spot an academic engineer? They had three identifying features, none of them definitive on their own: their *affiliations*, their *positionality*, and their *principles*. (In Appendix A, I list fifty-three academic engineers, most of whom shared all three signifiers.)

Affiliations are the simplest clue. The GEB and the CFAT were organizations with explicit mandates for systemic higher education reform; being a member of their boards or their staffs prior to 1920 was a pretty sure sign that you were an academic engineer. It was not a lock; in chapter eight I will describe members who served as counterweights on those boards and eventually helped bring the reform movement to a close. Foundation membership was also not a requirement. Many people were academic engineers but lacked the prominence to be affiliated with the big foundations. Others were excluded from the boards because of their race or gender. At least two people are firmly identifiable as academic engineers due to their prominence, position, and principles and would have surely joined one or both boards if they had been white men: Booker T. Washington of Tuskegee Institute and M. Carey Thomas of Bryn Mawr College.

Positionality is more abstract. The academic engineers were self-styled *outsiders*. Their goal was to reform the mainstream of American higher education, and they emphasized that they were not part of that mainstream. This ostensibly made them disinterested parties, in alignment with Progressive Era ideals about management by neutral "experts."

One hallmark of outsider status was an education that took part literally outside of the United States. Specifically, many academic outsiders had attended graduate school in Germany. In the late nineteenth century, German universities were considered the best in the world. Nearly ten thousand Americans traveled to them to study, in some cases earning PhDs, which were not yet commonly offered in the United States.[9] Many of them returned as reformers, claiming their knowledge of a supposedly more modern postsecondary system as expertise. Sinclair, their antagonist, was well aware of this fact and spat it back in their faces in the aftermath of World War I. After deriding their elitist dogma, he explained, "One after another of these academic drill-sergeants—Butler of Columbia, Berlin—Lowell of Harvard, Berlin—Smith of Pennsylvania, Goettingen . . . Angell of Yale, Berlin—Wheeler of California, Heidelberg—Wilbur of Stanford, Frankfurt and Munich—every one of them learned the Goose-step under the Kaiser!"[10]

The other type of outsider positionality came from the opposite end of the social spectrum: an origin on the margins of American society. Many academic engineers had humble childhoods, and they invoked this to distinguish themselves from an entrenched Eastern Seaboard higher education establishment that was wedded to the status quo. This old guard was absolutely a straw man—plenty of people who opposed reform had modest origins, too—but the distinction was a powerful one, not least because it helped connect the reformers with their famous benefactors. Carnegie had been a working-class immigrant with a grade-school education, and Rockefeller had been born into poverty in far-upstate New York. Although the industrialists do not fit in the academic engineering category themselves because higher education reform was merely a side project for them, the fact that they were throwing their money at the cause despite their humble backgrounds (which did not include college) was symbolically powerful for the movement.

The third sign of an academic engineer is principles, derived from engineering. The reformers revered—even fetishized—the discipline, which had been formalized only in the 1880s.[11] Engineering furnished the central principles of the effort to reshape the form and function of higher education: systemization, efficiency, and utility. "Efficiency," above all, was a ubiquitous buzzword for the reformers. They viewed colleges and universities as engines with inputs and outputs. Efficiency meant conserving a low ratio of the former (expenditures, both from philanthropic giving and from tax dollars) to the latter (the production of human capital and useful knowledge).

The academic engineers applied the same logic, with even more force, to the nationwide higher education "system."[12] Unlike an early generation of leaders that sought primarily to expand the capacity of American higher education, the academic engineers in many cases thought that the sector had *too much* capacity, leading to duplication of effort, wasted resources, and something they called "insincerity," which meant that institutions were not staying in the lanes that the reformers had ordered them into. They believed that top-down control, coercive and normative, was needed to instate an efficient system. And, of course, the reformers believed they should be the ones wielding that control. This, too, was not lost on their contemporary critics, one of whom argued that the academic engineers' "methods of centralization and outside control" were ruining American higher education.[13]

But as the academic engineers saw it, all three signifiers combined to justify their authority. In their telling, they were disinterested outsiders who had a vision for American higher education and a mandate, expressed through the foundations, to implement it. Wallace Buttrick, a longtime GEB staffer and its eventual president, habitually described his organization as "the layman's contribution to education."[14] It was a ridiculous statement to make about a board that at times included a half dozen university presidents. But in the strange logic of the Progressive Era, a "layman"—at least an imagined one—with the right ideology was the best possible person to implement reform.

THE ENGINEERING IDEAL

History best remembers the CFAT for its famous "Bulletin Number Four" on medical education, also known as the Flexner Report (discussed later in this chapter). Less attention is paid to "Bulletin Number Five," also issued in 1910. It was titled "Academic and Industrial Efficiency," and its author certainly met the definition of a "layman" when it came to higher education: Morris Llewellyn Cooke, described by his biographer as the archetypal "progressive engineer."[15]

Cooke was an engineer with ideas. His first ideological inspiration was the "Social Darwinist" philosopher Herbert Spencer, whose works he would read aloud to his wife. (Carnegie was also an ardent disciple of Spencer.[16]) But he was even more inspired by his neighbor in Philadelphia, Frederick W. Taylor, who became his mentor. After a period of informal study, the most famous engineer of the day chose Cooke as his special assistant when he was elected president of the American Society of Mechanical Engineers in 1906. Cooke absorbed Taylor's immensely popular gospel of "scientific management" and sought to extend it beyond the factory floor. As Jean Christie writes, "To lead the way toward social betterment was, in his eyes, both the social responsibility and the professional opportunity of engineers."[17]

Engineering was both a set of skills and, as Taylorites argued, a philosophy for the administration of organizations and of society itself. Henry Pritchett, who ran the CFAT for its first twenty-five years, explained that "the engineer today is no longer a mere specialist; he is also the executive officer, the manager, the agent, the director of great business enterprises."[18] The logic ran both ways: engineers could apply their vision to many different domains in need of reform, but administrators of all stripes, including those (like the academic engineers) who had no training in the discipline, could also pick up the mantle of the engineer whenever it suited them.

In 1909, Pritchett wrote to Taylor and asked him to write a report on higher education; Taylor declined but recommended his protégé.[19] Cooke promised to be a clear-eyed, impartial judge whose engineering expertise qualified him to make sweeping judgments about how to reorganize whole sectors of economy and society. In the preface to "Bulletin Number Five," Pritchett declared that the "standpoint" from which the author had conducted his investigation "is the same which Mr. Cooke takes when he examines a manufacturing concern." He explained that while the college should be "viewed from a different standpoint than that of factory efficiency, it is still true that all large and continuing causes rest upon formal organization and upon some assumed machinery of administration. . . . In any event, only good can come to an organization—whether it be commercial, educational, or religious—when a friendly hand turns the light of public scrutiny upon its methods, resources and aims."[20]

On behalf of the CFAT, Cooke delivered the goods. His introduction blithely declared that the challenges of American higher education were universal and thus simple: "Every college feels that it has problems unlike, and of greater difficulty of solution than, those to be encountered at other colleges. As a matter of fact, from the standpoint of organization, uniformity in collegiate management is a much easier problem than it is in most industries, because in any industry which I know about, the individual plants vary considerably more than do the colleges."[21] That uniformity, however, extended only to the *form* of the American college and not to its internal or external functioning:

> Perhaps the most notable feature of collegiate administration is the entire absence of uniformity or accepted standardization. . . . At nearly every institution progress has been made along certain lines, but generally it has been a "lone fight;" one institution doing one thing and another doing another, without any of the mutual help and coöperation which is given in the business world. Indeed, it is not going beyond the facts to say that in the college world there is less real coöperation than one finds in those industries where competition is the most intense.[22]

Cooke went on to detail numerous sins in institutional management, including an overreliance on faculty committees, an absence of rational financial accounting, and the inefficient use of buildings and classrooms. In a particularly memorable chapter titled "The College Teacher as a Producer," he challenged the practice of professorial tenure as only a true outsider could: "The question is whether the community secures more efficiency from college professors by guaranteeing to them as a class a life tenure in their offices as long as the service of any one of them remains above the level of an inefficiency that is notorious, or whether more general efficiency would be secured by fixing their tenure at that which obtains in the outside world, that is, guaranteeing to the professor the possession of his chair only so long as he remains the best man obtainable."[23]

Cooke was far from the only person applying the rhetoric of industrial efficiency to higher education. Clarence F. Birdseye, a prominent New York lawyer and reformer, was blunt in a 1909 lament: "These terrible losses in educational efficiency and results come from the unwillingness of the

American college to learn from and in part to pattern after the American factory."[24] In 1912, a group of actual engineers organized a symposium in Boston on "Scientific Management and Efficiency in College Administration." Some participants were harsh on leadership: "The manager of the factory knows that he knows nothing about the best way of running a factory and therefore calls in outside expert assistance; the manager of the college thinks he knows it all, and therefore has no need of advice."[25] Others turned to the question of students, acknowledging that the college had some advantages ("It would be to any industrial organization an asset of untold value to have among its employees and esprit de corps at all approaching 'college spirit'"[26]) but also pointing out that many students squandered their college years on frivolous pursuits that wrecked their efficiency ratios, which were weighted down with heavy inputs in terms of time and tuition.

The academic engineers, however, did not think much about students or even about individual administrators. They focused on institutions and systems. In doing so, they patterned themselves after the idealized civil engineer, as described in 1910 by Hugo Münsterberg, a Leipzig-trained Harvard psychologist who ran in the academic engineering circle: "He does not care for that individual who will pass over the bridge or rush through the tunnel. . . . The chance demands of individuals are submerged in the forward striving of all humanity."[27] Pritchett made his submergence of the individual clear in a 1906 speech:

In mechanics, the term "efficiency" has a definite and distinct meaning. It is the ratio of useful work performed by a prime motor to the energy expended. A prime motor—or, as the old English phrase better expresses it, a prime mover—is a machine which receives force as supplied by some natural power, as a water wheel, or a steam engine, and modifies it for the purposes of industry. . . . A college is one of the prime movers in our social order. Into it is poured an enormous stream of human energy: the energy of devotion, of high scholarship, of unselfish service, and the potential energy of wealth. . . . But is the college an efficient prime mover in education? Is its product in proportion to the energy poured into it? Is its co-efficient of efficiency high or low?[28]

Pritchett would keep asking those questions throughout his career. And the fact that he controlled a huge endowment made his take on the matter particularly salient. Cooke took note of this in his report, explaining that efficiency was not just an end in itself but also a way to impress men with deep pockets: "Everyone likes to feel that the money which he devotes to educational and charitable and philanthropic purposes is well expended; and other things being equal, that [institution] which has an organization making possible the highest efficiency, will in the long run receive the greatest consideration from such public benefactors."[29]

FOLLOW THE MONEY

Speaking of benefactors, to understand the academic engineers, we need to understand the men who bankrolled them. It is not trivial that the money that would fuel reform came from Rockefeller's and Carnegie's massively successful industrial trusts. Standard Oil and Carnegie Steel served as models both for the foundations themselves and for the new vision of what American higher education should look like: national in scope, vertically integrated, optimized for efficiency, and managed by experts. Friends of colleges and universities needed to assimilate this ethos if they were to get the funds they so ardently sought.

Higher education reform found Rockefeller and Carnegie, and not vice versa. By 1890, the men were nationally famous for being rich and found themselves constantly besieged by friends and strangers alike seeking gifts for various causes. Colleges and universities were very much in the strangers group, and they were very much part of the siege.

The institutional form that the two industrialists developed to moderate the cycle of asking and giving, the endowed foundation, predates the establishment of the Rockefeller Foundation (1911) and the Carnegie Corporation (1913), their two massive general-purpose philanthropic organizations. In fact, this archetypal form of American philanthropy—the permanently endowed foundation—began with the explicit mission of reforming the nation's colleges and universities.[30] Although Rockefeller and Carnegie had begun major personal giving in the late nineteenth century (especially for Baptist causes and public libraries, respectively), their first endowed philanthropic institutions were all primarily focused on higher education: Rockefeller's GEB (1902), the Carnegie Institution of Washington (1902), and Carnegie's CFAT (1905).[31]

Rockefeller and Carnegie were not giving out of the kindness of their hearts, nor out of their desire to see their names inscribed in marble. Historians of philanthropy have recently begun casting aside long-standing assumptions of generic benevolence in early philanthropists, construed in the historiography first as saintliness and then as witlessness.[32] In the updated telling, as explained by Olivier Zunz, their project was "a capitalist venture in social betterment, not an act of kindness as understood in Christianity."[33] Their largesse took the form of what Judith Sealander calls "scientific giving." They were interested not in relieving social ills but in resolving them: "Philanthropy should seek causes and cures. It should find a remedy for a disease, rather than build a hospital to treat its victims."[34] In the realm of higher education, the diseases were disorganization, inefficiency, impracticality, and low standards. The "hospital" remedy would have been to build new colleges and universities, as many philanthropists (including Carnegie and Rockefeller) did. But that was a side project, not the main affair. In the pursuit of causes and cures, more sweeping initiatives were required.

John D. Rockefeller Sr.

Rockefeller engaged with higher education first. It was a surprising interest, since he had only the slightest personal experience with it: ten weeks at something called Folsom's Commercial College in Cleveland in the summer of 1855. Rockefeller picked up the essentials of accounting, penmanship, and commercial law there, but this training did not translate easily into a job; it took six weeks of pounding the pavement before he found an unpaid apprenticeship as a bookkeeper.[35]

That apprenticeship famously turned into one of the largest commercial fortunes in history, driven especially by Rockefeller's domination of the North American oil market. After the 1911 dismemberment of his great industrial trust, Standard Oil, Rockefeller's personal net worth surpassed $900 million—about $24 billion in today's dollars.[36] Even his fiercest critic, Ida Tarbell, had to marvel at the firm, using engineering language to call it "as nearly a perfect machine, both in efficiency and in its monopolistic power, as ever had been devised"; at the same time, she employed the metaphor to argue that Rockefeller had cheated his way to success: "the whole system of discrimination has been nothing but violence."[37]

From the time his wealth became an object of press attention (much of it negative) in the 1870s, Rockefeller was under siege by individuals and causes seeking handouts. The oil baron was notoriously tightfisted and for many years made only modest gifts, almost exclusively to Baptist causes.[38] He was a devout, "born again" member of the Baptist Church—and the church was integral to his second rebirth, as a higher education reformer.

The first guide toward that transformation was a clergyman: the Reverend Augustus Strong. Rockefeller knew Strong from his pastorage of his hometown church in Cleveland, before the minister became the president of the Rochester Theological Seminary, which Ron Chernow calls "the citadel of Baptist orthodoxy." Strong was also the chairman of the board of trustees of Vassar College, where Rockefeller sent his oldest daughter, Bessie. Most importantly, they were family; Bessie married Strong's son in 1889.[39]

The many close connections between the two men yielded some financial support for Rochester and Vassar but not for Strong's great dream: the creation of a flagship Baptist university in New York City. As designed, the institution would have stood at the apex of a unified system linking together hundreds of Baptist schools and colleges across the nation. I will return to this idea in chapter three, but the operative point for now is that Strong introduced the idea of systemic higher education reform to the oil baron—and then overplayed his hand. According to Chernow, the reverend "contended that he had a 'divine mission' to promote [the flagship university]—and he badgered Rockefeller about it at every turn. . . . [He was] overbearing, as if trying to bully him into endorsing the project."[40]

Rockefeller passed on the project and parted ways with his in-law, but his interest was piqued. It turned out that Strong was not the only person pushing the Baptist "super-university" idea, and New York was not the only candidate for its location.[41] By 1888, a movement was underway in the Midwest to resurrect the defunct University of Chicago, a small Baptist institution that had perished due to financial mismanagement, and build a new research university along the cutting-edge lines of Johns Hopkins.[42]

The cause's champion was another Baptist minister: Frederick Gates (known to all as Fred), the executive secretary of the newly formed American Baptist Education Society and one of the most foremost academic engineers (I will describe him at length later in this chapter). Kenneth Rose gives Gates sole credit for persuading Rockefeller to pledge $600,000 for the Chicago effort. In written reports and personal conferences, Gates convinced the oil baron that New York was already well served by Baptist colleges and universities, in contrast to the "problem area" of the western states, of which Chicago was considered the capital.[43]

Gates also recruited William Rainey Harper, a prominent Yale professor and a fellow academic engineer, to be the first president of the new university. This helped seal the deal with Rockefeller, who knew Harper from mutual interests at Vassar, where they "were often seen cycling around the campus together."[44] Harper helped Rockefeller develop an expansive view of the potential of higher education. In a 1929 retrospective interview about his philanthropy, the industrialist explained, "Following the principle of trying to abolish evils by destroying them at their source, we felt that to aid colleges and universities, whose graduates would spread their culture far and wide, was the surest way to fight ignorance and promote the growth of useful knowledge."[45] Even though this was revisionist history—the GEB worked hard in its early years to *limit* the number of college graduates—Rockefeller had certainly embraced the idea that higher education had a broad social purpose.

Rockefeller split with Harper in 1897 over the president's excessive spending at the university. In a letter that year, Gates explained that the industrialist's newfound ardor for higher education made him all the more concerned with its wise financial management. Rockefeller, he wrote, "feels that an institution of learning should be far more conservatively managed than, for instance, a bank, or even a savings bank or a trust company. These companies need only assure the depositor or investor that his funds will be duly cared for during the limited time in which they may be deposited. But a university invests the funds of those who are seeking to make an investment of money for the good of humanity, which shall last, if possible, as long as the world stands."[46]

"As long as the world stands" was not a familiar concept in the nineteenth-century world of philanthropy, which revolved around immediate gifts of cash to alleviate suffering, as opposed to what Rockefeller called destroying evils "at their source."[47] Philanthropy in the twentieth century would increasingly move toward the latter model, most notably in the form of the permanently endowed foundation. Education gave the impetus for this dramatic switch. Much of the credit is due to the growing belief in the United States that education was the most effective vehicle for long-lasting social change. As Michael Katz writes, this was in direct contrast to European nations (even those with conservative governments), which in the late nineteenth century were building the infrastructure of the social welfare state rather than pinning hopes on their ancient universities.[48]

Rockefeller embraced the idea of Chicago as an institutional source of reform, but he was not particularly interested in it as a university. He rarely visited it and declined to have either the institution or any campus buildings named after him. The same was true for the first permanent philanthropic foundation he established—which was, in fact, the first permanent foundation that anyone established.

The General Education Board did not bear Rockefeller's name, and he was not a trustee (although his namesake son was). Nevertheless, he endowed it lavishly and repeatedly. He had faith that the academic engineers he had placed at its helm would successfully prosecute its reformist goals—first among them Gates, who dominated the foundation for two decades after its 1902 origin. Rockefeller Jr. later described himself as the conduit between the reverend's ideas and the industrialist's money: "Gates was the brilliant dreamer and creator. I was the salesman—the go-between with father at the opportune moment."[49]

Although historians of education largely associate the GEB with primary and secondary schooling, especially for Black children in the South, that was not its main purpose during Gates' leadership.[50] Higher education was, especially after Rockefeller donated $10 million to the foundation (ten times the amount of his founding gift) in 1905, for a program of reform targeted squarely at higher education.[51]

The GEB's activities run throughout the rest of this book. The foundation and its counterparts maintained a relentless emphasis on accountability, efficiency, and thrift that came straight from Rockefeller's core. Even more importantly, they drew on his incredibly successful business model in their belief that broad, integrated national systems would be as transformative in the higher education sector as they had been in industrial capitalism.

Andrew Carnegie

An interest in higher education was even less likely for Carnegie than for Rockefeller. His schooling had ended upon his immigration to the United States at age twelve. What further education he had took place in the Pennsylvania telegraph offices and railroad depots in which he first proved himself as a businessman. By age sixty-five, he was a steel magnate, the richest private citizen in the world, and a proud autodidact.[52] And yet, over the last twenty years of his life he gave away enormous amounts of money earmarked for higher education.

As I have argued elsewhere, Carnegie underwent a profound transformation in his attitude toward colleges and universities, with four identifiable stages.[53] Early in his philanthropic career, he dismissed higher education as effete and impractical. Around 1895, he started to embrace a bifurcated system that included high-level research and low-grade technical training but little in between. After the turn of the century, he turned to the middle ground, with a reformist agenda for baccalaureate colleges. Finally, in the last decade of his life he embraced the institutions he had once disdained, giving lavishly to a wide variety of colleges and universities. Carnegie's agenda evolved, but he always had one, and he was willing to pay to see it enacted.

First came antipathy. Standing on the steps of the newly opened Carne-

gie Library of Braddock, Pennsylvania, in 1889, Carnegie addressed the assembled steelworkers and influential Pittsburghers on an odd topic. While
he extolled the value of the knowledge contained within the library, the
first of 1,679 that he would finance across the United States, he took time
for a digression on the value of college education. His words were harsh
and worth quoting at length:

> Men have sent their sons to colleges to waste their energies upon obtain-
> ing a knowledge of such languages as Greek and Latin, which are of no
> more practical use to them than Choctaw. . . . They have been "educated"
> as if they were destined for life upon some other planet than this. I do
> not wonder that a prejudice has arisen and still exists against such educa-
> tion. In my own experience I can say that I have known few young men
> intended for business who were not injured by a collegiate education. Had
> they gone into active work during the years spent at college they would
> have been better educated men in every true sense of that term. The fire
> and energy have been stamped out of them, and how to so manage as to
> live a life of idleness and not a life of usefulness, has become the chief
> question with them.[54]

Carnegie's antipathy toward college-going extended beyond the classics
and the traditional liberal curriculum to skepticism about the worth of
anyone who did not learn "in the trenches" as he did. In 1885, addressing
the graduates of a Pittsburgh "commercial college" that trained business
clerks and did not award the bachelor's degree, Carnegie advised, "Look
out for the boy who has to plunge into work direct from the common
school and who begins by sweeping out the office. He is the probable dark
horse that you had better watch."[55] Writing in the New York *Tribune* in 1891,
he was blunter: "The almost total absence of the [college] graduate from
high position in the business world seems to justify the conclusion that
college education as it exists is almost fatal to success in that domain."[56]

Carnegie's criticism of college-going was hardly unique. Other influential leaders, especially those in the business realm, displayed a strong
antipathy to holders of the bachelor's degree. They perceived college as the
domain of "weakly children" and the institutions themselves as esoteric
and impractical.[57] While undergraduate study was becoming a prerequisite
for professions like medicine and law, college graduates were commonly
judged unfit for careers in the complex bureaucratic organizations emerging at the forefront of the American economy.[58]

It is notable that Carnegie's 1889 diatribe occurred in front of a library.

His library-building, for which he would soon become internationally famous, was an ideological project designed to facilitate the type of autodidacticism on which he prided himself. He never tired of telling the story of Colonel James Anderson, a Pittsburgh notable who opened his private library to the young Carnegie and other "working boys" in the 1850s.[59] He described his reasoning for pouring his fortune into public libraries: "The fundamental advantage of a library is that it gives nothing. Youths must acquire knowledge themselves. There is no escape from this."[60] The chasm between this model and the didacticism he saw in college education was considerable.

The colleges, however, were undeterred. After Carnegie announced his intent to become a philanthropist in his widely circulated 1889 essay "Wealth," the solicitations from college leaders came quickly: for music halls, dormitories, teaching salaries, and unrestricted endowments. Almost all appear to have been refused, often with a friendly but firm explanation: "I am clearly of the opinion that I can do most good by selecting one field and sticking to it, and that field, as you know, is Free Libraries for the people."[61] Some tried particularly novel tactics. George W. Atherton, the president of Pennsylvania State College, maintained a constant campaign for support that yielded only modest contributions for student aid. In an 1895 letter asking for $200, he made a bold entreaty: "I cannot give up the hope that you will think favorably of making this institution Carnegie University."[62] Needless to say, the effort was unsuccessful. Atherton's cross-state rival, the chancellor of Western University in Pittsburgh, tried a different form of flattery in the cause of a campaign arguing that "it is manifest destiny that this great city must have a great school like Columbia, like Cornell. . . . We ought to begin now to plan big things."[63] A part-time lepidopterist, the chancellor named a newly discovered species of moth (*Carnegia mirabilis*) after the man with deep pockets.[64]

Andrew Dickson White offered a more valuable prize, one that Carnegie accepted and valued for years: his friendship. White was a historian, a politician, a diplomat, and the founding president of Cornell University, from 1866 to 1885. He had first shown his prowess in the difficult joining of business and higher education by convincing the telegraph magnate Ezra Cornell to endow the university that would bear his name.[65] In the 1880s he turned his attention to Carnegie. White was perhaps Carnegie's first friend to be so intimately associated with higher education. By 1890, he had cajoled the industrialist into joining White on the university's board of trustees. This did not yield the former president's hopes for a donation, however. Writing to White the next year to deny his request for a music hall on campus, Carnegie gave his standard demurral: "I have taken Free Libraries as my line, and I believe in concentration."[66] Within a few years, however, that concentration was fracturing, as the business leader became more intimate with other higher education leaders. He remained a critic of college-going, but he began to realize that reform was a more promising strategy than disavowal.

The following chapters detail many of the higher education reform efforts that Carnegie bankrolled, but two are worth mentioning briefly at this point. The first was the Carnegie Institution of Washington. This entity is a perfect example of the "scientific philanthropy" code: it came from an effort to enlist Carnegie to endow a new university but ended up as a mechanism to improve the efficiency and strength of existing ones.

In the last few years of the nineteenth century, a handful of prominent Americans including White began agitating to establish a national university.[67] Such an institution, located in Washington, DC, and patterned on European universities like the University of Berlin, would surely have a powerful effect on the nation's higher education institutions through its normative influence at the top of a newly delineated national hierarchy. (I will return to this idea at length in chapter three.) Carnegie considered White's request to endow the project but had mixed feelings about establishing a new institution when so many others existed. Writing to White in 1901, he explained, "You suggested National University at Washington, Washington's desire, several have; but while this does, as you say, ensure immortality to the Founder, it has hitherto seemed to me not needed, and this puts immortality under foot. . . . Don't care two cents about future 'glory'. I must be satisfied that I am doing good wise beneficial work in my day. Better come to Skibo and confer."[68]

White did come to Skibo, Carnegie's newly built castle in Scotland, that summer, along with Daniel Coit Gilman, the founding president of Johns Hopkins. This brain trust worked out a new scheme with efficiency at its heart. Instead of a new university, national or regional, Carnegie would instead endow an institution dedicated to advancing pure scientific research within the existing higher education framework. It would distribute grant money to professors and universities, organize research projects, publish findings, and sponsor conferences, thus reducing wasteful competition and overlap between institutions while spurring them to new heights of scholarship. As Carnegie explained to President Theodore Roosevelt that fall, "For some time I have been considering the propriety of fulfilling one of Washington's strongest wishes, the founding of a University at Washington, but the conclusion reached was that, if with us today, he would decide that under present conditions greater good would ensue from co-operation with, and strengthening of, existing universities throughout the country, than by adding to their number."[69]

His friend and fellow industrialist-turned-reformer Abram Hewitt put it even better. Carnegie's gift of $10 million establishing the Carnegie Institution of Washington (which had Gilman at the helm) would serve as "an educational fly wheel, [and] will give a vigor and achieve results which otherwise would be impossible."[70] His imagery, derived from a mechanical device integral to the efficient operation of a steam engine, was a good preview of the engineering ethos that was beginning to prevail over the rhetoric of higher education reform. Furthermore, engineering was a curricular centerpiece of both halves of Carnegie's bifurcated vision, at research universities like Cornell as well as at the sub-baccalaureate schools like the Carnegie Institutes of Technology in Pittsburgh, which Carnegie had created the year before, and Cooper Union, which both Carnegie and Hewitt had generously endowed.[71]

In 1905, Carnegie turned fully toward reform. In that year, he gave another $10 million to endow another institution dedicated to higher education progress, the Carnegie Foundation for the Advancement of Teaching (CFAT). Much of the following chapters revolve around the activities of this foundation, so I will describe only its origins here.

Carnegie's gift was ostensibly earmarked for a very unlikely cause: a fund to provide pensions for retiring college professors. This was a misdirect. Reform was the unequivocal goal, and the pensions were merely carrots dangled in front of colleges that needed it. Historians typically (but incorrectly) attribute the CFAT gift to Carnegie's humanitarian "impulse"[72] and a special concern for poorly paid college professors dating back to his instatement on Cornell's board of trustees.[73] This is unlikely. Up to 1905, Carnegie never expressed any affection for college faculty.[74] His sentiment ran toward mockery, as he expressed in a 1900 speech in England: "I have walked over the moors with more than one learned professor who did not know the lark from the thrush . . . perhaps in American slang I may be allowed to say, he didn't know beans."[75]

These were not the words of a man eager to reward the efforts of college instructors. But while Carnegie was not interested in professors, he was finally interested in colleges. This was largely in response to an onslaught of aid requests. By 1905, Carnegie's secretary estimated that "three or four hundred such applications in regard to colleges" were on file.[76] Many cash-strapped colleges organized extensive letter-writing campaigns in the hopes of victory through overwhelming force. Coe College in Iowa, for example, sent over twenty letters in a single week, representing students, alumni, local business leaders, presidents of neighboring colleges, US senators, the postmaster of Cedar Rapids, and the president of the National Biscuit Company. By 1904, Carnegie wrote to White to complain about all the "begging," leading to a reproach from the former administrator, who himself had spent many years asking for such gifts.[77]

These small colleges requested endowments, libraries, classroom buildings, and even entire academic departments, but one category was conspicuously absent from the wish lists: professorial pensions. Instead, the idea for a nationwide pension fund came directly from Carnegie, and it was designed as an instrument of reform. Along with Henry Pritchett, Carnegie imposed two critical features on the fund. The first was that an individual professor could not apply for a pension; everything had to be regulated by the professor's college or university. The second feature was that in order to participate in the pension program, institutions had to comply with strict regulations set by the CFAT. Each of the regulations had a reformist goal, including remaking the academic ranks, exorcising religion from colleges and universities, setting minimum institutional standards, and broadly promoting accountability and efficient management. The pensions were merely a means to these ends.

If Carnegie had any doubt about the potential of his scheme, it must have been assuaged by the rousing congratulations that poured in immediately after he announced the gift. Jacob Schurman, president of Cornell, described the fund as "the wisest thing ever conceived in the interest of higher education in America."[78] Harper of Chicago deemed it "one of the most brilliant things that has been conceived in the history of American education" and later called the first meeting of the CFAT trustees "an occasion which seems to me to be one of the most significant in the history of modern education."[79] (Harper had, in fact, proposed an organization called the Carnegie College Institution the previous year.[80] It was a version of an idea that he had in 1902 to create a blue-ribbon board of "men of national reputation" who would raise and spend money to promote "practical economies on the educational side as well as on the financial" for American colleges.[81])

Carnegie's reformist crusade in higher education faded in the last decade of his life.[82] As he aged, he softened, and by the 1910s he was giving unrestricted funds to colleges and universities. This denouement, however, should not distract us from the zealous focus that informed his earlier philanthropy. We cannot understand the first movement for systemic reform in higher education without acknowledging its origins in monopolistic, vertically integrated capitalism. We also cannot tell this story as one of internal changes driven by campus administrators, which is the theme of classic analyses of elite universities like Lawrence Veysey's *The Emergence of the American University*.[83] For the vast majority of the higher education sector, external, top-down reform backed by outsiders like Rockefeller and Carnegie was the dominant force of the day.

The rest of this chapter provides sketches of six exemplary academic engineers who served as arbiters of that benefaction. They were not by any means the only members of this group. I have already mentioned some individuals who epitomized every signifier I mentioned earlier. Nicholas Murray Butler studied in Germany, sat on the CFAT board, and fully embraced the college-as-a-problem mantra. So did David Starr Jordan of Stanford. So did Arthur Twining Hadley of Yale. Harper sat on *both* the CFAT and the GEB boards and was perhaps the leading reform theorist of the cohort. While he did not do any graduate study in Germany, that was because he was even more of an educational outsider than his peers; he had been a child genius who entered college at age ten and earned a Yale doctorate at nineteen.

But the most interesting academic engineers are the ones who never ran elite institutions. Since they did not already think of themselves as members of a new American aristocracy, their commitment to top-down reform is even more remarkable. Their outsider status was more pronounced, and so was the force of their vision.

Frederick T. Gates

The Reverend "Fred" Gates is best described as Rockefeller's consigliere on philanthropic matters, and he was a close business advisor as well. The industrialist trusted Baptist ministers. Although Gates's pastoral days ended before the two met, he retained the spirit of the evangelical revivalism of upstate New York's "burned-over district," where both men had been born before moving to the Midwest as children.

He was a striking character. Sealander opens her analysis of philanthropy's turn to "scientific giving" with Gates in full form: "arms waving, long white hair flowing wildly . . . characteristically banging a table with the flat of his hand" in front of a group of Rockefeller confidants.[84] Chernow describes his "prosecutorial zeal and ministerial fervor."[85] John Boyer calls him "a tough-minded rationalist with little patience for soft-hearted social causes."[86] Fosdick, who worked with him as a young man, calls him "a dominating and sagacious man . . . fundamentally a figure of ardor and zeal, with little humor—either about himself or anything else—and with very few doubts."[87]

Although he later became closely identified with other Rockefeller causes, including medicine, Gates's first and most ardent passion was higher education reform. Most notably, he relentlessly sought to systemize and strengthen American colleges and universities, reserving special scorn for weak institutions in isolated locations.

His contemporary Sigmund Freud would have had some psychoanalytical fun with this obsession, given Gates's personal background in higher education. His first alma mater was something called Highland University in rural Kansas, which can be described only as an extraordinarily modest institution. In his memoirs, Gates admits that it was just a single building, "two stories, of fifty by eighty feet. . . . We had no great and splendid groups of buildings, no long line of distinguished alumni, presidents, professors, and trustees. We had none of the pride of age or wealth."[88] He spent eight years at the institution.

At age twenty-two he entered the University of Rochester, which held only slightly more claim to the moniker of "university"; it had less than two hundred students and offered no real graduate training. Gates remembered it as "then a small college under Baptist auspices."[89] Fosdick is blunter, calling it "a Baptist institution whose search for candidates was not handicapped by considerations of academic standards."[90] Gates was blasé about his experience, writing, "My college course simply confirmed me in habits of study, reading, and reflection. I can truthfully say little else for it." He echoed Carnegie's brand of book-based autodidactism, based on his experience of teaching himself classics, which "confirmed in me the belief that with modern textbooks a man with reasonable independence and self-reliance need not be dependent on a college classroom."[91] He did not earn a bachelor's degree and instead transferred his studies to the affiliated Rochester Theological Seminary.

Gates next spent eight years as a minister in Minneapolis and then in 1888 was chosen as the first executive secretary of the newly founded American Baptist Education Society, largely on his reputation as a tireless fundraiser for Minnesota schools and churches. The organization had oversight of hundreds of loosely connected institutions serving all ages, but Gates immediately fixed his reformist eyes on the top of the jumbled pyramid. Within months he had thrust himself forcefully into the cause of establishing a flagship Baptist institution, issuing a report called "The Need for a Baptist University in Chicago, as Illustrated by a Study of Baptist College Education in the West."

The document is perhaps the ur-text of academic engineering. Gates argued for far more than the endowment of a new institution. Brimming with hastily gathered statistics, charts, and maps, the report laid out a scathing criticism of existing Baptist higher education, which existed in "a state of destitution" and desperately needed top-down reformation. The primary function of a new university would be a normative one, Gates explained: "Before its walls were reared, before its foundations could be laid, the mere assurance of such an enterprise made certain by means provided would lift up the heads of our colleges and clothe them with renewed vigor and larger influence."[92] His 1888 vision of a dynamic hierarchical system set the tone for much of the academic engineering project. So did his goal of using that ethos to yield philanthropic dollars, as he revealed in a letter to a colleague that same year: "A scheme so vast, so continental, so orderly, so comprehensive, so detailed, will in my view capture a mind so constituted as Mr. Rockefeller's is."[93]

Rockefeller was soon on board for the project of forming what Chernow calls "an educational trust of Western colleges."[94] More importantly, his pocketbook was open to the cause of academic engineering, and the fingers in that pocketbook were Gates's.

The utmost expressions of that relationship took place in the workings of the General Education Board, which I will continue to analyze throughout this book. For its first decade, Gates ruled it with an iron fist and used it to advance his vision of higher education reform to unprecedented heights. In his memoirs, he took care to gloat about the GEB's congressional charter, one of the few ever given to a philanthropic organization, which allowed the board "authority to hold limitless capital and to do anything whatever which could be construed to be directly or even remotely educational."[95] He also admitted to ghostwriting Rockefeller's gift letter for his 1905 pledge, which earmarked $10 million for efforts to "promote a comprehensive system of higher education in the United States."[96]

Gates always insisted that the GEB's grants be made with an eye to fostering a balanced national system of colleges and universities. He was especially obsessed with the geography of this hoped-for system. His official GEB obituary noted, "The great map of the United States which hung on the walls of the General Education Board Room and to which he frequently turned to make graphic his thought and expression symbolized the large way in which his mind worked. Thus he would mark the great fortresses and the outposts of higher education in this country."[97] Gates aimed to spread institutions so that they would not compete with one another, a task that would require eliminating hundreds of existing schools. He wrote an internal memo for Rockefeller Jr. that explained his restrictionist theory of action:

> I want to see a hundred colleges in this country so planted as to cover the whole land and leave no part destitute, each of them planted in a fruitful soil, each so planted that it shall not be overshadowed by others, each conducted under such auspices as will take care of it, see that it is watered, particularly in its earlier years, see that it is properly fertilized, see that the forces of destruction which always fasten themselves on institutions shall be pruned away.[98]

This hundred-college vision, of course, did not come to be. Still, in his memoirs Gates flatly credited the GEB with the successful wholesale reform of American colleges and universities. In 1905, he recalled, "I had a reasonably clear bird's-eye view of the whole field and, while there was much to encourage, there was much also to regret. The picture was one of chaos." In 1926, after two decades of the academic engineering project, he could say of the United States, "Clearly we have the most efficient system of higher education in the world."[99]

Henry S. Pritchett

Of all the academic engineers, Henry Pritchett experienced perhaps the most dramatic fall from fame to obscurity. We have only three significant explorations of the life and work of the man who served for twenty-five years as the CFAT's first president: a 1943 biography by a close friend and two histories of the CFAT, in 1953 and 1983.[100] These were not impromptu scholarly inquiries; all three were commissioned by the Carnegie Corporation. What other latter-day mentions of Pritchett we have almost always discuss him primarily in the context of the famous Flexner Report on medical education, which he commissioned.[101] And the close friend who wrote his biography, it is worth mentioning, was Abraham Flexner.

And yet, Pritchett was well known and highly influential in his day, especially in the key years from 1905 to 1915. As the foundation's president, Pritchett had a bully pulpit. He authored book-length annual reports, gave countless speeches, and published constantly in news magazines. Lagemann, in her 1983 CFAT history, writes, "His rhetoric, embroidered with facts and statistics, was often stirring and earnestly moral. His opinions derived from principle and were tenaciously argued and adhered to."[102] Flexner is even more generous but still hints at his dogmatic streak: "He had a consciousness of what was right which never deserted him. He had 'the prepared mind,' upon the importance of which Pasteur had insisted, but how it was prepared is not known."[103]

On the topic of mental preparation, Pritchett's higher education was decidedly haphazard. Whether or not he held a bachelor's degree is in dispute: Flexner claims he did, Lagemann says he didn't, and his own unpublished memoir doesn't mention one.[104] His undergraduate training took place in rural Missouri at an institution variously known as Pritchett School Institute or Pritchett College, operated by his father. He left at age eighteen for training in astronomy at the Naval Observatory in Washington and returned to Missouri four years later to take a job as the director of an observatory in his hometown. He parlayed this opportunity into an observatory job at Washington University in St. Louis and eventually a professorship there. Finally, at age thirty-seven, he rounded off his education with a PhD earned at the University of Munich. According to Flexner, he completed the degree in just eight months, during which time he also toured Europe extensively with his teenage sons.[105]

At forty-three, Pritchett found himself the president of a low-status urban technical college commonly called Boston Tech. Its full name was the Massachusetts Institute of Technology, but it was years from being MIT in terms of both nomenclature and prestige.[106] It was in this capacity that Pritchett first got to know Carnegie, who had a strong interest in technical higher education. The industrialist consulted with him often on matters related to the Carnegie Institution of Washington (which counted astronomy as one of its chief foci) and in fact lobbied for him to become the institution's president upon Daniel Coit Gilman's retirement in 1904. In that year, Carnegie wrote to a trustee that "I was very favorably impressed with my friend Pritchett. . . . He seems one of the men who can do things."[107] Pritchett actively pursued the opportunity, but the trustees ultimately passed him over in favor of someone whom another trustee predicted "would meet with the general approval of the Scientific men of the Country to a much greater extent than would that of Dr. Pritchett."[108] Still, Carnegie did not give up on finding a leadership role for his friend.

The two men saw eye to eye on the vision of a bifurcated system of higher education. When Pritchett took the reins at MIT, it was located in cramped quarters in the city of Boston and served commuter students who came to study applied technical fields. This was a situation most unbefitting the research university the young president aspired to lead. Working with the Boston philanthropist Henry Lee Higginson, in 1904 Pritchett convinced Carnegie to contribute $400,000 to establish a new technical school in Boston. Pritchett's brilliant apparatus was to convince the industrialist to match a century-old bequest left to the city of Boston by Benjamin Franklin. The association with the most famous American autodidact proved too great to resist, and Carnegie put up the cash to establish the Franklin Union in the city's working-class South End. Thus divested from the burden of training Boston's industrial workers, Pritchett was free to pursue his plan of relocating the institute to Cambridge and the academic halo of Harvard.[109]

The next collaboration came soon after, with the establishment of the CFAT. In 1904, Pritchett was seeking contributions to MIT's modest pension fund.[110] Other more robust, universities had better-endowed pension plans, including Columbia, Yale, Harvard, and Cornell; German universities also had a long history of professorial pensions.[111] Carnegie did not contribute to the MIT fund but proposed a much farther-reaching plan to extend pensions to dozens of institutions. In February of 1905, Pritchett jumped on board with Carnegie's proposal.[112] He agreed to run the numbers on what such a scheme would entail, working with Frank Vanderlip, a bank president and Carnegie confidant, as actuarial advisor. Two months later, the research was done but lightly considered; Carnegie donated his usual $10,000,000 to the still-unnamed foundation, with the clear expectation that professorial pensions would be used as coercive carrots spurring reform in colleges and universities.

Pritchett would spend the rest of his professional life using the CFAT to advance the academic engineering agenda. He openly touted this power, boasting in a 1906 essay in *The Outlook* that the foundation would become "a centralizing and standardizing influence" that would fundamentally reshape the American higher education sector, especially by "clearing our ideas of educational administration and bringing in right standards."[113]

Pritchett's primary goal in wielding that "standardizing influence" was to restrict the ambitions of colleges and students. Like Gates, he held a special perverse antipathy toward humble colleges like the one he had attended himself. In 1908, Pritchett wrote, "We have founded many more colleges under this system than we can possibly maintain, colleges which are colleges in name only and which will for many years continue to demoralize our standards of education and to place before our people false ideas of what education is. Ultimately, perhaps, the weaker and more objectionable of these colleges will disappear."[114] His highly visible post also earned him the most enmity of any academic engineer, as I will show in chapters 6 and 7.

Generally, though, Pritchett operated with impunity, and he knew it. Writing late in life to his successor, he gloated, "One of the fine things about the presidency of the Carnegie Foundation is the great freedom of speech the president has. He has no constituency like a great body of alumni on his back. The trustees have got pretty well inured to the notion that the president can take up any subject in education he pleases. . . . Whether it is wise for a man to have as great freedom to air his opinions as all this comes to is another matter."[115]

Frank Vanderlip

Pritchett's partner in the actuarial framing of CFAT certainly fit the description of an outsider who had made it big. Frank Vanderlip, vice president and soon-to-be president of the enormous National City Bank in New York, had been born in rural Illinois. He was immensely proud of his rustic roots, even titling his 1935 memoir *From Farm Boy to Financier*. He is best remembered as a member of the secretive Jekyll Island group that created the Federal Reserve system in 1911, but he took plenty of time along the way for the cause of academic engineering.

Like Pritchett, whom he called "my closest friend," Vanderlip had a spotty higher education.[116] It took place at the University of Illinois, his second choice of institution after an initial dream of studying electrical engineering at Cornell. He made it through just one year of college before taking a correspondence course in shorthand and landing a job at a local newspaper. This turned into years as a business reporter for the *Chicago Tribune*, a position in the Treasury Department (where he first met Pritchett, who was also in Washington at the time), and eventually bank leadership in Manhattan.

Vanderlip was an autodidact who could veer into plain anti-intellectualism. Carnegie revered libraries as hubs of self-directed learning, but his banker friend described their limits in a 1905 speech: "Book covers contain much knowledge, but may also shut out from a too close student much wisdom, —much of that sort of wisdom which is gained by experience in the world." [117] And he was blunt about social realities, the kind of bank president who could tell a gathering of bank clerks, "Certainly you cannot all be bank presidents. We need many privates, and comparatively few generals. Not a few of you, filled with ambition though you may be to-day, will go on year after year in faithful regularity . . . never advancing to the highest positions."[118]

He was equally blunt when it came to a favorite topic: education reform.

In May 1905, he claimed that the cause of many higher education controversies was that "the solution of the problem has been left too largely in the hands of educators."[119] Instead, he suggested that he and his outsider peers had the disinterested expertise to whip the nation's colleges and universities into shape. They also had the money to do it. In the same speech, he predicted the beneficent influence of "a great central fund, the object of which should be so to distribute the income as to give effective force to an impulse toward co-ordination of our whole system of higher education. If such a fund were in the hands of the wisest body of men that could be brought together for that purpose, it could be so used that it would stimulate the educational system to a symmetrical growth."[120]

That fund, of course, was CFAT, which he had helped establish the previous month; the "wisest body of men" comprised himself, Pritchett, and their fellow academic engineers. Vanderlip frankly explained the CFAT pension program as "in the interest of highest efficiency" but went on to explain that the foundation's work would go far beyond that, into organizing a rational system of higher education along the lines of an ideally engineered machine. "The highest possible success," he declared, "for an institution of learning is to become a perfectly efficient unit in a perfectly co-ordinated scheme."[121]

And speaking of coordinated schemes, Vanderlip is emblematic of the interlocking directorate of academic engineers. A muckraking author calculated in 1914 that Vanderlip sat on twenty-one corporate boards, plus the New York University board; on these he overlapped with many fellow CFAT trustees.[122] In addition to his Carnegie connections, he was also enmeshed in the Rockefeller circle. He was a business colleague of the senior Rockefeller's brother, and his close collaborator on the Federal Reserve plan was Senator Nelson Aldrich, the junior Rockefeller's father-in-law and the force behind the congressional charter for the GEB. This type of social capital underlaid the concentrated power of the academic engineering movement.

Abraham Flexner

Many of the academic engineers can be simply described; Abraham Flexner cannot. More than anyone, he managed to be both a relentless gadfly criticizing higher education and a moth drawn continually to its flame.

We can certainly classify him as an outsider. He hailed from Kentucky, and his parents were Jewish immigrants from Germany. He and his siblings, however, were secular, as he recalled in his memoir: "For us Herbert Spencer and Huxley, then at the height of their fame and influence, replaced the Bible and the prayer book."[123] Flexner's worship of Spencer, a former civil engineer who went on to become the father of social Darwinism, echoed Cooke's and Carnegie's. All three thrilled at Spencer's assurance that human society could become continually more robust through the attrition of its weaker links. This theory would be foremost in Flexner's mind when he turned to the study of educational institutions.

At age seventeen, Flexner enrolled at Johns Hopkins, then just eight years old and branded as the only true university in North America. Late in life, he claimed the influence of Hopkins' founding president "in all I have done or tried to do."[124] Gilman's hardheaded empiricism was always a touchstone for Flexner: "There was no froth in the Johns Hopkins University of my time. . . . I never heard President Gilman or any member of the academic staff urge that the supreme end of a college education is 'citizenship' or 'character,' the slogans under which much modern inefficiency is cloaked."[125] He certainly took the efficiency ethos to heart as an undergraduate, earning his bachelor's degree in two frenzied years and returning to Louisville before he could even receive his diploma. By his own admission, he made just one friend among his classmates.[126]

Flexner embarked on a high school teaching career in his hometown and eventually opened his own private college prep school.[127] He married well; his wife, a lapsed Baptist who had attended Vassar a few years after Bessie Rockefeller, wrote a hugely successful play that debuted in New York in 1904. *Mrs. Wiggs of the Cabbage Patch* brought in enough money for Flexner to shut down his school and resume his own higher education. He went first to Harvard, studying under Hugo Münsterberg, an experimental psychologist; Flexner quit his lab after a few months and Harvard itself after one year.[128] The next stop was Europe, where he toured Oxford and Cambridge and enrolled at the prestigious universities of Berlin and Heidelberg. He never earnestly pursued a degree, however. Instead, he pursued a job.

In Heidelberg, when he should have been writing a dissertation, Flexner wrote a slim volume called *The American College: A Criticism*. Published stateside in 1908, it was a scathing attack on undergraduate education. Some of his comments were simply cruel: "our college students are, and for the most part, emerge, flighty, superficial and immature, lacking, as a class, concentration, seriousness and thoroughness."[129] But elsewhere he appeared to be plainly appealing to Carnegie and Vanderlip's self-made man ideal. He wrote of the graduate, "The college leaves him 'soft'; he has had no such discipline, no such biting realization of consequences as one gets out in the rough and tumble of the world. . . . Practical life with its intense, narrow urgencies binds up the shattered personality, focuses the dispersed energies."[130] Other passages appealed to the broad ethos of academic engineering. The elective system of undergraduate study, he wrote, "impoverishes and isolates by excessive and premature specialism where it does not waste by aimless dispersion."[131] In its place, he called for "a more intelligent, systematic and fearless experiment" in college education.[132]

In his memoir, Flexner noted that a copy of *The American College* "fell into the hands of" Henry Pritchett. In reality, it appears to have been written directly for him, citing him throughout and plainly appealing to his sense of educational efficiency. The plan worked; within months, Flexner was on the CFAT payroll, heading a major reform project and working on "an unlimited expense account."[133]

His assigned target for this first project was not undergraduate education, the subject of his 1908 book. In the outsider spirit of academic engineering, Pritchett tasked Flexner with a study of medical education, a field in which he had no experience.[134] Like with the Cooke report, a neophyte's perspective carried more weight than an interested insider's. Armed with cash and a cause, in less than two years he personally inspected every medical school in the United States and Canada. His research methods were cursory at best; he wrote in his memoir that "in the course of a few hours a reliable estimate could be made respecting the possibilities of teaching modern medicine in almost any one of the 155 schools I visited."[135] His final report, published in 1910 as the CFAT's "Bulletin Number Four," was a sustained denouncement of most medical schools, finding low standards and shoddy instruction at all but a handful of institutions (the exceptions, of course, included his own alma mater). His prose was cutting, but it slashed with wit rather than stridency. Of the prospective medical student, he wrote, "Her choice is free and varied. She will find schools of every grade accessible: the Johns Hopkins, if she has an academic degree; Cornell, if she has three-fourths of one; Rush and the state universities, if she prefers the combined six years' course; Toronto on the basis of a high school education; Meridian, Mississippi, if she has had no definable education at all."[136]

The "Flexner Report" propelled its author to sudden, lasting fame. It had other major effects, too. The report is generally credited with the wholesale reform of medical education; within two years of its publication, 30 percent of medical schools in the United States had shut their doors, and the others were frantically taking steps to modernize their curricula and facilities.[137] (The casualties included all but two schools open to Black students, resulting in a decades-long dearth of Black physicians.[138]) Carnegie was delighted with the results, writing to Charles Eliot of Harvard that he welcomed the uproar: "I am quite prepared for the wrath of all the quacks, vendors of patent medicines, teachers in cheap medical schools, and victims of the 'healing' delusions. . . . The bogus 'Colleges' and even 'Universities,' so cald [sic], will soon be things of the past."[139] The report also put the potential of academic engineering on full display, not just for educators and the public but for funders as well. In 1913, Carnegie donated another $1.25 million to the CFAT for a Division of Educational Enquiry that would produce similar reports.

Flexner's career as an academic engineer was just beginning. After he authored two more reports for the CFAT, Gates poached him in 1912 to join the staff of the GEB. He soon became a GEB trustee, too. Flexner produced voluminous work there on higher education reform for nearly two decades before leaving for other pursuits including the founding of the Institute of Advanced Studies at Princeton. By that point he was increasingly focused on promoting basic research, which he called "the usefulness of useless knowledge."[140] He never lost his zeal, however, and reinserted himself into the higher education debate at age sixty-four with a book, *Universities: American, English, German*, that reprised many of his themes from *The American College*. Like its predecessor, it brought recognition to its author but had nothing of the impact of his report on medical education. In 1994, Clark Kerr memorably called the book important but "so wrong": "Flexner was too addicted to all-out criticism as a mechanism of change. This led him to look mostly for items to criticize in American universities. This led him to unbalanced views. This led him to unbalanced judgements about needed reforms—too drastic."[141] An assessment of one man but also an assessment of an entire movement.

John G. Bowman

Flexner was not the only young man who turned academic engineering into a lifelong career. John Gabbert Bowman matched him for that as well as for imperiousness.

Like his peers described above, Bowman was born far from the metropole, in Iowa. Unlike them, he had a normal undergraduate education: four years at the University of Iowa leading to a BA, which he followed up with a master's degree at the same institution in 1904. Shortly after, he made his way to New York and a job at Columbia University. The few historical references to Bowman describe him as a professor,[142] but the 1906–07 Columbia catalog lists him as a tutor in the English department.[143] Regardless, teaching was not in the cards for Bowman. He seems to have caught the eye of Columbia's president, Butler, who was by that point an influential CFAT board member. By mid-1907, he was on the foundation's staff, serving as secretary.

The CFAT archives indicate that Bowman's job there was to be Pritchett's enforcer. When professors or college presidents wrote to the foundation to protest its policies (typically in relation to their status on its list of schools approved for pensions), Bowman conducted the back-and-forth. He was stubborn and fond of rules, many of which he appears to have made himself on an ad hoc basis. He could even be a stickler on the topic of classics, which Carnegie despised and Pritchett spent little thought on. A series of increasingly distressed letters from the registrar of Bowdoin College reveal a typical scenario. In yet another demand for higher admission standards, the low-level foundation staffer wrote, "I do not wish to insist upon any dogmatic method of stating requirements" but quickly continued:

> In regard to the requirement of Elementary Greek as stated in the Bowdoin catalogue, I fail to see wherein a student must prepare more thoroughly Book II of the Anabasis than a student who prepares Book II and in addition Books I, III and IV for admission to some other first class college. . . . I should like, further, to have you forward to us all of the examination papers together with the marks of the examiners which were offered by the present Freshman class and, if possible, by the Freshman class of a year ago. If it is evidenced then that your standard for Book II of Xenophon is distinctly higher than the standard required, let us say, at Columbia University where four books are required in satisfaction of the Elementary Greek, there will be no further difficulty in the matter.[144]

After four years of this type of nit-picking in New York, Bowman was ready for a new job. He found one at his alma mater—as its president. The Iowa Board of Education had forced out the university's president and needed a new one. According to Stow Persons, it took them just a month to offer the job to the thirty-three-year old Bowman, based a bit on his Iowa pedigree but mostly on the weight of his CFAT affiliation: "Clearly, no very extensive search had been deemed necessary. President Pritchett's recommendation of Bowman had been sufficient to secure the appointment."[145] He didn't last long. I will return to Bowman's tenure at the University of Iowa, which Persons calls "brief and unhappy," in chapter three. For now, a contemporary's description of him will suffice: "an exceedingly tough, ruthless individual, 'a little Napoleon.'"[146]

After being forced out of office in 1914, Bowman temporarily left the world of higher education reform. His successor at CFAT wrote after his dismissal from Iowa that there was "no thought either on Mr. Bowman's part or that of the Foundation of his returning to our work."[147] He spent six years running the American College of Surgeons before reemerging as a university leader.

His new job was as the chancellor of the University of Pittsburgh. Surely, Bowman's CFAT pedigree helped, as did his reputation as a hardheaded reformer. Pittsburgh had low status and massive debt, and it needed a savior. One of Bowman's conditions for taking the job was the end of academic tenure, which he replaced with one-year contracts for all professors. The move was emblematic of his autocratic tenure. Christian Anderson writes that students saw him as "a tyrannical patriarch" while the American Association of University Professors repeatedly censured him for repressing the faculty's academic freedom. However, he remained on good terms with the university's trustees and the Pittsburgh business community. These groups (which overlapped, of course) enthusiastically supported his signature project: the building of the forty-two-story Cathedral of Learning, whose construction occupied more than a decade of his tenure.[148] Bowman conceived of the tower as a symbol of the lofty status of the research university, which was a constant obsession in the academic engineering movement.

In many ways, Bowman was the last academic engineer. His chancellorship at Pitt lasted until 1945, three decades after the movement had peaked and well after its slow fade was complete in 1936. His final years, however, were spent in isolation. The trustees' patience had been tested in 1939, when he suddenly instituted a series of restrictions designed to cripple the university's storied athletics program, including ending athletic scholarships and defunding the football recruiting program.[149] (Attacks on extracurricular pursuits, especially football, were a side project for many academic engineers.[150]) But by 1939, Bowman's assault was too much, too late; the trustees transferred almost all of his duties to the university provost, leaving Bowman marginalized and ignored.[151] The last of the reformers, who had cut his teeth in the heart of the movement, was finished.

Booker T. Washington

The final academic engineer I will profile here is likely the most unexpected. Booker T. Washington is also the only one of the group who remains a household name. Today, he is remembered as a leading voice on turn-of-the-century race relations, especially in the context of his famous rivalry with W. E. B. Du Bois. In reality, the rivalry was largely one-sided: Du Bois thought a lot more about Washington than vice versa. Furthermore, they were not having the same conversation. Du Bois, who held a PhD from Harvard, was an intellectual while Washington, who published and lectured constantly but lacked academic training, was a pragmatic fundraiser and reformer. His friend and first biographer, the influential philanthropist and higher education leader Anson Phelps Stokes, realized the distinction as early as 1936: "Booker Washington treated the 'Intellectuals' with respect, but believed that they were dominated by theories derived in Northern universities, rather than by facts which one could study first-hand in the rural South."[152]

Academic engineering fit Washington well. Recently, he has routinely come under fire for being a "two-faced"[153] "accommodationist"[154] due to his ability to quickly switch between the worlds of poor African Americans in the South and wealthy white businessmen in the North. But he was hardly unique in that type of insider/outsider code switching; Carnegie famously played the role of the genial, simple-minded Scot when it suited him, and the other academic engineers routinely invoked their rural or backwater roots, especially when they were in the field, visiting backwater institutions.

That said, among the outsiders Washington had no equal. He had not been born on the family farm; he had been born on James Burroughs' farm in Virginia, as his slave. The Civil War ended when Washington was nine years old. As his hugely popular autobiography, *Up from Slavery*,[155] explained, after emancipation he found work as a child laborer in a West Virginia coal mine before making his way to the Hampton Normal and Agricultural Institute, founded by a Union Army general to educate freed slaves. (Washington called the general "superhuman" and "Christlike."[156]) We cannot call the Hampton that Washington attended a college; it did not offer academic degrees. But like the colleges of its day, it enrolled young adults starting at age sixteen and it looked like a college, with recitation halls, debating societies, intermural athletics, and an active alumni association. James Anderson emphasizes that in terms of academics it served

primarily as a normal school, preparing its students to teach in the segregated Black public schools of the South.[157]

Washington did exactly that for two years before returning to his alma
mater for an administrative position. Then, at age twenty-five, he was
tapped to serve as the first leader of a new institution in Alabama, designed to replicate the Hampton model. Washington would spend the rest
of his life at the helm of Tuskegee Institute, steering its dramatic growth
and leading the way for a much broader program of education for African
Americans across the South.

It may seem inappropriate to group Washington with the academic engineers, since he often appears in the historical record not as their peer
but as a sycophant asking for their money. Indeed, much of his correspondence with the philanthropists concerned appropriations for Tuskegee;
Carnegie even funded a personal pension for Washington and his wife.[158]
But he also had the signifiers of an academic engineer: he was an outsider pulled to Manhattan (where he fundraised relentlessly and where he
convened most Tuskegee board meetings, typically in the GEB offices[159]),
and he was obsessed with efficiency and control. He shared the academic
engineers' passion for practical study over the traditional curriculum;
Washington declared in a commencement address that there was "just as
much to be learned that is edifying, broadening and refining in a cabbage
as there is in a page of Latin."[160]

And he shared their commitment to systemization. Du Bois famously
criticized the "Tuskegee Machine," which was not a lightly chosen phrase,
with its vivid imagery of interlocking parts and ruthless efficiency.[161] Washington's most important biographer, Louis Harlan, extends and mixes the
metaphor with language borrowed from contemporary critics of the great
industrial trusts: "the octopus-like Tuskegee Machine."[162] This apparatus
relied upon Tuskegee graduates who maintained their loyalty to Washington and his ethos. Some of these were active in politics or journalism
(an area of special concern for Du Bois), but many went on to run pseudo-
colleges for African Americans across the South, looking to Tuskegee for
leadership in much the same way that Gates and Harper envisioned Midwestern colleges lining up behind the University of Chicago. Arnold Cooper offers a vivid picture of the machine at work in his case study of the
Utica Normal and Industrial Institute in Mississippi. As he explains, defer-
ence to Tuskegee on matters of curriculum and growth reflected Washington's position as the "sole arbiter" of philanthropic largesse, which meant
life or death for the subordinate schools.[163]

Washington was also fully on board with the academic engineers in their goal of choking off support for weak institutions. Harlan writes that Washington "had dreamed for decades" about conducting a systematic survey of Black higher education institutions, much in the style of the Flexner Report. Washington's words echoed Gates' and Flexner's when he collaborated with Stokes on plans for "a pretty thorough study of the entire field with a view for selecting schools that are physically located in the right place, and secondly, those that have such backing as to insure them a reasonable future. . . . The killing out of the poorer schools would have to be done very gradually and through a process of placing emphasis upon the efficient ones."[164]

I will return to Washington's tremendous influence over Black higher education in chapter five, especially his insistence on "industrial training" for low-status students, in lieu of academic study. But it is important to introduce him here as evidence that the powerful social capital at the heart of the academic engineering movement traded on ideology, not class. Washington, a formerly enslaved person, was very much a part of the interlocking directorate, leading Tuskegee board meetings that included many wealthy white reformers and sitting alongside them on the boards of Fisk University and Howard University. The color of his skin always mattered, but it did so less than his ideas and tactics: the curious mix of outsider agitation and top-down control that made the academic engineers so iconic—and so controversial.

ROMANS AT THE GATES

Given the outsider status of these reformers, a logical alternative title for this book might be *Barbarians at the Gates*. And in fact, that would also be a compelling title for a book about contemporary higher education reform. One strain of thought about current efforts to change the form and function of American colleges and universities is marked by academic dismay that laymen (especially politicians but also business mavens, philanthropists, and the ever-present "thought leaders") are attacking the nation's redoubts of culture and wisdom. This conjures images of Visigoths massing at the Porta Appia, torches in hand.

Before there were barbarians, however, there were Romans. Operating out of a compact capital city, the Romans spread out and conquered most of the known world. With them, they brought order, rule of law, infrastructure, and culture. But the Romans were also capable of wanton cruelty and ruthless disregard for local cultures and ways of life. When the Romans came to the gates of your village in Gaul or Iberia, you had some reason to be hopeful—and even more reason to be concerned.

People like Gates, Pritchett, Vanderlip, Flexner, Bowman, and Washington were not barbarians. They were Romans. Yes, they were onetime outsiders who had relocated themselves in the metropole, but like religious converts, they were the most zealous believers of all. They had wealth, power, and a self-ordained mandate to spread their vision for the world; in a word, they were elites. And they were builders. The connections they sought to build between institutions and the foundations' headquarters were commensurate to the Roman aqueducts and roads, and they had a plan to organize the provinces that extended out from the city limits. They were obsessed not just with order but with *hierarchical* order. Manhattan may have been at sea level, but in the reformers' minds it was as lofty as Rome's seven hills, an excellent perch from which to rule over an empire.

The Romans are gone. You don't hear much Latin anymore. We gawk at their gluttony and mock their pagan gods. And yet, you can't swing a stick in most of Europe without hitting Roman infrastructure, both monumental and mundane. And you certainly can't claim to understand Western civilization without studying Rome.

The elites who animate this book are long gone too, but they left behind major infrastructure and a logic of reform that lives on today. Their decline and fall came much quicker than Rome's, and their imperialism conquered far less territory. But once you start studying their efforts and arguments, you see vestiges of them everywhere you look in American higher education.

2: TOWARD SYSTEM

Writing to his fellow GEB trustees shortly after Rockefeller's $10 million donation, earmarked "to promote a comprehensive system of higher education in the United States," Fred Gates lingered on a single word in the letter that accompanied the gift: "This word in the letter is a word about which every other word turns—this word 'system.' That word is the pivot of the whole conception."[1]

In the rhetoric of the academic engineers, "system" may have even outranked "efficiency" in prevalence. It spoke to their desire to emulate best practices from Taylorism and the great industrial trusts.[2] But most importantly, it spoke to their hunger for ongoing control of colleges and universities. Engineers design systems, but they also tend them. The reformers, from their offices in Manhattan, would do that tending.

Pritchett elaborated on what systemization should mean, arguing in *The Atlantic* that the chief fault of American colleges and universities was their lack of coordination. Without it, they were doomed to friction and waste:

> In great continuing movements, such as the education of a nation, organization is indispensable. In no other way can continuity and efficiency be had. Not only is this true, but organization which is wise, which respects fundamental tendencies and forces, which separates incongruous phases of activity, may not only add to the efficiency of a national educational effort, but may offer a larger measure of freedom than can be hoped for in chaotic and unrelated efforts to accomplish the same ends. . . . To-day our schools, from the elementary school to the university, are inefficient, superficial, lacking expert supervision. They are disjointed members of what ought to be a consistent system.[3]

This chapter is about the quest for a system but not about the design of the system itself; I will address that in the book's next section. Above all, this chapter is about the *obstacles* the academic engineers perceived as standing in the way of their systemic reforms.

First, they were convinced that there were too many institutions attempting to do the work of higher education. This situation had developed in the nineteenth century, when laissez-faire policies had allowed hundreds of schools across the nation to set up shop and offer degrees, with little oversight. The academic engineers' solution was to reduce the numbers of colleges and universities through attrition, consolidation, and demotion. They would use their money and influence to pick winners and losers among institutions, rewarding the robust ones and shaming the weak ones into either giving up their degree-granting status or shutting down entirely.

Second, they believed that American colleges and universities were servants to too many masters, many of them incompetent. The academic engineers sometimes spoke as if the systems they designed were the first ones ever imposed on American colleges and universities. They were not; some states and many religious denominations had already begun the work of connecting institutions and developing oversight schemes. The reformers had to reckon with these existing power structures and did so in different ways. They attacked religious control but tried to harness and improve the power of state control.

The reformers believed that once these obstacles had been removed, they could create and maintain an efficient higher education system that was ready to help in the work of organizing American society, just as it had been organized itself.

AGAINST THE MARKET AND FOR SOCIAL CONTROL

To understand the academic engineers' feelings about centralized control, we need to understand their economic worldview. It is a foreign one from ours. Today, in a world in which neoliberal economic theory is broadly accepted by business leaders and government officials, we might be forgiven for assuming that elites in the early twentieth century loved the free market. We even have a widely used term—"the market system"—that seemingly offers a logical end result for the academic engineers' systemization project. The reformers and their benefactors were closely intertwined with capitalism, so they must have revered the invisible hand of the marketplace as the wellspring of efficiency. Right?

Not so fast. First, as John Kenneth Galbraith explains, the term "market system" is an oxymoron and a dodge that emerged only after the Great Depression in response to public disgust at the excesses of the prior decades: "Reference to the market system as a benign alternative to capitalism is a bland, meaningless disguise."[4] Instead of a neutral marketplace, he argues, the United States has an economy in which both supply and demand are tightly controlled by powerful corporations that are the heirs to the great industrial trusts of the early twentieth century.

More to the point, the leaders of those trusts *hated* the free market. Instead of gentle supply and demand curves, they saw ruthless competition that gutted prices, lowered quality, and led to endless replication of effort. The monopolistic trusts were construed as an antidote to the madness of the market. Ron Chernow goes so far as to compare Rockefeller's economic worldview to communism: "At times, when he railed against cutthroat competition and the vagaries of the business cycle, Rockefeller sounded more like Karl Marx than our classical image of the capitalist. Like the Marxists, he believed that competitive free-for-all would eventually give way to monopoly and that large industrial-planning units were the most sensible way to manage an economy."[5] The simple difference was who would control those units. Marx thought it should be the proletariat; Rockefeller thought it should be Rockefeller.

This connection was not lost on contemporary critics of the industrialists and the academic engineers they bankrolled. One prominent opponent of the "educational trust" argued in 1911:

> The resemblance between the avowed purpose of this richly-endowed educational agency and the professed purpose of socialism is curious. . . . We have the same use of the word 'competition' in an offensive sense to disparage individual enterprise. . . . They can conceive of no unity and coherence that is not brought about by a central efficient causality. To them consolidation, either through control by the community or by a powerful corporation, is the ultimate form of progress.[6]

The proponents of anticompetition were motivated by recent economic history. As Harold Faulkner explains, in the first decade of the twentieth century a consensus formed that laissez-faire economics, based on free-market principles, were hopelessly irrational and had largely caused the depression that crippled the nation from 1893 to 1897. Coordinated government intervention in the nation's economy came not out of Populist protest or democratic action but rather as a response to "the demands of the most powerful economic groups."[7] The trusts were understood to be doing their part to eliminate the inefficiency and friction of the free market by consolidating and vertically integrating scores of smaller businesses.[8]

The academic engineers applied this logic directly to their vision for higher education. As Frank Vanderlip explained in a 1905 speech on "the co-ordination of higher education," Carnegie and Rockefeller had been doing virtuous work in building their trusts, which the education sector should admire: "The pervading economic tendency of the day, the tendency toward combination and away from useless competition, is a tendency which has been set in motion as a protest against waste. It is, I believe, in its potentiality for the improvement of the condition of men among the foremost of all economic influences ever brought into being." In his 1908 book, Abraham Flexner made the case that the prevailing type of undergraduate education in the United States, like laissez-faire economics, represented a transitional phase that had produced some positive effects: "It performed in education the sort of service that laissez-faire performed in economics and politics: it battered down artificial and harmful restrictions." Its time, though, had passed. "The educational field is now free for constructive effort: for a positive, not a negative, doctrine."[9]

The academic engineers certainly had a positive doctrine in mind, from another area of the social sciences. We can call it social control. That term comes from Edward Alsworth Ross, a sociologist closely associated with a number of academic engineers, who developed it in the 1890s.[10] Ross described social control as a prerequisite for the engineering ideal and the dream of systemization: "It is, in fact, impossible to reap the advantages of high organization of any kind—military, political, industrial, commercial, educational—save by restraints of one kind or another. If the units of a society are not reliable, the waste and leakage on the one hand, or the friction due to the checks and safeguards required to prevent such loss on the other hand, prove so burdensome as to nullify the advantages of high organization and make complicated social machinery of any kind unprofitable."[11]

Ross's vision of social control focused on individuals, which led him to eugenics advocacy and latter-day disrepute. Many academic engineers also dabbled in eugenics, most notably Ross's patron, Stanford president David Starr Jordan. Not coincidentally, the movements had strikingly similar arcs, each soaring in the early 1910s before dissipating in the '20s.[12] But their failures came on different terms. Instead of individuals, academic engineering focused its social control efforts on institutions. As such, it was less morally repugnant. But that focus also meant that its targets—colleges and universities—turned out to be more formidable foes than the largely marginalized and disenfranchised victims of the eugenics movement.

The reformers had a specific model in mind when they described their dream of an educational system built for social control: Germany. Their deep admiration of Germany was especially fitting since it was a nation that had systemization at its heart. In just a few decades at the end of the nineteenth century, a small handful of Prussian leaders consolidated a vast array of independent principalities into Europe's most powerful nation-state.[13] Pritchett explained his fondness for German education and, especially, its systemic form:

> We have barely the framework of what might be called a national system of education, as that is conceived in the more advanced civilized countries. In Prussia, for example, there exists a system of education which begins with the elementary schools. . . . The organization is complete from the beginning to the end, and while the system in some respects to us appears rigid, it nevertheless has greater elasticity than our more incomplete and desultory system, while offering at the same time an enormously greater number of opportunities to the children of the commonwealth for educational advancement.[14]

Writing to President Theodore Roosevelt, he lauded the educational policies of "that remarkable executive, the German Emperor." He was referring to Kaiser Wilhelm II, who was less than a decade from unleashing the horrors of the First World War. "As he himself tersely puts it: 'I intend to develop a system under which each individual citizen shall be trained to be an effective economic unit, and I intend to organize these units into the most effective organizations.' It is the carrying out of this policy which has made Germany the power it is to-day."[15]

Pritchett also triumphantly sent Carnegie an article from the *Berlin International Journal of Knowledge, Art, and Science* that praised the CFAT, writing, "It is to me a great encouragement to find the authorities in education admitting so generously as they do to-day that the Foundation has been the agent for bringing into our school system a wider co-operation. Universities, colleges, and schools have been led in some measure, at least, through the Foundation to stop considering themselves as independent of all the rest and have gone to work to co-operate helpfully with the others."[16]

ACADEMIC ENGINEERING AND THE ORIGINS
OF THE ENDOWED FOUNDATION

For Pritchett, "the authorities in education" were German, and within Germany they had direct access to the kaiser and the apparatus of the state in enacting their vision of social control. The academic engineers in the United States yearned for similar state authority. In a 1908 *Atlantic* article, Pritchett even invoked the growing regulatory power against industrial trusts as a blueprint: "The good college has everything to gain by a scrutiny of higher education if carried out by able men under a system free of political interference. . . . Universities and colleges are to all intents educational trusts. They have the same advantages to gain from fair and wise oversight on the part of the state which other trusts have to gain by such oversight."[17]

Such governmental regulation over higher education was always fleeting, however, as I will discuss at more length in the next chapter. While some individual states did take active oversight of colleges and universities at the urging of the academic engineers, many did nothing, and the federal Bureau of Education lacked any power besides issuing toothless reports. As an alternative, the reformers took matters into their own hands.

In doing so, they developed a completely new mechanism for social control: the permanently endowed foundation. My language here is intentional. The academic engineers did not adopt the apparatus of the foundation for their purposes; they personally developed it. The GEB and the CFAT predated and established the organizational pattern for the landmark general-purpose foundations that Rockefeller and Carnegie set up in the 1910s.

Among other things that set them apart from the charitable funds of the nineteenth century, the two foundational foundations were explicitly *not* benevolent, and neither were the Carnegie Corporation and Rockefeller Foundation. They were designed as elite agencies that would do what the state could not. As such, their early years were marked by controversy, not gratitude. The foundations were styled as devices that promoted the public good, but they were also vast concentrations of wealth, untouchable and untaxable in perpetuity. Most famously, the federal Commission on Industrial Relations held hearings on the Rockefeller Foundation in 1913, questioning its intents and ultimately causing the foundation to withdraw its bid for a congressional charter, which the GEB and CFAT had each received eight years earlier.

One line of criticism focused on the money-hoarding nature of the foundations (1913 also marked the ratification of the Sixteenth Amendment, authorizing a federal income tax), but another focused on the opposite issue: that the foundations would *use* their money. Americans were only just coming around to the idea of the federal government having an active role in society, and to further pass the baton to unelected, unaccountable foundations was a step too far. Of course, the irony in the argument that private foundations were an affront to the prerogatives of the state is that they were founded as a second-best alternative to state control itself.

The academic engineers set goals of control and organization that would be major tasks even for a powerful national ministry of education like Germany's. After Rockefeller's $10 million gift to the GEB, Gates immediately proposed using the money to create a comprehensive national system of higher education. His platform had four planks, emphasizing that colleges and universities "must be comprehensively and efficiently distributed," that they "must be related to each other harmoniously and helpfully and not hurtfully," that they "should be each within its assigned compass," and finally that "the scheme, as a whole and in all its parts, must be essentially stable and permanent and not temporary or fluctuating."[18] These goals were vaguely worded, but together they envisioned a pared-down network of institutions spread evenly throughout the country so as to not compete with one another for students and resources. Stability for the chosen few would be ensured through permanent endowments, padded by the foundation.

The CFAT's stated purpose was less ambitious, and from first appearances it seems like a ruse. Carnegie's $10 million gift was earmarked exclusively for awarding pensions to retiring college professors, but he had no fondness for professors or their work. Therefore, the pension scheme seems like a smokescreen hiding an ulterior plan to control colleges and universities.[19] But this interpretation is wrong on two counts. First, the pension scheme was not a subterfuge at all but rather an important part of the efficiency project. Second, the foundation never hid its desire to control American higher education.

The CFAT pensions were not advertised as benevolent. Instead of easing the golden years of aged professors, they were expressly designed to usher them out the door in the name of efficiency. In a public letter announcing his gift, Carnegie wrote that without guaranteed pensions, "Able men hesitate to adopt teaching as a career, and many old professors whose places should be occupied by younger men, cannot be retired."[20] Writing to thank him, the president of McGill University explained to Carnegie exactly how pensioning would reform his institution: "I have met with no greater difficulties in the course of my administration than those which are involved in a decision to take action in regard to superannuation. The demand for efficiency must, of course, be paramount, and yet, of course, on the other side of the account are the services of the individual often rendered most ungrudgingly through long periods of depression."[21] The CFAT pensions offered institutions a way out of this dilemma. Gates called the plan a gambit "to increase the efficiency of college teaching . . . by pensioning off inefficient college teachers so that their places may be supplied with younger and better instructors."[22] Vanderlip, characteristically, was also blunt, publicly describing the foundation's goal as "retiring faculty members who have passed their day of usefulness and who, in the interest of highest efficiency, had best make way for others."[23]

And the reform worked, judging from a letter sent by a Tufts professor seeking a pension:

> I shall be 81 years old next September and shall then have been connected with Tufts College 60 years. I am still obliged to teach Greek in the Senior & Junior Classes to make a living but for the last 10 years my salary has been reduced to $600. I have tried in vain to get some outside work, but my age is against me. . . . I should like to be able for the time that may be allotted to me yet to be free from teaching and yet to be able to look to the future without anxiety.[24]

Carnegie, who held special scorn for the classics, was presumably delighted to oblige the professor's request. Clearing out this type of dead wood from the academic ranks was critical to his plan to modernize higher education. That said, the CFAT leaders saw some value in promoting the idea that Carnegie funded the pensions because he was sympathetic to professors. Their effort seemed to resonate in the news media, including with a *New York Evening Post* journalist trying to put together an exposé in 1910. He wrote urgently to Carnegie announcing that Pritchett was subverting the industrialist's supposed wishes:

> As the result of an inquiry addressed to each of the professors who have thus far availed themselves of the service pension, it appears that a considerable proportion were either expressly or practically forced out by the college administration, and this fact seems to have made a great impression on the president of the Foundation. "It has been urged," he says, "that one of the benefits of the Foundation consists in the opportunity thus afforded the colleges to get rid of teachers who have worn out their usefulness or who have lost interest."[25]

There is no record of Carnegie's reply, but it is safe to say that he was unmoved by the revelation.

As important as cleaning up the professoriate was, the CFAT's mission went much further. Just like the GEB, the foundation's leaders transparently sought to control and reform American higher education at a systemic level. From the start, Carnegie granted the agency expansive power to promote systemization and standardization in the sector. The CFAT charter established firm criteria for admitting institutions into the pension system, and Carnegie's widely reprinted gift letter authorized the board to impose additional "terms and conditions" on participating schools, "in case two-thirds of the Trustees decide that times have so changed that the form specified is no longer the best way to aid the cause we have all at heart."[26]

The CFAT's goal was to deny money and status to subpar institutions, whose choice would be to shape up or perish. To establish a starting place for that denial, the foundation quickly announced a minimum definition of a college, requiring that participating institutions have at least six full-time professors, an endowment over $200,000, and an admissions policy that required matriculating students to have completed a specific sequence of high school coursework. (This final provision is the origin of the now-notorious Carnegie Unit.[27])

The foundation was thus much more than a pension fund, and it never tried to cover up that fact. As Pritchett explained in 1906 in a national magazine, it was "a central agency in educational administration" that would promote the progressive ideal: "The idea of the scope of the Carnegie Foundation for the Advancement of Teaching as a centralizing and standardizing influence in American education promises to outweigh in importance the primary purpose of the fund [i.e., pensioning], great as that primary purpose is."[28] A decade later, longtime CFAT official Clyde Furst credited his organization and the GEB with having transcended parochial interests in the spirit of social control: "The educational foundations represent an even broader view of universities and colleges, approaching them not only through their institutional history and functions, but chiefly from the point of view of social need."[29]

Today, we are familiar with the idea of philanthropic foundations exerting tremendous influence on American society. That influence has increasingly come under critical examination, especially when it turns to educational matters. When institutions like the Gates Foundation and the Broad Foundation have attempted to use their funds to spur education reform, there has been considerable resistance, particularly from educators themselves. It is useful to remember that the very first national foundations were also chiefly concerned with education reform and that they also inspired an angry backlash.

WINNERS AND LOSERS

The GEB and CFAT had plenty of money, and they both had explicitly stated goals of reforming the hodgepodge collection of American colleges and universities into a centralized, standardized system. What they needed was a strategy to turn the former into the latter.

At the most basic level, we can describe the academic engineers' theory of action as picking winners and losers. They couldn't pass legislation to regulate institutions, so instead they sought to use their money and prestige to reward the colleges and universities that fit into their plans and to deny such blessings to the ones that did not. The foundations would thus boost efficient, virtuous schools while the others died off. The Rockefeller and Carnegie endowments allowed the reformers to play not necessarily God but something closer to the depersonified natural selector they imagined when reading Darwin and Spencer.

Social control theory had already set the stage for this sort of approach. "The way to create a short-clawed feline," Ross wrote in 1901, "is not to trim the claws of successive generations of kittens, but to pick out the shortest-clawed cats and to breed from them. Similarly it is only certain happy siftings that can shorten the claws of man."[30] This eugenicist logic rejected Lamarckism, an incorrect offshoot of Darwinism that held that physical changes experienced during an organism's lifetime could be passed on to its offspring. In its place, Ross held that progress came only when powerful experts picked winners, thus hastening the slow work of evolution. When the reformers read this in the context of higher education, it meant that they should reward schools that were already doing well, and instead of trying to fix inefficiencies at retrograde institutions, they should simply let those losers die off.

Gates, always the most forthright of the academic engineers, spelled out his strategy for "happy siftings" in higher education explicitly in a letter to his fellow GEB trustees:

> [There are] some four hundred and fifty institutions of learning calling themselves colleges or universities. . . . If our directions were not explicit, we could do little more than stand and hesitate amid a din of discordant voices, for all want money. Shall we try to help all of these schools or some of them only—if some, which, and how shall we help these best? Happily our founder has explored the ground before us. . . . WE ARE TO SELECT FOR OUR BENEFACTION NOT ALL COLLEGES AND UNIVERSITIES, BUT ONLY SUCH AGENCIES OF LEARNING AS MAY JUSTLY CLAIM A PLACE IN A SYSTEM

OF HIGHER EDUCATION, AND WE ARE TO CHOOSE SUCH WAYS OF AIDING
THESE SELECTED AGENCIES AS IN OUR JUDGMENT WILL BE BEST ADAPTED
TO PROMOTE SUCH SYSTEM.[31]

Pritchett, writing to Vanderlip in 1905, held the same position about the
CFAT bounty: "I am sure that if this is to be a practical thing you must
confine it to a limited number of institutions."[32] This limitation was not
an unfortunate consequence of limited resources; it was the heart of the
enterprise. Over the coming years, Pritchett would spend much of his time
curating a highly visible list of institutions that met the foundation's standards. Later, Clyde Furst explained the idea: "The educational foundations,
through their careful selection of beneficiaries, have encouraged the elevation of university and college standards. . . . The knowledge that they
recognize and support only institutions that genuinely meet generally recognized standards has been widely influential in encouraging the adoption
and enforcement of such standards."[33] At other times, Furst used blunter
language to explain the other side of the strategy: "At least one-half of our
so-called colleges . . . are unnecessary, and at least one-fourth of them are
a hindrance to education. They give their students inferior training, they
reduce the support of reputable colleges and high schools, and they injure
the cause of education by lowering its repute."[34] These were the losers that
had no place in the new system.

The CFAT trustees made clear from the start that the point of pensioning wasn't about helping professors, writing in their second annual report:
"The true task of this board is not to pass upon the merits of individuals
but of colleges."[35] They began working on the accepted list of institutions
even before the foundation was formally founded. In early 1905, Pritchett
directed MIT's registrar to compile statistics on institutions that were of
high grade and eligible for pensions under the terms of Carnegie's gift,
which excluded denominational and taxpayer-supported institutions.
Twenty-five universities, fifty-six colleges, and eleven technical schools
made the cut.

The next year, the new foundation went much further, creating a comprehensive categorization of American institutions, circulated in a memo
stamped "confidential." There were five groups, two of which were cat-
egorically ineligible for pensions because they were either denominational
or public. The other groups were marked "apparently eligible" (sixty total
schools, fewer than in the 1905 survey) or "possibly eligible" (with more
information needed), and at the bottom were schools that met the minimum criteria but were "below the educational standard." Only fifty-one

were in this pitiful category, although a huge percentage of the institutions in the denominational group surely would have also been judged as subpar. Many schools in the bottom group quickly disappeared (including Pritchett College), though others gained better footing and remain today (including Randolph-Macon College and Tulane University).[36]

That analysis was confidential but the CFAT officials didn't keep the project quiet for long. Starting in 1906, the foundation's widely circulated annual report included an "Accepted Institutions" list of colleges and universities whose professors were eligible for pensions. Everyone quickly understood that pensions themselves weren't the point; a number of institutions fought for a place on the list but never pursued the actual pensions. Instead, the accepted list was an instant *Who's Who* of the winners in the higher education system.

Extramural actors like CFAT get little acknowledgment for instigating the stratification of American higher education. Historians have generally credited the Association of American Universities with casually starting the process in 1900. Indeed, in that year, 14 PhD-granting institutions (many of them headed by academic engineers who would soon sit on the CFAT board, including Jordan and Harper) joined together in a voluntary association. Their ostensible primary goal was to improve the transfer of credits and credentials with European universities, but as Hugh Hawkins and others have noted, the most momentous result of the AAU's formation was a self-identified elite tier of universities.[37] But that was far from all; in its founding document, the AAU declared its intent to "raise the standard of our own weaker institutions." They meant to do so not by helping them earn elite status but by reforming them and increasing their efficiency and utility.[38] This top-down project was exactly in line with the academic engineering ethos, and the connection was not just ideological. By 1908, the AAU was convening its official meetings in the CFAT offices in New York.[39] Shortly after, the AAU began publishing an annual list of colleges whose bachelor's degrees were acceptable for graduate study at AAU member universities. Not only did this effort closely resemble the CFAT accepted list, but internal correspondence shows that the AAU's list was actually created by CFAT staff.[40]

The CFAT picked its winners and losers in full view of the public. The GEB, by contrast, did that work behind the closed doors of its offices. (Although word of Gates's geography obsession leaked to a *New York Tribune* writer in 1907: "on the maps in the William Street office of the Rockefeller fund the little colored pins will probably seal the fate of many a college."[41]) There was no official GEB accepted list, and the foundation published no public reports until 1915, when Flexner authored a comprehensive account of over a decade of its activities.[42] But they certainly played the role of selector, even if their criteria for picking winners were opaque. Buttrick proudly reported that the foundation had no "application blanks"; colleges that wanted money had to write free-form narratives about their "aims, plans, and desires."[43] Gates explained to John D. Rockefeller Jr., why he had refused a suggestion from Charles Eliot (who sat on both boards) to issue a formal definition of a college, like the CFAT had done: "we were seeking to build up a great system of higher education and that to define a college at the present time would be simply to embarrass us and becloud the issue."[44]

Gates's reluctance to define the college had two key components. The first was that declaring formal benchmarks would limit his ability to use his own subjective judgment in picking winners and losers. The second was a fear of formalism. By setting down minimum standards, institutions could come up with ways to game the new system, appearing robust on paper even if they were fundamentally weak in the eyes of a discerning reformer. Gates stated, "I am not content that Mr. Rockefeller's money shall be frittered away. . . . Apples are good. I think people ought to eat apples—the apples of education. Dr. Eliot's plan is to buy them at a dollar a bushel and distribute them. My plan is to plant apple trees."[45]

CONSOLIDATION

Gates spoke often about using the GEB's resources to plant brand-new colleges and universities in areas where supply was not meeting demand, like he had done with the University of Chicago. But in actuality, the academic engineers cared far less about planting new institutions than they did about weeding out the ones already rooted in the soil. Since they hated marketplace competition and wanted to eliminate friction and duplication of effort, the path forward was to pare down the number of institutions. Furst's assessment that half of the nation's colleges were "unnecessary" may have been extreme, but every academic engineer believed that an efficient system required eliminating many of the roughly five hundred institutions that existed in 1905.

That said, even the brashest reformers knew that publicly demanding that dozens or hundreds of colleges shut their doors was politically untenable. Furthermore, in some cases the institutions they viewed as needlessly duplicative were robust schools that competed with other robust schools. The obvious solution was to encourage them to consolidate their operations.

Pritchett was making this case even before the CFAT's founding. In a 1904 speech he called for the merger of two strong institutions in the same metropolitan area. Competition, he told the crowd, had "been the parent of innumerable ills, the author of waste, and still more of insincerity in education. . . . The co-operation of these two great American institutions for a common end, on terms that shall be just and generous and fair, would bring forth fruits for civilization and for education sweeter than those which competition and rivalry can offer."[46]

He was talking about the Massachusetts Institute of Technology and Harvard University. In that year, Pritchett was MIT's president, and he wanted to consolidate operations with the nation's oldest and most prestigious university. This was a deeply controversial proposal. It meant both literally and symbolically giving up the institute's long-standing identity as Boston Tech in order to move across the Charles River to Cambridge, abandon its mission of training working-class technicians, and join the refined academe of Harvard.[47]

Pritchett and Charles Eliot, who backed the plan from the Harvard side, never publicly described the project as a legal combination of the schools into a single institution. They constantly reassured their respective constituencies that in any agreement made, each would retain its distinctiveness and autonomy. The next year, Pritchett spoke to the MIT alumni association, invoking his benefactor in his justification for the plan: "There were some hundreds of years of discussion in Scotland as to whether Scotland should ally with England. My friend Mr. Carnegie says Scotland finally annexed England, not England Scotland. . . . Is the freedom which Scotland has in alliance with England not a wider one and a better one than it could have as a separate kingdom?"[48]

What Pritchett didn't point out was that while Scotland retained its *cultural* identity after the 1707 Treaty of Union, it abandoned its political autonomy, and its citizens immediately became dwarfed by their new English compatriots. It seems likely that the same would have happened if Boston Tech had joined forces with the much larger, much richer, and much more prestigious Harvard.

Eliot's formal proposal for the plan certainly suggested as much, describing it in positive terms: "The Institute of Technology shall move to the land on the right bank of the Charles River, as nearly as practicable opposite the present site of Harvard College. . . . The students in the Institute of Technology shall be deemed students in Harvard University so far as access to and use of the present dormitories, dining-halls, playgrounds, museums, and libraries of the University are concerned."[49] Fellow academic engineers enthusiastically supported the plan. Nicholas Murray Butler predicted that it would quickly yield a single institution: "I cannot but think that the result would so commend itself to everyone that before many years there would be no objection whatever to the most complete merger that may be legally possible."[50] Vanderlip saw the potential merger as evidence that technical education was finally getting the recognition it deserved: "We find even intellectually aristocratic Harvard inviting, perhaps vainly, a great technical school to share in its endowments and enjoy the lustre of its honored name."[51]

As we know, the plan was unsuccessful, although it was approved by the MIT board, which proceeded to relocate to Cambridge even without an agreement with Harvard. Both schools continued to offer competing programs along the same two-mile stretch of Massachusetts Avenue, including, most notably, engineering. It is safe to say that the duplication of effort did not diminish either institution.

Other cases were temporarily unsuccessful but eventually led to celebrated mergers decades later. One was in Cleveland, where Pritchett noted that the Case Institute, a robust technical school, and Western Reserve University, a liberal arts institution, were immediate neighbors: "Here side by side on the same campus stand an Engineering School and a University, each under its own board of control; each sympathizing as the spirit and needs of the time may require, and yet so actuated by ties of daily life and friendly association as to make possible an unusual cooperation."[52] Despite efforts toward consolidation by Charles F. Thwing, Western Reserve's president and a founding CFAT board member, the two remained separate until 1967, when they finally merged to create Case Western Reserve University.

A similar effort took place in Carnegie's adopted hometown, where the technical school he endowed and the newly rebranded University of Pittsburgh (formerly Western Pennsylvania) were actively exploring merged operations in 1910. Uncharacteristically, Pritchett frowned on the idea in a letter to Carnegie, perhaps in recognition of his benefactor's fondness for pure technical education: "the Technical School should be careful not to invade the field of college work. . . . It should keep its purpose clear to teach the applied sciences to those who are to use them for vocational purposes."[53] Unlike in Cleveland, nothing came of the proposal even after decades had passed, although in 1967 Carnegie Tech did merge with the research-focused Mellon Institute to become Carnegie Mellon University.

Many smaller colleges merged during the heyday of academic engineering. Some of them are identifiable by their hyphenated names, like Baldwin-Wallace College, the product of a 1913 merger, and Birmingham-Southern College, which resulted from a 1918 merger. In other cases, the merger meant the disappearance of the less reputable school: In Iowa, Morningside College absorbed Charles City College in 1914 and Coe College absorbed Clark Leander in 1919. Some of the most prominent examples were among Black colleges. As I will describe in chapter five, these schools were constant subjects of the academic engineers' reform ideas. This was especially true in the 1920s, when the reformers had lost their national eminence but retained sway over Black institutions that depended on financial support from Northern philanthropists. Bethune-Cookman was the product of a 1923 merger, and Dillard came out of the 1930 merger of Straight College and New Orleans University.[54]

These were exceptions. Very few mergers actually happened, despite a conviction about their efficiency that has persisted from the academic engineers to today's thought leaders.[55] But the consolidation idea was merely one of many levers to pull in the effort toward systemization. A news magazine writer perceived this in 1907, describing the GEB as "the Standard Oil Company plan of consolidation and concentration applied to educational institutions. . . . In other words, the Board will decree, so far as it has power, where new institutions should be located, what standards of efficiency they ought to conform to, what institutions are needless and should go out of existence."[56]

THE PROBLEM OF THE SMALL COLLEGES

When the academic engineers made the case for merging institutions, they were usually talking about two robust schools in close proximity. Consolidating would mean less friction and duplication of effort, and hence more efficiency. These cases were the exception, however, to the general rule governing the desired reduction in the number of higher education institutions. Instead of merging—a legally and politically difficult process—the reformers often simply sought to eliminate undesirable schools. This was particularly true for the small baccalaureate institutions that we today call liberal arts colleges.

In 1906, Pritchett wrote to Carnegie to address a situation with a group of colleges in eastern Tennessee, all of them small, all of them affiliated with the Presbyterian Church, and all of them asking for pensions from the foundation or direct gifts from Carnegie himself. Of Washington College, Tusculum College, and King College, he wrote, "These three institutions, weak, contending, ill-equipped, are all pretending to give a college education which no one of them can give."[57] Pritchett wanted Carnegie to deny funds to these schools in the hopes that they would die, but he did not intend to leave the area without any higher education. Instead, he picked a winner, urging Carnegie to support a fourth Presbyterian institution, Maryville College: "It is a vigorous institution, growing, is in a strong community, and will be able to do the college work for the whole region." (Tusculum and Washington ended up merging two years later, but then separated again in 1912 after an acrimonious lawsuit.[58]) Pritchett's letter mentioned that he intended to continue sending such assessments, which "might help you to make your gifts count enormously for education, and particularly for sincerity in education."[59]

"Sincerity in education" was an even more amorphous and generously defined term than "efficiency." This was by design. When the strict metrics of minimum standards failed to separate winners from losers, applying a vague test of "sincerity" could do the trick. At times, Pritchett equated it with simple modernity, telling an audience in 1908 that "we need now not more colleges, but colleges that shall be sincere and honest and thorough. In a word, we have come to an older stage of our educational activity, and what might have been entirely justifiable fifty or even twenty-five years ago may require today serious revision."[60] Other times, he described it as a more ineffable quality best ascertained by experts empowered by the government: "The time has come when, in all states, those who stand for sincerity in education should demand the passage of law safeguarding the degree-giving power, and providing an agency for the expert oversight of higher education."[61]

Most often, the reformers used "sincerity" in the context of encouraging liberal arts colleges to limit their ambitions. Today, we might call this an attempt to curtail "mission creep," especially in the context of adding functions beyond undergraduate education. The academic engineers constantly criticized small colleges that attempted to develop law schools and medical schools. But they also readily criticized institutions that in their view were not even doing college-level work, as Pritchett argued: "There is only one honest course, and that is to do sincerely the work which is feasible. If that is the work of a secondary school, then the institution should frankly call itself by the right name."[62]

The reformers were obsessed with nomenclature. Flexner railed against "the indiscriminate use of the terms college and university in America," and Pritchett complained that "educational sincerity has been hurt, not helped, in many localities when a good academy or high school is made impossible by the effort to conduct a sham college; or when a good college is sacrificed in the attempt to sustain an imitation university."[63] All of the reformers enjoyed mocking modest institutions that branded themselves universities, as Pritchett did in a 1910 *Atlantic* article describing a visit to a particularly humble "university": "After meeting the Dean of the College, and the Dean of the Scientific School, I was introduced in rapid succession to the Dean of the School of Education, and finally to the Dean of the Graduate School. With some hesitation I inquired of this last functionary what the duties of Dean of the Graduate School in such an institution might be. The Dean spoke up like a man. He said that he taught elementary Latin to those beginning that study."[64]

The academic engineers were cautious about demanding the outright closure of small colleges, even though they had at best a tenuous place in the grand plans for a higher education system, located somewhere between elite universities and technical schools for the masses. In some cases, the baccalaureate schools were prestigious institutions with prominent, loyal alumni; the reformers would have a difficult time calling for Amherst or Williams to shut down. And to that point, they always intended to pick winners among the small colleges; Rockefeller's 1905 GEB gift was "designed especially for colleges as distinguished from the great universities."[65] The idea, though, was not to support modest institutions in continuing their modest missions. It was to select robust colleges and help them grow while their lesser peers died off.

Some leaders of baccalaureate colleges sat on the foundation boards; the presidents of Oberlin, Smith, Colorado, and Allegheny Colleges were CFAT trustees. Still, these men did not oppose letting many of their peer institutions die. William Slocum, an Amherst alumnus and president of Colorado College, wrote in 1915, "It is not maintained that all the colleges of the West are fitted for the work to which they are called. Many of them ought never to have been instituted, as is true of other educational establishments. Others have so far departed from that to which they were called that they cannot recover, and should drop out of existence."[66]

One tactic was to isolate the colleges in function, thereby preventing their growth in both size and mission. This meant restricting them to the four traditional years of college, with neither graduate training nor secondary work allowed. Both the CFAT and the GEB doggedly criticized colleges for running high school level academies, claiming that they drained time and resources from the institutions' core mission. The CFAT was more dogmatic on the postgraduate question, however, as Pritchett made clear in a 1910 letter to Buttrick. He was angry that the GEB had given a grant to Saint Lawrence University, which had just 203 students on its far-upstate New York campus but also maintained "incongruous educational enterprises" including "a theological school, an elementary agricultural school, and a low-grade law school in Brooklyn." With its grant, Pritchett scolded, the foundation was in "danger of confusing in the public mind the conception of what a college is. Does the General Education Board, for example, approve of an American college in the northern part of New York running a cheap law school in Brooklyn?"[67] His idea was not necessarily to kill off Saint Lawrence, only its auxiliary features. That said, Pritchett likely did not expect an isolated college of 203 students to survive very long.

Sometimes, the academic engineers did make an explicit case for institutional death. These types of calls grew louder after the dramatic impact of the 1910 Flexner Report, which led to the rapid closure of dozens of medical schools. Furst used Darwinist language in an article that proposed to extend Flexner's approach to baccalaureate colleges: "Naturally some of the unfit struggle to survive, but the burden of proof is upon them to justify their existence according to the elaborate standards set by the obviously best 50 or 60. If they cannot do this, they must look forward to death from inanition, unable to acquire further support."[68] Shortly after, another CFAT staffer extended this analysis directly to what he called "the small college problem": "I have seen four of these schools and am chiefly impressed with the general ignorance, even on their own part, of what they are really doing. A mere comparative array of the real facts would, if generally understood, be the death blow of several of them."[69]

THE JUNIOR COLLEGE

There was an alternative to death, which allowed the small college a place in the academic engineers' idealized system. In his 1906 letter to Carnegie on Tennessee's competing Presbyterian colleges, Pritchett wrote that "the proposition has been made that they combine into a single junior college which should not pretend to give the full college education, but only that of the first two years, and this solution is undoubtedly a good one from the standpoint of education and of the region itself, and particularly from the standpoint of sincerity."[70] Washington, Tusculum, and King would not only be consolidated; they would be recast as an institution doing thoroughly different work than that of a university or even a standard college.

A robust literature debates the educational and social functions of the two-year junior college, which we now call the community college.[71] For its creators, however, it had one primary purpose: to serve as a consolation prize for subpar baccalaureate colleges.

William Rainey Harper, president of the University of Chicago and one of the foremost academic engineers, is widely acknowledged as the creator of the junior college.[72] He laid out the framework for the new type of institution in *The Prospects of the Small College*, a 1900 book dripping with contempt, especially for the devotees of baccalaureate colleges:

> The love of an alumnus for his alma mater is something sacred and very tender. Does the true son think less of his natural mother because she is, perhaps, poor and weak, or even sick and deformed? The true college man is and will be all the more devoted to his spiritual mother, if, perchance, in the varying tides of human vicissitude, she has become low; or, if in spite of long and weary years of struggle, she has failed to grow into full and perfect vigor. There are scores of colleges which live today, and in God's providence will continue to live, because of the devotion, even at terrible cost, of a few teachers, or a few alumni.[73]

Harper's assessment of colleges as weak and sick had an obvious conclusion, to which he alluded in stating that "in the development of institutions we may confidently believe in 'the survival of the fittest.'"[74] But he did not call for a mass extinction. Of the roughly four hundred small baccalaureate colleges in the United States, he wrote, 25 percent were robust and should survive. The rest needed Darwinism in reverse: a devolution. Harper declared that another 25 percent should become high schools, and the remaining 50 percent should become two-year junior colleges: "There are at least two hundred colleges in the United States in which this change would be desirable. . . . The pretense of giving a college education would be given up, and the college could become an honest institution."[75]

The other academic engineers embraced Harper's idea. Butler echoed him in a 1902 article, stating that "it would be an unmitigated advantage if one-third of the nearly five hundred colleges in the United States would give a two years' course and that only."[76] Pritchett routinely responded to colleges complaining about their exclusion from the CFAT accepted list with the suggestion that they consider dropping the last two years of their curricula and embracing the efficiency and sincerity of the junior college model. Furst extended the consolation prize to women's colleges, arguing that only 10 percent of them were doing true collegiate work. Of the remainder, he argued, "Most must become content, sooner or later, to adopt the name of institute, junior college or secondary school, which really describe their work. The earlier they arrive at this decision, the better for all concerned."[77]

Jordan, who replicated Harper's efforts in the Midwest by working to establish California's early junior colleges, went the furthest.[78] His vision was that the new model would allow Stanford and Berkeley to fully divest themselves from the burden of teaching young undergraduates: "I am looking forward, as you know, to the time when the large high schools of the state in conjunction with the small colleges will relieve the two great universities from the expense and from the necessity of the two first university years."[79] He also argued that the nation's normal schools, which were increasingly seeking to become four-year teachers colleges, should instead be confined to junior college status.[80]

The drive to push small colleges to drop their latter two years of instruction met some success, at least temporarily. In 1925, Leonard Koos calculated that at least half of the nation's roughly 175 junior colleges at that point had reached their status through demotion: "less well-established institutions have taken recourse to the junior-college status as a means of finding a recognized place in the school system."[81] A "recognized place" sometimes meant a direct connection to elite institutions. Harper, again, established this trend by cultivating a network of small Baptist colleges to affiliate with Chicago; they could transfer their best students to the university after the two-year course.[82] Other notable examples included Oxford College, a two-year school that occupied the former Emory College campus in rural Georgia when its progenitor left for Atlanta and university status, and Seth Low Junior College in Brooklyn, created by Butler and controlled by Columbia University.[83] Columbia also gained control of the struggling St. Stephen's College (now Bard) for a short period in the 1920s and '30s. All of these paired small, low-status colleges with large metropolitan universities, offering their students a nominal transfer path into the elite institutions. Simple mathematics, of course, prevented the vast majority of students from doing so, leading to what critics have called "the diverted dream," a trend that only intensified with the growth of public junior colleges in the midcentury and their shift toward terminal vocational degrees.[84]

For some institutions, the consolation prize of junior college status was welcome. In 1916, an author profiled several of these in the *Methodist Review*. At Martin College in Tennessee, "the students like two years of real college work that is respected, better than the old course that no standard authorities would respect. . . . The surrender of the degree-conferring power has in nowise injured the school." At Weaver College in North Carolina, since becoming a junior college, "attendance has almost doubled, the friends of the school are more active, having received in gifts more in the last year than in the ten preceding years. President Newell says: 'Our diploma with a degree was a joke; our diploma without a degree is now accepted everywhere without question.'" The author went on to cite the Methodist Commission on Education's embrace of the stratification of higher education as well as the academic engineers' emphasis on sincerity: "that the honor of a school is in the character of work that it does, not in the class of schools to which it belongs; that a Junior College doing its work well is entitled to as much honor and esteem as a great graduate university."[85]

There was plenty of criticism for the movement, however. Koos noted resistance to the junior college push and admitted that the original idea came from the "forces of reorganization in higher education," which often clashed with the desires of students and institutional leaders.[86] That said, one of the most pointed complaints came from within the foundations. Charles Eliot, nearing retirement and increasingly the odd man out on both the GEB and CFAT boards, wrote urgently to Pritchett in 1908: "'Junior College' was a Chicago invention—a dangerous one. . . . In my judgment, the adoption of this nomenclature and this practice would be a long step toward the total abolition of the American college; therefore I am strenuously opposed to it."[87]

For many of the academic engineers who surrounded Eliot, of course, the abolition of the American college was exactly the point. The junior college concept allowed baccalaureate institutions to save face while being permanently demoted to a status in which they would never compete with research universities. The icing on the cake was the promise of sloughing off the freshman and sophomore years onto the junior colleges as well as the task of plucking gifted students out of the masses.

That vision did not hold. No US university successfully eliminated the first two undergraduate years, and, as I will explain in chapter eight, by the 1930s many institutions that had downsized to junior college status returned to offering the bachelor's degree. Furthermore, as Robert Pedersen has shown, most of the growth in new two-year institutions was driven by parochial interests like civic development, not acquiescence to the designs of elite reformers.[88] After all, while the academic engineers were willing to confer a form of legitimacy to the schools, they didn't supply the resources to build them. "It simply strains credibility," Pedersen argues, that communities "took on the cost of a junior college primarily to allow some distant university to be rid of troublesome freshmen and sophomores."[89]

Still, the establishment of the junior college—now called the community college—is a signature legacy of the academic engineers, and its origin as an exclusionary device is an important clue to understanding the many challenges that face students who start their college careers in two-year institutions.

BATTLING DENOMINATIONALISM

The problem of the small colleges was not simply one of institutional weakness. It was also wrapped up in the academic engineers' ardent desire for control over the higher education sector. Before they could execute their plans, they needed to wrest that control away from its current holders.

Often, and especially in the case of the small colleges, control was in the hands of religious denominations. Mainline Protestant denominations like the Baptists, Congregationalists, Methodists, Episcopalians, and Presbyterians, as well as the Roman Catholics, maintained regional and national governance agencies overseeing dozens of affiliated colleges that had been founded in the name of the church in order to train clergy and spread the faith.

The academic engineers had to reckon with these existing systems, which were large. When Vanderlip and Pritchett surveyed private colleges and universities in 1905, they found that of the 329 institutions that responded, 120 were clearly "denominational" while another 109 were "denomination questionable." Only 74 were fully free of denominational control.[90]

Of the two foundations, the GEB was much less hostile toward the denominations. This made sense: Rockefeller was a devout Baptist, and Gates had previously led the American Baptist Education Society. Still, Gates could grow frustrated with them, as he expressed in a letter to Harper grousing about the abundance of small colleges in Iowa: "What is the special claim of the 25,000 Iowa Baptists on us by which they should be favored with five educational institutions, one in front of each man's door yard, when no other 25,000 Baptists in the country can properly claim more than one? . . . I think we will have to let time clear the air, and proceed on the principle of the survival of the fittest."[91] Later, he indicted all of the Christian denominations for contributing to an oversupply of colleges that was "destructive of higher education":

> Each sect reasons that its efficiency as a sect depends upon retaining the higher education of its youth in its own hands, and that the establishment and support of a college or colleges under its own control is a necessity of its competitive growth, if not indeed of its continued existence. I suppose that with reasoning of this kind the General Education Board can have nothing to do. . . . We aim to assist [these colleges] only when as educational forces they are needed, and not only needed, but have within themselves and their constituency a reasonable promise of growth, permanence and power.[92]

The root of this overabundance, as Gates saw it, was that naive churchmen were falling victim to greedy interlopers who wanted to launch colleges as part of land development schemes: "[M]any, if not all of these colleges, originated in the minds of the children of this world - in the imagination of real estate speculators and town site promoters who flattered the vanity and beguiled the simplicity of the children of light. . . ."[93] Pritchett echoed this theme, using almost identical language in a scolding speech to the Conference on Education of the Methodist Episcopal Church: "This weakness of the denominational relation to education has been taken advantage of by the children of the world to impose upon the children of light many educational ventures which are sometimes little better than real estate schemes."[94]

Gates, though, was ultimately sanguine about the issue. In a 1906 GEB report, he argued that in their mission to create a national system of higher education, "We should work harmoniously with the denominational agencies. . . . Religion is the foster-mother of education."[95] He invoked the spirit of anti-denominationalism that was at the forefront of liberal American thought but believed that the Protestant orders could help the larger project: "We may deplore sectarianism. But the sects exist. They harness the powerful motives of religion to the educational chariot. They are the mightiest agencies possible, ready made to our hand."[96]

The CFAT, by contrast, had no sympathy for denominational control. Nor could it have, given its benefactor's long-standing views on the subject. Carnegie was a well-known skeptic of organized religion who viewed religious sentiment as premodern and irrational. As he wrote for an address at St. Andrew's University, he explained that after abandoning the Presbyterian Church as a young man,

> No creed, no system, reached me, all was chaos. I had outgrown the old and had found no substitute. . . . Here came to me Spencer and Darwin, whom I read with absorbing interest, until laying down a volume one day I was able to say, 'That settles the question'. I had found at last the guides which led me to the temple of man's real knowledge upon earth. . . . I was upon firm ground, and with every year of my life since there has come less dogmatism, less theology, and greater reverence.[97]

Herbert Spencer, whom Carnegie befriended and corresponded with for decades, was an ideal prophet for the industrialist.[98] Spencer represented everything that Carnegie admired: he was an engineer-turned-philosopher who eschewed religion and strongly advocated pacifism. Most importantly, he was the thinker most closely identified with the social Darwinism that undergirded Ross's writing and much of the ethos of Progressive Era reform. And he was a well-known agnostic and critic of organized religion.

The academic engineers applied Spencer's antipathy to church-controlled colleges. Harper complained about the "denominational bosses" who governed institutions and blamed sectarianism for the fractious marketplace of higher education. Often, he wrote, "on account of the rivalry between different sects, more institutions have been crowded into a particular territory than the territory could possibly support. Death in these cases is of course a blessing—not only to the institutions that have died, but to the world about them."[99]

Carnegie ensured that denominational colleges would automatically fall into the "losers" category. His gift letter establishing the CFAT pension fund specifically excluded colleges and universities "under control of a sect or require Trustees (or a majority thereof), Officers, Faculty or Students, to belong to any specified sect, or which impose any theological test."[100] Very few denominational schools denied admission to students from outside of their sect—tuition dollars always superseded theology. Almost all, however, required their trustees to be members of the church, and this fact allowed the foundation to ban them from the accepted list until they gave up their ecclesiastical oversight. Even otherwise robust institutions were subject to the requirement. Carnegie held firm in a letter to the president of Northwestern University, who had complained about the Methodist-affiliated institution's exclusion: "So many colleges have seen fit to broaden their views and become participants in the Pension Fund that it is best to adhere to present conditions, hoping the reform may soon be complete."[101]

The policy had a quick and noticeable effect. Within four years of CFAT's founding, at least fifteen institutions had severed their ties to religious denominations, and within a decade the total rose to at least thirty-seven—roughly 12 percent of the religiously affiliated four-year institutions that existed in mid-1905. While this subset was definitely a minority, its members were distinctive. They included many institutions that we know today as elite liberal arts colleges, among them Bates, Bowdoin, Carleton, Colby, Colgate, Grinnell, Pomona, Swarthmore, Trinity, and Wesleyan, as well as ones that would become research universities, like Rochester, Syracuse, and Vanderbilt. Even Chicago, which Gates and Rockefeller had established as a denominational institution, severed its formal ties to the Baptist Church during this period.[102] Writing to Carnegie in 1907, Pritchett claimed victory: "It has been the misfortune of the world that wherever the organization called the church has tried to deal either with educational affairs or with politics is has proved both autocratic and a corrupter of all parties, and it is a great good fortune that we are now rid of any such connection."[103]

The reformers often endorsed a generic form of Christian morality,[104] but they insisted that it could emerge from nondenominational, nontheological college education. Pritchett argued in a 1908 speech that the church should "take the position that all colleges and universities, being influential agents in the training of men, are also agencies for moral and religious influence." Having settled for this secular definition of Christianity, the church could "make itself a religious influence in all institutions of the higher learning without assuming their control or support."[105] This distinction proved too heretical for some, most notably the deeply religious politician William Jennings Bryan, who publicly resigned from the board of Illinois College (his alma mater) in 1907, after it severed its ties to the Presbyterian Church in order to qualify for the CFAT list. He wrote in his resignation letter, "Our college cannot serve God and Mammon. It cannot be a college for the people and at the same time commend itself to the commercial highwaymen who are now subsidizing the colleges."[106] Bryan's invocation of "God and Mammon" was not metaphorical, as it usually is. In this case, the choice was literal.[107]

Some college presidents were enthusiastic about severing their denominational ties and embraced the CFAT decree as a means to that end. Pritchett smugly wrote to Vanderlip, "I am getting many curious communications these days from college people. . . . Many of the brethren are troubled in their souls over the sectarian provision attached to their institutions, and I am inclined to think many of them are getting ready to change."[108] One of these was the president of Pomona College, who wrote to Pritchett about the dilemma and opportunity CFAT presented in terms of severing his institution's ties to the Congregational Church: "We have been discussing changing that rule ever since I knew the college; that is four years ago. We have never got to it. . . . Now we face the embarrassment of being charged with mercenary motives, as if we should make the change because of this Carnegie Foundation. I do not know any way out of it, however, but we must go straight ahead and accept the implication that we are ready to make any sort of a rule in order to get in under some money."[109]

A short-term loss of face was worth a long-term change in governance. A similar process played out at the University of Rochester, where President David Jayne Hill struggled throughout the 1890s to diminish the institution's well-known Baptist affiliation. His successor, Rush Rhees, accomplished the improbable task in June 1906, convincing the board of trustees to sever its denominational ties in order to qualify for CFAT approval.[110]

The CFAT staff went through reams of paper negotiating with college leaders about the nuances of their ecclesiastical control. In some cases, like Pomona and Rochester, both sides were aligned. Denominational ties were often nominal, and sometimes even less than that. In 1907, Pritchett asked the president of Beloit College why his institution was listed in the Congregational Year Book as an affiliated institution, despite his assurances that the college had become nonsectarian. The president frantically wrote back to New York that "the editor of this annual has no right to do so and has not been authorized by us to do it" and promised to remedy the error immediately.[111]

In other cases, however, college leaders waged long battles with the foundation to prove that they were not controlled by a church. Henry A. Buchtel, the president of the University of Denver, fought for years over his institution's Methodist affiliation. Even though the church had powers of appointment over its board, he argued, the university should get credit for its diverse student body, which included Catholics, Theosophists, and "a Jewess of exceptional intellectual alertness."[112] That liberal admissions policy, he claimed, should supersede other considerations: "No institution in America, not even Harvard, is more thoroly [sic] free from sectarian spirit than is the University of Denver. What more could you ask to be said in a charter than that 'NO TEST OF RELIGIOUS FAITH SHALL EVER BE APPLIED AS A CONDITION OF ADMISSION INTO SAID SEMINARY'?"[113]

Still sulking about Denver's continued exclusion two years later, Buchtel groused to Bowman about the foundation's support of colleges that employed leftist professors: "It seems almost wicked to give the sort of generous recognition which you will give to socialists who are incipient anarchists, and then to refuse it to institutions like this one . . . which makes purposeful men and women by the train load."[114] In his final letter, he gave up the fight, telling Bowman, "Some day your people might be able to see with clear eyes."[115]

On some campuses, the anti-denominational campaign provoked internal turmoil. Coe College, a small Presbyterian-affiliated institution in Iowa, had long eyed Carnegie's largesse as a solution to its financial woes. Some of the people it dispatched to write fundraising letters to him even made the mistake of assuming that the Scottish-born industrialist was a practicing Presbyterian. The connection was not so tenuous, however; in 1905, Coe's president, Samuel McCormick, left for the chancellorship of the University of Western Pennsylvania (now the University of Pittsburgh) in Carnegie's adopted hometown, as well as a seat on the CFAT board.

His replacement at Coe, William W. Smith, was a former businessman and the college's first president who was not a clergyman. He fought hard to get Coe on the CFAT accepted list by cutting its denominational ties. His position was that while the institution had needed the church in its formative days, it was time for its control to end: "I believe in autonomy for a college when its character and permanency have become established, as I believe in the legal freedom of a youth when he attains his majority."[116] He managed not only to sever the relationship on the college's end but also to persuade the Presbyterian Synod of Iowa to condone the separation. Smith's efforts paid off in earning Coe the right to CFAT pensions in 1908 as well as a Carnegie-funded science building and a $50,000 GEB grant. They proved too much, however, for the college's board of trustees, which forced him out that same year. They replaced him with a Presbyterian minister. In fact, its next three presidents were Presbyterian ministers, and the college reestablished ties with the church.[117]

Some CFAT trustees were lenient on the issue; William H. Crawford of Allegheny College expressed hope that Carnegie would consent to a modification of the foundation charter "to take in all of the really liberal and educationally efficient institutions of higher learning so far debarred by the denominational restriction."[118] Others, like Jacob Schurman of Cornell, insisted on strict application of the mandate: "I am opposed to the Board of Trustees making any exceptions. If we once begin, these deviations from the rule will return to plague us."[119]

This type of rigidity was on full display in Pritchett's long-running correspondence with William DeWitt Hyde, the president of Bowdoin College. Hyde largely played ball with the foundation, quickly convincing his board to remove itself from the control of the Congregational Church. This was not enough to earn Bowdoin a spot on the accepted list. The foundation's hesitation may have been inspired by Hyde's publicly stated opinions, which could be read as hostile to external reform. The president had recently published a book that included strong words about the role of outside donors in the academic affairs of a college: "A donor has no more right to dictate what views an institution shall teach than a stockholder of a steamship company has a right to direct the pilot how he shall steer the ship to which a thousand lives have been intrusted. . . . It were better that a million dollars should be sunk in Boston Harbor, Lake Michigan, or San Francisco Bay, than that the donor of it should influence, in the slightest degree, the utterance of a professor at Cambridge, Chicago, or Berkeley."[120]

It is not clear whether Pritchett had read the book, but he soon flipped Hyde's logic on him. Several decades earlier, he discovered, Bowdoin had accepted a gift from a Mrs. Stone, endowing a chair in moral philosophy. Stone mandated that the chair's incumbent "shall always be in doctrinal and religious sympathy with the Orthodox Congregational Churches of New England." This clearly was an infringement on the very autonomy Hyde had defended. Pritchett encouraged him to remedy the situation, adding a threat: "It does seem to me important that Bowdoin move in this matter some time within the next six months, because I feel sure it will mean a great misfortune to the college not to have a place on the list of accepted institutions, and as time goes on there will finally come a limit to the capacity of the fund."[121]

Pritchett was not suggesting that the college ignore the terms of the endowed chair—quite the opposite. Writing to a Bowdoin trustee about the Stone Professorship the next year, he championed donor intent, continuing his threatening tone: "It is most essential that American colleges should make it evident that they expect to deal with absolute fidelity with any gifts which are accepted. . . . In my judgment, the support of higher education will depend in no small measure on the completeness with which college boards of trust comply with the evident wishes of givers."[122] The solution, he argued, was that Bowdoin should renounce the gift and relinquish the endowment. This posed two problems for Hyde. The first was that Bowdoin was struggling financially, and he could hardly afford to throw away an endowed chair. The second was that the current occupant of the Stone chair was William DeWitt Hyde.

Hyde continued his efforts at double self-preservation, trying to convince the foundation that the college could have its cake and eat it, too. "We have secured the moral support of releases from twenty-nine out of thirty-one heirs of Mrs. Stone," he wrote, giving them leeway to ignore the theological test.[123] But there was no persuading the reformers, and as Hyde admitted, "the funds involved should be considered as merely the dust in the balance in comparison with the benefits of being placed on the Carnegie Foundation."[124] Furthermore, the problem was quickly compounding: the GEB had pledged a large gift to Bowdoin, contingent on the college raising $250,000 in matching funds by March 31, 1908. The college had hit this number, including in it a personal pledge of $50,000 from Carnegie himself,. However, Hyde had received a letter from the steel baron's secretary declaring him "astonished" to have learned about the Stone chair situation and withdrawing his pledge until the situation was resolved.[125] Carnegie, of course, got his information from Pritchett, who had in fact drafted the letter.[126]

Pritchett's twist of the knife accomplished its goal. Before January was up, Bowdoin divested itself of the Stone gift, donating it (with interest) to the Phillips Academy in Andover, Massachusetts. Hyde quickly got to work making up with the reformers, writing to Carnegie, "Your withdrawal of your offer to give $50,000 came to us at first as a severe blow: but it has helped to clear the air and has put us in a way we possibly might not have reached otherwise to secure admission to the benefits of the Carnegie Foundation."[127] The same day, he sent a sycophantic letter to Pritchett: "Thank you for the patience and courtesy you have shown in bringing to our attention the uniform requirements which you make of all institutions in the interests of the largest educational efficiency. As Mr. Carnegie has been informed of the obstacle which recently existed to prevent our admission to the benefits of the Carnegie Foundation, may I trouble you to kindly inform him that the obstacle has been satisfactorily removed?"[128]

THE PLACE OF THE PUBLIC COLLEGES

Public colleges and universities quickly emerged as the academic engineers' most important arena for systemic reform efforts, but the reformers were split about how to treat them. They could not agree on whether public institutions were the problem or the solution.

Gates was largely in the "problem" camp. He worried that tax-supported institutions were too vulnerable to the whims of the voting masses, in contrast to "colleges and universities amply endowed and holding and teaching truth whatever may be the passions of the hour."[129] He wanted to direct Rockefeller's money only toward these autonomous private institutions, with the hope that they would exert a normative influence on their public peers. Gates also took care to boast that the GEB and CFAT themselves had a direct role in pushing the public sector toward "truth." "The private foundations," he wrote, "will so enlighten and direct popular opinion at all times that there can never ensue a conflict between the democracy and its state universities."[130] Pritchett and the CFAT trustees were less suspicious of public colleges, but since Carnegie had forbidden them from issuing pensions to any tax-supported school, their hands were tied.

The academic engineers saw the real problem of public institutions, even more than their weak academic will, as their tendency toward proliferation. The Christian denominations had theological purposes for building unneeded colleges, and state legislatures had political purposes for doing the same. The CFAT trustees made the connection clear: "In both state and denominational promotion of colleges, local and personal considerations have been allowed to have in many cases too much play."[131] The greatest sin in the public sector was when politicians scattered multiple public institutions across their states instead of consolidating their efforts on a single, maximally efficient university.

I will return to this theme at length in the next chapter, with case studies of several states, but will briefly illustrate the phenomenon here with the case of Montana. Despite its sparse population, Montana was home to three public higher education institutions by 1905, each located in a politically important location: the University of Montana in Missoula, the Montana College of Agriculture and Mechanical Arts in Bozeman, and the Montana School of Mines in Butte. This wealth of institutions was not a result of demand; combined, they enrolled just 322 students.[132]

The academic engineers bristled at this triplication of effort, especially since it was in the form of public institutions. When private colleges competed, that was inefficient, but when taxpayer dollars were involved, the offense was much graver. Jordan declared himself to be on record for this point: "As I said to the people of Montana some years ago, their separation of the agricultural college at Bozeman from the State University at Missoula was a piece of folly which would deepen into a crime."[133]

By 1912, help was on the way in the form of the academic engineer Edwin Craighead. A founding CFAT board member, Craighead had served as president of Clemson and Tulane before his appointment to lead the University of Montana. Shortly after taking office, he reported back to Pritchett, "We have under consideration a plan for the consolidation at one place of our four higher educational institutions now separated and located in different places."[134] His tally included the Montana State Normal School in Dillon, which had recently declared itself a college. Craighead convinced the state Board of Education to endorse the consolidation, with the three abandoned campuses becoming high schools. His local newspaper was also enthusiastic, since Missoula would be the most likely spot for the combined institution, and suggested that a committee including "educators of national reputation" be brought in to advise the board on the project (unsurprisingly, they named Pritchett, Butler, and Jordan as potential members).[135] But the legislature, wary of alienating constituencies, blocked the consolidation plan, and when the proposal made it to a statewide ballot initiative in 1914, the voters overwhelmingly rejected it. Still, Craighead continued pushing consolidation, and in 1915 the exasperated Board of Education fired him.[136] All four of the Montana higher education institutions remain today, in the places where they were founded.

Thus, the problem of dividing scarce resources turned out to be just as acute for public higher education as it was for the private colleges. Craighead understood this parallel well and in fact was on record as arguing that the fiscal distinction between public and private institutions was meaningless. At Tulane, he had waged a long and ultimately unsuccessful campaign for appropriations from the state of Louisiana, arguing that its educational functions were a public good and thus deserving of public support. It made no sense, he argued, for a leader like him to spend his time seeking private support: "Shall the President spend his time tramping the streets of New Orleans begging the mere maintenance of an all-important state institution? No, Tulane is a public institution, entitled to state aid."[137]

Craighead's demand for public appropriations to a private institution had precedent. Harvard, for example, had a long history of taxpayer appropriations; as the historian Herbert Adams noted in 1889, until recent years "Harvard was really a State institution. . . . She was brought up in the arms of her Massachusetts nurse, with the bottle always in her mouth."[138] Many other private institutions benefited from public funds, including some Black universities: Atlanta University received a subsidy from the state of Georgia from 1874 to 1887, and Howard has received an annual appropriation from the US Congress since 1879.[139] The most notable case, however, was that of Cornell, one of several privately endowed universities to receive public support in the form of a federal land grant. This was not enough for President Jacob Schurman (a future CFAT trustee), however. He dedicated the entirety of his lengthy inaugural address to demanding public appropriations (at least $150,000 annually) from the state of New York: "Cornell University is a very important part of the body politic, and why should it alone be deprived of the nourishing life of the organism? ... No one can fail to recognize the justice of our claims upon the state."[140]

But others saw a clear dividing line between the public and private halves of the higher education sector. They included Carnegie, who insisted on language in the CFAT charter excluding all public institutions from pension eligibility, snubbing them alongside the denominational colleges. Carnegie had long been wary of putting his largesse toward public purposes that he viewed as the responsibility of taxpayers. For example, although he donated thousands of public library buildings, as a rule he never funded operating budgets or the purchase of books. The same principle applied to higher education, where he frowned on inviting public resources and mandates into the private sector. He wrote Andrew White to congratulate him on Schurman's inauguration but noted, "He is no doubt just the man for Cornell but astray about Government aid for such Institutions—can't manage that in a Republic yet."[141]

Carnegie's exclusion of public institutions from the CFAT accepted list was the flip side of this policy. Writing in reply to Charles Eliot's dismay at his decision, he explained that "it was the opinion of those around me whom I could consult, that leaving out the State Universities would stimulate the States to do something for them."[142] The idea was that taxpayers should provide more funds to public institutions, starting with professorial pensions, and that CFAT would serve as a normative influence encouraging just that. A Stanford trustee wrote him to confirm this reformist logic, alongside the effects of the denominational restriction: "It will cause all public institutions to provide adequate retiring allowances, and tend to liberalize and bring ineffective sectarian colleges up to a higher standard of efficiency."[143]

Furthermore, in Carnegie's view, public institutions were of minimal importance; in 1905, despite recent growth, they enrolled just 28 percent of the nation's students. This underrepresentation was especially true in the two states he knew best. His adopted home of New York had twenty-eight private colleges and universities in 1905 but only a single public one: City College, which enrolled 8.3 percent of the state's undergraduates. His adolescent home, Pennsylvania, also had just one public institution (Penn State), versus thirty-nine privates. It enrolled only 6.5 percent of the state's undergraduates.[144] Carnegie saw no point in wasting time and money on a small sliver of higher education, especially one that he thought should be the responsibility of the taxpayers and legislators who had created it.

This stance would grow into a rift between the industrialist and the head of his foundation. Shortly after the gift announcement, Pritchett wrote to Vanderlip, hinting at brewing trouble: "Talking with several of the heads of the larger state institutions I find they are a little sore at being omitted."[145] A month later, Carnegie heard from Elisha Benjamin Andrews, the chancellor of the University of Nebraska, a staunch academic engineer, and the president of the ten-year-old National Association of State Universities.[146] Andrews was more than a little sore. Public institutions, he explained forcefully, were the worthiest recipients of Carnegie's largesse: "In nearly every state having a state university this institution is doing more for the people than any other of the kind; in most states more than all others. Every increase to the efficiency of such an institution is a vast public benefit."[147]

Pritchett agreed with Andrews, writing in *The Atlantic* the next month, "No one interested in education can repress a thrill of exultation as he looks forward to the future of the great state universities."[148] He saw no reason why they shouldn't be included in the CFAT pension scheme. In May of 1906, he assured Eliot, "I am in touch with President Buckham, of the University of Vermont, and that institution will undoubtedly share in the benefits of the Foundation. It is entirely possible for him now to make a request of the trustees at any time in his own case."[149] This was a clear attempt at subverting Carnegie's intent, and it failed; Vermont did not appear on the accepted list for several years. But Pritchett was not done. In March 1907, he released a bold pamphlet under the CFAT name: *Bulletin Number One: Papers Relating to the Admission of State Institutions to the System of Retiring Allowances of the Carnegie Foundation.* He included in it verbatim letters from public university leaders, as well as Andrews' association, as prologue to his own twenty-seven-page memorandum on the topic. His measured words built a case for including public institutions in the pension fund before abruptly declaring the idea impossible on the grounds that it would deplete the foundation's endowment.[150]

This problem was solved, it seemed, by an unexpected change of heart by Carnegie. In January 1908, Pritchett met with "all the state university presidents" at a private conference in Chicago, assuring them that the CFAT board was working to remedy the situation.[151] Two months later, he had something to show for his efforts: a letter from Carnegie suggesting in noncommittal language that he was open to contributing an additional $5 million to the CFAT endowment in order to expand pensions to public institutions.[152] Pritchett took this as a green light and quickly rallied the board to start adding these to the accepted list. Among the first to make the cut was the University of Nebraska. But to Andrews's great chagrin, native Nebraskan William Jennings Bryan showed up in Lincoln and convinced the legislature to refuse the honor, calling the CFAT scheme "the most insidious poison that has ever entered the body politic."[153] Similar problems emerged in other states as well, as I will explain in chapter six.

And there was a bigger problem: Carnegie soon seemed to either forget his offer or change his mind. Pritchett wrote to his benefactor in May, asking him to transfer the $5 million to the foundation's account, only to receive this response: "I am particularly anxious that nothing should be done to give the slightest support to the idea that we officiously wish to render aid to State University Faculties, who are employees of the State. I admire the State that says 'This is our duty' and performs it."[154]

These were not the words of a man with an open pocketbook, and indeed Carnegie did not transfer any new money to the foundation. Two years later, Pritchett wrote again in search of the allegedly promised donation, touting the normative function of including public institutions: "If we establish in a single institution of the state a retiring allowance system, it produces great pressure on the state to do the same thing for the other institutions with which we do not deal, and we can see that this pressure is already beginning to have its effect."[155] Nothing came of it. The next year, he wrote yet again, explaining that the foundation was now paying the pensions of dozens of public university professors and was rapidly depleting its funds. The handwritten response from Carnegie: "I don't see how the Foundation can pension 72 men from State Universities when these institutions were excluded by me."[156]

The impasse was somewhat resolved later in 1911, when Carnegie finally sent a fraction of the suggested gift—just $1 million—to the foundation, to fund pensions at public institutions. But the incident revealed two important facts about the academic engineers. The first was that some of them, including Pritchett, were less committed to hard and fast rules than they publicly claimed. They enacted their reforms under the imprimatur of what their contemporary Max Weber called "rational-legal authority," but in reality, they craved flexibility to pick winners and losers based on more personal, subjective criteria of institutional worth.

The second fact is that by 1911, the academic engineers were learning that their vision of reform would not be so simply executed. Not only did their internal disagreements hinder their progress, but they also were increasingly running up against serious skepticism about their work: from prominent foes like Bryan, from peers like Eliot, and even from their own benefactors. Pritchett acknowledged as much in an unusually contrite November 1911 letter to Carnegie: "I have tried, my dear Friend, to give to the problems of the Foundation the best thinking I was capable of. Of course, such mistakes as have been made are my mistakes. But on the whole, as I look back over these six years, I feel that the important things have been decided well. If I have fallen short of your expectation, it has been from no lack of devotion to the things you wish to accomplish."[157]

PART TWO

The Program of Reform

3: THE HIGHER EDUCATION PYRAMID

The academic engineers lived in a world obsessed with modernization and rationalization. The historian Robert Wiebe described the Progressive Era as a "search for order": an attempt by elites to organize the provincial, chaotic society of nineteenth-century America into rationalized harmony.[1] Daniel Rodgers followed up by pointing out the incorrectness of the notion that Progressivism was a grassroots attack on big business and bureaucracy. On the contrary, it was a top-down attack on the disorganization of the American grassroots.[2]

Academic engineering was exactly that sort of attack. At the turn of the new century, the reformers looked at the landscape of higher education and saw a morass. Too many institutions, too much catering to the chaotic marketplace, too much pretension on the part of modest schools, and no clear sources of authority.

They intended to impose order, and order meant hierarchy: a stratified system in which the upper strata set the rules for everyone else. On one level, they believed that their reforms would mean that the higher education sector would shape American society, rather than respond to it. Gates explained, "When the spirit of education shall be changed, as it will be, then the direction in which the machine works will be reversed, and the colleges will studiously employ themselves in carrying civilization with all its blessings downward to the people on the soil."[3]

But on another level, the reformers saw hierarchy as something that needed to be imposed upon the higher education sphere itself. The first step was clearing up the pecking order of institutions. The legacy of laissez-faire policies in American education meant that any school could operate as it wished. Some high schools issued master's degrees, some colleges issued PhDs, and some universities issued neither. In Pritchett's words, the chief task of the foundations was the "work of standardization, with clearer ideas of what the function of the various grades of institutions ought to be."[4] But classification was only the beginning.

The academic engineers were eager to design hierarchical systems, but they also knew that they lacked the capacity to maintain them without help. They pursued several top-down mechanisms in the service of delegating that maintenance work: the bureaucratic authority of the federal government, the normative influence of a national university, and the legitimating power of elite private universities. These went nowhere. The one idea that had some staying power was the effort to cement the role of public "flagship" universities at the top of state-level hierarchies. But even this, as I will show in four case studies, was deeply controversial.

THE VISIBLE HAND OF HIGHER EDUCATION REFORM

The best possible business sector analogy for what the academic engineers were trying to do was not Rockefeller's oil trust or Carnegie's steel empire but the national system of railroads. The reformers flattered themselves with the comparison. Building the nation's rail system was the work of actual engineers, a purposeful project conducted by technocrats. These engineers enabled miracles like the ability to travel from Florida to California in the same rail car, a feat until recently unthinkable across a hodgepodge of locally owned, nonconforming tracks. It was a triumph of efficiency.[5]

Pritchett used the analogy in a 1907 essay:

A generation ago railways began to push out through the west into all parts of the then undeveloped country. They were built with little regard to standards. They were pioneers of commerce and created the trade upon which they were afterwards to live. To-day, however, pioneer days in railroading are over. Railroad lines are cutting down grades, straightening curves, and everywhere conforming to fixed standards. Only a limited number are developed into trunk lines, but all conform to a standard gauge.[6]

He and Gates often talked about the "pioneer days" of American higher education, by which they meant the laissez-faire era. Their self-appointed task was to transcend those bad old days by creating a standard gauge of institutional status and then deciding which institutions would be the equivalent of "trunk lines"—the main intercity routes that provided the framework of the nation's rail system—and which would be the marginal "branches" that fed into the trunks.

Rail was not just a convenient analogy; it was the center of the American economy at the turn of the century. The business historian Alfred

Chandler describes railroads as "the first modern business enterprises" in the United States: "They were the first to require a large number of full-time managers to coordinate, control, and evaluate the activities of a number of widely scattered operating units."[7] The academic engineers were obsessed with this type of management. Just as railroad managers would oversee nationwide networks of trains and depots, they would oversee interconnected and standardized colleges and universities across the nation. Chandler famously analyzed "middle managers," whom he described as the irreplaceable foot soldiers of big business, but he also analyzed their superiors, whose role in structuring massive corporations and cartels was far from ancillary: "The perfecting of internal organization and the coordination of flows across and between roads had been largely the job of middle management; system-building was almost completely the task of top management."[8] The latter category was a good description of the Manhattan-based reformers; in turn, they sought to install right-minded people—college presidents, trustees, and even faculty—as their middle managers.[9]

For Chandler, the American economy became modern when the "invisible hand" of the marketplace was overtaken by the "visible hand" of managerial capitalism. That switch reflects the academic engineers' determination to transcend laissez-faire, along with many of their other preoccupations: the quest for consolidation, the sense that competition was ruinous, and the creation of new organizations to exert normative and coercive control over the components of a would-be system. The reformers' vision aligned with the business concept of vertical integration, which enabled a handful of corporations to become enormously profitable around the turn of the century—most notably the Rockefeller and Carnegie trusts. As Chandler shows, by aligning all aspects of production, sales, and distribution, firms could transcend both the whims of the free market and increasing government regulation. Their efficiency made them big, and their bigness[10] allowed them to further dominate their sectors by gobbling up some smaller players and running the rest out of business. Even after federal antitrust legislation became law, large enterprises "remained successful because administrative coordination continued to reduce costs and to maintain barriers to entry."[11]

These two goals—efficiency of costs and benefits, and a halt/reversal of the proliferation of institutions—were hugely important to the academic engineers. Managerial hierarchy and vertical integration provided the template for their vision of a rationalized higher education system.

SUBORDINATING THE HIGH SCHOOL

The academic engineers started their stratification project by dealing with the bottom of the hierarchy. Today, we take it for granted that the high school occupies a rung below the college on the educational ladder, but that was not always the case. David Labaree reminds us that starting in 1849, the Pennsylvania legislature authorized Philadelphia's Central High School to grant bachelor's and master's degrees; its teaching faculty also called themselves professors.[12] This may have been an extreme example, but the common description of the high school as "the people's college" reveals the fine line between the two institutions.[13] Mark VanOverbeke shows that throughout the nineteenth century, high schools and colleges competed for the same students. Both primarily enrolled fourteen- to eighteen-year-olds and often offered indistinguishable curricula.[14] As late as 1907, Pritchett felt the need to argue that "the college should be superimposed upon the high school."[15] Even the term "higher education" itself, with a built-in hierarchical connotation, was not yet consistently used toward the end of the century; frequently, it was used to refer to both secondary and collegiate institutions.[16]

The work of differentiating the high school and college is typically framed in the context of the administrative progressives, who were focused on K–12 schools.[17] But the leaders of the high school reform project more frequently came directly from the higher education sector. When the National Education Association convened its famous "Committee of Ten" (officially the Committee on Secondary School Studies) in 1892 to create the first national set of standards for the high school curriculum, half of its members were college and university presidents. Three of them went on to become CFAT board members and a fourth, US Commissioner of Education William Torrey Harris, was an academic engineer closely interlocked with the GEB and CFAT circles.[18]

VanOverbeke describes the primary goal of these reformers as "articulation" between the institutions: a coordination of curricular standards designed to facilitate the college admission of high school graduates. Even that very premise, however, points to the subordination effort. By framing the high school as the *gateway* to college, the academic engineers effectively formalized an institutional hierarchy. Harold Wechsler describes the rapid spread of the "certificate system" in the 1880s and '90s, which further cemented the status strata.[19] Whereas all colleges had previously admitted students only by examination, many now offered admission by certificate, in which students who held a diploma from an approved high school were automatically accepted. Making this system work required a very visible display of managerial hierarchy: college and university professors coming into a high school to quiz teachers and principals about their curriculum and rigor. It was finally clear who was the boss.

The certificate system's shift—from judging students to judging schools—sounds a lot like the CFAT mantra I quoted in the last chapter: "the true task of this board is not to pass upon the merits of individuals but of colleges."[20] And in fact, the foundations played a role in reforming K–12 schools, at least indirectly. For example, historians have emphasized the importance of the Carnegie Unit, a precise measure of time-based high school instruction that became an indelible part of the "grammar of schooling."[21] The name came of course came from the foundation, not from Andrew Carnegie himself, who had no interest in high schools. The CFAT board created the Carnegie Unit as a ruler by which they would measure *colleges*—specifically, to assess the rigor of their admissions standards under the certificate system. The goal was not to reform high schools but to crack down on unscrupulous colleges that accepted unprepared students from lousy secondary schools.

Sometimes, those lousy schools were directly connected to the unscrupulous colleges themselves. The academic engineers hated the fact that many baccalaureate colleges maintained "preparatory academies" on their campuses, which confused the hierarchy. In 1905, CFAT board member Samuel McCormick wrote a memo describing the types of college that would be particularly impervious to reform, with "the college with preparatory department" as exhibit A: "This is perhaps the source of greatest perplexity for in many cases the Academy is practically the whole thing, though a four year College course is offered."[22]

The idea of college professors spending their time teaching low-level courses to high school students smacked of inefficiency and low standards. And McCormick was speaking from experience. He had once been the president of Coe College, the Iowa school that begged for a place on the CFAT accepted list. Coe maintained a high school on its campus, and a few years later Pritchett told McCormick's successor to give it up: "I find it hard to convince myself of a real necessity for the existence of such a school. It serves only one purpose, so far as I can see, and that is to bring a few students to the college."[23]

Small colleges weren't the only sinners in this category. Writing to a fellow academic engineer in 1909 about why the University of Illinois was excluded from the CFAT accepted list, Pritchett explained that "the University maintains a large preparatory school, containing some five hundred students. This is inextricably mixed with its college students being at the same time in both schools. I have visited Urbana and tried to understand the basis of the continuation of this school, but I have been unable to."[24] Soon, however, Illinois got with the program. Nine months later, the university's board of trustees unanimously voted to shut down the preparatory academy, and it was on its way to a spot on the accepted list.[25]

In one sense, the academic engineers' disgust at in-house preparatory schools points *away* from an interest in vertical integration. Shouldn't they have celebrated the efficiencies inherent in housing a complete set of educational units, from kindergarten to graduate school, on one campus and under one set of managers? But this was not how the reformers thought.

When they spoke about efficiency and systems, the academic engineers were not speaking about the internal dynamics of any particular institution. The CFAT trustees were clear on this issue, writing, "It is the work of the Carnegie Foundation to present the problems of education not from the standpoint of an isolated school, but as far as its officers and trustees are able to do, from the standpoint of a continent."[26] Thus, the systems they imagined were continent-wide, and so were their models of vertical integration. Their hierarchical ideal was not that University of Illinois's preparatory academy would be aligned below the University of Illinois's baccalaureate division; it was that all secondary schools would be aligned below all colleges.

FEDERAL MANAGEMENT

The foundations were not the logical arbiters of such a continent-wide system. They had great wealth and power, but not as much wealth and power as the US government did. The academic engineers saw foundations as the instigators of higher education reform, but they wanted the long-term managers of the movement to be civil servants in Washington, DC.

Vanderlip, Pritchett, and other reformers had held federal jobs and were aware of the potential strength and reach of the federal government. And as in all things, they looked across the Atlantic for a role model. As early as 1874, Andrew D. White (who went on to a career in the State Department after leaving the Cornell presidency) praised the German system of higher education, which derived from "a State whose central administration is thoroughly orthodox, and exercises strong political control." He went on to denigrate the United States by contrast, mostly for the inability of its government to regulate the spread of institutions: "The main condition of advanced education is concentration of resources. England sees this, and has but four universities; imperial Prussia sees it, and has eight; the United States has not seen it, and the last Report of the Bureau of Education shows that we have over three hundred and sixty institutions bearing the name of 'college' and 'university.'"[27]

The United States Bureau of Education, in fact, was at the heart of the problem, because of its impotence. The bureau had been organized only in 1867, as a small division within the Department of the Interior, and for its first decades it was staffed by political hacks with little expertise in education. Even those hacks, however, could sometimes speak the language of academic engineering, as did N. H. R. Dawson, a well-connected Alabaman appointed commissioner by Grover Cleveland who wrote in 1890, "Higher education needs to be centralized and harmonized."[28]

A precedent existed for government involvement in higher education reform: the celebrated 1862 Morrill Act, which offered federal largesse to the states in order to bring practicality to higher education, in the form of land-grant colleges. But the land-grant project was hardly a resounding success, as I will describe in the next chapter, and some critics wanted the government to take a much more active role than handing out grants.

At the dawn of the academic engineering movement, Johns Hopkins professor Herbert Adams pressed the case for increased federal power in a report for the National Education Association. Adams praised the German model of state control and noted that the recent gifts to American higher education were only a start: "Private philanthropy will do all it can, but public interest demands that the State should do its part." Most forcefully, he called for an enhanced role for the nascent educational bureaucracy: "The Bureau of Education ought to become a ministry of public instruction, with a recognized place in the Cabinet, and with a constantly energizing influence proceeding from the capital of this country throughout the length and breadth of the land, stimulating the colleges and the universities, as well as the school systems of the whole country."[29]

William Torrey Harris, Dawson's successor as Commissioner of Education, moved the bureau in that direction. He was a classic academic engineer. A Germanophile who wrote a book on Hegel, he never earned a bachelor's or any other degree (he had dropped out of Yale after two years) but always insisted on being called Dr. Harris due to an honorary LLD from the University of Missouri.[30] After a stint as a K–12 administrator, he became commissioner and turned his attention to higher education.

Harris turned the bureau into a reform agency by mastering the art of data collection. In his inaugural report as commissioner, he explained, "The legitimate function of the Bureau of Education is the collection and distribution of educational information. Each place should know the fruits of experience in all other places."[31] Every year, he submitted to Congress a Statistical Review of Higher Education, which provided constant grist for the academic engineering mill. Harris also worked with Vanderlip and Pritchett on the groundwork for the CFAT pension scheme.[32] Upon his retirement in 1906, the foundation took the highly unusual step of awarding him a CFAT pension on the basis of "meritorious service."[33] Even though he had never worked at a college or university in any capacity, he received $3,000 a year for the rest of his life, out of a fund earmarked for retired professors.

Harris's successor as commissioner was even more aligned with the academic engineers. Elmer Brown held a German PhD and went to Washington from the Berkeley faculty. Shortly before his federal appointment, he had been elected president of the National Council of Education, whose leadership included other academic engineers like Harper, Butler, Thwing, and Harris. The council was the research arm of the NEA, authorized to conduct surveys and investigations, often with a reformist agenda.[34]

At the bureau, Brown took this work to the next level, commissioning a report that brought to life an academic engineer's most pleasant dream: a government-sanctioned stratification of colleges according to strength and standards.

It was a debacle. The stratification report generated an uproar that eventually required the president of the United States to intervene. As Samuel Capen, a fellow reformer, recalled, this "startling and momentous document, which originated in 1911, flitted like a comet across the educational firmament, left a trail of deadly meteorites falling behind it, and suddenly vanished from the purview of the naked human eye."[35] Pritchett used slightly less vivid language to argue that "politics" killed the reform attempt: "The moment the nature of its contents became known, the local institutions in many States appealed to their Congressmen and Senators, and they in turn to the President. The report was suppressed. It reposes peacefully upon the shelves of the Bureau. There it will continue to repose."[36]

The 1911 report was distributed "semiconfidentially" for review and comment from educational experts. Chief among these were deans of graduate schools at elite universities, who themselves had provided much of the qualitative data for classifying the colleges. The report also acknowledged its debt to "helpful interviews with the officials of the Carnegie Foundation for the Advancement of Teaching, and of the General Education Board."[37] Needless to say, those officials were not just helpful but instrumental in creating the rationale and impetus for such a report.

The document's author, Kendric Babcock, was the bureau's first "Specialist in Higher Education" and the former president of the University of Arizona. He made the case that a neutral bureaucracy in Washington, and not a foundation in Manhattan, was the best agency to impose order on American higher education: "Having no funds to give or withhold and no special propaganda to promote, and having a reasonable probability of the acceptance of its judgment both at home and abroad, the bureau already feels assured of a cordiality of cooperation in its investigations which has not always been granted to other investigators of like purpose."[38] The officers of CFAT and the GEB, who were under increasing public scrutiny by 1911, agreed and enthusiastically backed the report.

Babcock sorted 344 colleges and universities into four categories. The robust Class I category contained 59 schools, almost perfectly replicating the CFAT accepted list of the previous year, with the addition of certain denominational institutions like Northwestern and Brown, plus a few women's colleges. The bulk of schools fell somewhere in the two middle categories. The dismal Class IV comprised 40 institutions whose diplomas Babcock deemed basically worthless.[39] They included many small denominational colleges, of course, but also some public institutions that would rise to prominence later in the century, including Georgia Tech, the University of Maryland, and Texas A&M.

Babcock's prediction of "a cordiality of cooperation" was comically wrong. The contents of the fifteen-page report spread quickly, and angry responses followed from spurned colleges and universities as well as their defenders in the media. The Catholic periodical *America* compared the effort to the "similar effort of the Carnegie Educational Trust's officials to set up classifying standards, [which] has met with widespread opposition." It went on to attack Babcock and Brown and to suggest that they were receiving their comeuppance: "the Bureau of Education has wrought grievous injury to more than seven-eighths of the higher institutions of training in the country. . . . The storm that has broken over the heads of the Bureau officials responsible for the circular is proof enough of the contempt felt for the paltry achievement."[40]

The chancellor of Syracuse University, whose institution had ended up in Class II, went further, publishing an irate letter in the *Boston Evening Transcript* that personally attacked the "obscure man by the name of Babcock," whom he viewed as an illegitimate judge: "By what authority? Not by law, for no such authority is given the Department at Washington. Not by justice, for we had been granted no hearing. Not by competency of the classifier for he is unknown to the educational world and is without experience or expert ability and knowledge."[41] The chancellor's criticism was based partially on Babcock's newcomer status. Perhaps a figure like Pritchett or Gates, both of whom were widely known in the higher education sector by 1911, would have passed muster. But the other charge—a lack of authority—applied even more to the unaccountable foundation officials in New York than to a bureaucrat in Washington.

The criticism continued to mount. As Capen described, "The bureau learned that there are no second and third and fourth class colleges; that it was an outrage and an infamy so to designate institutions whose sons had reflected honor on the state and nation. The clamor reached Congress and grew louder."[42] Finally, President William Howard Taft issued an executive order in February 1913 that stopped the bureau from issuing any more reports on the subject.[43] This was the suppression that frustrated Pritchett, and it apparently meant the end of Babcock's tenure in Washington as well. Three months later, he left for a job as a dean at the University of Illinois. Capen was his successor. He never attempted anything so audacious, and in fact, as I will describe in chapter seven, he would soon play a major role in ending the influence of academic engineering in Washington.

The bureau's ineffectiveness was a disappointment for the academic engineers, but the situation ended up bolstering their position. As John Thelin has observed, in the 1910s the CFAT was "no less than the de facto Ministry of Education" in the United States, and the GEB took on a regulatory function as well.[44] Today, we distinguish between the authority of the state and the lesser power of "third sector" nongovernmental agencies like foundations, but during the crucible of reform that rank order was often reversed.

THE NATIONAL UNIVERSITY

The Bureau of Education's failure to exercise any kind of oversight of American colleges and universities was a major embarrassment for the academic engineering movement. But bureaucratic authority was not their only hope for federal influence.

Some, though not all, of the reformers wanted to create a national university. Such an institution, located in Washington, would go far beyond mere regulation. Modeled on European universities—especially Berlin, but also Paris—it would instantly become the elite of the elites, exerting a powerful downward influence on the entire higher education sector. The effort was strong enough to merit a series of congressional hearings in 1914, at which the president of the University of Illinois argued for establishing "the kind of a university which the Federal Government can build and which shall stand, so to speak, at the apex of our educational pyramid."[45] Another reformer testified that the nation's colleges and universities were disorganized, leaving them deprived of "economy, efficiency, and achievement." He went on:

> How shall all these varied agencies be brought into mutual harmony and systematic collaboration, to the end that they may accomplish the most and the best for American education? . . . Gentlemen, the answer is—and there is but one possible answer—through a national university, founded and maintained by the Nation at the seat of Government, which shall stimulate, elevate, standardize, co-ordinate, and supplement them all, and be the capstone of a truly national system of education that shall be the admiration of the world.[46]

The organized push to establish a national university began around 1890, due to the efforts of John Hoyt, the president of the University of Wyoming. He believed in a federal role in education, as did an even more prominent advocate who joined the cause around 1890: Andrew D. White, who had long been associated with the land-grant movement. Hoyt moved to Washington to lobby full-time for the cause, and White was often there as well in his new role in the State Department (which included an overseas stint as ambassador to Germany).[47]

The two men brought the issue to Congress, working to spur the creation of the Senate Committee to Establish the University of the United States in 1896. They offered a potential cause célèbre: George Washington, it turned out, had called for a national university during his presidency and had set aside some invested funds (which had zeroed out a few decades later) in his will to support it. The centennial of Washington's death was fast approaching in 1899; what better way to memorialize the great national leader than to honor his wish for a great national university?

The university's proponents presented statements of support from many early academic engineers. Most stressed the theme of hierarchy, from David Starr Jordan of Stanford ("a national university would mean the setting of higher standards and more worthy ideals in all branches of higher education"); Martin Kellogg of Berkeley ("[the national university] should bear to the existing universities and collegiate institutions a relation such as a university bears to the secondary schools. That is, it must be above them and far superior to them"); Charles Thwing of Western Reserve ("The University of the United States should bear such a relation to universities already established as they bear to the colleges"); and George Atherton of Penn State ("all the elements of a magnificent system lead up to one institution which should crown and dignify and inspire the whole").[48]

Also included were six separate letters of support from William Rainey Harper of Chicago, who, after the 1896 effort fell short, went on to head a special NEA committee that assessed the national university idea between 1899 and 1901. By the end, David Madsen reports, Harper's enthusiasm for the idea had diminished, and he now regarded it as impractical and duplicative of existing university work.[49] This shift presaged a growing split between the academic engineers, based on whether the centralizing and standardizing effect of a national university outweighed the reality that it would be yet another university in a nation that already had too many.

By the time of the second set of congressional hearings in 1914, the divide was on full display. Some academic engineers, including John Bowman (then president of the University of Iowa) and Charles Van Hise (president of the University of Wisconsin and a CFAT trustee), went on record in strong support of the effort. Others, including Butler of Columbia and Lowell of Harvard (both also CFAT trustees), opposed it. Lowell made the case succinctly: "we suffer at present, not from too few, but from too many institutions of higher learning which are competing to a greater extent than is necessary to preserve their efficiency."[50]

Here we can see a growing divide, even within the academic engineering ranks, between the leaders of public and private institutions. The most forceful remarks in favor of a national university at the 1914 hearings came from Edmund James, the president of the University of Illinois, who was speaking as a representative of the National Association of State Universities. The NASU had officially supported the idea since 1907.[51] Public institutions had a natural interest, beyond systemization, in the normative influence of a national university. By setting a federal precedent for taxpayer largesse, they could then hope for better support from their respective state legislatures, which were far from reliable when it came to appropriations.

By contrast, the elite private institutions had something to lose from the establishment of a new university at the top of the pyramid—especially those that already saw themselves as serving a national student body and acting (as Woodrow Wilson had declared for Princeton) "in the nation's service." James picked up on this point and attacked it: "Neither Harvard, nor Yale, nor Columbia, nor Princeton, nor all of them taken together, great as is their function, great as is their service, can hope to do this particular service for this country. Nor Mr. Rockefeller nor Mr. Carnegie nor both of them together though multiplied by five and animated even still more fully than at present by patriotic unselfishness and farsighted motives, can do this thing for the Nation, which after all only the Nation can do for itself."[52]

Whether or not Carnegie *could* "do this thing for the nation" didn't matter because he had already said that he *wouldn't*. In 1901, White asked him for a major gift to the cause, to get the ball rolling and inspire Congress to act. Carnegie declined, citing Washington's proximity to Johns Hopkins, which most academic engineers regarded as the most elite university in the country, and referred to a frustrating situation on the other side of the continent: "Gov. Sanford [*sic*] made a useless rival as you and I saw when in San Francisco, to the State University. I could be no party to such a thing."[53]

The industrialist instead took the opportunity to endow the new Carnegie Institution of Washington, the great "educational fly wheel"[54] designed to fuel collaboration and efficiencies among existing universities. That was as close to the University of the United States that the reformers would ever come.

THE RESEARCH UNIVERSITY IN CONTROL

The quixotic national university movement fell flat, but it did show the academic engineers a new model of control. There was only so much that the Manhattan-based foundations could do, given their limited manpower and a growing line of criticism about their antidemocratic nature, and even less that federal bureaucrats could do. Instead, the reformers increasingly sought to award control of the higher education pyramid to the institutions that sat at its apex: a handful of research universities, many of them conveniently run by academic engineers.

Historians have written extensively about the turn-of-the-century American obsession with research universities, typically describing it as an attempt to replicate the empiricism and research production of the German universities.[55] What they gloss over, however, is that these institutions—including the German ones—were never envisioned as stand-alone entities. They were always meant to be tightly coupled to the lower tiers of colleges, institutes, and secondary schools. Furthermore, in the United

States they almost without exception included an undergraduate division, which belies the notion of them as fixated on inquiry.[56] The research mission was important, but the primary theme was hierarchy.

At the turn of the century, American universities were trying to justify the word "higher" in their name. They raised their admission standards above those of the high school and prioritized faculty who held "higher" degrees (which led one prominent critic to decry "the increasing hold of the Ph.D. Octopus" on universities).[57] In many cases, institutions even made the effort literal. At least four schools in the New York area sought to relocate to higher ground, ideally with the word "heights" in the name. In 1894, NYU opened a new campus in University Heights in the Bronx. Columbia moved from a flat midtown campus on Forty-Ninth Street to Morningside Heights in 1897. City College moved uptown from Twenty-Ninth Street to St. Nicholas Heights in 1907. Stevens Institute of Technology expanded its campus to Castle Hill on the Hudson River in 1910. This last move was jointly sponsored by CFAT and the GEB, each of which donated to the land purchase.[58] In a speech to Stevens alumni, Pritchett claimed that the "noble hill" of the new site "is one of the most imposing sites for an educational institution which could be found in the world. The possession of it would mean in twenty years from now an enormous difference in the power and influence of the Institute."[59]

Not all institutions could seek this higher ground, though, literally or symbolically. First of all, the academic engineers made clear that in the top rank of the new order, there would be no place for baccalaureate institutions. Pritchett explained that while in the nineteenth century the college had been "the crown of our educational organization," it was now subordinate: "For the future, the college is to be a part of a general system of education; and the university, with its professional schools and its schools of research, is to rest upon it. In no other form of educational organization is the college likely permanently to survive."[60]

But not all universities would hold high status. As the academic engineers loved to point out, in the laissez-faire era it didn't take much for a modest college to rebrand itself as a university and start offering advanced degrees. Some of them knew this personally; Gates's alma mater, Highland University in Kansas, consisted of a single two-story building. Still, it somehow managed to issue at least one PhD, in 1899. That same year, the University of Wooster issued six PhD., and Taylor University in Upland, Indiana, with ninety-one total students, issued fourteen.[61] Pritchett railed against "weak but ambitious colleges [that] call themselves universities" and routinely made a point of telling presidents of "universities" to change their schools' names to "college."[62] One of these, the head of a Southern institution, acknowledged the misnomer but begged for more time to prove himself, promising that in his region, "the few institutions of higher learning that are now in the lead will soon justify names that are as yet only provisional and prophetic."[63]

Nomenclature was only a small skirmish in the larger battle. A very limited number of universities had to be designated as unquestioned leaders. There would be no national pyramid capped by a national university, but there could be several pyramids across the country, each capped by a university in control of the colleges below it. Ironically, the precedent for this plan came from one of the Protestant denominations that so exasperated the academic engineers. These religious orders were a challenge to systemic reform but they also offered an entrée to it.

In the late 1880s, Gates was pursuing what Joseph Gould calls "the Baptist dream of a super-university." It was more than a dream; it was an active struggle between two regional camps to establish a research university that would sit at the top of a nationwide pyramid of Baptist colleges and high schools, exerting downward control. The first camp was led by the Reverend Augustus Strong, Rockefeller's in-law and an ardent advocate of establishing the super-university in New York City. In his estimation, such an institution in such a place would not just serve an organizing function. As he wrote to Rockefeller in 1887, they had an opportunity to make the first "true University" in the United States a Baptist one and, in doing so, "take the wind out of the sails of Yale, Harvard and even Johns Hopkins."[64]

Gates, as the founding leader of the American Baptist Education Society, liked the idea. Richard Storr reports that he backed and expanded Strong's plan in concept: "Gates suggested that the institution should be not merely a local university but a complete educational system, graded from the home upward, symmetrical in its extension and broad enough to cover the whole land: a Baptist university with its head in New York and its corporate parts extended over the whole land."[65] His academic engineering instincts, however, soon gave him pause. New York was already saturated with universities, and introducing yet another one would be a step backward.

Gates's hatred of duplication led him to support a rival faction that was agitating to establish the super-university in the Midwest, where higher education was much less developed. He threw the weight of the American Baptist Education Society behind this push and convinced Rockefeller to back it with a $600,000 establishing gift. In Gates's estimation, the University of Chicago would "at once remove so many difficulties, restore so many disaffections, reduce to harmony and order so many chaotic elements."[66] He employed the physical hierarchy theme, even though Chicago was utterly flat: Rockefeller's largesse would "lift so far aloft a Baptist college as an intellectual and religious luminary, that its light would illumine every state and penetrate every home from Lake Erie to the Rocky Mountains."[67]

Gates was also instrumental in recruiting William Rainey Harper to serve as the university's first president. He saw a kindred spirit in the budding academic engineer, who in 1888 was a thirty-two-year-old professor on the Yale faculty. Harper shared Gates's systemic vision for the institution: "let it be a university made up of a score of colleges with a large degree of uniformity in their management; in other words, let it be an educational trust."[68] The metaphor and the direct appeal to Rockefeller's sensibilities were powerful.

At the outset, Harper's vision of multiple colleges that comprised a university was likely based on the traditional English conception. Oxford University, for example, was not a teaching institution; its function was to award degrees to students educated in its adjacent constituent colleges. Some American institutions replicated this model in the late nineteenth century, although they differentiated their colleges by discipline, not by culture and status. Chicago itself, for example, established a College of Liberal Arts, a College of Literature, and a College of Science. Notably these shared a single campus, just as the Oxford colleges shared a town.

But Harper soon developed a much more expansive model that would extend well beyond that campus: an affiliation program. His goal was to bring existing stand-alone Baptist colleges across the country under the wings of the new university. In Storr's description, "affiliation would convert an accumulation of separate institutions into a rationally organized and elevated structure."[69] Harper hoped that Chicago's sudden emergence in a burst of wealth and prestige would stun the older colleges and convert them into disciples.

His first choice to run the affiliation program was Gates himself, who declined the offer.[70] As an alternative, he recruited someone with first-hand knowledge of the small colleges: Albion Small, a sociologist who had studied in Germany and earned a PhD at Johns Hopkins before becoming president of Colby College in Maine, a modest Baptist institution. Small quickly warmed to his new job and to the University of Chicago itself, describing it with a metaphor that mixed electrical engineering with banking: "Its mission is to help make every educational institution within the circuit of its possible influence stronger, and more efficient than it could be without the co-operation of a great central educational clearing house."[71] He went on to predict that what Chicago was doing for Baptist colleges would soon spread nationwide; it was the start of "a co-ordinating process which will in time take in every University and college in the country, in a perfectly adjusted federation."[72]

The affiliation program's results did not match its ambitions. The primary problem was that colleges thought they had more to lose than to gain by coming under the Chicago umbrella. The president of Des Moines College reported to Harper that his board of trustees was balking at the affiliation, concerned that the college "is no longer an institution under the auspices of the Baptists of Iowa, but it is a Chicago school, run for the benefit of the University there."[73] By 1902, only four baccalaureate colleges had joined the program: Des Moines, Kalamazoo in Michigan, Butler in Indiana, and Stetson in Florida. Harper explained the slow progress: "In the minds of many, the act of affiliating an institution is equivalent to absorbing the institution and taking away its independent existence." He went on to note "the fear, in many cases, that the first step will be followed by a second which will consist in the removal of the last two years of the college course and the withdrawal of the privilege of conferring degrees."[74] Any protest Harper made against this "misconception" was futile; his 1900 book had plainly called for the demotion of most of the nation's small colleges to junior college status.[75]

Chicago was not the only privately endowed university to attempt an affiliation scheme. Columbia pursued a similar program with small colleges in New York City, including Adelphi College and the Packer Institute.[76] Baylor University had a formal affiliation program with four baccalaureate colleges, all in Texas.[77] And Harper personally assisted David Starr Jordan in convincing baccalaureate colleges in California to affiliate with Stanford, in some cases by dropping down to a two-year curriculum.[78]

A rare successful effort to create a regional hierarchy came late, in the Atlanta University Affiliation, a GEB-driven project in the 1920s that I will discuss in detail in chapter 5. Its origins were an inversion of the scenarios at Chicago and Stanford, in which a new, robust university reached a paternalistic hand down to weaker baccalaureate institutions. Here, Atlanta University was the weak partner while two baccalaureate colleges (Morehouse and Spelman, both supported directly by the Rockefellers) were much more robust. The project's leader on the ground was John Hope, the Black president of Morehouse who also became the simultaneous president of Atlanta, even as the two maintained a legal separation.

Hope was no academic engineer, but he anticipated many of their positions in 1904, when he wrote an essay calling for reform of Atlanta's Black institutions, including two other small colleges. He lamented the existence of preparatory academies in the colleges (a necessity due to Georgia's refusal to fund high schools for African Americans). He criticized church control in the subtle manner required of the president of a Baptist college, predicting that "denominational pride and pressure" would fade and "give place to a larger freedom of choice." Most momentously, he called for "a division of labor" among the Atlanta institutions, with Atlanta University as a graduate-only institution and the four colleges arranged as baccalaureate-level subordinates leading into it. "Without some such division," he predicted, "competition may result in an unseemly struggle for existence."[79]

Hope would oversee this very reform twenty-five years later, and the Atlanta affiliation scheme would last for several decades. It was, however, an arrangement much closer to the Oxford model than the Chicago model in that the Atlanta colleges were physically adjacent to the university and retained their own independent identities. The same was true for a similar project in California: the Claremont Colleges consortium, which also came together in the 1920s under one research university (Claremont Graduate University) and had lasting success.

But these later affiliations were not what the academic engineers originally had in mind. They incorporated aspects of hierarchy, but only up to a point—especially when it came to prestige. Morehouse and Spelman were always more prominent than Atlanta; Pomona and Scripps were always more prominent than CGU. The baccalaureate schools were benefitting from the renewed status of liberal arts colleges that followed the crucible of reform, which I will describe in this book's final chapter.

But that renewed status was particular to *private* baccalaureate colleges. Public higher education was a different story. Not surprisingly, that was where the academic engineers turned their attention once it became clear that institutions like Chicago, Columbia, and Stanford would not be topping any formal pyramids.

A TURN TO THE STATES

The federal government would not serve as the top-down organizer of American higher education, and neither would the private research university. The academic engineers had one more hope: the states. As Gates declared in 1906:

> Our national system will be little else than the sum total of the state systems. This fact, while it may interfere slightly with symmetry, is as desir-

able as it is inevitable. It is this free local play of elemental forces that has produced our present educational development, not indeed perfect, but widely distributed, vast, precious and powerful. It is fortunate too for us as a Board. It simplifies our problem.[80]

The wrinkle was that many states lacked systems. In many cases, they maintained the hated laissez-faire policy of awarding college and university charters to all comers and then forgoing any oversight of the institutions. And where state standards did exist, they often did not align across borders, as Pritchett explained with yet another railroad metaphor: "This multiplication of college standards results in what practically amounts to an educational tariff between different institutions and between different states. . . . The situation is a little like that which existed in transportation relations between New York and Pennsylvania when their railroads used different gauges."[81]

The academic engineers were skeptical of most elected officials in the states, whom they considered petty and myopic. These people were not to be the arbiters of higher education. Instead, the reformers saw singular public research universities as the focal points that would direct state systems. This idea had the most potential in the states outside of the Northeast, which had relatively few prominent private institutions, clearing the way for a public leader. Gates explained in 1909, "The ideal thing to do is to establish one institution of higher learning under the patronage of the state and support it by taxation in which all, from the highest to the lowest everywhere shall be obliged to contribute some small part. Let all the educational forces work together to this one end and establish one central college so supported." So doing, he argued, should obviate the demand for small religious colleges: "Let the religious denominations turn in and aid this school, sending their sons and daughters to it freely."[82]

This model had some potential in the nine states that had just a single institution with any claim to university status at that time.[83] But it is much harder to imagine it working in a state like New York, with twenty-six institutions that offered the bachelor's degree (not counting teachers colleges), eleven of them calling themselves "university."

But New York, oddly, was actually the academic engineers' ideal. It did have a singular, powerful, public university that capped the state's educational system. But the University of the State of New York was somewhat different from, say, the University of Michigan. For example, it had no faculty and no students.

USNY (not to be confused with the SUNY system, established in 1948) dates to 1784, when the New York legislature chartered it and awarded it oversight of all higher education institutions in the state. This was not a systemic intervention, since there was only one such institution at the time: King's College, which became Columbia (initially, the USNY regents acted as the private college's trustees).[84] By the end of the nineteenth century, however, New York was home to forty-eight colleges, universities, normal schools, and technical institutes, all of them accountable to USNY, which set the definition for each category and controlled all degree-granting privileges.[85]

In an acknowledgment of the institution's legitimacy, when the CFAT established a formal definition of a college in 1906, they borrowed their criteria, word for word, from USNY.[86] The next year, they described it as "almost the only effective agency in any state in the Union which has the power to supervise or even to criticize institutions devoted to higher education."[87] And academic engineers dominated the USNY Board of Regents. In 1902, several of them reached out to Carnegie, asking him to become the chancellor of the university.[88] He declined, and they instead ended up with Whitelaw Reid, a close associate of Andrew White as well as a Stanford trustee. This type of interlock was everywhere in New York, sometimes formally instituted. The state's superintendent of public instruction was, automatically, a USNY regent and a trustee of both Cornell and Syracuse, in addition to his day job overseeing the state's normal schools and the baccalaureate-level Normal College at Albany.[89] In 1904, the connection became even tighter with the passage of the Unification Act, which consolidated control of K–12 and higher education under a single Education Department. USNY retained its authority, however, and it was clear that the higher education sector would continue to call the shots; the first state commissioner of education, Andrew S. Draper, was recruited from the presidency of the University of Illinois.[90] He served until 1913, when he was replaced by the president of the City College of New York.

In 1900, the Johns Hopkins political economist Sidney Sherwood wrote a glowing summary of USNY, comparing it to German institutions in its design and admiring its "power of life and death" over higher education institutions, even privately endowed ones. He went on to summarize its past in horticultural and mechanical metaphors: "It is difficult to place this university in any known category of institutions. In its origin it had the form of an English educational corporation; but upon it were ingrafted the powers and functions of a modern State department of education. . . . It was at first a rude machine. But it worked, and a century of use and improvement has perfected it."[91]

As much as they may have admired USNY, the academic engineers knew it was an anomaly. Flagship universities needed to be recognizable to citizens, and that meant maintaining a teaching mission. Harper saw virtue in this, in that the institutions would outmatch baccalaureate colleges due to their superior facilities, prestigious faculty, and low or free tuition: "the state university presents an inducement to the prospective student which the smaller college cannot under any circumstances duplicate."[92] Pritchett added that public institutions were the logical leaders of affiliation schemes as well: "There are in almost every Western state private colleges and universities whose development has been practically stopped, and which must in the end become feeders to the great state universities."[93]

The leaders of public universities were more than happy to get with the hierarchy program. In 1903, the president of the University of Iowa addressed a meeting of the USNY regents, where he predicted that the future of higher education was in Chicago-style affiliation schemes: "The grouping about all these universities of the so called detached colleges by means oftentimes of formal affiliation, will conserve as well as uplift the small college. . . . A happy promise is thus given of the unification of the higher and highest education in the interests of the best traditions of the American college and genius."[94]

The Iowa president's words, however, glossed over a looming problem that would bedevil the academic engineers for years. Iowa certainly had its share of duplicative private colleges, but their travails would soon no longer be the state's most pressing problem. Iowa had three robust public colleges. Only one called itself a university, but the others were not going to submit to its authority without a fight. In the 1910s, a fierce controversy emerged among the three, which were increasingly competing for status, students, and appropriations. Similar struggles played out in many other states.

The academic engineers so often thought that the sheer brilliance of their ideas would outweigh local politics and traditions. As I will show in case studies of Iowa and three other states in the next section, and again in chapters 6 and 7, they were very wrong.

CREATING STATE-LEVEL HIERARCHIES

Challenging the authority of clergymen was one thing; doing the same to taxpayers and their representatives was quite another. But this was a fight that the academic engineers wanted. One of the great successes of the early Progressive Era had been civil service reform, which divorced bureaucratic control from party politics, especially in cities but also in state and federal government. In that context, the reformers saw democracy less as an expression of the will of the people and more as an inefficient market system unfit for the twentieth century.

Like so many phenomena in the United States, the public sector of higher education varied dramatically from state to state. The most obvious pattern as far as the academic engineers were concerned was the split between states with a single public institution and multiple competing ones. The difference dated at least to the 1862 Morrill Land Grant Act, in which the federal government gave large onetime gifts to the states in the form of land that could be used or sold in order to finance colleges focused on "such branches of learning as are related to agriculture and the mechanic arts." In the Northeast, legislatures often allocated these gifts to strengthen private colleges. New York directed the funds to Cornell; Massachusetts split its grant between a new agricultural college in Amherst (today's University of Massachusetts) and MIT; and Rhode Island gave its land grant funds to Brown for more than three decades.[95]

Outside of the Northeast, however, land grants went to public institutions, which is where the divide really began. In states like Wisconsin, Minnesota, and California, the assets went to strengthen monolithic flagship universities; the CFAT praised them for their "wise forethought, concentrating their efforts into the development of one great institution."[96] But in others like Michigan, Iowa, Montana, and Colorado, they established or propped up new agricultural colleges. In Washington State, the Morrill Act funds went to create a new agricultural college in Pullman, on the eastern border of the state, as far as possible from the flagship in Seattle. This division had a certain amount of logic, but it also spurred mission creep. By 1915 Henry Suzzallo, an academic engineer who ran the older institution, attacked the increasingly liberal curriculum at the Pullman school, accusing its "slyly ambitious" leaders of threatening his vision of "one great university and one great vocational college for agriculture" in the state.[97]

The existence of multiple public institutions within a single state infuriated the academic engineers. Pritchett complained, "This whole process of competition between state colleges is demoralizing. It means low standards, political log-rolling, and waste of the state's money. . . . The common sense and patriotism of those who direct the state governments, and of those who direct education in the state, should join to do away with such a situation."[98] The competition ramped up even more in the 1910s, when public normal schools began converting into teachers colleges that offered the bachelor's degree.

The process of setting up and reforming state systems is one of the few aspects of academic engineering that has received sustained attention from historians of higher education. Megan Connerly details how the institution now known as the University of Northern Iowa, driven by isomorphic forces, broke out of its ordained sub-baccalaureate role as a normal school during the first decades of the twentieth century, despite dogged attempts to constrain it.[99] Scott Gelber takes a broader view of the same period, explaining how "academic Populism"—the political demand for greater access and utility in higher education—shaped the reform narrative in agrarian states like Kansas and Nebraska, helping to preserve and expand the mission of normal schools and agricultural colleges.[100] Other accounts appear in institutional histories or in statewide survey histories of higher education, like Michael McGiffert on Colorado and David Sansing on Mississippi.[101] Lois Fisher offers a rare comparative case in her examination of Idaho and Washington State. She finds that Idaho hewed closely to the academic engineering ideal of limiting competition, directing all resources to a single university in Moscow, while Washington spread itself thin over a half dozen institutions. She concludes that despite what the academic engineers would have thought, Washington's model was more efficient: it "was accessible to citizens throughout the state and was responsive to changes in their needs and demands. Idaho's system was not, resulting for many years in wasted resources."[102]

The demands of citizens did not concern the academic engineers, except when they posed a challenge to their ideal systems. The reformers saw ordinary voters and taxpayers in the same frame as the pious "children of the light" who they thought had been swindled by real estate developers into sponsoring denominational colleges. Their intentions were pure but naive. Somehow, after overhearing lots of talk about the importance of higher education, they had gotten the idea that they deserved some of it—maybe even in their own town.

The academic engineers' solution to state-level systemization was the same as at the regional or national level: hierarchy. They started at the top. Establishing forty-six singular universities to cap forty-six state pyramids would limit competition and facilitate top-down control.

There were two ways of dealing with states that had multiple public colleges and universities. The most common was to subordinate all but one institution to sub-baccalaureate status. I will discuss this option in detail shortly. A more elegant solution, however, was to collapse all public institutions into a unified university. David Starr Jordan of Stanford was a leading proponent of this strategy. He aided Pritchett in his quest to make public institutions eligible for the CFAT accepted list but argued

> that the agricultural and mechanical colleges should not be included if they are under separate control from the university itself, and that those professors who might be engaged in teaching low-grade or preparatory work should not be included, and that the institutions themselves should be standardized just as other institutions are. . . . If by chance this should have the result of forcing these side institutions to become unified with the state institutions it would be an enormous advance.[103]

Events in Mississippi illuminate this idea. As Sansing describes, Mississippi at the dawn of the twentieth century was still emerging from Reconstruction and its politics retained a heavy element of outside reformers. One of these was Julius C. Zeller, an Illinois native who had done graduate work at Chicago. After a stint as the president of the University of Puget Sound in Washington State, Zeller landed in Mississippi, where he served as a superintendent of schools and won election to the state Senate. His national profile was well below that of the Manhattan-based reformers, but he was an academic engineer nevertheless.

Zeller was aghast at Mississippi's public higher education sector, which was split between three institutions serving white students. The eldest was the University of Mississippi at Oxford, founded in 1848. Mississippi Agricultural and Mechanical College in Starkville was the state's land-grant institution, founded in 1878, but in Sansing's description, it "had become for all intents and purposes a liberal arts college." The third was the Mississippi Industrial Institute and College in Columbus, dating from 1884, which held the distinction of being the first public women's college in the United States and also offered a liberal arts curriculum. In 1910, the state legislature had abolished the individual boards of trustees for each college and consolidated control under a single statewide board "composed mostly of businessmen." However, this board was almost entirely ineffective in streamlining operations and encouraging noncompetition between institutions.[104]

In 1919, Zeller spearheaded legislation to dissolve all three institutions and organize them into a new unified university in Jackson, the state capital. He argued that the three existing campuses were in disrepair and that it would make more sense to build an entirely new institution "than to repair old, worn-out buildings." But Zeller's idea went beyond infrastructure as he explained in a speech: "This is the psychological moment for the legislature to realize that if we are ever to have a great university, an institution that will compare favorably with universities in other states, we must build anew, locate the institution at a center of population, broaden the scope of its work, and make it a University in something more than a name."[105] Zeller also suggested that the academic engineers in New York would financially back the project. If Mississippi "shows a willingness to build a Greater University," he argued, "the authorities can then go to the General Board of Education [sic], present their plans, and it is almost certain that substantial assistance will be given."[106]

Zeller's bill, however, was soundly defeated, most likely due to local constituencies furious about losing their institutions to the state capital. A subsequent bill to preserve the three colleges but move the University of Mississippi from Oxford to Jackson was also defeated. Zeller's reform efforts were not entirely unproductive, however. In 1922, he authored successful legislation that established Mississippi's system of junior colleges.[107]

Clearly, the consolidation strategy was politically impossible, since it involved actively taking away public colleges from communities that had come to rely on them. But the alternative solution—to firmly establish one institution at the top of the state pyramid while letting the others live on in subordinate positions—would be equally controversial, as events in Ohio proved.

To the academic engineers, Ohio was the most vexing state of all, with a long-standing reputation for the quantity, if not the quality, of its postsecondary institutions. Writing in *The Atlantic* in 1910, Pritchett decried the situation:

> Perhaps there is no other state in the Union in which the unlimited competition between denominational, state, and local institutions has so fully done its perfect work as Ohio. . . . It is certainly true that Ohio is the most becolleged state in the Union. Over fifty institutions have been chartered by that generous commonwealth with the power to confer the learned and professional degrees. . . . The state itself helps along in this matter by sustaining three state universities, which carry on a three-corned campaign for students and for appropriations. Under such conditions it is not to be wondered at that the public-school system of the state is inferior to that of nearby states.[108]

The three "corners" dragging down Ohio's entire education sector were distributed throughout the state. In the far eastern foothills was Ohio University, founded in 1804. On the far western border was Miami University, five years younger and home to Ohio's leading teacher training program. The most recently founded was the land-grant school: Ohio State University, which in 1870 opened its doors smack in the middle of the state, in Columbus, the state capital. The geographic dispersal did nothing to assuage the academic engineers' concerns about duplication of effort, and to make matters worse, the two older institutions were tainted by denominationalism. A contemporary observer explained that "for many years an unwritten law has conceded the presidency of Miami U. to the Presbyterians and of O.U. to the Methodists."[109]

In 1906, banker and state representative Edwin L. Lybarger introduced a bill in the legislature to reform the situation by subordinating Miami and OU. His measure proposed to drastically defund them, limiting state appropriations to their normal school departments. According to Thomas Hoover, "By this act the liberal arts colleges at the older institutions would have become meagre adjuncts to the teacher-training departments, or would have been closed entirely."[110] That was exactly the point of the bill, which would have clearly established OSU as the acme of the state's pyramid. A pamphlet authored by the dean of the OSU College of Engineering made the reformist case for the Lybarger bill:

> Each session of the Legislature for many years has developed into a constant struggle among the competing forces, and this has resulted in a waste of public money, a lowering of educational ideals and a general failure to make the progress which the expenditures should have produced. . . . Ohio can not take a creditable place on the educational scale. This reflects not only upon state pride, but also on the efficiency of the training which our youth can receive.[111]

An intense lobbying effort by the presidents of Miami and OU, who also proposed a counter-bill that would have restricted the curriculum at OSU to its original land-grant mission of agricultural and mechanical education, beat back the Lybarger bill and allowed the older institutions to maintain their status as real colleges. The reformers succeeded, however, with a new bill a month later. This was in theory a compromise measure, but it plainly set up a hierarchy by restricting graduate education and research activities to OSU. To cement matters, the new bill granted an annual state appropriation to the land-grant school that was four times that given to the older universities.[112] OSU was clearly at the top of the Ohio pyramid.

Even this was not enough for Pritchett, who weighed in on the matter three years later in a letter to Ohio governor Judson Harmon. The letter denied participation in the CFAT pension fund to all three institutions, complaining that in Ohio "the firmness and consistency that could be maintained by a single university capping the educational system is, of course, out of the question."

> Such overlapping as is here represented is not only wasteful, but it results in competitive bidding for students. It demoralizes the institutions concerned. . . . It is quite evident that the three state universities are not all real universities. That designation may be fairly conceded to Ohio State University, and if relieved from the pressure of state competition, it would no doubt assume within a reasonable time the efficient and orderly development of such an institution as the University of Wisconsin.[113]

OU president Alston Ellis led a voluble counterattack. He distributed Pritchett's letter (which the governor had forwarded to him) to newspapers around the state, along with his rebuttal, which directly condemned elitism and the academic engineers' project of top-down reform:

> The cry of the Foundation is for standards, STANDARDS, STANDARDS, with constantly increasing emphasis on the term. . . . What does it concern the Foundation how many colleges and universities the State of Ohio sees fit to establish and support? The fact that Ohio works along an independent line in this matter presents a condition so 'extraordinary' that the President of the Foundation feels called up to tell the Governor of Ohio 'who's who and what's what. . . .' At the risk of forever barring the doors of the educational aristocracy, sought to be established, against my admission, I must record my doubt of the ability of the Carnegie Foundation to order educational affairs in Ohio more wisely than our people are now directing them.[114]

This astonishing broadside was a strong indication that the CFAT had overstepped its bounds. Not everyone shared the academic engineers' passion for efficiency and systemization. Nor did everyone assume that the business acumen of leaders like Carnegie and Rockefeller was an untarnished good. The pushback was not limited to defensive college presidents like Ellis; the editorial board of the *Columbus Evening Dispatch* weighed in on the controversy with strongly populist language: "Better that the Carnegie millions should be thrown into the sea than there should be this centralization of educational control in the hands of millionaires or their representatives."[115]

The millions were not thrown into the sea, but they did not accomplish their full goals, either. Miami and Ohio both still exist today as full universities, and by 1917 Ohio State was admitted to the CFAT accepted list, despite Pritchett's threats. Just as with the national university and the Chicago and Stanford affiliation schemes, hierarchies that looked good on paper were not so readily implemented.

So consolidation didn't work, and neither did outright subordination. The academic engineers had one last stand to make: defending the status quo in states that had established the ideal of a monolithic university. Chief among these was California. In 1910, Pritchett praised the state for holding firm against the urge to scatter institutions across its vast territory:

> From this temptation the University of California is happily delivered. When the law-makers of 1868 provided for a state institution to crown its public-school system, they wisely made the school of agriculture and the school of mines parts of a single institution. It may be that California virtue is so high that it might have dealt successfully with a divided university. But if the history of other states points any moral, one may suspect, at least, that, had the wise law-makers of that period established a state university at Berkeley and a college of agriculture and mechanic arts at Los Angeles, the state would by this time have upon its hands two weak competing institutions instead of a single strong university which stands to-day in the very first rank of American institutions of the higher learning.[116]

Pritchett's admiration made sense from the efficiency mindset of the academic engineers, but it certainly did not make sense as a practical matter. Two years later, Los Angeles passed San Francisco as the state's largest city, and there was no sign of its growth slowing down; within two decades its population would quadruple. The state offered no public option for the young people of this exploding metropolis to get a bachelor's degree other than to travel to Berkeley, four hundred miles away.

There were two obstacles in the way of a public university for Southern California. The first was the University of California's Board of Regents, a group that matched the reformers' dream of centralized control. The regents' role was enshrined in the state constitution as having "full powers of organization and government" over public higher education, subject to legislative oversight only regarding certain fiscal matters. The second obstacle was the UC president, who had the regents' strong backing: Benjamin Wheeler, an academic engineer who held a PhD from Heidelberg and took a year's leave from his presidency to teach at Berlin. (In 1911, he nominated Kaiser Wilhelm for the Nobel Peace Prize.[117]) Wheeler fully subscribed to the idea that higher education needed to be insulated from the demands of the public, as expressed through elected officials. He described the regents with a metaphor from electrical engineering:

> Politics as represented by the legislative is in mood and manner so radically estranged from education and research as represented by the university, that is, the voltage is so different, that the two must in operation be firmly differentiated and a transformer introduced between them. This transformer has been found in the form of a commission called the Board of Regents, and the mechanism has been mounted and used—on the whole with most beneficent results.[118]

In 1915, legislators from the southern tier of the state introduced a bill to inaugurate a wholly new university in Los Angeles. They recognized that the regents were firmly opposed to anything that challenged the supremacy of Berkeley atop the state's hierarchy, so the bill also proposed a new, independent governance board for the institution. Their colleagues, however, were hostile both to the idea of a new institution and to expanding college education in general; one prominent senator from San Francisco exclaimed, "This country has gone higher education mad, creating a generation of all generals and no privates."[119] Wheeler testified against the bill, arguing that it would mean wasteful duplication and "academic mediocrity." It was soundly defeated.[120]

There was one regent who openly supported expansion: Edward Dickson, a newspaper publisher from Los Angeles who was the first Southern Californian on the board. He began promoting the idea of establishing a southern campus of the UC. Wheeler, of course, resisted this but in 1916 dangled the idea of offering a summer extension course in LA, in which UC professors would offer a taste of the university: "We cannot offer a school like the one at Berkeley, for library, equipment, and atmosphere will be lacking, but we can bring the men."[121] Later that year, though, he killed the idea, explaining that it would cause a "distinct rivalry"—not with Berkeley but with the University of Southern California.[122]

Meanwhile, other Angelenos were preparing to try the legislature again, this time by demanding the conversion of the local normal school into a four-year college.[123] A local member of the legislature began drafting a bill to create the "Los Angeles College University" on the site of the normal school.[124] Finally the regents realized that they needed to compromise and gave their support to a 1919 bill that created the awkwardly named Southern California Branch of the University of California.[125] This concession, notably, came shortly after Wheeler announced his resignation as UC president.

As Wheeler knew, there was only one way things would proceed once this foot was in the door. At first, the new institution was only a junior college, offering just the first two years of instruction. Students still had to go to Berkeley to finish their bachelor's degrees. Wheeler's successor suggested that the school be converted to an "Institute of Technology" that would offer a strictly practical education.[126] But the Los Angeles community had bigger things in mind. Support for a four-year course of study came from all sectors. The local chamber of commerce demanded a real college in the interests of "the moral, ethical, and material welfare of Southern California." At the other end of the status spectrum, a delegation of local high school students quoted the Gettysburg address in their petition: "In the spacious plains of California it is 'altogether fitting and proper' that there be two pathways leading to knowledge, light and understanding."[127]

In 1923, Robert Sproul, a sympathetic Berkeley administrator (and a future president of the campus), suggested to Dickson that getting his fellow regents on board was hopeless. Instead, they had to go back to an elected official: "My advice to the friends of the University in Los Angeles would be to bring the heaviest possible pressure to bear upon the Governor."[128] Dickson followed his advice—the newly elected governor was, in fact, a fellow newspaperman and was apparently very sympathetic. Two months later Sproul frantically wrote again, saying that the governor had gone overboard and was proposing to fund the full university in LA by slashing Berkeley's budget.[129] Shortly thereafter, a Berkeley committee endorsed the four-year expansion.

There would be no more obstacles to the new institution's progress. The timing was important; by 1923, the academic engineers were unquestionably fading from the scene, along with their ideas. As I will explain in chapter six, their authority had ebbed under the steady opposition of critics, many of whom were journalists. And, indeed, it was one of Dickson's fellow journalists—the editor of a rival LA paper—who provided the nomenclature that by itself sliced through the academic engineers' dream of a state higher education system capped by a singular university. "What do you think," he wrote to Dickson, "of having all the papers adopt a rule that would put the northern and southern divisions of the university on an equal plane by instructing all writers to use one form, namely, 'University of California (Berkeley),' whenever the northern site is referred to, and 'University of California (Los Angeles),' whenever the southern division is being written about?"[130]

And with the swap of a comma for a parenthesis, that is exactly how UCLA is still known today.

BOWMAN IN IOWA: A CASE STUDY IN FAILURE

In the Mississippi, Ohio, and California efforts, the leading academic engineers stayed in their foundation offices in New York, preferring to wage their battles via the mail, the media, and like-minded proxies in local positions of power. But occasionally, they got their hands dirty.

In chapter one, I profiled John G. Bowman, describing him as "the last academic engineer." He is best known for his tenure in the 1920s and '30s as the chancellor of the University of Pittsburgh, where he built the forty-two-story Cathedral of Learning: a literal monument to educational hierarchy. First, though, he was the president of the University of Iowa, his alma mater, where he attempted to bring the academic engineering model home.

Bowman had no credentials for the Iowa job other than his connections to the reformers. He had worked at Columbia in his early twenties and caught the attention of Nicholas Murray Butler, who brought him into the world of higher education reform. Bowman cut his teeth with four years as the CFAT's secretary from 1907 to 1911, a powerful post that made him the lead enforcer of the foundation's rules. When institution leaders wrote to Pritchett to seek a place on the accepted list, it was often Bowman who wrote back, pointing out their shortcomings and suggesting changes that would improve their standing.

Sometimes, however, the perceived problems lay with the leaders themselves, and that was the case with the University of Iowa. Since 1899, its president had been George MacLean, who held a German PhD but fell short of expectations. He was a religious man who had fired professors for agnosticism, he directed resources away from the sciences, and he proudly expanded the university's intercollegiate athletics program.[131] All of these were sins in the academic engineering movement. Worst of all, he had failed to establish his university as the unquestioned apex of Iowa's higher education sector. Things were moving in the wrong direction: Iowa State College, the state's land-grant institution, was rapidly duplicating all of the university's academic programs, and the Iowa Normal School had successfully rebranded itself as a college.[132] (This latter change was a direct result of the unintended consequences of reform. In their appeals to the state legislature, the normal school leaders had explained that their primary motivation for the elevation in status was to qualify for the CFAT accepted list.[133]) Adding to the problem was MacLean's opposition to the creation of a unified state board governing all three institutions, in the model of the USNY Regents.[134]

In 1909, after years of attempts, the Iowa legislature finally created such a board, with strong oversight powers. One of its first acts was to invite Pritchett to Des Moines to consult with them on building a cohesive system of higher education. He accepted and spent three days on the ground there in early 1910. In short order, the board fired MacLean and asked Pritchett to suggest a replacement. He tapped the CFAT's secretary. No other nominees were seriously considered, and less than a month later, the thirty-three-year-old John Bowman was on his way back to Iowa.[135]

The new president should have had immediate success. The state oversight board made immediate attempts to advance the academic engineering agenda, proposing a plan that would eliminate the liberal arts programs at the teachers college and land-grant college and setting the stage for consolidating the three institutions on a single campus.[136] They also proposed to demote the former normal school to a two-year junior college.

But these moves were not enough for Bowman, and his frustration with the board soon turned to animosity. He was particularly annoyed by the board's decision to remove the engineering program from the university, designating it the domain of the land-grant college. Although this made sense from a curricular standpoint, it was a clear step away from the supremacy of the university, especially since engineering itself was such a symbolically important discipline.

By early 1914, things had come to a head. The CFAT officials were well aware of the conflict, and they arranged to have eyes and ears on the ground. Pritchett put Will Learned, a low-level staffer, on a train to Iowa. He kept New York informed with a steady stream of letters, which are a window into the limits of Bowman's leadership and the limits of the academic engineering movement itself.

Learned's first order of business was keeping a low profile. Of his dealings with the oversight board, he reported, "The members themselves I expect to see one by one at their homes. I should like to meet them here [at a hotel] tomorrow but rather think it wise to keep the Foundation clear of the present decidedly strained situation. It would look as though we had hurried a man to the spot intentionally."[137] (Which was, of course, exactly what they had done.) He also met with faculty members at the university and found a mixed opinion of Bowman. They were "perfectly aware of his faults: lack of tact, impulsive temper, poor or at least hasty judgement of men, but all appreciate his absolute honesty, his open mindedness, and, above all, the perfect soundness of the principles for which he stands."[138]

Those principles were ultimately what sank the president. Learned reported that Bowman's jealousy was well placed: the land-grant school had "smuggled in" a liberal arts curriculum, and the teachers college was attempting to replicate the work of the university's graduate-level pedagogy department.[139] But he had gone too far in promoting a plan to reassert his institution's supremacy: "Bowman was fairly obsessed by it and wished to father it publicly but was prevented by Boyd [an ally on the board] who warned him to keep out of trouble."[140]

Before Learned had left Iowa, Bowman had turned in his resignation, which seems to have come as a relief to all parties. In Learned's estimation, the issue was partially due to politics but especially to a failure of leadership: "Here three schools are struggling in constant rivalry and no president can be unpartisan. The only way out, retaining the one-board plan, is, in my judgement, to give the board a first-class man as secretary, or State Commissioner. . . . The whole system should be coordinated under one board with a Snedden as its executive and responsible for the whole public educational system."[141]

Learned's reference to the K–12 reformer David Snedden—whose name is shorthand, even today, for social efficiency—was telling.[142] What worked for K–12 reform was far less tenable when it came to colleges and universities. Learned was also becoming disillusioned with the idea of a central board itself. Despite the best hopes of civil service reform, there were only so many experts around to fill bureaucratic positions. The vacuum allowed hacks to claim authority. There was danger, Learned wrote, in "throw[ing] the final deliberation wholly on the shoulders of this 'lay' board. One might as well expect a board of nine preachers and three blacksmiths to build a bridge."[143]

Bowman left Iowa in 1914, never to return. He also didn't return to CFAT, which declined to rehire him.[144] Instead, he spent six years in exile from higher education before landing at Pittsburgh, an institution deep in debt and desperate for forceful leadership. He lasted much longer there but wore out his welcome just the same, managing to alienate almost every constituency on campus by 1939, when even national magazines like *Time* published editorials calling for him to be fired.[145] But by then, academic engineering was completely finished; Bowman's first ouster is more telling. The crucible of reform was fading fast in 1914, and with it faded the reformers' moment of impunity.

4: "THE PRACTICAL LIFE"

As we have seen throughout the last three chapters, a key tenet of the academic engineers' dogma was that the supply of colleges outstripped demand, in the form of students. This may have been true in certain isolated locations, but it was completely wrong on a national level. More and more students were seeking higher education. College enrollments grew 278 percent between 1870 and 1900 and over the next two decades, when the academic engineers were most active, enrollments grew another 152 percent.[1]

This growth was largely due to the wild success of the American high school during the same years. As William Reese has shown, although communities debated the usefulness of the high school through much of the nineteenth century, by the 1880s the question was settled and high schools had spread "to nearly every town and city" in the nation.[2] A large percentage of the graduates of these new schools inevitably sought to continue their education. Their object was college, the rung on the educational ladder that by 1905 had been set firmly above the high school. Demand was strong.

These facts betrayed the academic engineers' logic but did not change their goal of limiting access to the bachelor's degree. Their solution was to double down on the concept of stratification; they would accept broad access to postsecondary education but would make sure that it took place within a tiered system of postsecondary institutions. By design, many students would be directed away from college and toward sub-baccalaureate schools and institutes. This redirection strategy would especially dampen the opportunities for college success available to marginalized populations like women, students of color, and immigrants.

Redirection was a gentler alternative to the approach of simply warning subpar students away from college, as some academic engineers did. Kendric Babcock, the federal higher education expert, argued in 1914 that "no institution has an unlimited capacity of men, means, and equipment, and when it gives its time to those ill disposed to work and unfit it is wasting energy."[3] Ernest Hopkins, who became president of Dartmouth in 1916 following a career as "a consultant on industrial relations," declared in a speech that "too many men are going to college. . . . There is such a thing as an aristocracy of brains, made up of men intellectually alert and intellectually eager, to whom increasingly the opportunities of higher education ought to be restricted." He went on to warn of the danger posed when inferior young people are "withdrawn from useful work to spend their time profitlessly" in college.[4]

Hopkins' sentiment, memorably restated more recently as "the world needs ditch diggers, too," was too alienating to have much effect.[5] Most academic engineers chose the gentler approach of advocating alternatives to college. If a large percentage of the young adults clamoring for higher education were destined to be ditch diggers, why not foster some schools that could teach them how to dig those ditches?

This approach also fulfilled their preference for putting direct restrictions only on institutions, not on students. It was closely related to the junior college idea in the sense that it sought to create a category of sub-baccalaureate schools that would serve as a consolation prize for under-performing colleges and, indirectly, a systematic dumping ground for undesirable students. But on paper at least, the junior college was different; it offered a liberal education, and students could use it as a stepping-stone to pursue bachelor's degrees at other institutions. Many of the inferior institutions fostered by the academic engineers would not even make that modest enticement.

The academic engineers took special interest in institutions that *looked* like colleges but did not offer liberal programs of study, did not offer the bachelor's degree, and did not offer a route to that degree. They saw these as alternative pathways for students past high school age who wanted further education but weren't "college material." By supporting existing schools in this model and encouraging weak colleges to drop their baccalaureate programs and join them, the reformers believed they could accommodate the growing demand for higher education while simultaneously walling off true colleges and universities from the masses. They were wrong, though. Students never stopped seeking the bachelor's degree, and institutions of all stripes would soon rise to the occasion by practicing "mission creep" and becoming full colleges.

A PAEAN TO PRACTICALITY

The turn-of-the-century business leaders whose money fueled the higher education reform movement loved to invoke practicality. Often, this took the form of bashing the liberal arts. Andrew Carnegie did so gleefully. In a 1904 speech at Penn State, he leaned on humor to make the case that the students assembled before him shouldn't waste their time on abstract philosophy: "The young Scottish shepherd asks his elder, 'Donald, what is metaphysics?' The reply was, 'Metaphysics, Sandy, is one man trying to tell other men all aboot a thing he knows nothing aboot himself.'"[6] In an earlier speech in a Pennsylvania mill town, he was more direct, describing college graduates as ruined by their studies: "They have in no sense received instruction. On the contrary, what they have obtained has served to imbue them with false ideas and to give them a distaste for practical life."[7]

The academic engineers whom Carnegie and Rockefeller bankrolled could play this game, too, as Abraham Flexner did in 1908, writing that "soft" college graduates lacked the lessons of "practical life with its intense, narrow urgencies."[8] Sometimes they veered into plain anti-intellectualism. "Book covers contain much knowledge," explained Frank Vanderlip in a 1905 speech, "but may also shut out from a too close student much wisdom—much of that sort of wisdom which is gained by experience in the world."[9] Frederick Gates, meanwhile, paraphrased the gospel of Luke in a GEB memo: "Beware of the scribes, which desire to walk in academic gowns and receive salutations in the marketplaces and the chief places in the synagogue and the first places at social functions. Their learning, their doctors' degrees, their academic gowns, find their end in livelihood, in personal distinction, in social advancement, and not in the enrichment and uplift of the common life."[10]

Proponents of education for "practical life" and "common life" gained a pedagogical platform with the takeoff of the "manual training" movement in the 1880s and '90s. As Herbert Kliebard explains, this movement sought to shift the education of adolescents and young adults away from the traditional liberal curriculum and toward craft work, taught through manual arts like forging, carpentry, and technical drawing. Manual training's proponents described it as a path to "moral redemption," especially for impoverished or otherwise marginalized students.[11]

Carnegie was actually the direct heir to this pedagogical tradition. His grandfather, Thomas Morrison Sr., was a Scottish radical who published an influential essay titled "Heddekashun and Handication," in which he argued for manual training as a liberating alternative to traditional education, which he claimed propagated servility in working-class children.[12] Carnegie and other reformers bought into this vision of "uplift," perhaps most closely associated with his friend Booker T. Washington's defense of manual labor as the first step toward full citizenship for African Americans. Washington went so far as to invoke the antebellum plantation as a place where enslaved Black people were trained as artisans and thus held more respectability than they did after emancipation, when they foolishly began to seek a liberal education:

> As a generation began to pass, those who had been trained as mechanics in slavery began to disappear by death, and gradually it began to be realized that there were few to take their places. There were young men educated in foreign tongues, but few in carpentry or in mechanical or architectural drawing. Many were trained in Latin, but few as engineers and blacksmiths. Too many were taken from the farm and educated, but educated in everything but farming. . . . The pushing of mere abstract knowledge into the head means little. We want more than the mere performance of mental gymnastics. Our knowledge must be harnessed to . . . the every-day practical things of life. [13]

It is impossible to miss that Washington's claim, like most of the claims about the dignity of manual arts and the "practical life," starts to sound like an economic argument for the necessity of low- and mid-skilled labor just as much as it does a moral argument. This brings us back to "the world needs ditch diggers, too." And indeed, Washington's Tuskegee Institute offered courses on topics like laundry and bricklaying. As Kliebard describes, manual training quickly gave way to vocational training, which "projected a distinctly more explicit commitment to economic benefits. . . . It was the economic message that attracted the crucial support of a coalition of politically powerful interest groups."[14]

The most prominent members of this coalition were, like Carnegie, titans of business. The railroad magnate Collis P. Huntington made the case explicitly in an 1899 speech at a society banquet: "The years from 15 to 21 are immensely valuable, for they are years of keen observation, individuality and confidence. In many cases—quite too many—they are spent in cramming the mind with knowledge that is not likely to help a young man in the work he is best fitted to do."[15] But the idea went well beyond plutocrats, even to the social reformer Jane Addams, who wrote that "one of the most pitiful periods in the drama of the much-praised American who attempts to rise in life, is the time when his educational requirements seem to have locked him up and made him rigid. . . . He is bowed down by his mental accumulations and often gets no farther than to carry them through life as a great burden."[16] And, of course, the academic engineers made the case as well. Woodrow Wilson, in his 1902 inaugural speech as president of Princeton, made clear that he favored a liberal education for "the managing minds of the world"—that is, the privileged young men arrayed before him. As for the rest, "The college is not for the majority who carry forward the common labor of the world, nor even for those who work at the skilled handicrafts which multiply the conveniences and the luxuries of the complex modern life. It is for the minority who plan, who conceive, who superintend."[17]

That said, the obsession with practicality was not solely about diverting would-be students away from college and into mundane jobs. Many reformers saw a liberal education as pointless for white-collar careers as well. In 1904, Charles F. Thwing, soon to become the CFAT board secretary, published a book based on his survey of dozens of executives about their opinions on college education as preparation for business careers. Many, he found, were skeptical, especially of the purported hubris of college graduates. A railroad executive explained, "A college education, I believe, leads a young man, on entering railroad service, to think that he 'knows it all'. . . . Anyone that has such an idea rarely succeeds."[18] Carnegie himself argued that "The almost total absence of the [college] graduate from high position in the business world seems to justify the conclusion that college education as it exists is almost fatal to success in that domain."[19] And there were some academic engineers who celebrated college education but emphasized that it must be practical above all. Edmund J. James, at his 1905 inauguration as president of the University of Illinois, argued that the university must "stand simply, plainly, unequivocally and uncompromisingly for training for vocation, not training for leisure—not even for scholarship per se . . . but training to perform an efficient service for society."[20]

James was an exception; the academic engineers' obsession with practicality was most obvious when they turned to doing something with the college-aged Americans who weren't destined for a baccalaureate education.[21] Henry Pritchett noted in a 1902 article that "there are sixteen million persons in the United States between the ages of fifteen and twenty-four," most of whom were not college material. "Can a rational and feasible plan be devised by which this large majority of the youth of our country may have opportunity to better themselves by further education, and to increase their efficiency by effective training given in schools such as they can find time to attend?"[22] He and his fellow reformers had some answers to this question.

THE OLD STORY: LAND GRANTS AND NORMAL SCHOOLS

It is important to note that practicality was not only for low-status schools. Utility, according to Laurence Veysey in his study of elite universities, was one of the three prevailing conceptions driving the new university model that emerged at the end of the nineteenth century. However, the utility of institutions like Harvard and Stanford was not about preparing students for the labor market: "emphasis was placed upon utility in a sweeping social sense rather than in a precisely vocational one." This emphasis took the form of lofty visions of preparing students to be model citizens and lending faculty expertise to solve social problems.[23]

Practicality in the form of vocational training would fall to other institutions: ones that were much lower down on the academic engineers' intended hierarchy and, therefore, served students whose status was also low. Two of these types of institutions are well known as progenitors of postsecondary workforce preparation: land-grant colleges and normal schools. The academic engineers saw little value in the former but attempted to use normal schools as part of their stratified system.

Land-grant colleges should have been the easy answer to Pritchett's question about postsecondary education for the masses. The Morrill Land Grant Act, passed during the Civil War, tied the first federal support of higher education to specific vocational missions: each state that received the support had to maintain at least one college that taught "such branches of learning as are related to agriculture and the mechanic arts . . . in order to promote the liberal and practical education of the industrial classes in the several pursuits and professions in life."[24] The traditional historiography of higher education has accepted these goals as lasting facts; in Nathan Sorber's words, many scholars view land-grant colleges as "products of a burgeoning industrial education movement that [was] premised on displacing the old collegiate order with practical education suited to the industrial classes."[25]

The problem, as Sorber and other revisionists have pointed out, is that most land grants in the nineteenth century did a terrible job of preparing students for practical work. Eldon Johnson describes how student demand for studying agriculture and mechanical arts was essentially nonexistent and how the land-grant colleges responded by minimizing those programs in favor of traditional ones: "The manpower training done by these new colleges turned out to be, both by student choice while in college and by employment choices after graduation, much more conventional than expected—it was chiefly for liberal education and for the common professions."[26] In 1910, Penn State, a proud land-grant institution, still required fifteen units of Latin for the bachelor's degree—more than any other public university in the nation.[27]

Furthermore, many states had made the decision to award their land-grant funds to existing colleges, including elite schools in urban locations. Cornell was famously a land-grant institution (and still is), but so were Brown, MIT, and Yale. Sorber explains the saga of the Connecticut land grant, which belonged to Yale until 1893. In that year, the legislature, heavily influenced by the agrarian "grange" movement, transferred the appropriation to the recently established Storrs Agricultural School in a rural part of the state. (Yale sued, and the state eventually had to pay it $150,000 in damages.) However, the newly christened Connecticut Agricultural College didn't last long. After just six years, it dropped "agricultural" from its name, and its new president set about firing the old agriculture faculty and replacing them with PhD-holding academics.[28] It would soon become the University of Connecticut.

This type of "mission creep" helps explain why the academic engineers didn't embrace land-grant schools as a practical form of higher education for students who weren't cut out for true colleges. Everywhere they looked, land grants were attempting to elevate themselves to university status, exacerbating the duplication that the engineers despised. Connecticut didn't need a new university, they reasoned; it already had Yale. And, not surprisingly, the reformers scorned the climbers when they sought status. After the CFAT opened its accepted list to public universities, they admitted only one land-grant school that was not also a flagship: Purdue. The trustees admitted Indiana University at the same time, falsely describing the two schools as "component parts of a single state university."[29]

The teaching of engineering was a particular sticking point. The reformers insisted that it was a science, distinct from the "mechanic arts" described in the Morrill Act. Like-minded allies in state governments helped to enforce this idea. In 1909, the Kansas legislature forbade the state's land-grant school from teaching engineering, reserving it for the University of Kansas.[30] Three years later, the Iowa state Board of Education attempted to prevent duplication in the opposite manner: by taking engineering away from the University of Iowa and giving it exclusively to its land-grant institution in Ames. The board asked Pritchett for his opinion on the matter, and he responded that their logic was exactly wrong:

> The strongest reason of all for leaving the teaching of engineering to the University, is that only in this way will the teaching of agriculture have a

fair chance. . . . The two kinds of education are incongruous and do not go well together. The engineering school under such conditions always tends to overshadow the school of agriculture. It appeals to the students who come to the school as being something higher than agriculture, and many of them who come to the school with the intention of following an agricultural calling are led off into engineering.[31]

Pritchett, of course, agreed with the students that engineering was in fact "something higher than agriculture." That meant it belonged in the university, and the university alone.

The Iowa board also consulted another academic engineer, who plainly stated that the fundamental solution to their problem was to consolidate the university and the land-grant college. The controversy over engineering was, he said, "the penalty of having two institutions instead of one."[32] This consultant was Charles Van Hise, CFAT trustee and president of the University of Wisconsin. His opinion should have come as no shock since his institution was both the state's research university and its land-grant institution. In fact, in addition to the northeastern states that awarded their land-grant funds to elite private institutions, many states simply gave them to their existing public flagship universities. These notably included California, which the academic engineers held up as an exemplary case for its pre-1919 commitment to housing all of the state's university functions in Berkeley.

Wisconsin, though, was the truest expression of the academic engineering ideal. Not only did the state have a single public university and no stand-alone land-grant college but there were also no robust private institutions to compete with it for students and resources. Furthermore, under Van Hise's leadership, the university's faculty worked closely with state officials to create public policy, a system that became celebrated as "the Wisconsin Idea."[33] Gates described it in 1910 as a mutually beneficial stroke of brilliance:

> In the State of Wisconsin, now the best governed of all our states, the University writes every law that goes on the statute books, University professors guide and control every department of state administration and inquiry; nor is there a limit to the financial resources which a grateful people are placing at the disposal of learning, thus consecrated to the service of the commonwealth.[34]

The state itself participated in the celebration, commissioning in 1913 a massive 957-page report on the university that opened with declarations that "the University of Wisconsin has performed a large and splendid service" and that "the University of Wisconsin in its present form is much more than an institution for the 'education of youth.'"[35] This institution was a shining example of a crown at the top of an educational pyramid as well as the epitome of Veysey's notion of utility. But the university in Madison, along with the land-grant movement itself, most definitely did not fulfill the academic engineers' goal for a practical, vocationally oriented fallback for the masses.

A better bet lay forty-five miles down the road, at the Whitewater Normal School. This very different institution had no pretensions of competing with the university; it did not offer the bachelor's degree and in fact, in 1913, even stopped offering the first two years of a collegiate instruction (i.e., a junior college course), under pressure from state officials.[36] The school existed for one purpose only: to prepare students for jobs.

The jobs on offer to the students at Whitewater, and at the rest of the 281 normal schools that existed across the country that year, were largely teaching positions in elementary schools. The tremendous success of the common school movement of the nineteenth century had created free public schools in every American community, which needed teachers to staff them. Normal schools, both public and private, arose to meet the need. As Christine Ogren shows in her definitive history of the normals, these institutions excelled at—and prided themselves on—educating nontraditional students, including older students, people of color, and, above all, women.[37]

For this reason, the normal schools were much less of a threat to the top of the educational pyramid than the land grants were, and the academic engineers embraced them accordingly. They saw them as a ready-made bottom rung on the postsecondary ladder: vocationally oriented, sub-baccalaureate schools for students who had no business enrolling in a real college. Those students, in Ogren's description, were "the masses and not the classes."[38]

This logic also applied to the "masses" of postsecondary institutions. In the 1906 effort to reform Ohio's public higher education system, normal school status was used as a dumping ground for inefficient colleges. The controversial Lybarger bill, backed by academic engineers and their allies in the state legislature, sought to build up Ohio State University as the only true university in the state and to restrict any state appropriations at the much-older Ohio University and Miami University to their normal school departments. The bill's defenders were compelled to explain that their proposed law did not actually force the older institutions to become pure normals, even though the subtext was clear:

It does not provide, as the daily press reports, for the conversion of Ohio University and Miami University into Normal Schools. This the State cannot do. The bill does not seek to restrain them from continuing their university and college work *on their own foundation*. It simply says that the State will support this part of their work no longer, but that it is willing to build up their normal school work more energetically than ever before. The State needs better teachers for the rural schools and many more of them, and is anxious to perfect its machinery for creating such teachers, but it does not regard the money spent in building up the university work at Ohio and Miami as being well spent for this end.[39]

In Iowa, a similar situation played out in 1912, although reformers there were working to maintain the stratified status quo rather than create a new hierarchy. As Megan Connerly describes, while it was determining which colleges could offer engineering degrees, the Iowa Board of Education was attempting to make sure that the state's normal school at Cedar Falls kept its lowly status. The members moved to restrict the school's course of study to two years, prohibit it from offering degrees, and ensure that it remained "distinctly a professional school." With these edicts, the board argued, the normal school (which had very recently rebranded itself as the Iowa State Teacher's College) would be prevented from inefficiently duplicating the work of the University of Iowa.[40]

Efforts to impose these types of restrictions became common during the crucible of reform; Ogren calls the 1910s the "dark ages" of the history of normal schools. Following an era of growth in which they developed a robust liberal curriculum that offered marginalized students a real shot at social mobility, in that decade "the overall displacement of the liberal arts by vocationally oriented instruction allowed little opportunity for normalites to reach beyond their 'distinct social limitations.'"[41] Ogren ascribes this devolution to a "mission leap" in which normal schools tried to emulate full-fledged colleges but instead "lessened the intellectual vitality that had inspired earlier students."[42]

Of course, it was not the "mission leap" itself that caused normals to double down on their vocational mission; it was the deliberate top-down reform efforts of the academic engineers and their allies to limit their ambition. They had good reason to want to hold back the low-status institutions. In 1908, the Normal School Division of the National Education Association passed a resolution encouraging its members to remove the word "normal" from their names and call themselves "teachers colleges," as the Iowa school did the following year. More tellingly, the division also resolved to encourage its members to require a high school diploma for admission and to offer a four-year course of study.[43] These standards, conspicuously, were two of the requirements for getting on the CFAT accepted list.

Pritchett, alarmed by the ambitions of normal schools, wrote to Wallace Buttrick in 1911, suggesting that the GEB and the CFAT collaborate on "a thorough-going study such as Flexner made of the medical schools" that would show "the very wide fluctuation in the function of the normal schools" and offer "a constructive recommendation for the future of a feasible sort."[44] A Flexner Report for normal schools never came to be, but it would have presumably been its inverse: instead of making the case for raising standards and killing off the schools that refused to do so, it would have made the case for *lowering* standards.

That said, the academic engineers didn't rule out killing off some normal schools. In 1913, the state of Vermont commissioned the CFAT to conduct a study of its entire educational system. The result was overwhelmingly critical and notably included a call to shut down the state's two low-grade public normal schools, at Johnson and Castleton, and create a brand-new central training school to prepare teachers. The report generated a major backlash, which I will describe in chapter 6. While it did emphasize the idea that normal schools should be low status, the report also insisted that they be high quality in terms of *how* they offered sub-baccalaureate training for the practical life.

Elsewhere, in the name of a quality low-status education, reformers worked to gain outright control of rogue normal schools. In Pennsylvania, the state government had been in the practice of subsidizing a number of privately owned and operated normal schools. A 1911 overhaul of the state's School Code directed the Board of Education to purchase those private normal schools and make them its direct agents. As William Issel argues, this law was an unequivocally top-down reform that sought to ensure "social efficiency" by making Pennsylvania's educational apparatus "conform to the standards of efficiency being created in the modern corporation."[45] In other words, it was the product of the academic engineering ethos. Ernest O. Holland, a PhD student at Columbia studying under the academic engineer Henry Suzzallo, wrote a dissertation that leveled an outright attack on the old Pennsylvania system:

[The] normal schools are controlled by lay boards that look upon these institutions largely as business ventures, and are primarily interested in their financial prosperity and indifferent to their educational influence. . . . Their mismanagement and inefficiency are undoubtedly due to the greatest defect of the Pennsylvania school system; namely, that of leaving the direction of education to local initiative and control. . . . Costly conflicts and duplication of work will continue until a unified system is established and large supervisory powers are given to educational experts appointed for the state. Since this is true, the state should immediately assume control of the normal schools and radically change them.[46]

This reform, he noted, would "give adequate educational facilities to the children of the poor as well as the rich."[47] He included a pyramidal graphic of the organization of education in "the most progressive states," in which the normal schools occupied the same tier as baccalaureate colleges, but with a clear distinction that they were two-year institutions and not four-year ones. Furthermore, he made clear that part of the new regime should be urging students to choose the inferior institutions: "every encouragement will be given to the local community to provide high school education in preparation for professional training in the normal school."[48]

Holland (who three years later became president of Washington State College, a land-grant school) got his wish. Pennsylvania purchased the private normal schools, forming the basis of what is now the Pennsylvania State System of Higher Education (PASSHE), a fourteen-campus middle tier of nondoctoral institutions situated between the state's community colleges and its three public research universities.[49]

In some states, allies of the administrative progressives ran up against popular opinion when it came to the regulation of normal schools. In Washington between 1913 and 1917, Ernest Lister, a governor who Lois Fisher calls "committed to economy and efficiency" in higher education, pushed to curtail the state's three normal schools' curricula and even to defund one of them after it had been damaged in a fire. The legislature repeatedly overruled him with veto-proof majorities.[50] The reform movement had better luck during the same years in neighboring Idaho, which, according to Fisher, "established a more completely centralized system than that of any other state." A compliant legislature consolidated all degree programs in the state university, shut down two normal schools, and converted a third into "a two-year vocational collegiate institution."[51]

During the crucible of reform, the normal schools served the same function that the academic engineers had designated to junior colleges: dumping grounds. The head of the Illinois State Normal School embraced the metaphor, with no bitterness, in describing his institution's role: "The normal school is a place where the waste product of other institutional efforts may be so treated and so directed as to bring the wastage to the irreducible minimum."[52] The "waste product" largely consisted of low-status students. As Ogren explains, "The majority [of their students] were women, and among both the female and male students, many were from minority ethnic and racial groups and families that were struggling financially. . . . The state normal schools opened a form of higher education to those types of students who would struggle for full access to mainstream higher-education institutions for decades to come."[53] Which was, of course, exactly the point.

But the restrictions imposed during the "dark ages" did not last. As Alden Dunham shows, after 1920 the NEA's suggestion that normals rebrand themselves as "teachers colleges" took off. By the 1960s, he could find only one remaining two-year normal school (in Idaho, not surprisingly). Dunham describes the transformation as a natural process: "as the state seeks to respond to increasing demands for higher education," the normal school becomes a teachers college and then "a multipurpose state college and perhaps a university."[54] That gentle evolutionary narrative, however, misses the actual story: the attempts of the academic engineers and their allies to limit the normals, and the active resistance and insistence of the institutions to expand their missions, as I will describe in the last section of this book.

THE HEIGHT OF PRACTICALITY: TECHNICAL SCHOOLS

Due to their mission creep, normal schools and land-grant colleges failed to be pure expressions of practical education. For true practicality, the academic engineers looked to a new type of institution, one that had been conveniently fostered by their wealthy benefactors: the technical school.

In 1899, years before he gave any monetary gifts to a traditional college or university, Andrew Carnegie made his first two donations to higher education. Fifty thousand dollars went to the Stevens Institute of Technology in Hoboken, and $100,000 went to the Cooper Union for the Advancement of Science and Art across the river in lower Manhattan.[55] Each was a school that served college-aged students but did not offer anything resembling a liberal education. In fact, this type of school was, by design, an anti-college. Carnegie had been in attendance at the 1891 dedication of the Drexel Institute, a technical school in Philadelphia, when the railroad executive Chauncey Depew explained the idea and its macroeconomic benefits:

[The college's] course of study must be mainly for the minister, the lawyer, the doctor, the journalist, and the business man. For the vast army which must live by labor, and upon the results of whose labor depends the welfare of the country, no adequate provision has yet been made. This splendid Institute of Art, Science, and Industry leads the column and points the way. . . . Disciplined intelligence and harmoniously cultivated minds and muscles will give the economy in the use of materials and skill in the handling of tools which will command the markets at home and abroad.[56]

Technical schools were typically founded by plutocrats. Anthony Drexel earned his millions as a part of J. P. Morgan's banking empire. Edwin Stevens was a railcar and shipbuilding magnate. Charles Pratt, who founded a tech school in Brooklyn, made his fortune in oil while Philip Armour, who founded one in Chicago, made his in meat. Inevitably, the steel baron got into this game as well, donating $1,000,000 in 1900 to found the Carnegie Institutes of Technology in his adopted hometown of Pittsburgh.

None of these millionaires had gone to college, and each made sure that their largesse was going to a new form of higher education, distinct from traditional academic spaces. Carnegie's trustees appointed a committee of four men to design a plan for the Pittsburgh school, two from universities (Cornell and Wisconsin) and two from existing technical schools (Armour and Rose, founded by a railroad mogul). They proposed a full-time engineering-focused college that offered a four-year degree. Carnegie rejected this outright. As he explained to the chairman of the unbuilt school's board of trustees, he had nontraditional students in mind, in particular the ones who had to attend night classes: "I believe it is chiefly from the ranks of those who work with the hand during the day and improve their brains at night that the future inventors and successes are to come and that is the class I had in view mainly when I offered to build and endow a technical school."[57] A second committee, drawn exclusively from the faculty of technical schools, not universities, proposed a far more satisfactory plan in 1903. The new institution would focus exclusively on manual and industrial training, would be coeducational, and would not offer the bachelor's degree. This model was exactly what the philanthropist was looking for.

The wealthy benefactors clearly intended these technical schools to serve working-class students, but class was not the only consideration. Politics was another. Later in his speech, Depew included a stunning claim about the future Drexel student: the institute, he explained, "will so equip him and open avenues for his energies that instead of dynamiting the successful, he will be himself a success."[58] This was a barely veiled reference to the Haymarket Square protest in Chicago five years earlier, in which a dynamite bomb killed seven police officers during an otherwise peaceful workers' rally. The idea that technical education could assuage radicalism was a powerful one, and it even extended to the notion that similarly "practical" schools could repress the social and political ambitions of African Americans in the South, as I will discuss in the next chapter.

And there was one more aspect to the intended student body of the technical schools, intertwined with the political one. The accused Haymarket conspirators were immigrants, as were many other radicals, and it was clear that the technical schools were largely designed to serve the new Americans arriving in huge numbers in major cities in the late nineteenth century. Carnegie, an immigrant himself, made the case in 1906 that education was the key to suppressing foreign-born radicals: "The hundreds of thousands of ignorant immigrants now reaching our shores from the backward nations of Europe would soon prove a menace to our peace and happiness were their children not attended to and instructed in our ideas."[59] Other reformers put a more positive spin on things, like the CFAT official Clyde Furst, who praised the tech schools "recently developed for adults and, especially, for immigrants, particularly in Massachusetts and New York. From one point of view this popular and practical movement seems to point away from all of the higher cultivation, but it has the most intimate relation to that idealism which makes our nation hold that its citizenship may rightly include anyone from the four corners of the earth."[60] That said, there was also a flip side to this logic. According to James Watkinson, some nativist backers of technical schools were motivated by "the recurring fear that foreign laborers were grabbing the lion's share of skilled labor positions, those that 'should' have gone to American boys."[61]

Whether or not immigrants were their intended targets, the technical schools held tremendous promise for training and socializing working-class students and turning them into useful economic actors. Critically, the schools also kept them away from colleges and universities. Tech schools played directly into the academic engineers' pyramidal notion of the American occupational hierarchy. Elite forms of higher education were great places to train the upper echelon, explained Pritchett. "But, after all, the number of leaders who are needed is limited; and it is worth while asking what is being done in America and what can be done for training the sergeants and corporals and privates of the industrial army, the superintendents and foremen and skilled workmen who man our mines and mills, who build our roads and bridges, who make and transport our manufactured products."[62]

Before he became CFAT president, Pritchett was integral to the creation of a new technical school, when he convinced Carnegie to help fund Boston's Franklin Union as "an evening school for the training of men and women in the practical arts of life, such as you suggest."[63] The committee behind the new school called it "an institution on the general plan of the Cooper Union."[64] In Carnegie's letter announcing the gift, which Pritchett personally delivered to the committee, the industrialist heaped praise on Cooper, of which he was by then a trustee, as well as "the class who not only spend laborious days but who also spend laborious nights fitting themselves for hard work."[65] Practical people—not scholars.

Pritchett wasn't the only academic engineer who helped launch a technical school. William Rainey Harper not only was integral to the 1897 founding of the Bradley Polytechnic Institute, devoted to teaching the "practical and useful arts" to prepare students for an "industrious and useful life," but he was also the president of the school for its first decade, at the same time that he was running Chicago.[66] But Pritchett wasn't the president of an elite research university. He was the president of an *existing* technical school in Boston. His advocacy for the new institution wasn't a case of the hated duplication, however. Pritchett had no intention for MIT to remain in the lower ranks of the higher education pyramid; that was the place of pseudo-colleges like Franklin Union. Instead he wanted MIT to be a real university—or, more specifically, part of an existing real university.

Pritchett pushed hard for an alliance or merger with Harvard. The idea was that MIT would relocate to Cambridge and become the university's school of applied science, with a focus on engineering. This consolidation was hardly a natural one, given Harvard's long-standing disdain for Boston Tech. As Bruce Sinclair writes, although Charles Eliot was open to the idea of a merger, other Harvard administrators emphasized the vast distance between the two schools, writing of MIT and its peers using "old prejudices, speaking of 'trade work' and learning directed at 'immediate utility,' culturally one-sided technical school graduates trained in 'craft sense' for 'particular tasks,' and an approach to education dominated by 'the uncivilized humor of monetary enjoyment.'"[67] There was external opposition, too, from local interests who wanted to preserve the Boston Tech identity and not lose it to the university's elitism. Once Pritchett's scheme came to light, newspaper editorialists railed against it. The *Boston Transcript* called it "pernicious" and illogical, since the two institutions "must always continue to be different and to appeal to different species, if one may so express it, of young men." The *Boston Advertiser* declared it unthinkable that MIT could ever cross the river to join Harvard: "its site will always be in Boston, its work will be done here, its dormitories and branch shops will be in this city."[68]

Of course, MIT did cross the river, where it remains today. And while it remained independent of Harvard, its gleaming neoclassical campus indicated a clear break from its practical roots, toward the university ideal. In describing the campus's 1916 opening ceremony, the school's official journal declared, "The necessity of concentrating on the purely utilitarian has passed; the chrysalis has lived out its time and the butterfly of art has crept out to try its wings."[69]

In a sense, then, Pritchett's MIT was a cautionary tale. Like the normal schools and land grants, some technical schools also embarked on mission creep toward a liberal curriculum and university status. Cooper Union began quietly offering the bachelor's degree in the 1890s, and the Carnegie Institute in Pittsburgh did the same in 1912, with no apparent protest from its founder. The Cooper board of trustees fired the school's academic director in 1922 because he stood in the way of their plans to use "intelligence testing" in moving toward more selective admissions. The director, who frantically corresponded with GEB officials as his job was on the line, cited the school's historical mission to serve working-class students and protested that "we shall be in danger of changing Cooper Union into quite a different kind of institution from that contemplated by the founder and from that which has found so useful a place in the community."[70] He lost his battle, Peter Cooper's grandson resigned as treasurer in protest, and the school took a major step toward elitism.[71]

Perhaps the most stunning transformation happened in southern California, at the Throop Polytechnic Institute in Pasadena. Pritchett described the shift in a letter to Carnegie's personal secretary: "Until five years ago it was an institution of low grade and with a most confused medley of departments. It had, for example, a normal school department. Since Hale went on the board, and particularly since Dr. Scherer took the presidency the institution has been completely remade. It consists now of a high grade engineering school with admirable buildings and laboratory equipment." George Ellery Hale was a kindred spirit for Pritchett, a fellow astronomer who had also done graduate study in Berlin. He and James Scherer, the Throop president, did indeed remake the school, which rebranded as Throop College in 1913, began offering the PhD, and then rebranded again in 1920 as the California Institute of Technology.[72]

Today, CalTech is an internationally renowned research university, as are MIT and Carnegie Mellon, while Cooper Union offers one of the most elite undergraduate engineering programs in the country. Drexel slowly built its status and in 2018 became an R1 university in the Carnegie Classifications. However, these triumphs of mission expansion did not negate the place of the technical schools as low-status alternatives to college. Many of the ones that did not make the leap to elitism remained at the bottom of the higher education pyramid, like the Franklin Union, which exists today as an open-access trade school offering programs in automotive technology and HVAC repair.[73]

Ultimately, though, the tech schools failed to replicate the broad swath of vocational, antiliberal postsecondary institutions that existed in nations like Germany. The idea had been to offer a practical alternative to college that had a level of prestige but no aspirations to elitism. Instead, a model that had seemed so promising in the 1890s dissipated within two decades, splitting into a tier of soon-to-be elite universities and a tier of very low-status trade schools. This failure must have been a sore disappointment for the academic engineers, who pinned so much hope on the schools—not merely as alternatives to traditional colleges but as role models for them. Charles Thwing declared in a 1903 speech at Stevens that "the technical school is to teach the college and the university the lesson of efficiency."[74] His fellow CFAT board member, Vanderlip, made the point more acerbically: "The schools that are most tenacious of classical tradition should hardly feel proud of the fact that practically the only institutions of learning in the country that demand a full and honest return of work done in exchange for the honor of their degrees are the technical schools."[75]

CLOSE, BUT NO CIGAR: JUNIOR COLLEGES AND UNIVERSITY EXTENSION

The academic engineers had envisioned the technical school as a clear alternative to college. Like the land-grant and the normal school, it transcended its design and ended up adding to, not subtracting from, overall college enrollment. But what if there were other alternatives that would be structurally blocked from mission creep, not because they were distinct from elite universities but because they were intimately connected to them?

One such alternative was the junior college, whose origins I described in chapter two as a consolation prize for demoted four-year institutions. But the junior college was also designed as a net for catching subpar students and keeping them away from the university. Alexis Lange, a Berkeley administrator who worked closely with David Starr Jordan to promote junior colleges in California, made this case with stunning directness, describing the junior college movement as "in the educational interests of the great mass of high school graduates who cannot, will not, should not, become university students."[76] Ray Lyman Wilbur, who succeeded Jordan as president of Stanford in 1916, was equally frank: "Let the junior colleges try their hand at the double job of preparing better the ones who enter the upper division, and discouraging others from going to the university at all. The junior college forms a logical stopping point for many who should not go farther. It is a try-out institution."[77]

The institution did offer a possible pathway to the university for those who escaped the net. But Leonard Koos, who published a comprehensive survey of junior colleges in 1925, found little enthusiasm for this opportunity in the writings of the leaders who promoted the schools. It was primarily marketing: the transfer function was "the one most commonly put forward in the catalogues, but not in the remaining literature."[78] Instead, as Stephen Brint and Jerome Karabel argue, "university presidents," a category that included many academic engineers, "sponsored the development of junior colleges as a means of diverting the flow of students away from their own institutions."[79] A. Lawrence Lowell, the academic engineer who became Harvard's president in 1909, saw a restrictive benefit in junior colleges: "one of the merits of these new institutions will be the keeping out of college, rather than leading into it, young people who have no taste for higher education."[80] A Berkeley faculty committee wrote in 1915 that the university had an "obligation" to only selectively admit students applying to transfer from junior colleges: "to refuse to allow any student to enter upon work for which he is not competent, to attempt to erect a superstructure on a foundation incapable of supporting it." The committee took pains to note that this exclusion was "for the protection not so much of the University, or of any University department, as for the protection of the student himself."[81]

The earliest incarnations of the junior college did not claim to offer a practical education. This made sense, given that they were largely produced by what one observer called the "decapitation" of existing four-year liberal arts colleges.[82] These schools, many of them denominational and very traditional, could hardly be expected to suddenly start offering vocational coursework. Soon, though, junior colleges were frequently offering "terminal degree programs" geared toward "semiprofessional" jobs that required some higher education, just not the liberal variety. Brint and Karabel argue that in the late 1910s and '20s, a second generation of reformers worked to develop "a coherent counterideology that could blunt the continuing appeal of the explicitly academic ideology still favored by many junior college educators. This vocational counterideology celebrated 'practicality' and 'realism.'"[83] The academic engineer Lange stated this position plainly enough in 1918: "The junior college will function adequately only if its first concern is with those who will go no farther, if it meets local needs efficiently, if it turns many away from the university into vocations for which training has not hitherto been afforded by our school system."[84]

In short, the junior colleges shifted their orientations from liberal to vocational in order to absorb the "practical" mantra cast off by land grants, normal schools, and technical schools as they shifted in the opposite direction. And this trend stuck. Ever since, two-year schools—today's community colleges—have been tasked with the lion's share of vocational training within the American higher education system. That said, they have never abandoned the promise of access to a baccalaureate education and beyond. Critics like Burton Clark point out that retaining the transfer function causes community colleges to perform a bait-and-switch, in which students intending to transfer out and get a bachelor's degree are gradually coaxed away from their ambitions and toward vocational programs. This, he suggests, quietly and effectively serves to keep undesirable students far away from the university.[85] Exactly as the junior college's original backers intended.

In order to perform that bait-and-switch, which Clark calls "the cooling-out function in higher education," the two-year school had to maintain its ties to elite institutions, which it typically did within the public sector of higher education, through formal articulation agreements with the universities at the top of a state's hierarchy. And the academic engineers doubled down on those connections even more profoundly in another innovation that appeared to offer access to the top of the higher education pyramid, while in actuality keeping the masses at arm's length. It was called university extension.

Extension was an idea supposedly borrowed from British universities in the 1880s that met little initial success in the United States. (In reality, its first American proponent was a Johns Hopkins professor, the Heidelberg-trained historian Herbert Baxter Adams, who based his conception on models from German universities.[86]) After the turn of the century, the academic engineers rediscovered extension and added it to their agenda. The movement sent professors and other university-affiliated instructors out into communities to deliver lectures and short courses (almost always non-credit bearing) to anyone who showed up and paid a fee. It perfectly performed a function central to the academic engineers' program of reform: showing the worth of the research university while keeping unwanted students far from its gates. It also had a built-in hierarchy to it, which Gates extolled: learned men descending from the ivory tower to offer "the extension downward of the blessings of civilization through the masses of our own people."[87]

There was a specific political motivation that contributed to extension's takeoff around 1905: public universities were calling on taxpayers for more and more support, and they had to offer something in exchange.[88] A rapid expansion of seats in their undergraduate classes was not on the table. Instead, extension offered a taste of university-branded education as a token of appreciation for tax dollars. Louis Reber, an academic engineer and the pioneer of extension at the University of Wisconsin, explained in 1911:

> The state university is a public service corporation. It is supported by the public presumably *for* the public. . . . Is not the public justified in demanding that this great expenditure be made to serve the entire state as its student body? Nor should the fact be overlooked that the extramural activities of university extension create an attitude in the people of the state, that will not fail to be reflected in greater loyalty and more generous financial support—conditions that may be counted upon not only to insure the spread of university benefactions, but to more rapidly advance the interests of the conventional and long-established forms of higher education work.[89]

The idea that extension could be a source of profit did not escape private universities, either. A 1907 *Journal of Education* article about Brown University's forays into the field noted that extension students were "spared the mortification of being in any sense charity students," since they were charged course fees in addition to an entrance fee and a "certificate fee." The author explained that the program was meant "to obliterate to some degree the long-standing distinction between 'town and gown'" but also made clear that the obliteration did not mean access to actual academic credentials for the townies: "One fear has been expressed that there would be a necessary cheapening of academic degrees by this new method of instruction. But these degrees have been and will be sacredly guarded."[90]

Two years later, Harvard entered the game with force, under the new leadership of Lowell, who made establishing an extension division one of his first acts as president.[91] He did not go it alone: in 1910, he spearheaded the creation of a "permanent Commission on Extension Courses," which linked eight Boston-area colleges and universities in coordinating their extension offerings. In addition to promoting the academic engineers' ideal of noncompetition, this linkage allowed Lowell sufficient cover to offer most Harvard Extension classes in Boston rather than Cambridge.[92] Doing so ensured that these second-class Harvard students would remain safely across the Charles River, the same body of water that Pritchett and his successors at MIT were so eagerly trying to cross in the opposite direction.

Surprisingly, Harvard Extension promised that its courses would lead to a degree. Less surprisingly, that degree was *not* the bachelor's. Instead, Harvard, Tufts University, and Wellesley College jointly announced that extension students could pursue the associate in arts degree. This credential had up to this point been offered only by junior colleges, most notably those affiliated with the University of Chicago. At Harvard and its Boston-area peers, however, it was a four-year degree, equivalent to a bachelor's in terms of required credits.[93] Thus, by semantics as well as geography, Harvard drew firm distinctions between real students and those who were ushered in the back door for financial and political reasons.

The idea of America's most elite university offering a second-class degree to second-class students was perhaps the purest expression of a new type of college for "other people." James Ropes, the founding dean of Harvard Extension, explained that with the collaborative effort, "there is now in operation in Boston a kind of extension college, giving courses which lead to an adequately guarded degree." James Moyer, a mechanical engineer and a close ally of Ropes who became the director of University Extension for the Massachusetts Department of Education in 1915, predicted that only 1 percent of Americans were destined for enrollment in a traditional college. "The other ninety-nine," he wrote, "must depend on extension teaching, either in classes or by correspondence instruction, for their growth and their fuller realization of life."[94] And in the end, even the creation of a new second-class degree to dangle in front of the 99 percent wasn't much of a concession; in its first dozen years, Harvard Extension awarded only thirteen associate's degrees.[95]

The extension movement was most potent in the Upper Midwest, where public universities were declaring themselves to be core components of the social contract between state governments and citizens. Louis Reber's boss, the academic engineer Charles Van Hise, epitomized the University of Wisconsin's role in this with his famous, though misattributed, declaration: "the boundaries of the campus are the boundaries of the state."[96] His interpretation of the Wisconsin Idea, however, was far more elitist than that line suggested. As David Hoeveler argues, Van Hise believed in a "doctrine of power" that held that ideas, reforms, and even morality should flow downward from the university, which therefore had to remain pure and isolated from the mundane, pecuniary, and denominational interests of ordinary people.[97] The public would benefit from the high standards of the university, as long as they waited for it to come to them and not vice versa.

This logic certainly applied to extension, as Van Hise explained in his keynote address at the inaugural University Extension Conference, held at Madison in 1915. Lowell, a fellow extension pioneer, had threatened to boycott the conference if its proceedings were published, indicating that frank statements would cast an unfavorable light on the movement.[98] Van Hise was indeed somewhat critical in his remarks, noting that the traditional lecture-based model of extension was overly patronizing, leading to "this class of work being dubbed 'second rate at second hand.'" The newer program of correspondence-based extension courses, conducted via the US mail, had more promise, he said, but also had dismal completion rates. Van Hise said the programs were best suited to "vocational work," particularly among "apprentices and artisans" who "desire to gain knowledge of the industry in which they are engaged whether it be pattern making, plumbing, machine work, foundry work, etc." He assigned the most potential to "systematic instruction at other places than the university," noting his own university's large presence in Milwaukee, the diverse city a safe eighty miles east of Madison.[99]

Another speaker at the conference expounded on a variation of this theme, linking it to the political necessity of proving the university's value to taxpayers. Richard Price, the director of extension at the University of Minnesota, described his institution's practice of University Weeks, a sort of college road show:

> There are two ways in which the people who support a state university may find out what it is doing and what they are getting for their money. One way is to read the annual reports and the various bulletins of the institution. . . . The other way is to have selected members of the faculty and student body spend a week every year in each of a number of towns scattered over the State, meeting with the citizens, delivering popular and scientific lectures, putting on plays, giving concerts and having good fellowship. . . . The community finds that the university professor is a man and a brother and not a high-brow or a fossil. Best of all the community, usually absorbed in business, experiences a widening of the horizon and learns to think in terms larger than the local unit.[100]

This "larger" thinking of course included a willingness to keep sending tax dollars to support the far-off university. But University Weeks, which continued in Minnesota for at least five years, had much deeper origins than political expediency. The idea bore a striking resemblance to another type of road show: a phenomenon called "circuit Chautauqua," which was a traveling version of the educational program of the Chautauqua Institute, established in upstate New York in the 1870s.

This was not a coincidence. Price's boss, University of Minnesota President George E. Vincent, knew a lot about the Chautauqua movement. In fact he had grown up in it, since his father, John Vincent, had created it. The elder Vincent, a Methodist minister, had gotten his start in education as a reformer of religious education, including his leadership of a normal college for Sunday school teachers established by the Methodists in New York City.[101] He would continue to emulate higher education after his establishment of the institute in 1874. According to Andrew Rieser, he soon set up the Chautauqua Literary and Scientific Circle, a four-year correspondence-based education program: "The CLSC offered a full curriculum, textbooks, structured discussion sections, and correspondence exams. The CLSC mimicked the formal education process, right down to its elaborate graduation ceremonies and symbolic diploma."[102] In 1883, Vincent went a step further with the establishment of the Chautauqua College of Liberal Arts, commonly called Chautauqua University.[103]

The founding leader of this "university," which conducted its education by correspondence, was a twenty-seven-year-old college professor: William Rainey Harper. (Herbert Baxter Adams was also active in Chautauqua in this period.[104]) Harper continued to be involved with Chautauqua until his death, although after Rockefeller tapped him as president of the University of Chicago, he stepped back from administrative duties and primarily engaged as a lecturer. His fellow academic engineer George Vincent, however, fully took over the institute from his father and remained as its president even after he was named president of the University of Minnesota in 1911. He did not relinquish the position until after his final promotion in 1917—to the presidency of the Rockefeller Foundation.

Thus, Chautauqua was intimately associated with academic engineering. In addition to its Rockefeller ties, Andrew Carnegie was also a major supporter of the institute.[105] And when Harper, Vincent, and others applied the model to extension, it took on an increasingly practical character. Vincent predicted in 1904 that "university extension dealing with culture studies, not with professional pursuits, cannot be made permanently self-sustaining."[106] After he became Minnesota's president, the university's extension division statistics bore this out: in the fall of 1913, 612 students enrolled in business classes (where Salesmanship was by far the most popular course), while only 417 enrolled in academic classes. Even this breakdown was deceptive, though. The most popular course in the second category was something called Labor and Life, with Public Speaking not far behind. And also classified as an academic course? Swimming.[107]

Years later, Vincent frankly described his mixed feelings about education for "the great masses of mediocre people." He compared his education at Chautauqua and at Yale as rent between a focus on catering to those masses and on training young men primed for leadership. This bifurcation continued into his time on faculty at Chicago, when he saw the bifurcation in his mentor, Harper, who was trying to run an elite university that also had "university extension and correspondence courses and downtown courses"—things that his fellow professors thought were "dangerous experiments." Ultimately, Vincent was able to reconcile the two visions by deciding that the purpose of extramural education for the "mediocre people" of a democratic society lay in "enabling them to choose wisely the persons to whom they turn over the working out of those [societal] problems."[108] A perfect summation of the academic engineering attitude: the masses can have some limited fun with higher learning, as long as they remember that experts run the world.

Today, university extension is most closely associated with its offshoot cooperative extension, which focuses on disseminating agricultural best practices developed in land-grant universities out into rural communities. The 1914 federal law that established it described cooperative extension's purpose as "diffusing among the people of the United States useful and practical information on subjects relating to agriculture and home economics" and specified that its beneficiaries were to be "persons not attending or resident in said colleges." Van Hise summed up the idea more bluntly: "it is necessary to go out, and figuratively to knock the farmer over the head with agricultural knowledge in order to get him to apply it."[109]

But the broader vision of extension lives on, too, at hundreds of American universities, both public and private. Nontraditional students continue to take classes at night, on the weekends, and increasingly online, under the aegis of the research university but without its highest blessings. Along with the community college, it is an enduring infrastructural legacy of the academic engineers that continues to serve its original purpose of bestowing just enough higher education to the great masses to satisfy them while still walling off the elite center of the system.

5: SEPARATE AND UNEQUAL

The early years of the twentieth century were a time of intense division in the United States. Not necessarily ideological or political division but rather literal division of Americans along demographic lines.

This followed a period of hope that the nation would become more egalitarian following the Civil War. As C. Vann Woodward famously demonstrated, de jure segregation between Black and white Americans had been largely unknown before it emerged in the 1890s, giving cover to increased racial violence and the return of long-dormant terrorist organizations like the Ku Klux Klan.[1] After decades of permissive immigration policy, the US Congress passed increasingly harsh limitations between 1891 and 1924, with the greatest restrictions applying to immigrants from Asia. The fight for civil rights for women, so hopeful following the establishment of equal rights associations in the 1860s and early achievements in western states, experienced defeat after defeat through the 1890s and 1900s when activists sought women's suffrage east of the Mississippi.[2]

The timing of these developments does not indicate that racism and sexism were novel to the Progressive Era—far from it. Instead, it has much more to do with the end of laissez-faire and the new establishment of top-down control by "experts" and other elites. Segregation and its even more sinister cousin, eugenics, were ostensibly backed by "expert" social, legal, and scientific reasoning, which helped them become state policy in parts of the nation.

The shift from laissez-faire to elite control also underlay the rise of academic engineering. And much of the new systemic discrimination found its way into higher education reform, too. The sub-baccalaureate, "practical" variety of higher education that led away from academic study was designed for students who weren't "college material"—and those students were disproportionately members of marginalized demographic groups. Women, immigrants, and above all African Americans and other racial minorities were frequently the intended enrollees of sub-baccalaureate institutions. In many cases the academic engineers who ran elite universities actively supported or created lower-tier schools in order to use them as dumping grounds for undesirable types of students who wanted access to those universities. And even when they weren't relegated to second-class schools, these groups faced rampant discrimination at elite universities, as did Jews and Catholics.[3]

The academic engineers generally avoided making overtly bigoted statements, but the patterns embedded in their reforms are unmistakable. Preserving the ivory tower meant keeping it white, and male, and economically privileged. Still, while the reformers and so many of their contemporaries were plainly racist, sexist, and classist, we need to look beyond simple prejudice to understand the second-class status of institutions like historically Black colleges. The academic engineers certainly had subordination on their minds, but their vision for the hierarchical ordering of education, and of society itself, came first. As such, this chapter focuses on systemic bigotry rather than individual bigotry.

That said, we can't write prejudice out of the story. Curiously, the academic engineers contemplated the idea of stratified pyramids within the *othered* sectors of higher education. Even within the so clearly separate and unequal Black colleges, the reformers allowed that research universities might develop, with tiers of baccalaureate colleges, junior colleges, and vocational schools arrayed below them. This vision, and similar ones that pertained to colleges for women or religious minorities, is a clear tip-off that their efficiency ethos was half-baked. Maintaining separate systems was the definition of the much-scorned "duplication" problem. And yet, the academic engineers supported this grossly inefficient policy because the doctrine of segregation demanded it. They were bigots after all.

And finally, as a later generation would report, "separate educational facilities are inherently unequal."[4] Even though the reformers entertained the idea of elite forms of higher education for marginalized communities, the separate systems would of course always be inferior to the system for privileged white men. At best, they would occupy the lower tiers of a pyramid of pyramids.

A WOMAN'S PLACE

For a perfect example of the regressive trend toward division and subordination, consider the 1909 vote of the Wesleyan University board of trustees to overturn a policy that some members called "an anachronism." That policy was coeducation.

Wesleyan had started admitting women in 1872, a decision that met very little opposition. For more than two decades, the number of women students was small, never exceeding 10 percent of the student body. But around 1898, some of the university's constituents became alarmed by fast-rising numbers of admitted women. The board agreed to a 20 percent cap on female enrollment, but that was not enough to placate agitators (led by alumni groups) who demanded that women be excluded entirely. At the height of the crucible of reform and one year before Wesleyan made it onto the CFAT accepted list, the board did just that.[5]

The academic engineers never argued that women shouldn't attend college. They certainly didn't subscribe to the late nineteenth-century pseudoscience that claimed that too much education would damage women's reproductive capabilities, nor the ideas of Clark University president G. Stanley Hall, who believed that women should be educated only for motherhood.[6] Some were amenable to "race suicide" theory, most famously espoused by Theodore Roosevelt, a friend of Andrew Carnegie and many academic engineers, which raised the alarm that as more white, Anglo-Saxon women went to college, their birthrates would decline precipitously.[7] Others were anxious that increased female attendance would alienate men and make higher education a feminized space, a phenomenon Harold Wechsler calls "group repulsion."[8] These fears usually manifested in limitations on collegiate women rather than outright bans. Stanford University maintained a strict quota of five hundred undergraduate women from 1899 to 1933, coinciding almost exactly with the academic engineering era, and Michigan and Cornell also imposed quotas on women around the same time.[9]

Segregation was a more common solution than quotas. Woodrow Wilson called coeducation a "gratuitous folly" and argued that single-sex education would serve as good preparation for domestic life for women, and for men as good preparation for leadership.[10] A number of elite universities refused to open their doors to women but sponsored affiliated—and smaller—women's colleges literally across the street from their main campuses. Columbia opened Barnard College in 1889; Brown opened Pembroke College in 1891; Harvard opened Radcliffe College in 1894. Less elite institutions got into the game as well. Tulane opened its subsidiary, Newcomb College, in 1888, the same year that Western Reserve University opened its College for Women. Tufts, which had been coeducational, shunted its female students into the affiliated Jackson College for Women, opened in 1910. Rochester had also been coed since 1893 but instituted segregation in 1913 with the launch of its subordinate Women's College.[11]

As Lynn Gordon argues, most of these schemes to establish separate colleges "simply excluded women, without offering them any advantages."

Rochester's president, the academic engineer Rush Rhees, was openly hostile to female students and presided over budget cuts and other indignities to the Women's College after it opened.[12] The state of Florida drove the point home even further. In 1905, its legislature turned the coed Florida State College (today's FSU) into the Florida Female College and made the University of Florida, which had also been coed, into an all-male institution. Amy Thompson McCandless explains that the lawmakers "intended the university for men 'to be the major institution in the state' and envisioned the female college as primarily a normal and industrial school."[13]

The University of Chicago, meanwhile, claimed that separate could be equal. In 1902, after a decade of full coeducation, it made all of its undergraduate classes and its extracurriculum single-sex. William Rainey Harper justified the split in his 1903 presidential report, using vague terms: "The general ideal or standard of university work is injuriously affected by mixed classes and common community life. . . . The tendency is to admit too much of the personal element into interests which should be cultivated for their own sake." He gave himself cover by including a letter from Fred Gates, who claimed that despite the commitment to gender equality in the university's charter, John D. Rockefeller himself endorsed the idea "that the demand for the education of women would be sufficiently met if the institution admitted both sexes on equal terms, without requiring the institution to give instruction to both sexes in the same class-room."[14]

Harper's involvement suggests that elite universities' relationships with subsidiary women's colleges like Barnard and Radcliffe were a prelude to the affiliation schemes launched at Chicago and Baylor and contemplated elsewhere. Chicago's version was even called a "junior college," although the two gender-segregated junior colleges that Harper set up on his own campus (the men's division was also "junior") were of course of a far higher status than the ones in Des Moines or Kalamazoo. And even though most of the other affiliated women's schools offered the bachelor's degree, there was no doubt that they were—by design—in the shadows of their far more prestigious, all-male parent institutions.

However, other academic engineers went the other direction, embracing coeducation because of its association with progressive educational thought. William T. Foster had a snappy response to a New York reporter's question about including women in his plans for the launch of Reed College, a pet project for the GEB: "Co-educational? Why, of course. All western colleges are that. It's funny how provincial and unprogressive New York is in some ways."[15] Others also emphasized the prevalence of coeducation in the American West, like the journalist Edwin Slosson, who linked the policy to other types of inclusion: "the exclusion of students from educational facilities because of sex or money is repugnant to Western ideals."[16] In some Western universities, the policy was more accidental. As one commenter said of the University of California, "No one expected women to attend the university and therefore no plans were made to keep them out."[17]

The academic engineers' openness to varying forms of coeducation should not obscure the fact that they could be jaw-droppingly sexist. Pritchett showed this plainly in a 1907 speech at a college graduation:

> I have the conviction that a man has a distinct and lasting advantage over a woman when it comes to the profession of the law, or of politics, of the soldier, or of most of what we may call the great professions. . . . The same thing is true with regard to the great business places which come to men. The manager of the great corporation, of the great railroad system, of the bank, will in the long run be a man, and the woman who is ambitious for power must clearly look these facts in the face. . . . When it comes to the winning of a place in the vocations, the survival of the fittest is likely to play a large part in the fierce competition for a livelihood and for power and for influence which goes on in our social order. . . . In the end and by and large, those win the rewards who can; and measured by the same standards men will always have for these professions an immense advantage.[18]

Pritchett was speaking at Simmons, a women's college in Boston. He went on to note that not all hope was lost for the young graduates arrayed before him: "For the educated woman—and it is concerning the educated woman, and particularly the college woman, of whom I speak—the opportunity seems to me greatest in what might be called the 'semi-professional' vocations, such as those of the teacher, of the librarian, of the secretary."[19] Simmons was a good venue for these sentiments. Although the college, which opened in 1902, was a four-year institution, its founding president described it as "a technical college of high standard" and it had vocationalism at its core.[20]

Pritchett's approval of Simmons was an exception; stand-alone women's colleges typically came in for scrutiny, since they were often examples of the inefficient small colleges that the academic engineers despised so much. Most fit the description of failure in Harper's *Prospects of the Small College*: underenrolled, underendowed, provincial, and denominational. Harper also added a demerit unique to women's colleges—that they wouldn't be able to hire quality professors: "the strongest men will not consent to devote their lives to work in a women's college."[21] Woodrow Wilson perhaps inspired his criticism; the future CFAT trustee despised his first professorial job at Bryn Mawr, writing that "lecturing to young women of the present generation on the history and principles of politics is about as appropriate and profitable as would be lecturing to stone-masons on the evolution of fashion in dress."[22]

Harper's book didn't argue that all small colleges were lousy—just most of them. And this logic also applied to women's colleges, including in the halls of the federal Bureau of Education. As David Webster explains, while the bureau did not attempt to publish a "full-fledged stratification" of men's colleges and universities until the explosive Babcock Report in 1911, it had been publicly stratifying women's colleges since 1890.[23] The commissioner of education's annual report listed the institutions into two groups: Division A and Division B. For example, Commissioner Elmer Brown's report for 1907–08 listed sixteen women's colleges in the first group, including all of the famous Seven Sisters, and placed the overwhelming majority—ninety-three colleges—in the second group. The underlying statistics were telling. Just 19 percent of the Division A schools were denominational; 71 percent of Division B schools were. All but three in A were on the Eastern Seaboard between Virginia and Massachusetts; the B colleges were scattered everywhere, with more in Missouri than in Pennsylvania and New York combined. The first group had far larger enrollments, averaging 487 students each, while no college in the second group had had more than 350. Nine of sixteen colleges in Division A had endowments over $500,000, with five exceeding $1 million; the largest endowment of the ninety-three in Division B was just $177,000 and most had no endowment at all. It was very clear which ones were the winners and the losers.[24]

As for those losers, the academic engineers had their standard prescription in mind: demotion or deletion. Clyde Furst, the CFAT official, made this case explicitly in a 1915 speech:

> The degrees of not more than a dozen colleges exclusively for women are accepted by our foremost universities. Of the remaining nine-tenths, some are approaching the characteristics of a true college; some, apparently, can hope to attain these characteristics only through consolidation with stronger institutions. Most must become content, sooner or later, to adopt the name of institute, junior college or secondary school, which really describe their work. The earlier they arrive at this decision, the better for all concerned.[25]

His logic was echoed by other reformers like Benjamin Wheeler, whom Gordon reports advocated the expansion of junior colleges in California largely because he thought they would draw women away from Berkeley.[26] A 1930 survey showed how junior colleges were often gendered spaces: out of 279 total two-year schools, 41 percent were for women only while only 15 percent were for men only.[27]

The leaders of elite women's colleges also showed some interest in relegating the Division B schools to junior college status. In 1913, five of the stand-alone institutions—Vassar, Wellesley, Mount Holyoke, Smith, and Goucher—cooperated with the Virginia Association of College and Schools for Girls to put in place a "scheme of standardization" that would facilitate transfers from that state's low-status women's colleges into the Northern four-year institutions.[28] There is no record of whether the transfers ever happened. Even if they did, they would have been only an imitation of the academic engineers' vision of upward transfer, which always involved transferring to a university with graduate-level training.

In fact, the lack of graduate education at the elite women's colleges indicated that a separate pyramid for women's higher education was not really on the table. Many academic engineers were plainly sexist, but they did not extend their sexism to the graduate level. There was no effort in the United States, as there was in England in the 1890s, to establish a research-oriented "Women's University."[29] Even universities that vehemently defended their male-only undergraduate divisions, like Yale, allowed women into graduate programs.[30]

There was only one stand-alone women's college that awarded the PhD: Bryn Mawr. The Pennsylvania school was run by M. Carey Thomas, Flexner's sister-in-law and an academic engineer in her own right, with a doctorate from Zurich.[31] According to Helen Horowitz, Thomas aimed to make the college "the outpost of Leipzig in America."[32] She authored a monograph, commissioned by Nicholas Murray Butler and full of Gatesian charts and maps, that suggested that a handful of the Division A schools should be considered the "four great colleges for women: Vassar, Smith, Wellesley, Bryn Mawr," with two lower tiers arranged below them.[33] Thomas also proved herself as part of the overtly bigoted subset of academic engineers, like Harvard's Lowell, by working to exclude Black and Jewish students from her institution.[34]

But while Bryn Mawr earned the attention of the academic engineers (Gates heaped praise on it), it remained an outlier, and it never capped a segregated women's pyramid.[35] The reformers looked down on the vast majority of women, but they also acknowledged that some brilliant women—Thomas, first and foremost—could rise to the top to join them in that very looking down.

RELIGIOUS MINORITIES

Even in a period of increasing secularization, religion still loomed large in the early twentieth century. As indicated by the academic engineers' scorn for the duplicative efforts of Methodists, Baptists, and other denominations to establish and run colleges, before 1905 American higher education was an overwhelmingly Protestant space. Many colleges maintained religious litmus tests for trustees, administrators, and faculty. While these rarely extended to students themselves, the messaging was clear: if you are outside of the denomination, and certainly if you aren't a Protestant, this place is not for you.

The academic engineers thought it was ridiculous for a college to draw divisions between Protestant groups, but their feelings about dividing non-Protestants were much more mixed. The experiences of Catholic and Jewish students tell two sides of a segregation story. Both were minorities that experienced widespread discrimination, but their faiths approached their exclusion differently.

As Wechsler describes, elite universities never had to formulate a plan to keep out Catholics because many Catholics voluntarily segregated themselves.[36] Extreme anti-Catholic prejudice in schools and society throughout the nineteenth century, capped by the virulent Know-Nothing movement, had led them to create a separate, parallel educational system. Starting with primary schools in which students would not be forced to read Protestant scripture (as was the case in many public schools), the system quickly extended into higher education.

The word "system" is appropriate. The Catholic Church is famously hierarchical, and its leaders in the United States applied the institution's logic to schooling. By 1905, the church had divided the nation into fourteen ecclesiastical provinces, each led by an archdiocese with smaller dioceses arrayed below it. Similarly, nearly every province had one university or elite college, typically run by the Jesuit order, with lower-tier colleges and academies arrayed below it, often with affiliation agreements in place.[37]

This was, of course, the same idea as the academic engineers' dreams of regional or denominational higher education pyramids. Just as Gates had pitched the University of Chicago as the pinnacle of a Baptist pyramid, Catholic leaders put their energy behind the Catholic University of America, which had opened three years prior in Washington, DC. Both were designed as super-universities at the apex of a widespread religious community; both were meant to focus on research and graduate training (Catholic didn't admit undergraduates until 1904); both were founding members of the elite Association of American Universities; both launched formal affiliation schemes with lower-tier colleges (Philip Gleason calls Catholic "a single-institution accreditation program"[38]); and both were blessed at their outset by a famous and powerful man (Chicago had Rockefeller, Catholic had Pope Leo XIII).[39]

Despite these parallels, it didn't take long for the academic engineers to infuriate the Catholics. Their antagonism to religious control made them suspect, and their support for public education systems was a threat to the nation's largest nonpublic education system. Pritchett bragged to Carnegie that "our Catholic friends" were increasingly concerned about the CFAT's work in this regard: "They really would like to get rid of any general system of education and they find it very difficult to tolerate the idea of a public system of education free of sectarian control."[40] This was certainly an overstatement and, in fact, the inverse of the reality in many states, in which Protestant majorities were advancing compulsory school laws that essentially banned Catholic education, until the US Supreme Court ruled the laws unconstitutional in 1925.[41]

In 1910, the National Catholic Educational Association voted to express alarm about "the encroachment upon liberty of education by what may be styled in current parlance 'Education Trust,' and notably what is called the Carnegie Foundation, acting without mandate from the people, without justification from circumstances and without responsibility to any tribunal save themselves."[42] Every annual meeting of the group for several years thereafter featured broadsides against the academic engineers. A 1911 speaker derided them for their fixation on "academic efficiency" and accused the CFAT of making itself "a permanent, self-perpetuating, central bureau of education" that aimed "to get practical control of the higher education of the country."[43] A 1913 speaker called the foundation "an officious, meddlesome institution which grasps half notions about education and attempts to foist them on everybody."[44] A 1914 editorial by Thomas Edward Shields, a Catholic University professor and leading educational theorist, described the effect of the rise of academic engineering as "simply a change of masters. The god Mammon was substituted for Jesus Christ."[45]

Yet another NCEA speaker in 1912, though, attacked the academic engineers in a way that indicated that the treatment of Catholic higher education was not that much different from what small Protestant colleges were experiencing:

> To use a homely expression, they are in the process of freezing out the smaller colleges. In accordance with this process we hear jeremiads anent the excessive number of colleges and universities; the inefficiency born of poverty of resources. In accordance with the process, we perceive larger institutions uniting in a great educational trust. They are strong enough to obtain and hold vast privileges from the State, and, ironical as the situation may seem, they crowd the weakest to the wall after the manner of an older and pagan civilization. *Vae victis!* The exiles from the weaker colleges will eventually swell their ranks.[46]

That concern, though—that small Catholic colleges would lose their students to big universities—showed that Catholics were not *so* alien that they needed their own schools.[47] As Noel Ignatiev and others have shown, anti-Catholic sentiment waned in the late nineteenth and early twentieth centuries; in 1928, the Democrats would nominate a Catholic man for president.[48] It was a sign of their acceptance that Catholic Americans were now considered mainstream enough that their colleges could be squashed by the academic engineers.

Not so with American Jews during these years. Associated with recent immigration from Eastern Europe and considered foreign not just ethnically but attitudinally, Jewish students were ostracized by their peers and flagrantly excluded by college administrators. As Marcia Synott and Jerome Karabel have shown, Harvard, Yale, and Princeton went to great lengths to limit the number of Jews in their undergraduate classes, but anti-Semitic admissions policies were hardly unique to the "big three" in the early twentieth century.[49] David Levine has documented flagrant discrimination at Williams, Dartmouth, Virginia, North Carolina, and even the Massachusetts Agricultural College, while Zev Eleff cites Jewish quotas at two dozen institutions.[50]

Unlike the Catholics, American Jews never developed a parallel higher education system. Part of the reason was organizational; Judaism is a largely decentralized religion, in stark contrast to Catholicism. But a more important explanation involves timing. Most Jewish immigration came a full generation after the first big wave of Catholic immigration, meaning that it emerged alongside the rise of public higher education, which offered more access for marginalized groups. That was particularly true at the two public colleges in New York City, the center of American Jewish life. A 1911 study found that Jewish students made up an astonishing 74 percent of the all-male City College while the public Hunter College, a former normal school, was similarly dominated by Jewish women.[51]

That said, there were movements toward segregated Jewish institutions at both ends of the status spectrum. At the bottom was the Hebrew Technical Institute in lower Manhattan, founded in 1884 as a vocational high school, which in 1903 expanded into evening classes for adults in exactly the same model as Cooper Union, located one block away.[52] At the top of the spectrum was the abortive push for a national Jewish university. First floated by G. Stanley Hall (who equated it directly to Catholic University), the idea came to prominence in the early '20s, especially after severe budget cuts to City College were proposed in 1922.[53] As Eleff argues, liberal Jews hated the idea, seeing it as unhelpful to their assimilationist goals, and many Gentiles attacked it for similar reasons. However, a purely Jewish college did launch in the '20s: Yeshiva University. This institution was backed by the Orthodox movement of American Judaism, and unlike the proposed Jewish research university it was an explicitly sectarian institution. Yeshiva gained the backing of prominent academic engineers like Nicholas Murray Butler and Ray Lyman Wilbur, who saw it as a good location for unassimilable Jews who had little to contribute to the universities they ran.[54]

Those endorsements of Yeshiva presaged a more disquieting turn in the academic engineers' treatment of Jewish students. As Wechsler shows, Columbia administrators, led by Butler, were dismayed by the increasing percentage of Jews in the university's undergraduate ranks throughout the 1910s. This increase had been driven by those students' excellent scores on the entrance examination on which Columbia based its admissions decisions. In an effort to curtail the trend and stymie the "invasion" of Jews, in 1919 the university invented what we now call the "holistic" model of college admissions, in which interviews, letters of recommendation, and personal questions are considered in addition to grades and test scores. This model allowed behind-the-scenes discrimination. Other institutions soon followed, often backing up the new system with explicit quotas limiting the number of spots available to Jewish students.[55] Exams were still considered, but differentially. A 1922 article in *The Nation* slammed colleges for telling "a Cohen, whose average on the college board examinations was 90, that he cannot enter because there are too many Jews there already, while a grade of 68 will pass a Murphy, or one of 62 a Morgan."[56]

But the academic engineers never simply excluded undesirable students from elite institutions; they knew that they had to provide alternatives. And Butler devised just such an alternative: Seth Low Junior College, which opened in downtown Brooklyn in 1928. The two-year school was a satellite campus of Columbia, and it served an overwhelmingly Jewish student body. Many Jewish students offered anecdotal evidence of being rejected by Columbia but encouraged to apply to Seth Low. The school was unquestionably a second-class institution. Like other junior colleges, it did not offer the bachelor's degree, and while some opportunities existed for continuing their studies at the university's Manhattan campus, Butler ensured that Seth Low transfers could never be enrolled as members of Columbia College and could never earn a bachelor of arts degree at the university.[57]

Seth Low lasted only eight years, and it had no imitators. The rise of Nazism in Europe turned a harsh light on anti-Semitism in the United States, and private junior colleges were fading fast anyway. But its creation by one of the leading academic engineers, well after the crucible of reform was over, indicated the enduring allure of separate and unequal institutions designed to divert undesirable students and therefore protect the top of the higher education pyramid.

"THE NEGRO PROBLEM"

As was the case with Butler and many others, the leaders of elite institutions often cultivated second-class schools into which they could divert undesirable students. The clearest and most distressing example came with the education of African Americans. Even leaders who claimed to be perfectly egalitarian promoted racial segregation. Take the word of the president of Amherst, who declared that Black students had every right to a college education but went on, "Where shall they obtain a liberal education? With few exceptions, I think it should be in the Southern colleges. The color line is so sharply drawn in Northern colleges (unfortunately) that a Negro is at great disadvantage."[58] What he failed to say, of course, was that however sharp the color line may have been in the North, nearly every single college and university in the South was absolutely segregated.

Furthermore, the Southern schools that Black students could attend were not just single-race; they were also largely sub-baccalaureate and vocational. Another elite New Englander, the president of Williams, echoed his Amherst peer but applied the anti-duplication logic of academic engineering, showing how much the "dumping ground" plan would limit the opportunities of Black students. Although he allowed for the usefulness of a few true Black colleges, he clarified, "The multiplication of universities of the higher sort is not desirable in comparison with the multiplication of training schools for all the trades and manual activities."[59]

Nowhere was the dichotomy between a liberal education for the elite and a vocational education for the masses clearer than in Black higher education during the crucible of reform. Even more than for women, who were facing strong opposition in their campaign for full citizenship, even more than for immigrants, who were coming under increasing scrutiny from the federal government, the "Negro problem" was perceived as an issue of national importance in the first decades of the twentieth century. And when that "problem" dovetailed with the debate over higher education for the masses, seemingly everyone had an opinion.

The two most famous opinions were best articulated in an edited volume from 1903 titled, not surprisingly, "The Negro Problem." All of the contributors were Black, and the first two essays went to Booker T. Washington and William Edward Burghardt Du Bois. Their titles alone made clear the dueling arguments: Washington penned "Industrial Education for the Negro" while Du Bois's contribution was "The Talented Tenth," shorthand for his idea that 10 percent of African Americans deserved a liberal college education.

We can credit some of the two men's famous ideological differences to biography. Washington was born into slavery in the South while Du Bois was born after the Civil War in Massachusetts. Washington's extreme hardship as a child may have informed his belief that incremental progress for the Black community was the most realistic goal, whereas Du Bois had the privilege of impatience. Their educations are even more telling, if we are to believe that loyalty to alma mater has real meaning. Washington's higher education took place at the Hampton Normal and Agricultural Institute, a sub-baccalaureate industrial school in Virginia. Du Bois held a PhD from Harvard.

That said, the most important difference between them was that Washington was an academic engineer and Du Bois was a college professor who revered the liberal arts and sciences. Today, we hold the men to be equal interlocutors, but in 1903 the professor was small potatoes next to Washington, unquestionably the most famous and powerful Black American of the time. Washington was personal friends with Theodore Roosevelt and Mark Twain. Andrew Carnegie cherished their close relationship and even funded a personal pension for Washington and his wife.[60] And Washington was fully enmeshed in the academic engineering circle. While he never sat on the CFAT or GEB board, he was a regular visitor to their Manhattan offices, seeking help for his own institution, Tuskegee, or offering his counsel on appropriations to other Black schools. He overlapped with other academic engineers on various committees and on other boards of trustees.

Since they embraced him, does that mean that Booker T. Washington's fellow academic engineers were not racists? No. They may have considered themselves enlightened, but by modern standards they were terrible bigots. Wallace Buttrick, the longtime GEB leader, flatly stated in 1903, "I recognize the fact that the Negro is an inferior race, and that the Anglo-Saxon is the superior race."[61] William Baldwin, the GEB's first president and a close ally of Washington's, stated that Black men were "best fitted to perform the heavy labor in the Southern States. . . . This will permit the Southern white laborer to perform the more expert labor, and to leave the fields, the mines, and the simpler trades for the negro."[62] David Starr Jordan offered a backhanded compliment: "I believe fully in the higher education of every man and woman whose character and ability is such as to make such training possible. There are relatively fewer of such persons among the Negroes than among the Anglo-Saxons, but for all of these the higher training is just as necessary and just as effective as for anyone else."[63] Woodrow Wilson was a notorious Ku Klux Klan sympathizer.[64]

But when it comes to understanding the academic engineers' treatment of Black higher education, we need to look further than these ugly facts; as Joan Malczewski argues, "a conversation that starts and ends with racism" tells us very little about educational reform in the South.[65] And after all, the academic engineers and their backers were not consumed by the question of race. Black education was a side project at best for most of them. Yes, many of the reformers visited Southern Black colleges and institutes, usually as part of the annual rail tours gently mocked in newspapers as "the millionaire's special," organized by the railroad executive Robert C. Ogden, a founding GEB trustee.[66] These sometimes had unintended effects, however. Eric Anderson and Alfred Moss report that John D. Rockefeller Jr.'s, participation on the 1901 trip caused him to conceive of the General Education Board as a broad, race-agnostic foundation: "Though he and his father had originally been thinking of establishing a Negro Education Board, the discussions on Ogden's excursion led the young man to conclude 'that an educational program geared to the needs of a particular race, would represent an unfortunate and perhaps impossible approach.'"[67]

Thus, the reformers' ideas about Black higher education tended to resemble their ideas about higher education in general. This was most true when it came to the notion that there were simply too many institutions doing the work of higher education and that winners and losers had to be selected. Flexner, speaking at a 1915 GEB conference, asked, "What would be the effect of selecting four or five Negro colleges and building them up, making them good, honest, sincere, effective colleges so far as they went, and letting the others along, not to suppress them or consolidate them but just to make them 'sweat,' would that tend in the long run to so stigmatize the inferior institutions that they would give up, the way the poor medical institutions are giving up?"[68] Flexner couldn't resist giving himself a pat on the back for his recent report on medical education, which was indeed having the effect of causing institutions to close—including all but two of the medical schools that served African Americans, causing a dearth of Black doctors that lasted decades.[69]

The next year, the academic engineer Thomas Jesse Jones authored a widely read study of education for African Americans, funded by the GEB-aligned Phelps-Stokes Fund and published by the federal Bureau of Education. Jones imitated Flexner's brand of ideological muckraking disguised as impartial study. His examination of curricula found dismal results: "Hardly a colored college meets the standards set by the Carnegie Foundation. . . . Only three institutions, Howard University, Fisk University, and Meharry Medical College, have student bodies, teaching force and equipment, and income sufficient to warrant the characterization of 'college.'" Writing like a true academic engineer, Jones criticized religious colleges, noting the "denominational interest in a duplication that makes for a low-grade and ineffective education." The solution, he advised, was a dramatic reduction in the number of schools trying to be colleges. There should be only three baccalaureate colleges for African Americans in the South, he argued—one in Richmond, one in Atlanta, and one in eastern Texas—in addition to Howard and Fisk, which deserved university status. His solution for the rest of the Black colleges was predictable: they "should be developed into junior colleges or institutions doing two years of college work."[70]

Louis Harlan reports that the idea for Jones's report originated in 1911, when Booker T. Washington suggested it, repeatedly, to Anson Phelps Stokes, a top Yale administrator who was in the process of launching his family's education-focused foundation. Borrowing the geographical fixation of Fred Gates, Washington asked the philanthropist, who would also become a GEB trustee the next year, to fund a "thorough study of the entire field with a view of selecting schools that are physically located in the right place." Washington made the implications clear in a cautionary postscript: "The killing out of the poorer schools would have to be done very gradually and through a process of placing emphasis upon the efficient ones rather than any direct attempt to have the poorer ones disappear."[71]

The notion that there were too many Black colleges was a response to their healthy growth. Their numbers had tripled between 1880 and 1915, from nine to twenty-seven, and the number of African Americans enrolled in college exploded shortly thereafter, growing eightfold between 1914 and 1926.[72] Demand for postsecondary education was clearly burgeoning in the Black community, just as it was elsewhere. The academic engineers' response was predictable: they sought to divert the bulk of Black young adults into sub-baccalaureate institutions.

The perceived urgency of the "Negro problem," coupled with pervasive racism, meant that the alternative to college for Black people— Washington's "industrial education"—was met with deep commitment and wide acceptance. Although the reformers turned to vocational forms of higher education as a solution for many groups, we see its fullest expression as a program specifically for African Americans. Scholars, most notably James Anderson, have given it a specific name: "the Hampton-Tuskegee Idea." Or, more directly, "education for servitude."[73]

Hampton was the original site of the idea. The Virginia school, founded in the immediate aftermath of the Civil War by a Union general, developed the program of semiskilled vocational training that would dominate Black higher education until the 1920s, and it nurtured future reformers like Washington and Jones, both of whom worked there. It also opened its doors to Native Americans, an important development that I will return to later in this section. But it wasn't until Washington brought what he had learned in Tidewater Virginia deep into rural Alabama, where he established Tuskegee, that the model became an object of intense interest for philanthropists and planners bent on systemic reform.

As soon as he began opening his wallet to higher education, Andrew Carnegie embraced Tuskegee. Just a few months after his first gifts to Cooper Union and Stevens Institute, he began making annual donations to the Alabama school, capping them with a $600,000 check in 1903. Speaking at Tuskegee in 1906, he described the schools as doing Cooper's same work of educating the working classes, with only demographic differences: "We, of New York, have a somewhat similar problem to that which so heavily burdens our Southern brethren: the hundreds of thousands of ignorant immigrants." These newcomers, Carnegie argued, needed "primarily industrial and scientific" forms of education in order to become useful and non-threatening members of society.[74] And the steel baron was not Tuskegee's only admirer. By 1903, the school had a Carnegie Library, but just steps away was Rockefeller Hall. In fact, the GEB's founding board had major overlap with Tuskegee's board, including William Baldwin, who chaired both.[75]

So, what was Tuskegee, this rural institute that inspired so much philanthropic activity? We know one thing it was not: a college. Although it had academic classes, it did not offer academic degrees. Until the 1930s, it called itself only an "institute," and Washington was never its president— only its principal, as though it were a high school.

And yet it *looked* like a college. Tuskegee's average student age in 1906 was nineteen. It had 1,600 students, far more than any high school of its time. Much like a college, it drew students from a wide area: only 28 percent were from Alabama, with another 22 percent from the neighboring states of Georgia and Mississippi. Fully half of the student body was from elsewhere, including 68 students from foreign countries.[76] It had several dormitories and a stately library paid for by Carnegie himself, open seven days a week. And students took academic classes, whose titles by 1915 included Botany, Psychology, and Management, and many courses in the liberal arts.[77]

But no one confused it with a college. This was because of its celebrated program of industrial training, which most students took on alternating days—academic classes on Monday, Wednesday, and Friday, and vocational education on Tuesday, Thursday, and Saturday. Defending this 50/50 balance, Roscoe Conkling Bruce, the Harvard-trained head of Tuskegee's academic division, had to explain in 1906 that "Tuskegee does not graduate hoe-hands or plowboys. . . . The distinctive feature of Tuskegee— adequate provision for industrial training—sets it upon a hill apart, but by a whimsical perversity this major feature is in some quarters assumed to be the whole school."[78] The reformers who loved Tuskegee's "practical" reputation could certainly be found in those quarters. Even Charles Eliot, the CFAT board member who had the most sanguine view of liberal education, saw only the vocational purpose of the school and its peers: "When one goes through the shops and schoolrooms of Hampton Institute, where hundreds of negroes and scores of Indians are under instruction, or through the working rooms of the Tuskegee Institute, thronged with negroes of all shades, one is struck by the eager application to the work in hand which is exhibited by the students."[79]

So again, what was Tuskegee? Anderson is clear: despite its low-skill industrial programs in fields like bricklaying and laundry, it was primarily a normal school. "The Hampton-Tuskegee curriculum was not centered on trade or agricultural training; it was centered on the training of teachers."[80] Bruce's 1906 essay backs him up: "The mission of Tuskegee Institute is largely to supply measurably well-equipped teachers for the schools—teachers able and eager to teach gardening and carpentry as well as grammar and arithmetic."[81] The goal of the industrial program, Anderson goes on to explain, was to inculcate "the appropriate values and character to teach the children of the South's distinctive Black laboring class."[82] Therein lies his point about "education for servitude": that the Tuskegee-trained teachers were meant to absorb a limited view of their potential and that of their students, thus perpetuating the racial caste system.

The academic engineers disdained normal schools, though, as we have seen earlier. They also largely disdained land-grant schools—and it turns out that Tuskegee was one of those as well, although it was not among the 1890 Land Grant Colleges, the shorthand designation for the group of historically Black colleges created out of the Morrill Act of 1890. (That legislation ensured that federal appropriations to Southern states did not flow exclusively to white-serving institutions but in doing so codified segregation in higher education.) Instead, in 1899 the US Congress made an appropriation of twenty-five thousand acres of "mineral lands" specifically for the benefit of Tuskegee, without allowing any discretion to the state of Alabama in determining the institution to be benefited, as was typically the case with land grants.

Northern elites, however, overlooked these categories and saw Tuskegee as something much more important. It's hard to imagine huge groups of wealthy New Yorkers gathering to attend boisterous fundraisers for a normal school or a land-grant college, as they did for Tuskegee at Madison Square Garden in 1899, and then again at Carnegie Hall in 1906. Instead, they believed that they were supporting a truly unique experiment that would direct young adults in an impoverished region toward semiskilled manual labor, thus solving both a racial problem and a workforce problem. In announcing the 1899 fundraiser, the *New York Times* described "The Tuskegee Idea" in social efficiency terms the academic engineers could certainly appreciate:

> Dr. Washington's conception is based on clear facts. The greatest need of the South is labor, and the greatest resource of the South is the labor of the negro race. The demand and the raw material for the supply exist together. To the degree that this raw material can be developed, that is, to the degree that the negroes can be made more profitable workmen in all grades and kinds of employment, the relations between them and the whites are bound to be improved. . . . Every dollar spent in this labor will

do a lasting and increasing good. It will not be wasted. It will not be lost. The returns from it will be, like compound interest, a steadily increasing profit to the Nation.[83]

The logic of raw materials and returns on investment spoke directly to the corporate class, who flooded it with money. By the time of Washington's death in 1915, the school's endowment totaled roughly $2 million—$50 million in today's dollars.[84] While small by present standards, this was six times the size of the endowment of Howard University, the most prominent Black institution that offered a traditional college education. Furthermore, Tuskegee's endowment was larger than that of many white-serving institutions, including New York University, Boston University, and Lehigh University, and was only slightly less than Vanderbilt's.[85]

Tuskegee's fundraising success was also due to Washington's brilliant repackaging of another mantra from academic engineering; he inverted the "don't come to us, we'll come to you" message that drove the university extension movement. Washington himself came to the philanthropists—he estimated that he spent two-thirds of his time fundraising in the Northern states—but his promise was that his Black *students* would remain far away from the North.[86] The "Atlanta Compromise" speech that launched him into fame in 1895 established the idea in its most memorable passage: reminding "those of my race who depend on bettering their condition in a foreign land" that they should instead "cast down your bucket where you are" and make a humble life in the South.[87] In a 1906 speech celebrating Tuskegee's twenty-fifth anniversary, he gave his institution credit for the fact that "the main body of the race has decided to remain permanently in the heart of the South in or near what is known as the Black Belt."[88]

This "we won't come to you" promise was not just geographical but also specifically educational. In his 1903 essay, Washington made the case that college education had harmed African Americans by opening the door to a life of the mind. Prior to the ascendance of the Tuskegee model, he wrote, "Too many were taken from the farm and educated, but educated in everything but farming. For this reason they had no interest in farming and did not return to it." He drove the point home further when it came to the education of Black women, writing with sickening sexism, "It is discouraging to find a woman who knows much about theoretical chemistry, and who cannot properly wash and iron a shirt." His promise was that if they supported his industrial school, philanthropists would be actively helping to steer Black students away from the ivory tower. In *Tuskegee & Its*

People, a widely distributed promotional book, he used the "practicality" obsession of the academic engineers and the anti-intellectualism of their benefactors to seal the deal: "The masses who are most helpfully reached by the Tuskegee Institute are coming to realize that education in its truest sense is no longer to be regarded as an emotional impulse, a fetish made up of loosely joined information, to be worshiped for its mere possession, but as a practical means to a definite end."[89]

That said, like his fellow academic engineers, Washington never made the claim that *no* Black students should get a liberal college education. Writing in *The Atlantic* in 1903, he touted Tuskegee's industrial model (including by comparing it directly to German vocational schools) but also stressed that "it was never meant that *all* Negro youths should secure industrial education, any more than it is meant that *all* white youths should pass through the Massachusetts Institute of Technology, or the Amherst Agricultural College, to the exclusion of such training as is given at Harvard, Yale, or Dartmouth."[90] Since Tuskegee was both a form of technical school and a land-grant institution, the analogy with MIT and Massachusetts's recently established land-grant college made perfect sense.

Washington's colleagues in the foundations agreed with him that there was a place for a very small number of true colleges for African Americans. Anderson, citing a 1907 GEB report on Black higher education, describes the logic of the reformist group he calls the "industrial philanthropists": "If a few outstanding back colleges were established, industrial philanthropists could use these institutions to pressure the remaining ones into discontinuing their collegiate courses because of their inability to keep pace with the rising standards of college-level work."[91] In other words, the academic engineers envisioned a normative pyramid of Black higher education, just as they envisioned for white institutions. The Black pyramid, however, would be even pointier at its top.

In 1916, a GEB committee made clear just how pointy it would be, writing,: "Of course, there are far too many Negro colleges and universities; and of this large number, not one is well equipped and manned on a sensible, modest scale. Wise cooperation with one or two institutions would be the most effective way of bringing order out of chaos, of distinguishing the real from the imitation."[92] According to Thomas Jesse Jones in his federally commissioned study the next year, there were indeed exactly two African American–serving institutions that could accomplish the task. The first was Howard, in the nation's capital and partially supported by an annual direct subsidy from the US Congress. The second was Fisk University in Nashville. Despite Howard's federal support, both were private institutions, which made sense. As the president of a private Black college noted at a NAACP meeting that year, the state of public higher education for Black students was abysmal: "It is a well known fact that collegiate students are not encouraged in the Negro State institutions of the South, and in one or more of them they have been discontinued after having once been introduced."[93] The 1890 land-grant colleges did offer a strictly practical postsecondary education to small numbers of Black students, but a publicly funded liberal education was off the table.

Howard and Fisk had something else in common, too: by 1909, Booker T. Washington sat on both of their boards. Washington's involvement with the two best hopes for academic excellence among Black colleges is an indication of the tensions surrounding Black higher education during the crucible of reform. Even these would-be elite schools had to contend with the specter of industrial training.

In 1905, according to Harlan, Howard's president "tried to introduce industrial education and had been ousted by a near-revolt of students and faculty."[94] His successor continued the trend, establishing a School of Manual Arts and Applied Sciences that led critics to accuse him of a plot to "industrialize Howard University."[95] He also courted Washington for a board seat in a 1907 letter, trying to appeal to his love of practicality: "Manual work is required of all our students and the course for A.B. can be completed with honor without either Greek or Latin."[96] Washington did join the Howard board that year, where, according to Joe Richardson, he was "appointed a 'committee of one' to confer with the Carnegie Foundation."[97] In 1912 he was heavily involved in selecting yet another president for Howard. His first choice was Thomas Jesse Jones, who was then on the Hampton faculty.[98] The trustees declined the suggestion and instead tapped the president of a white women's college in Maryland. Washington would keep trying to find a spot for Jones, however.[99]

Fisk, even more than Howard, offers an illuminating case study of the tortured attempts of Black colleges to get money and status by searching for the right balance between practical and liberal models. Unlike Hampton and Tuskegee, which were generously supported by Northern philanthropists, and Howard with its federal appropriation, Fisk had always struggled financially. Its major financial lifeline came in late 1871 when a small group of musically talented students went on a singing tour to raise money for the desperate school, which had less than a week's operating expenses on hand. The Fisk Jubilee Singers were a smash hit; eighteen months later they were singing for Queen Victoria in London.[100] The student group raised hundreds of thousands of dollars for the university, but it was disbanded in 1903 due to diminishing returns, caused at least in part by competition from other Black schools—including the Tuskegee Quartets, formed in 1884.[101]

According to Richardson, Fisk had held industrial education at bay until 1902, when it "halfheartedly offered domestic science courses." In 1905, however, the university's president, James Merill, accepted a gift from the GEB-aligned Slater Fund to create a new Department of Applied Science focused on strictly practical courses like animal husbandry, woodworking, and cooking.[102] The GEB itself made its first donation to Fisk the next year, to support the construction of a new Applied Science building. A Slater Fund official praised the school's new programs as "a much needed addition to Fisk's otherwise too exclusively literary course."[103] As Du Bois, a Fisk graduate, recalled later, this shift represented "the surrender of college training to the current industrial fad." He responded with an extraordinary public rebuke in 1908, the occasion of his twentieth reunion, in a public address on campus that also served as a broad critique of how American colleges were acquiescing to the demands of top-down reform:

> The personality of an institution is a peculiar thing. The apparently isolated—almost unconscious movements of individuals, guided by the outside pressure of powerful interests, easily bring that to pass of which they themselves had not dreamed. And so today this venerable institution stands before its problem of future development, with the bribe of Public Opinion and Private Wealth dangling before us, if we will either deny that our object is the highest and broadest training of Black Men, or if we will consent to call Higher Education that which you know and I know is not Higher Education.[104]

The speech, which went on to describe the Applied Science curriculum as "a series of lessons in the training of servants," had a devastating effect on Merill, who was already on thin ice due to his weak fundraising. By that summer, he was out as the university's president.[105]

Fisk dramatically changed course in selecting its next president; instead of dabbling in industrial education, it would now fully aim to become an elite institution. Its board chair consulted both Pritchett and Buttrick in making the selection of George Gates, the sitting president of Pomona College, who had previously helmed Grinnell College. Gates fit right in with the academic engineers: he had done graduate study in Germany after graduating from Dartmouth and happily accepted the CFAT's intervention in getting Pomona to cut its denominational ties. He was a proponent

of "sincerity" in higher education, specifically for the handful of baccalaureate institutions that could run the gauntlet and become elite. These
included Pomona, Grinnell, and—he hoped—Fisk.

Even before he was sworn in as president, Gates was already asking
the GEB for money using the new approach. He wrote to Buttrick to explain that he had accepted the job "in the hope that there would be a
strong movement to make Fisk University the preeminent institution in
the South for the higher education of negroes especially with the view to
train teachers, lawyers, doctors, and clergymen." His letter included an
endorsement from a Supreme Court justice, who said that while the vast
majority of Black students should be given industrial education, "still I
believe that there are a certain proportion of that race who ought to have
an opportunity of receiving the benefit of the very highest education which
they are able to receive. I therefore am of [the] opinion that Fisk University
has its place and ought to be the head and crown of all colored institutions for learning in the South."[106] The GEB responded to this hierarchical
vision with an immediate donation, followed by a larger $60,000 pledge
the next year.[107] Pritchett also offered an endorsement, writing to a Fisk
official using identical logic to the justice's, with his usual tut-tut about
nomenclature:

> I venture to say that while the great need for education amongst colored
> people in the South is in the direction of industrial training, it is also
> necessary to have a few institutions of higher learning for the training of
> leaders. Fisk University would seem to me to be one of the places which
> might expect to do the work of higher education with proper facilities. It
> is, in my judgment, a mistake to assume the name 'university' until true
> university work is being done. I wish now that it might be changed to
> 'college,' but I believe that there is a real opportunity for a good college
> for colored people in Nashville.[108]

Shortly after assuming the presidency, Gates moved decisively away from
vocationalism by shutting down the Applied Science department and by
merging Fisk's Normal department into its regular college course, meaning that it no longer offered a sub-baccalaureate track. And this merger
was not the only one he had in mind.

Gates was particularly concerned about the academic engineering
ideal of cooperation and noncompetition. Part of his enthusiasm for having Washington associated with Fisk was about having evidence that his
university and Tuskegee were playing together nicely, as he wrote to his

famous board member: "This point will be of value to the more thoughtful givers. It will particularly appeal to Dr. Buttrick and such men who you
know are always talking about institutions getting together and working
in harmony."[109]

Tuskegee's mission was too different to be a real partner for Fisk, but
early in his administration, Gates began pursuing the idea of a formal
merger between his institution and Atlanta University, a growing Black
college whose faculty had included Du Bois until 1910. Despite its proud
status, Atlanta was struggling financially, and its recently appointed president was adding practical programs like Mechanic Arts and Household
Arts in an attempt to attract the attention of philanthropists. Gates's plan
would involve abandoning the institution in Georgia and moving its faculty and students to Nashville along with its endowment, thereby creating an unquestionably dominant university at the top of the Black higher
education pyramid.[110] The New York philanthropist George Foster Peabody
(a founding member of the GEB) wrote to a Fisk trustee in 1911, endorsing
the merger on the grounds that it would create "one real university on a
good foundation at Nashville" and adding that "there ought to be a definite
basis of cooperation" between Fisk and Howard as well.[111]

Buttrick loved the idea but was pessimistic that it would work, writing
to Peabody, "I wish that the Fisk and Atlanta people might see their opportunity; but there, as elsewhere in educational affairs, institutions and
the pride thereof stand in the way of what is best."[112] The next year, the
Atlanta trustees proved him right, showing their "pride" in voting to reject
any merger plan that "contemplates the abandonment of the situs of the
plant at Atlanta University and the removal of the institution to another
state."[113] In 1913, a Fisk administrator visited the GEB offices in New York
to report that "the consolidation" with Atlanta was still moving forward.[114]
But it never happened.

When Booker T. Washington joined the Fisk board, Gates felt obligated
to make a public statement that the university was not becoming an industrial training school.[115] But when Washington had the opportunity to
help pick Fisk's next president following Gates's sudden 1912 death, he
forcefully steered it in exactly that direction.

Washington's first choice for the post was—surprise, surprise—Thomas
Jesse Jones. This time, the board *did* offer the post to Jones, but the industrial education expert turned it down in favor of a position in the federal
government.[116] The man who did become Fisk's president in 1915 also
had a pedigree in industrial education: Fayette McKenzie, who had spent
many years studying Native American education as both a practitioner and

a Penn-trained sociologist and was a well-known advocate for vocationally oriented training for indigenous Americans.

That was very much the model at Hampton, a historically Black institution that also maintained a semi-segregated program for Native Americans between 1877 and 1923, many of them forced to attend by the federal Office of Indian Affairs, which also provided the tuition for these conscripts through an annual grant to the school. Samuel Armstrong—the school's founder, Washington's mentor, and the man generally considered the progenitor of the push for industrial education for Black people—had grown up in Honolulu, the son of a missionary who promoted manual training schools for native Hawaiians.[117] At Hampton, faculty members including Jones preached that industrial education would lift indigenous peoples out of their backward ways, in part by convincing them to accept their "natural" dominance by white people as well as the supposed fact that (in Jones's words) "social organizations . . . are necessarily coercive if, in their membership, there is a great diversity of kind."[118]

That said, McKenzie also insisted that for the best and brightest (which he estimated at just 1 percent of Natives), a traditional college education should be an option.[119] In general, this would mean sending those students to white colleges. There was one institution in the United States, Indian University, that sought to serve indigenous nations directly. Located in Muskogee, in the territory that would become Oklahoma, Indian University was financially supported by the Rockefellers (independently of the GEB). However, despite its origins as a true liberal arts institution, the school began offering industrial training around 1905, downgraded itself to a college in 1910, and stopped offering the bachelor's degree.[120] In keeping with that trend, McKenzie never strayed too far from the world of industrial education, explaining that his ideal college for African Americans "should revive the spirit of Hampton in a school of more advanced requirements."[121]

Anderson argues that McKenzie "came to Nashville as a representative of industrial philanthropy," and the board members he recruited certainly supported that identification. Jones became the Fisk board secretary, and although Washington died shortly after McKenzie got the Fisk job, his successor at Tuskegee, Robert Moton, joined the board in his place. The chairman of the board's executive committee was William Baldwin III, whose namesake father had been the founding chairman of the GEB and a passionate Tuskegee booster as well as the source of a notorious quotation: "Except in the rarest of instances, I am bitterly opposed to the so-called higher education of the Negroes."[122]

To his credit, McKenzie did not try to downgrade Fisk into a vocational institution. While still giving effusive praise for industrial schools, he made the case for a traditional college education for the Black students in Nashville, in part by claiming it would support the broader goal of vocationalism. In a fundraising appeal to the philanthropist Julius Rosenwald, he wrote, "The success of Tuskegee and Hampton compels the creation of efficient higher training for those graduates who demonstrate the requisite capacity and quality. Tuskegee and Hampton must, moreover, in the long run have their efficiency determined by the efficiency of the colleges that provide Tuskegee and Hampton teachers." He went on to lament the divide between advocates of the liberal and the vocational, suggesting it would "wipe out a great schism and a great bitterness if some Trustee of Tuskegee would offer, say $100,000, to such a college as Fisk hopes to be."[123]

Rosenwald, who was, needless to say, that "Trustee of Tuskegee," declined to make the suggested gift. However, McKenzie was able to report in 1917 that "the two big boards" had jointly pledged $150,000 to Fisk.[124] In 1921, an even bigger prize came in the form of a letter from Pritchett, announcing that Fisk had been added to the CFAT accepted list, making it the first Black college to receive that distinction.

This approval from the academic engineers was surely genuine, but it was an exception that proved the rule. That is, the reformers believed there was a case to be made for a very small number of true Black colleges, as long they played nice and as long as the rest of Black education had no such aspirations. The proposed consolidation of Fisk and Atlanta was a move in this direction, as was the 1914 proposition of a GEB committee headed by Buttrick: "The committee raises the question as to whether the Board could not wisely take hold of the most promising Negro college— Fisk University—and endeavor to develop it until it is fairly adequate to its task. Diplomatic efforts to consolidate other institutions with it might be informally made by the officers. . . . A single institution thus rounded out would profoundly influence the general situation."[125]

This was an idea directly borrowed from the academic engineering playbook. Historians like Anderson have portrayed it as specific to the case of Black higher education, but while there is no doubt that this ideology injured Black colleges more than others, it was not unique to them. In the eyes of the academic engineers, most Black colleges were like the predominantly white colleges they also despised: small, struggling, denominational, and poorly staffed. Fisk, which had severed its religious ties in 1912 and enrolled more students than any Black college besides Howard, could be the Black equivalent of a Chicago or Johns Hopkins:

an elite institution that set the rules for the lower-status ones arrayed below it.

Anderson points out that there was a particularly sinister end to Fisk's newfound elitism, related to the school's commitment to training leaders for the Black community. He argues that the philanthropists were committed to "training Black leaders to maintain a separate and subordinate Negro society."[126] Indeed, McKenzie's troubling policies as Fisk president confirm this. As Raymond Wolters describes, he maintained a policy of accommodation to the local white authorities, which he believed would lead to donations from both white Tennesseans and from the "secular foundations and educational boards that were closely attuned to the thinking of the white South. . . . McKenzie had to convince the men of wealth that Fisk had not departed too far from the Tuskegee ideal, that its students were not radical egalitarians but young men and women who had learned to make peace with the caste system."[127]

McKenzie's concern was real, as a letter from Rosenwald to Flexner about Fisk students showed: "There seemed to be an air of superiority among them and a desire to take on the spirit of the white university rather than the spirit which has always impressed me at Tuskegee."[128] McKenzie worked to combat this "air" by insisting that these future "leaders" bow to authority, especially his own. A white man at the helm of a Black institution was bad enough symbolically, but the president quickly became known for his actively authoritarian approach to the student body. He shut down the student government and the student newspaper and generally cracked down on dissent.[129] He also banned fraternities and suspended intercollegiate athletics, in line with the academic engineers' quixotic fight against the extracurriculum. Not all extracurricular activities were forbidden, however. In 1916, when racial tensions were spiking amid a lynching epidemic and the post-*Birth of a Nation* resurgence of the Ku Klux Klan, McKenzie brought back the Jubilee Singers, whose performances of slave-era songs for white audiences now had a vastly different symbolism than they did during Reconstruction.[130]

The situation was extremely tense when W. E. B. Du Bois once more stepped into the fray at his alma mater. In an address on campus in 1924, he slammed McKenzie in far harsher terms than he had used against Merrill sixteen years earlier. Du Bois recalled later that "the desperate attempt to get funds had led to a surrender to Southern sentiment compared to which the overtures of Dr. Merrill were but faint and unimportant. . . . The student discipline at Fisk had retrograded so as to resemble in some respects a reform school."[131] He spoke to a packed room of students, faculty, and alumni, with McKenzie sitting in the front row:

> For a long time a powerful section of the white South has offered to give its consent and countenance to the higher training of Negroes only on condition that the white South control and guide that education. And it is possible that for a million dollars the authorities of Fisk University have been asked either openly or by implication to sell to the white South the control of this institution. It is not the first time that a Corrupt Bargain of this kind has been attempted. Its earlier form at Hampton and Tuskegee included an understanding that these institutions were not to do college work and that they were to furnish servants for white people. . . . The Negro race needs colleges. We need them today as never before; but we do not need colleges so much that we can sacrifice the manhood and womanhood of our children to the Thoughtlessness of the North or the Prejudice of the South.[132]

The speech was devastating, kicking off a student-led revolt that forced the Fisk trustees to oust McKenzie the next year, an episode I will return to in the next chapter. Du Bois celebrated the victory, even though he acknowledged that donations might dry up, perhaps leading to the death of the university:

> Suppose we do lose Fisk; suppose we lose every cent that the entrenched millionaires have set aside to buy our freedom and stifle our complaints. They have the power, they have the wealth, but glory to God we still own our own souls. . . . Let us never forget that the arch enemy of the Negro race is the false philanthropist who kicks us in the mouth when we cry out in honest and justifiable protest.[133]

These twenty years of turbulence in Nashville were both a battle over the trajectory of one important college and a proxy war for opposing ideas about whether vocational training or true liberal arts education was the best hope for the Black community. To borrow a phrase from *The Souls of Black Folk*, Fisk was compelled to hold a "double consciousness" during the crucible of reform and its aftermath, balancing the top-down demands of the academic engineers with the bottom-up aspirations of its founders, alumni, and current students.[134]

However, there's a simpler way to sum up Fisk's double consciousness.

Booker T. Washington Jr., the eldest son of the great advocate of industrial education, earned a bachelor's degree at Fisk in 1913. And a decade later, Yolande Du Bois, the eldest daughter of the great critic of industrial education, did too.

CONSOLIDATION AND CONTROL OF BLACK COLLEGES

Jones's 1917 report, *Negro Education*, is the best possible example of applying the ethos of academic engineering to Black higher education. It reads like a greatest hits collection of the reformers' gripes about American colleges in general. Jones railed against the "duplication of college departments," the "desire of different denominations to have the pupils of their church attend their own colleges," the "tenacity with which they [the Black colleges] have clung to the classical form of the curriculum," and the "effort to maintain both a college and a secondary department with the small faculties available."[135]

His most characteristic call was to shut down or demote low-performing colleges and to concentrate all true higher education for African Americans on just five institutions: two universities and three colleges. Jones knew that a white man making such a suggestion would be viewed with suspicion, so he took great care to conspicuously cite a particular Black man's "strong appeal for cooperation to eliminate duplication." His authority on the matter was Nathan B. Young, a disciple of Booker T. Washington and the president of Florida's 1890 land-grant institution.[136]

However, Jones could have cited a different Black man who, in a 1910 report funded by the Slater Fund, called for "every effort towards cooperation between colleges in the same locality, and towards avoidance of unnecessary duplication of work." This author conducted a Flexnerian survey of every "colored college" and relied on CFAT standards to create a three-tiered ranking of schools, remarkably similar to the Bureau of Education's controversial Babcock Report, published the following year. These categories—First Grade Colored Colleges, Second Grade Colored Colleges, and Other Colored Colleges—represented a clear hierarchy.[137] The eleven schools in the top tier were a confirmation of the declaration made by the same author in a different report ten years earlier: that there were "entirely too many" Black colleges and only eight to ten should be maintained. The author explained, "This would mean that the college departments of 22 institutions be closed and that the college work be concentrated. . . . The smaller colleges would thus be left to develop as normal and industrial schools."[138]

This author was, surprisingly, Du Bois, whose conclusions demonstrate the ubiquity of the academic engineers' rhetoric and logic. In his 1910 report, however, he appropriated that logic to subvert their campaign against baccalaureate education for African Americans. Echoing the reformers' call for a balanced geographical distribution of colleges, Du Bois argued that there should be one "liberally endowed" Black college in every state, north and south. These would be baccalaureate colleges, not the research universities that the academic engineers envisioned capping state systems. Still, by co-opting this idea Du Bois was brilliantly using the reformers' reductionist logic to call for an *expansion* of Black higher education, since many states lacked even one true Black college.

Du Bois's vision did not come to pass, especially in the North, where Black students were fighting for admission to historically white institutions, not setting up new segregated ones. The idea of systemization was a runaway success, however. As Du Bois's strategy showed, the big question was who would control that system and, consequently, what form it would take.

Before 1915, there wasn't much doubt about how to answer that question. Booker T. Washington's control of Black postsecondary education was unquestionable.

To a casual observer, the extent of Washington's control may not be obvious given his reliance on wealthy and powerful people. The Tuskegee board of trustees, for example, was dominated by academic engineers, many of them representatives of the GEB.[139] But that interpretation ignores the fact that Washington was one of the reformers himself and that he unquestionably would have been a charter member of the GEB if racial prejudice hadn't made it a whites-only organization.[140]

Washington's system of control was perfectly described by Du Bois as "the Tuskegee Machine."[141] Summarized by Harlan as "an all-powerful control of every avenue of Black life," the Machine dominated the Black press, political patronage jobs for African Americans, and, of course, Black education. Since Washington was the most visible Black person in the nation, he became the go-to representative of his race for people with wealth and power, including philanthropists like Carnegie and politicians like Theodore Roosevelt and William Howard Taft. As such, he was a one-man choke point for benefactions flowing from New York and Washington into the Black community. As Henry Enck demonstrates, when it came to the many industrial schools enmeshed in the Machine, Washington was "almost the sole arbiter on questions of donations to Tuskegee's off-shoots."[142]

Washington's control, like many of his fellow academic engineers, could be both expansive and particular. Arnold Cooper demonstrates this in an examination of the Utica Normal and Industrial Institute in rural Mississippi, one of at least fifteen "miniature Tuskegees" founded by graduates of the mother school and scattered from Florida to Kansas.[143] Washington could be generous, doling out "Dear Friend" letters of reference to William Henry Holtzclaw, Utica's founder, and running interference for him with the GEB. But he could also be a micromanager, berating Holtzclaw about his unbalanced budget and the presence of "useless trustees" on his board, and even criticizing his autobiography. The protégé acquiesced at every turn and was rewarded with a 1912 letter from Washington to Rosenwald stating, "The school is being carried on along sane and practical lines. Cleanliness, order and system are to be found everywhere and Mr. Holtzclaw [is] striving hard to emphasize those ideals that we at Tuskegee emphasize. . . . All in all, I must say that I regard Utica as one of the very strongest of the Tuskegee off-shoots." Rosenwald immediately responded with a $5,000 gift.[144]

Holtzclaw also played a role in an incident that challenged the supremacy of the Tuskegee Machine. In 1913, a New York group headed by Oswald Garrison Villard, a prominent white journalist and the grandson of the abolitionist leader William Lloyd Garrison, formed a new organization that affiliated with the recently founded NAACP (of which Du Bois was a prominent leader). The Association of Negro Industrial and Secondary Schools claimed backing from businessmen and used the rhetoric of academic engineering in its published materials: "Its aim is the highest efficiency. . . . Undesirable duplication of schools in many localities where there is no obvious need and no reliable means of support entails waste, and, by placing an unnecessary burden on the public, hurts the whole cause of education among colored people."[145]

Washington, however, immediately perceived the ANISS as a plot to usurp his power. He was invited to participate but boycotted the organization and made sure that his counterpart at Hampton did so as well.[146] His suspicion made sense; one of the organization's first goals was the "establishment in New York City of a central office that shall be a general Bureau of Information concerning all colored schools."[147] Such an office already existed—the principal's office in Tuskegee, Alabama.

Villard protested, writing directly to Washington to explain that his goal was "to coordinate these rural schools, to weed out the unworthy, to insist upon standards of instruction and model curricula and proper accounting."[148] He also pointed out that Holtzclaw, of Utica Institute, was participating in the association. (He did not mention that Du Bois was, too.[149]) This fact initially angered Washington, whose secretary wrote to the protégé with a demand for loyalty: that "those persons who are allied with us and whom we are earnestly supporting in every way within our power not ally themselves with this movement. The purpose underlying at the bottom of the whole thing is all too apparent. . . . I am sure you can easily decide a method of relieving yourselves of any obligation to be present at the meeting." Holtzclaw skipped the meeting but then wrote again to Washington that to his dismay he had been elected as president of the association, in absentia. He offered to extricate himself, explaining that "I do not want to get mixed up in something that will not be best for this Institution and for what I will designate the general Tuskegee interests in the South." At this point, Washington appears to have had a change of mind and, as Cooper argues, decided to allow Holtzclaw to lead the association—as a "double agent" representing the Tuskegee Machine and relaying information back to his mentor.[150]

Six months before his death in 1915, Washington was still grousing about the ANISS. In a letter to a trusted ally, he called it "a fake organization . . . composed, for the most part, of nondescript little schools, those that are either humbugs or are doing the poorest work." He proposed sending another spy, his deputy Robert Robinson Taylor, "to go into their meeting and get on the inside so as to know what is going on."[151] He also wanted to get in front of the association by having the ally put out a statement announcing his forthcoming "investigation of schools," which Washington would help place in newspapers to serve as a warning to the "humbugs" that were trying to sap his authority.

His ally, of course, was Thomas Jesse Jones, whose report was well underway by that point. By 1915, Washington was in full support of Jones's project, although when he and Anson Phelps Stokes were conceiving it in the first place in 1912, he had proposed a different man for the job, who had "studied for several years in Germany" and, in contrast to Jones, had "the knack of meeting all classes of people in a way to get from them valuable information and at the same time not offend them."[152] Jones's reputation for stepping on toes surely reminded Washington of the exasperating Flexner, who had annoyed many of his subjects in compiling his survey of medical education.

The Flexner Report, in fact, was the direct inspiration for the Jones report, as Washington explained to Stokes: he wanted to expose schools where "the work is a mere sham" or were "pretending to do college work. . . . My idea is, that if your Board will provide the means, it would help these schools more than any one single thing that has ever occurred to have them thoroughly examined and let the public know just what they are doing much in the same way that the medical schools were recently examined under the auspices of the Carnegie Fund."[153]

The product Jones produced was the academic engineers' dream: a broad survey, jointly sponsored by the federal government and a New York foundation, that used data and "sociological" methods to indicate efficient ways for the wealthy and powerful to direct their benefactions. Stokes's introduction to the report drove the point home: "Thoughtful people of the South and the North, white and colored, are more and more puzzled as to the merits and demerits of the many appeals for money and sympathy in behalf of all sorts and conditions of institutions for the improvement of Negroes. . . . Every educational board interested in the colored people and almost every individual who contributes to this cause is calling for information."[154] Stokes praised Jones for his graduate training at Columbia and his "detached point of view" as well as (in contradiction) his eight years on the Hampton faculty.[155] He claimed that the author had done his work "without prejudice," a claim that would certainly be refuted by the historian Carter Woodson, who feuded with Jones for decades and summed him up in a good-riddance obituary as a "narrow-minded, short-sighted, vindictive and undermining" man who was "catapulted into fame among the capitalists and government officials. . . . When he said do not give here and do not help yonder, the 'philanthropic' element heeded his biddings. He became immediately successful as the most advanced agent of Negro control."[156]

Woodson also argued that Jones had emulated Flexner by picking one institution as an exemplar and weighing others against it. But while Flexner had chosen a true university—Johns Hopkins—as his benchmark, Jones did quite the opposite: "Taking the well established and amply supported Hampton Institute as his criterion, Jones reported as questionable and unworthy of support many of the struggling Negro schools which, although below standard, had educated and inspired thousands of Negroes who would not have received any education at all if these schools had not been established."[157]

There was another difference, too. While Flexner's report had without a doubt accomplished its goal of spurring the wholesale reform (including many closures) of medical schools, Jones's report did no such thing. By the 1920s, the Hampton model was unquestionably on the way out. Part of this disappointment can surely be attributed to the simple fact that in November 1915, the academic engineer with the most responsibility for Black postsecondary education died of kidney failure at age fifty-nine.

Without Booker T. Washington around as enforcer, Jones's recommendations had little impact.

But 1915 was also the end of the crucible of reform for reasons that included Washington's death but went far beyond it, as I will explain in the two chapters that follow. For the big foundations, the year marked the start of a slow progression toward acknowledging that a liberal education was appropriate for large numbers of African Americans. Du Bois recognized this adjustment after the fact. In a 1929 assessment of the work of the GEB, he explained that the board's first seventeen years had been devoted to efforts to "restrain and starve Negro higher education and to concentrate upon what they regarded as the Hampton-Tuskegee industrial plan." But then there was a shift, and the GEB "began with considerable reluctance but inevitable logic to help the Negro college. Their change in this last regard was a bitter pill for many of their older members, and it was not until several of these members, including Dr. Buttrick, died that comprehensive plans of Negro education were entered into and the abortive attempt to exclusive industrial training for Negroes practically surrendered."[158]

None of that changing of the guard, however, meant that the still-living academic engineers had abandoned their core ethos or logic. A GEB self-assessment published that same year explained that the foundation's recent work in Black higher education had been "focused upon strengthening university centers, such as Howard, Fisk, and Atlanta, and upon strengthening a small number of strategically located colleges which had prospect of obtaining adequate support and were disposed to do work of high quality."[159] The reformers were no longer concentrating on the bottom of the pyramid, but the pyramid itself was very much still standing.

The best example of this happened with a consolidation scheme in Atlanta. Jones had named the city as one of just five locations that should have a true college or university devoted to Black students, but he had conspicuously not named the specific institution, as he did for Howard and Fisk. This was because there were three schools—Atlanta University, Morehouse College, and Spelman College—that had a claim to the academic engineers' blessing. And that blessing was getting stretched thin, as a GEB official complained: "We're tired of giving out little dots of money first to one college, then to another, in Atlanta. There ought to be some way to bring them together."[160]

All three schools had appeared in Du Bois's grouping of First Grade Colored Colleges, but they were not on equal footing. Atlanta University was in the weakest position, as Vida Avery has shown. In 1928, the Phelps-Stokes Fund conducted a follow-up survey to Jones's, which criticized the university's ability to attract students and doubted its ability "to maintain instruction of a standard collegiate character."[161] These concerns had lingered since the failed attempt to merge it with Fisk fifteen years earlier. If anything, the situation had deteriorated. In Bacote's description, "Atlanta University, the pioneer in Negro higher education, the defender of racial equality and academic freedom, and the symbol of academic excellence, was on the verge of dissolution unless it could devise a unique program that would appeal to the foundations."[162]

Morehouse, an all-men's baccalaureate college, was in a much better position. It owed its success to its president, John Hope, a Brown University graduate who was the college's first Black leader. When Hope took over in 1906, only twenty-one college students were enrolled.[163] By 1928, there were three hundred. Most importantly, he knew how to speak the language of academic engineering. Shortly before he became president, he made a pitch for a "division of labor" among the Atlanta colleges, including Morris Brown College and Clark University, designating one as a school of technology, one as liberal arts college, one as an agricultural school in the land-grant fashion, and one as a graduate-only research university. He explained, "Without some such division, competition may result in an unseemly struggle for existence, causing untold detriment to defenseless students honest in their eagerness for learning but unexperienced to discern between the real and shoddy in matters educational."[164]

As a congratulatory gift upon Hope's appointment as Morehouse's president, the GEB gave $5,000 and Andrew Carnegie personally gave $10,000 to the school, which had never before received philanthropic money outside of the Baptist Church. Hope made sure that the gifts kept coming, capped by a banner year in 1920, when the GEB pledged $300,000 and the Rosenwald Fund chipped in another $100,000.[165] While his friendship with Du Bois meant that he wasn't a Washington-style accommodationist, the academic engineers nevertheless viewed Hope as a reliable ally.

Flexner wrote to Buttrick in 1918 with the usual praise for Hampton and Tuskegee but added that "nothing comparable in equipment or quality exists for the benefit of the smaller number of those [Black students] capable of and ambitious for intellectual advancement." Despite the casual racism, he wanted to open the GEB's coffers to a promising Black baccalaureate college. The one he had in mind was Morehouse, which he described as "the most efficient institution in Atlanta."[166] His endorsement surely helped pave the way for the board's major pledge two years later, and for Morehouse's continued ascent.

The third school, Spelman College, served a tremendously marginalized community—Black women—but it was actually in the strongest position. Its very name gives an indication of why that was: "Spelman" meant Laura Spelman, also known as Mrs. John D. Rockefeller Sr. The Rockefellers had been giving to the college for years. In an act of extremely paternalistic philanthropy, in 1906 Rockefeller created a pseudo-endowment of $250,000 for Spelman, to be held by the GEB and revocable at any time. By the late 1920s, though, the college had a real endowment, $2.5 million of which had come from the GEB and Mrs. Rockefeller's personal foundation.[167]

The links between the Rockefellers and Spelman went beyond money. In 1925, the college's longtime president announced her resignation in a letter to Trevor Arnett, who, in addition to chairing the Spelman Board of Trustees, was a GEB trustee.[168] Three years later, he became the foundation's president. He also happened to be a protégé of William Rainey Harper, having started his career as Harper's personal auditor at the University of Chicago.[169] Arnett and his colleagues in New York decided that Florence Read, an administrator in the Rockefeller Foundation, would be Spelman's new president.[170] Although her most recent work had been in international health, she was no stranger to higher education; in another link to academic engineering, she had been the reformer William T. Foster's right-hand woman in the creation of Reed College in Oregon.

The three Atlanta institutions were ideal candidates to test out the academic engineers' dream of consolidation. The GEB's in-house historian described the project as a "benevolent conspiracy" to forge an "educational Utopia" in Atlanta, including the creation of a shadow corporation to quietly buy up land on the west side of the city to create a continuous campus for the schools.[171] The final plan, written up in New York and signed by the three presidents in April 1929, called for "a co-operative educational arrangement in the nature of a University Foundation. . . . To co-operate in the advancement of college education and university training, both under-graduate and graduate, for colored people and also . . . to readjust the scope of their individual activities so as to increase the efficiency of all in the work they are doing and desire hereafter to do."[172]

In practice, this meant that Morehouse and Spelman would take on baccalaureate education for men and women, respectively, and that Atlanta University would drop its undergraduate division and become a graduate-only institution. The three would merge their libraries into a unified one, funded by the GEB (and named for Arnett). To further increase efficiency, the president of Atlanta immediately resigned and John Hope became the university's new leader—even as he remained the president of Morehouse.[173] Read became Atlanta's "superintendent" in addition to her role as Spelman's president. And the next year, the consolidation went even further when Hope and Arnett launched a plan to bring the two other local Black colleges, Morris Brown and Clark, into the scheme.[174] The schools were more than happy to do so, and the fact that they were located on the other side of town didn't prove to be an obstacle—the GEB paid for them to physically relocate their campuses to be adjacent to the others.[175]

The fact that these five schools served a marginalized student body and were always in need of financial support undoubtedly made it easier for the academic engineers to push them around. But the reformers' quest for an "educational Utopia" was certainly not unique to Black colleges. In fact, the Atlanta consortium bore a not-coincidental resemblance to the one forming in Southern California around Pomona College, which George Gates had led before he came to Fisk. The hallmark of that consortium, greatly admired by the New York reformers, was the 1925 creation of Claremont University College (today's Claremont Graduate University), which stood alongside Pomona and Scripps (a women's college) as a graduate-only institution.[176] This, in turn, harked to British-style institutions like Oxford and the University of Toronto, in which semi-autonomous colleges are organized under the umbrella of a degree-granting university.

In short, the academic engineers treated the Black colleges and universities of the South as a playground in which they could test out their ideas of higher education efficiency. This led to punishing restraints on the ambitions of both Black institutions and Black students. But this type of "efficiency" was not unique to Black colleges. It was academic engineering at its apex.

"THE MOUNTAINEERS": THE CASE OF BEREA COLLEGE

Wesleyan's dismissal of its women students in 1909 was one example of inegalitarian retrogression, but a more dramatic one happened five years earlier. Due to a new law passed by the virulently racist Kentucky legislature, Berea College dismissed all of its Black students.

Berea, founded as an integrated college by abolitionists before the Civil War, had been a bastion of racial inclusion. Under its longtime president Edward Fairchild, the student body was evenly split between Black and white students, who studied, played sports, and joined clubs side by side. Even interracial dating was allowed, so long as the couple didn't make "an offensive display of themselves."[177]

That egalitarian legacy had begun diminishing more than a decade before the 1904 Day Bill banned integrated education in Kentucky. (Berea, the only integrated institution in the state, was the sole target of the law.) We can pinpoint the beginning of the end to the day in 1892 when a letter arrived in Goettingen, Germany, offering Berea's presidency to William Goodell Frost, a proto-academic engineer who already held a doctorate from Oberlin. He gave up his continuing graduate studies to take the job.

Frost sought to shift the student body's racial balance toward whites. Like so many baccalaureate colleges, Berea needed to grow its enrollment, and the new president's initial idea was to work against group repulsion by recruiting white students from the North. His theory was that as the demographics shifted, more Southern whites would follow, putting the college on a better footing. When Frost took over in 1892, Berea was 52 percent Black. Twelve years later, when the Day Bill passed, it was just 16 percent Black.[178]

There is no evidence that Frost was an overt bigot. Washington reprimanded him in 1903 for telling a New York audience that "white men should be educated before negroes," but Frost had never said that Black Americans were unfit for college.[179] Publicly, he defended integrated education and protested the Day Bill.[180] (Berea's board of trustees sued the state, leading to a landmark Supreme Court case that affirmed the constitutionality of Jim Crow laws.[181]) Frost's defense was telling, however. Berea's integration policy, he argued, put it in "the same position as Johns Hopkins University, for example, and all great institutions outside the former slave States."[182] The wrinkle was that while Hopkins had no formal ban on Black students, Du Bois had reported a few years earlier that it had never actually enrolled one.[183]

Some trustees thought that if it couldn't be an integrated college, Berea should be a Black college.[184] Frost blocked any consideration of that idea; he had already cast his lot with white students. Despite a passionate student petition protesting any actions separating the races, at the end of the 1903–04 school year, Berea's Black students were told not to return.[185] Frost conceded, however, that the trustees had to use some of their endowment—much of which had been donated in an egalitarian spirit—to support Black higher education.

Frost's preferred plan, which he circulated just after the Day Law passed, was to establish a new college for Black students in the same town. In the spirit of academic engineering, it would be a subordinate institution, as Frost explained to the trustees: "The legal relations of the two schools would resemble those of Radcliffe College for Women and Harvard University."[186] But the legislature blocked that plan, too, with an edict that an institution could not sponsor facilities for Black and white students within twenty-five miles of each other. The plan now shifted to establishing a new school on the other side of the state, near Louisville.

But geography wasn't all that changed. As 1904 rolled into 1905, the big foundations splashed onto the scene. The calculus of small colleges across the nation quickly changed, as Frost demonstrated in a letter to Andrew Carnegie three days after the philanthropist announced the creation of the CFAT. Money was needed, he wrote, not for a four-year college but to fund "a colored school in this part of the country on the Hampton model."[187]

Berea College had once given a true college education to Black students alongside their white peers. Now it was shunting them off to an industrial school. Many advocates for Black higher education were outraged. William Lloyd Garrison Jr. called the plan "a monument to subserviency" and accused Frost of a "humiliating concession to the hateful spirit of caste."[188] The Black newspaper *New York Age* blasted Berea's "Jim Crow Annex."[189] Even the academic engineer and Tuskegee trustee George F. Peabody called Berea "dis-loyal to the Negro and lacking in moral courage" and argued that they should have followed the lead of Maryville College in Tennessee after it was forcibly desegregated in 1901. (Maryville had donated a chunk of its endowment to the Swift Memorial Institute, an existing Black secondary school, helping it turn into a residential, four-year college.[190]) Instead, Berea launched the Lincoln Institute of Kentucky, with the expectation that "it should be of the Hampton type, emphasizing normal and industrial work at first, and adding college work when the situation should so demand."[191] It never lived up to that promise. In October 1925, in the midst of protests by Black students across the country (which I will describe in chapter six), half of the Lincoln student body quit the school.[192] Within a few years, it was nothing more than a vocational high school.[193]

All of these developments were predictable: increasing racial division, a push for "practical" education for Black students, and dismay over the trend. What was not predictable was Frost's plan for Berea after segregation. It, too, would become a vocational school—for white people.

The Hampton-Tuskegee model was and always will be associated primarily with Black education. However, its pedagogy was similar to "practical" pseudo-colleges for white students, like the Franklin Union or the Hebrew Technical Institute. White educators saw the potential of vocational training for college-aged white students; the president of Southern Female College in Georgia visited Tuskegee and declared, "I am going back to Georgia and preach the necessity of industrial education for both races."[194] The *Colored American*, a Black newspaper in Washington,

DC, turned the table on racists who demanded second-class education for Black students by calling for industrial training for "poor whites" in the South: "A few white Tuskegees should be provided, to teach this poor class how to work."[195]

The white people in question at Berea had a special distinction. The college stood at the western edge of the Appalachian Mountains. Frost had started to take an interest in the residents of those mountains shortly after arriving at the college, and he increasingly understood them to be Berea's meal ticket.[196] "Have you ever heard of Appalachian America?" he asked a Cincinnati audience in 1895. "We have discovered a new pioneer region in the mountains of the central South just as our western frontier has been lost in the Pacific Ocean."[197] He didn't really discover the mountains, of course, but his message of novelty was appropriate; Henry Shapiro credits this speech, and Frost's further efforts, as the origins of "the vision of Appalachia as a legitimately discrete region defined by a particular pattern of culture as well as by its location. . . . Frost did not so much 'discover' Appalachia as invent it."[198]

At first, Frost had little interest in enrolling the people he dubbed "mountaineers" as Berea students. Instead, he saw them as a backward community to be *aided* by the college, in line with the university settlement movement that was rapidly developing in the 1890s.[199] Nathaniel Shaler, a Harvard professor notoriously associated with scientific racism, encouraged Frost to focus his work on helping "poor whites."[200] Frost's seminal 1899 article in *The Atlantic*, which brought his concept to a national audience, described Appalachians as "pathetically belated" and miserably impoverished. They could benefit most from learning "where they are" through "university extension lectures" on topics like hygiene, crop rotation, and "settling quarrels without bloodshed." The mountaineers were not beyond hope, Frost argued; he smirkingly praised their curiosity about the outside world by claiming that they would sometimes reclaim scraps of newspaper used as toilet paper by Berea's traveling lecturers as valuable reading material.[201] But he did not describe them as potential students. In a letter that same year, Frost emphasized his school's civilizing mission: "We consider Berea as much a missionary field as though it were in Africa."[202]

But stressing backwardness had its limits. Frost also took pains to help Northerners *identify* with the mountaineers, which he thought would bring in donations for the cause of aiding the population. He always trumpeted that they had fought courageously in the Revolutionary War and that they had remained loyal to the Union in the Civil War. And he made sure that Andrew Carnegie felt the love, describing Appalachia as the "American Scotland."[203]

Above all, he emphasized their purported racial purity as descendants of Anglo-Saxons who had been cut off from civilization and, therefore, retained unmingled blood. He often said they were "of British stock" and blessed them with a cultural legacy as well. In *The Atlantic*, Frost claimed that the mountaineers possessed "quite a vocabulary of Chaucer's words," which made no sense; he improved his sense of timing slightly when he told a Boston audience that "their speech glitters with Shakespearean English."[204] Eventually, he employed full-on nativism, with a regional flourish: "They are the purest Protestant American stock. . . . Ought they to have as good an educational chance as the foreign children of New York?"[205]

Frost's efforts to trumpet Berea's outreach efforts—seizing on multiple academic engineering passions, he described the school as "a kind of social settlement, Cooper Institute, and extension bureau"—did not do much to impress philanthropists.[206] With the Day Law and the dawning of the crucible of reform, however, an identity crisis produced a revelation. Without Black students, Berea would be just another struggling baccalaureate college, even with its special extension service in Appalachia. So Frost made two decisions. The first was that Berea would be a special-interest institution solely for mountaineers; the trustees rewrote the school's Constitution to identify its mission as serving Appalachia, and eventually they declared a moratorium on the admission of non-mountain students.[207] The second decision was that Berea would not be a college at all anymore.

Frost began actively touting Berea as a Tuskegee-style normal and industrial school for white mountaineers. He toured the Alabama institute as well as Hampton and inaugurated vocational courses in their model.[208] He launched a campaign to get participants in Robert Ogden's 1906 railroad tour of Black industrial colleges to visit Berea as well, prompting the philanthropist to tell Frost to stop bothering his guests.[209] And in a sign of how serious he was—or how nuts he was—Frost invited Booker T. Washington to become a trustee of Berea.[210] A Black man, trustee of an all-white school. In the South. In 1907.

Washington, not being nuts, declined the offer. But that didn't dissuade Frost from emulating him. He established a stand-alone Vocational Department at Berea, and by 1909 the school was offering a certificate course in bricklaying.[211] He also borrowed Tuskegee's use of student labor and Washington's portrayal of it as an emblem of efficiency and discipline. Starting in 1906, every Berea student had to work at least seven hours a week in a campus job, much of it manual labor. In 1917, the requirement was raised to ten hours. The labor program, according to a promotional periodical, taught students "punctuality, neatness, exactness, and fidelity."[212] This was no gentleman's college. Frost bragged about his "continual battle" to diminish Berea's collegiate division, which had been reduced to less than 10 percent of the student body by the end of his presidency, and scoffed at observers who "reproach us that we are not like Amherst or Vassar!"[213]

Frost also emulated Washington in fundraising strategy. He made the same rounds of Northern cities every year, and he stacked the Berea board with trustees from Northeastern cities (by 1917, the school had more trustees from New York and Boston than it did from Kentucky).[214] His splashiest emulation was a huge fundraiser at Carnegie Hall in 1911, in exact imitation of the Tuskegee event there. Five thousand people attended.[215] The evening was billed as an overview of "the varied educational and industrial work of Berea College for the vigorous and patriotic Americans largely of English and Scotch ancestry, who have been isolated in the Appalachian region."[216] The program opened with a speech by Seth Low, chairman of the Tuskegee Board of Trustees (and the soon-to-be namesake of Butler's subordinate junior college for Brooklyn Jews). But the keynote address went to a different academic engineer, who was rocketing to far greater national prominence.

"Berea is as much a national institution as if it were planted under the shadow of the Capitol at Washington," pronounced Woodrow Wilson at Carnegie Hall. "Its place of work is local, but its service is national."[217] Everyone recognized the rhetorical echo from the former Princeton president who had famously declared his university to be "in the nation's service."[218]

Wilson, a Southerner by birth, had been a Berea booster since at least 1899, and Frost leaned on him more and more as he became a CFAT board member and then a nationally famous politician.[219] He gave another keynote address at a 1915 fundraiser for Berea in Washington, DC, as the sitting US president. Wilson also directly petitioned Carnegie, again using the bully pulpit of the presidency, to fund Berea, which was educating "this great mass of people of our own stock and traditions" just as "Hampton is doing so effectively for the colored people."[220] Carnegie responded that he agreed that "industrial training is the most necessary education for the Southern mountain whites" but was going to wait for advice from Wilson's former colleagues on the CFAT board before making further donations.[221] (Pritchett followed up with Wilson the next month, claiming that "I have sought in every way to show Mr. Carnegie that the question involving the development of Berea College was a very much larger one than that of giving moderate assistance to the ordinary college."[222])

Frost, meanwhile, was fully embracing the language of academic engineering in his pitches. The Washington rally kicked off a campaign aiming to raise $1 million for an Efficiency Fund, a name that he later admitted was chosen to "appeal to business men."[223] He described the school's extension work as "a kind of moving Chautauqua."[224] In a direct letter to Carnegie, he called the Berea project "a big piece of patriotic engineering."[225] And he made inroads with some individual academic engineers. Philander Claxton delivered a commencement address at Berea, Flexner offered encouragement, and Pritchett praised the institution's "noble work . . . the work of an institution lower than the College, and I am very glad to see you frankly standing by this position."[226]

The foundations themselves, however, did not open their pocketbooks. As Frost repeatedly petitioned the GEB and CFAT for money, Pritchett suggested to Buttrick that the two foundations partner on a study of Berea to see if the school's "enthusiastic friends" were being "oversanguine"—a description that included Wilson's claim that Berea could become "a white Hampton."[227] But the study never happened, and no significant contributions came.[228] Part of the problem may have been that Frost launched the Efficiency Fund campaign at precisely the wrong moment—1915, when the academic engineers were coming under attack and scaling back their ambitions. Part of the problem may have been that the reformers' inherent bias made them always associate industrial training with Black students, and they couldn't bring themselves to support a white school in that model. And part of the problem may have been that Frost was proving himself to be an overweening crank.

Above all, the Berea idea was too convoluted to fit into the academic engineers' master plan for low-status students. Frost was making it an industrial school, but it still had that pesky word "college" in its name, and it was still issuing bachelor's degrees. He may have gotten some traction from turning it into a junior college, but he could hardly claim national importance under that designation. And despite Frost's efforts to name and promote a newly "discovered" disadvantaged group, Appalachian Americans just didn't fit into the *othered* categories that the reformers knew; they weren't Black, or Jewish, or Catholic, or indigenous, or immigrant. Berea served white Protestants, and those students didn't seem like a problem that needed solving, regardless of how poor they were.

By 1920, when Frost's presidency ended, Berea was still a small college in a marginal location—exactly the kind of place the reformers of 1905 despised. But in 1920, that position was not so tenuous anymore. As I will describe in this book's final chapters, the small liberal arts college made a comeback in the '20s—in status, if not in numbers. A new generation replaced the academic engineers, and new, liberal ideas replaced the worship of social efficiency and practicality. The changing of the guard was plainly apparent at the inauguration of Frost's successor, the Oberlin professor William J. Hutchins. After praising the outgoing president for his efforts in "supplying, as he puts it, the lower rungs of the ladder of learning, by which the humble may climb," Hutchins skewered the academic engineers and their hostility to tradition, using an old friend of theirs as a foil:

> In 1890 William II said, "It is our duty to educate young men and women to become young Germans, and not young Greeks and young Romans." The Kaiser, who no longer sits [as] the arbiter of the destiny of German education, made a distinction where there need be none. The man who masters a foreign tongue, whether ancient or modern, need not for that knowledge be less a good German or good American. Indeed, the new language is a key which unlocks the door of one of those great houses in which have lived and shall live forever multitudes of God's thinkers and fighters.[229]

Hutchins was previewing the kind of anti-practical education that his far more famous son, Robert Maynard Hutchins, would soon bring to the University of Chicago. In 1924, the elder Hutchins shut down Berea's vocational department.[230] After the walkout of Lincoln Institute students, he even urged that the Black school be reformed so that it could "serve Kentucky exactly as Fisk University serves Tennessee . . . a full four years' college."[231] President Emeritus Frost was irate, insisting to his successor that vocational education was "Lincoln's only hope and mission" and railing to an administrator that Berea was ruining itself by pursuing a "conventional, old-style, selfish plan to take people out of the vocational life into the professional, white-collar class."[232] Hutchins was unfazed. In the year he took over as president, Berea had awarded just five bachelor's degrees. In 1936, it awarded thirty times as many.[233]

But Hutchins's success actually relied on his predecessor's diligent fundraising work. The big foundations were the white whales that Frost never caught, but he reeled in plenty of individual-donor fish while pursuing them. During his presidency, he grew Berea's endowment from $100,000 to $3.5 million (the Efficiency Fund campaign met its million-dollar goal in less than two years).[234] And Frost's fundraising success kept paying off beyond his retirement; ten years later, the endowment was $9 million, largely due to bequests that he had secured.[235] That legacy continues; as of 2018, Berea had the eighty-third largest endowment of any higher education institution in the United States. At $1.2 billion, its endowment was larger than that of bigger, more prominent universities like Brandeis and the University of Miami, or of more elite liberal arts colleges like Wesleyan, Middlebury, and Oberlin.[236] That wealth allows all Berea students to attend college tuition-free.[237]

The fact that Berea and Fisk, among many other institutions that served marginalized students, were never stripped of their status as genuine colleges shows that even in an era of intense division along racial and socio-economic lines, a sense of egalitarianism persisted. But the story goes further than that. The two decades after 1915 witnessed the rolling collapse of the academic engineers' agenda. When it came to the question of second-class colleges, the fight would soon shift from preventing retrogression at existing colleges to *promoting* baccalaureate and even graduate education at schools that never had it in the first place. Normal schools, technical institutes, junior colleges for women and ethnic minorities, and even those great symbols of stymied Black progress, Hampton and Tuskegee, would soon flourish.

PART THREE

The Decline of Reform

6: THE COUNTER-REFORMATION

The crucible of reform, when the academic engineers operated as if they had impunity, lasted just ten years, from 1905 to 1915. The former date is marked by the massive gifts that kicked off the GEB and the CFAT. The latter date is marked by the launch of organized groups that sought to take back authority from the academic engineers and, in some cases, directly oppose their program of reform.

Informal resistance, however, was simmering well before 1915. After a honeymoon period of a few years, scattered voices began loudly decrying the growing top-down control emanating from New York and Washington. Before long, those voices became a chorus that included religious leaders, professors, college alumni, elected officials, journalists, and even students.

The first clear signs that the honeymoon was over came in 1908. Pritchett was trying to convince Carnegie to expand the CFAT accepted list to include public institutions, and he was promoting the anticipated expansion in the meantime. To qualify for the pension fund, every college or university's governing board had to sign off on a memorandum of understanding with the foundation. In private institutions those decisions were made behind closed doors, and any controversy was easily concealed—William Jennings Bryan's loud resignation from the Illinois College board being a notable exception. But public universities presented a different situation. Their governing boards held public meetings. Those meetings were attended by journalists. And those journalists wrote editorials.

"The canny Scot," wrote the *Oakland Enquirer* in July 1908, referring to Carnegie,

> sees in these subsidy schemes a shrewd method of entrenching the system of special privileges through which he has extorted millions of dollars from the wage earners and consumers of this country. . . . It is a crying crime against republican government to make our educational system dependent upon a servile system of patronage from the predatory Captain Kidds of industry. This scheme of "Carnegieizing" state universities and

other public institutions, together with the subsidy system of John D. Rockefeller, is doing more to demoralize and debauch public sentiment in this country, more to undermine democratic government than all the ravings of the radicals and agitation of the anarchists in a generation. . . . Better a thousand times that higher institutions of learning be closed as a confession of civic impotency than that they be made the training schools for the menials and serfs of a financial feudalism.[1]

Apparently, the largesse of the philanthropists was not always going to be welcomed with open arms.

More protest came from all over the nation. The *Springfield Republican* decried its state legislature's acceptance of the CFAT bargain in an editorial titled "Massachusetts the First to Kneel": "It ought to be clear that a private millionaire pension system for any class of state employees is a step toward the realization of the plutocratic ideal."[2] Other state legislatures refused to comply, and their newspapers celebrated. The *New Orleans Times Democrat* reported that the state senate killed an authorizing bill "on the theory that the State of Louisiana cannot afford to be put in the attitude of a mendicant."[3] Its cross-town rival, the *Daily States*, wrote that "if there was ever a [more] pernicious scheme to undermine the very foundations of higher education than is contemplated by Mr. Carnegie's proposition to pension university professors, we have never heard of it."[4]

Also in 1908, Carnegie became a trustee of the GEB, making it explicitly clear that the two powerful foundations shared an interlocking directorate. The Baltimore *Manufacturer's Record* railed against the "open combination of Mr. Carnegie and Mr. Rockefeller" in an "Educational Trust." Their work, the paper declared, "is a step in advance toward the greatest evil that could be inflicted upon the country. Unchecked, it will result in an education that will train coming generations away from basic principles of American life and cripple them in character."[5]

At the end of this tumultuous year, Pritchett published an article in the *Atlantic Monthly* that was sternly defensive. Noting that "even the older and stronger colleges have been disposed to resent any official inquiry into their organizations," he argued that the only institutions that should fear the CFAT and their fellow reformers in the GEB were garbage colleges that ought to be shut down. As for the rest, "the good college has everything to gain by a scrutiny of higher education if carried out by able men under a system free of political interference."[6]

Seven years later, in 1915, Pritchett rose again to defend his "able men" in a national newsmagazine, but his confident tone was gone. In an article titled "Should the Carnegie Foundation Be Suppressed?" he acknowledged that "various individuals and organizations have recently expressed doubts" about the role of the CFAT and claimed with a weird kind of self-deprecation that "I have even doubted at times whether the Carnegie Foundation was indispensable to the educational salvation of the country!" Mostly, though, he fumed about the widespread view of his organization as "a foreign corporation sitting in New York, issuing educational edicts." Pritchett and his fellow reformers were up against "the specter of a baneful educational influence exercised by a remote agency upon the policy of struggling colleges and universities."[7]

These aspersions, which so troubled Pritchett, were rooted in reality, and they would not go away. Pushback, ranging from subtle to virulent, would continue to haunt the academic engineers—never causing them to fold up shop altogether but rather to walk back, modify, or completely abandon large pieces of their program of reform. In the next chapter I will discuss formal organizations that emerged around 1915 and chipped away at the power of the big foundations and their allies. But first, I will show how outright resistance to that power was already forming seemingly everywhere.

THE ANTITRUST SPIRIT

To understand why resistance to top-down reform was more than reactionary grievance in individual colleges, we need to examine the broader policy context of the 1910s. That context can be explained through two trends: a slow-moving intellectual one and a fast-moving legislative one.

The intellectual trend is best exemplified by the rise of Louis Brandeis, a brilliant lawyer appointed to the US Supreme Court in 1916. In many ways, Brandeis's life was an alternate-reality version of the academic engineers'. Like Flexner, he was a Jewish outsider who grew up in Louisville; like Pritchett, he admired Frederick Taylor's theory of "scientific management;" and like so many of the reformers he studied in Germany. But there were key differences. Unlike the assimilationist Flexner, he embraced his Judaism and became a leading Zionist; unlike Pritchett, he viewed "efficiency" as something that should help individuals and small businesses, not society at large; and unlike the adult men who had dabbled in dilettantish graduate study in Germany, he had attended a rigorous secondary school there before enrolling directly in Harvard Law School at age eighteen.[8]

Brandeis's most famous text before joining the court was his 1914 book *Other People's Money*, which was about the banking industry.[9] (Frank Vanderlip, whose day job was as a banker, called its ideas "moonshine."[10]) Its chapter titles sound like indictments of the academic engineers: "How the Combiners Combine," "Interlocking Directorates," "The Inefficiency of the Oligarchs," and, most memorably, "A Curse of Bigness." Brandeis's political philosophy revolved around celebrating the virtue of the small against the rapacity of the big: private citizens against corporations, small banks against J. P. Morgan, localities and states against the federal government. His position, which gained him a national following, ran precisely counter to the "bigger is better" stance of the academic engineers and their fellow reformers in other sectors, who thought that consolidation and vertical integration would save the world. "Beware of centralization," Brandeis wrote, "and beware also of the mania of consolidating bureaus."[11]

Brandeis is not remembered in relation to higher education—other than that Brandeis University was named for him five years after his 1941 death. But he actually did have an opinion on the topic, and, not surprisingly, it opposed the academic engineers' vision. After he joined the court, he wrote to his brother with a typical complaint and a surprising solution: "The present tendency towards centralization must be arrested if we are to attain the American ideals. . . . The problem is a very difficult one; but the local university is the most hopeful instrument for any attempt at solution." As Jeffrey Rosen explains, he put his money where his mouth was by becoming a lifelong donor and booster of the University of Louisville, exactly the type of aspirational institution that the academic engineers scowled upon. His gifts emphasized the study of the classics, and he insisted that the school maintain a strictly local mission and local control: "an institution for Kentuckians, developed by Kentuckians."[12]

Brandeis was also a key ally of an erstwhile academic engineer, Woodrow Wilson. After Wilson left Princeton and the CFAT to become governor of New Jersey, his approach to policy shifted in no small part due to the influence of Brandeis, who advised his 1912 presidential campaign and provided cover for members of the progressive wing of the Republican Party to move to the Democrats.[13] His reward was a Supreme Court nomination, which was bitterly opposed by much of the political and corporate establishment, including William Howard Taft and New York Senator Elihu Root, Carnegie's closest political ally.[14]

Brandeis's advocacy of the small over the large influenced and was influenced by a broader trend against the anticompetitive ethos of the large industrial trusts and government-sponsored centralized control that quickly spun up and reached the halls of Congress by 1912, even before Wilson's election. As Martin Sklar explains, Roosevelt had taken pride as a "trust-buster," but he and Taft also had the conviction "that justice, social efficiency, and popular politics dictated a statist direction of the market."[15] In other words, the debate during those presidential administrations had basically been about whether New York corporations or Washington politicians would control national policy. The academic engineers would have been happy with either result.

But by 1912, it was suddenly politically popular to state, as Brandeis did in a brief for Wilson during the campaign, that "the Democratic Party insists that competition can be and should be maintained in every branch of private industry. . . . We believe that no methods of regulation ever have been or can be devised to remove the menace inherent in private monopoly and overweening commercial power."[16] Their position was bolstered by the landmark Supreme Court decision of the previous year, *Standard Oil Co. of New Jersey v. United States*, which broke up Rockefeller's oil empire.

In August 1912, the US House of Representatives formed the Commission on Industrial Relations, which was ostensibly meant to investigate labor rights but quickly became a forum for members of Congress to publicly berate captains of industry like Carnegie and Rockefeller, both of whom were called to testify. The election that November affirmed the popularity of anticorporate politics, with Democrats taking back the White House and the Senate and gaining a supermajority in the House. Their landmark legislative accomplishments came in 1914: the Clayton Antitrust Act and the creation of the Federal Trade Commission, which together gave the government power to ensure that the American economy would have competition at its heart.

The new suspicion of corporate power extended to the philanthropic sector as well. The GEB and the CFAT encountered no obstacles in gaining congressional charters in 1903 and 1905, respectively. But when the general-purpose Rockefeller Foundation applied for the same type of charter in 1911, with Fred Gates leading the charge, the situation had changed. According to Chernow, the foundation's deliberately broad mission statement was portrayed in the press as "a gauzy curtain behind which the evil wizard of Standard Oil could work his mischief."[17] When the charter encountered stiff competition in Congress, Gates offered a concession: that "a majority of the following people would have the power to veto appointments to the foundation's board: the president of the United States; the chief justice of the Supreme Court; the president of the Senate; the speaker of the House; and the presidents of Harvard, Yale, Columbia,

Johns Hopkins, and the University of Chicago."[18] Chernow calls this offer "extraordinary," but it of course was not. Gates had stacked the deck with academic engineers. (The 5-4 advantage held by elite university presidents would have been enough; to boot, their close ally Taft was the sitting US president and had appointed the chief justice. After his presidency, he joined the Yale faculty before becoming chief justice himself.) The charter push went nowhere, and in 1913 the foundation withdrew its request for congressional recognition and instead filed for a charter from the State of New York.

Inevitably, antitrust sentiment led to direct contempt for the academic engineers in their capacity as education reformers. In 1914, US Senator William Kenyon of Iowa introduced a bill to revoke the GEB's congressional charter. He was incensed that the United States might find itself complicit with the Rockefeller trust that funded the GEB, "one of the most contemptible concerns, so far as stifling trade is concerned, in existence in this country."[19] He insisted that the foundation was at the forefront of a vast conspiracy, arguing that Rockefeller was attempting "to build up his invisible government through the colleges . . . and in this way get control of the government. Through the General Education Board he has given some $43,000,000 to carry on this propaganda. . . . It is well for the people of this country to awaken to the realization that the invisible government is fast securing its clutches upon the very vitals of our public institutions."[20]

Kenyon's bill failed, but his anger and vivid imagery emblemized the growing tide of resentment at the concentration of elite power, which certainly included academic engineering. So did Brandeis's politically popular insistence that competition was a good thing and that the purported "efficiency" of big, centralized firms was pure myth. It was in this context that the crucible of reform grew dimmer and dimmer.

RELIGIOUS FUROR

Populist politicians and crusading lawyers were hardly the only people criticizing the higher education reform agenda. Given the academic engineers' hostility to organized religion—oblique in the case of the GEB, direct in the case of the CFAT—it is no surprise that Christian denominationalists were some of their most vociferous opponents.

In the pivotal year of 1908, Pritchett committed an act of near-literal hubris when he sent his protégé John Bowman to Atlanta to speak at a conference of the Southern Methodist Church. Looking out at a crowd of denominational Protestants, the CFAT staffer explained that denominational control of colleges "inevitably" produced "educational evils. . . . It is not too much to say that sectarianism has flourished generally where college standards were low, and as a college has raised its educational standards it has almost invariably dropped sectarian tests."[21]

As Bowman spoke, several audience members urgently passed notes to Bishop Warren Candler, who was sitting behind him on the dais, begging the powerful church leader to immediately rebut the young man from New York. Candler held his fire that day, according to a local newspaper, but after the speech, "instead of applause an expression of dissent went up from the main body of the audience."[22] The bishop eventually did make his rebuttal in a series of op-eds in the *Atlanta Journal*, which he collected in a widely distributed pamphlet in early 1909. People listened to Candler; in addition to his prominent position in the church, his brother was Atlanta's leading businessman, as the founder of Coca-Cola. The bishop was also the past and future president of Emory University.

His pamphlet's title left nothing to the imagination: *Dangerous Donations and Degrading Doles, or, A Vast Scheme for Capturing and Controlling the Colleges and Universities of the Country.* "An educational trust has been formed," he declared, "and it is operating to control the institutions of higher learning in the United States."[23] Would the academic engineers have objected to this statement? Certainly not. While they never appear to have described their foundations as "trusts," they certainly saw such conglomerates as virtuous, especially in their work to absorb and improve inefficient small businesses. A few years earlier, Pritchett had argued that "the spectacle of a trust buying up factories wholesale, while not without food for thought, is not so terrifying as many would have us believe. I have been told that if we took into account the number of scrap-heaps which have been sold to the trusts under the name of factories, one now and then might squeeze out a tear of sympathy for the syndicates themselves."[24] And control, of course, was the absolute center of their agenda.

Although the CFAT was more openly hostile to religious colleges, Candler focused his attack on the GEB, noting its origins in Rockefeller's tainted money and Gates's bold declarations that the board was creating a nationwide system of higher education: "Such a centralized educational system is perilous in the extreme, it is such a concentration of power in the matter of the highest interests of the nation as no fifteen men [i.e., the GEB trustees], however wise and virtuous, can be trusted to exercise without abusing it to the furtherance of their own views and interests and to the injury of those who do not agree with them in interest or opinion."[25] Again, the academic engineers would have gladly acknowledged the primacy of "their own views" in formulating their hoped-for higher education system.

Candler honed in, astutely, on the big foundations' practice of attaching strings to their gifts and often making those gifts revocable. He referred to this (with a sickening lack of self-awareness as a powerful white man in the Jim Crow South) as "the enslaving conditions prescribed by the Rockefeller Board for institutions to which it grants its humiliating doles." Not only would the GEB control the administrative operations of colleges, it would also "influence the character of the instruction given in the Board-fed institutions."[26] And Candler directly attacked Gates's obsession with the geographical distribution of colleges: "We want institutions freer than the Board-fed kind can be; and we mean to have them, and to put them where the Board's 'chain of colleges across the continent' cannot in any wise [sic] overcome them or make them afraid."[27]

Toward the end of the pamphlet, Candler attacked the two big foundations' collusion with each other and their hopes for full coordination with the federal government. He laid out a chain of logic about what would happen next, using quotes from the academic engineers and from New York magazines that endorsed their plans:

> Suppose now, that eventually, after many colleges have died and others have been wrested from any responsibility to state or church, "The General Education Board" and the "Carnegie Foundation" should unite on a "chain of colleges across the continent" independent of all authority or influence, except the control and influence of those two corporations endowed with the millions of Rockefeller and Carnegie; what then would be the "character of American education" as thus "determined?" . . . [Eventually] we must submit to Federal supervision, and with that subjection accepted, why not liaise the Bureau of Education at Washington to an executive department and make the Commissioner of Education a cabinet officer? Probably in such an event "The General Education Board," with its multiplied millions and national following, would have something to say about who should be chosen for the position of Secretary of Education. It could then fulfill the *Outlook*'s forecast when that periodical said of this "General Education Board," "It can do in many ways what the government does for education in France and Germany."[28]

Again and again, the bishop was perfectly astute about the academic engineers' best-laid plans. It's hard to imagine Gates or Pritchett objecting to anything in that analysis, other than its negative tone. Of course the reformers wanted to exert "control and influence" from coast to coast, of course they wanted "federal supervision" and sway over its administration, and of course they wanted to emulate the German model of top-down control.

I have quoted Candler here at length not because he was a brilliant detective but because he was restating plainly obvious facts from a position of outrage—which no one so prominent had done before his tract appeared in 1909. And it is doubly notable because his criticism came from a place of deep religious conviction, which was the only possible dam holding back the academic engineers' reservoir of secular conviction.

Candler made clear that he wanted nothing to do with the New York reformers, and under his watch Emory never sought a place on the CFAT accepted list. Other leaders of denominational institutions took a different stance, as we have seen before. One of these became an arch-foe of Candler's: James Kirkland, the chancellor of Vanderbilt. Kirkland was the son of a Methodist preacher, but he also held a PhD from Leipzig and was sympatico with the academic engineers on many issues about the modernization of higher education.

In 1905, when the CFAT declared that denominational colleges need not apply for recognition, Kirkland pushed his board to loosen its ties with the Methodist church. According to George Marsden, this was the beginning of a decade of "full-fledged warfare" between the chancellor and several "archconservatives" on the Vanderbilt board, including Candler himself, who personally accused Andrew Carnegie of being an "agnostic" who was attempting to make the university "a Carnegieized establishment in his own image and likeness."[29] The conflict ended up in the courts and was finally settled by the Tennessee Supreme Court in 1914, with a decision allowing the university to fully sever its church ties.[30] Soon after, Kirkland had a $300,000 endowment gift from the GEB and a seat on the CFAT board, and in 1919 Vanderbilt got full recognition as an "accepted institution."

Religious outrage was not just a Southern phenomenon. Just a few months after Candler published his pamphlet, the pastor of the prominent Marble Collegiate Church in New York made a similar attack on the CFAT at a national convention of the Presbyterian Church, declaring that "the Carnegie Foundation is the most significant movement in modern times in the interest of agnosticism in general education."[31] He also criticized Princeton, the erstwhile Presbyterian flagship university, for its increasing hostility to Christianity. A newspaper reporter tracked down Woodrow Wilson as he was about to board a ship to go on vacation. He gave no comment on the criticism: "I will not discuss that question at all at this time. I will talk to you about golf or the climate of the Bermudas, but as for anything concerning the university, I must ask to be excused."[32]

Nor was it just a Protestant phenomenon. As Philip Gleason explains, the control exerted by the foundations forced a major reckoning for Catholic colleges and universities. While some church leaders took the opportunity to modernize institutions, others pushed back hard on the reformers.[33] The most vocal of these was the Reverend Thomas Brosnahan, who had previously engaged in a much-noticed feud with Charles Eliot when he was president of Boston College in the 1890s. In 1911, he was a professor at Loyola of Baltimore, and he attacked the academic engineers at a Catholic convention in Chicago. The *Tribune* reported that he described the CFAT as a "menace" that "had developed into a trust to dechristianize education." Another newspaper quoted Brosnahan as calling the foundation a "self-perpetuating corporation, backed by millions of dollars, and irresponsible to the public whose one aim is to discredit and bring into disrepute schools under definite religious control of the higher education of the country, and finally to establish educational unity and coherency by an educational system which is necessarily hostile and skeptical in its attitude toward religious truth."[34]

Another controversy over religion played out at Syracuse. Its chancellor, James Day, was a Methodist clergyman "known for his powerful chapel preaching" at the mandatory campus services.[35] Like Kirkland, he fought hard for CFAT recognition, but unlike the Vanderbilt president he was unwilling to acquiesce to the foundation's insistence that Syracuse cut all church ties. He tried to negotiate on the issue for five years, but Day finally gave up in a scathing 1910 letter published in his city's leading newspaper. After explaining the CFAT's stubbornness, he wrote:

> It was in the face of these narrow and intolerant exactions that I replied that our loyalty was not for sale at any price; that there was not money enough in any man's hand to buy from us such an abject and craven attitude. Talk of "sectarian colleges!" Is there anything more narrow and contemptible than the administration of the Carnegie Pension Fund on these terms prescribed by Dr. Pritchett? . . . There is not space in this communication to show the degrading effect of such terms upon the colleges or to comment upon the insolence of Dr. Pritchett's offensive attempts to enforce his crude and faddish notions upon the universities and colleges of the country by the use of money. . . .

Other colleges may do as they please. If they wish to crawl in the dirt for such a price, that is their privilege. But no university can teach young people lofty ideas of manhood and forget its self-respect and honor or sell its loyalty and faith for money that Judas flung away when in remorse he went out and hanged himself.[36]

Strong words. And Day's biblical reference, equating the academic engineers to Pontius Pilate and college presidents like Kirkland to Judas, was no coincidence. Neither was Candler's reference to Esau's infamous transaction in Genesis: "Why should we barter away our birthright for a mess of potage from the predatory trusts?"[37] This type of religious backlash was not the only strain of opposition to reform, but it certainly was the most damning, in both senses of the word.

LOCALISM AND ITS DISCONTENTS

Candler's criticism was not coming only from a place of religious devotion. He also accused the GEB of a plot "to dominate especially the colleges and universities of the South." He went on with a Lost Cause screed: "Our people have risen up out of the desolation of war and the greater desolation of reconstruction. . . . For many years they have been lectured by their conquerors. . . . But now at last the effort to manage them takes a new direction. It is proposed to change their political thinking, religious beliefs, and social organization by a scheme to dominate their colleges and universities."[38]

The criticism that the academic engineers were New York elites oblivious to the traditions and values of American regions and localities became pervasive in the 1910s, well beyond the South. Opponents of reform in states across the country leaned on this argument as part of their pushback. Of course, such oblivion to context was a central tenet of the academic engineering ethos. They just called it impartiality. Pritchett had made this case in 1906, describing the CFAT as "a central agency in educational administration, which represents not a locality or a single institution, but which aims to take into account the educational needs of all sections."[39]

Not everyone saw the value in such an agency. The president of one of the Ohio universities that Pritchett wanted to demote to normal school status invoked local authority in his public retort: "Educational effort must have no plebian trend if it seeks recognition in New York City. . . . I must record my doubt of the ability of the Carnegie Foundation to order educational affairs in Ohio more wisely than our people are now directing them. At any rate, the people of Ohio will be in no hurry to give up sovereignty in that matter. They stand, at present, in no need of an educational wet nurse."[40]

Carl Kaestle describes localism as "one of the most enduring and pervasive sources of conflict in American educational history."[41] But it was also a source of strength. David Labaree gives credit to "the power of the parochial" as the way that low-resourced American colleges gained the nimbleness and popular support needed to rise to greatness in the twentieth century.[42] Since no one had attempted to direct American higher education at a national level prior to 1905, nineteenth-century institutions built local bases that sustained them through good times and bad.

The academic engineers tried to deny this, claiming that localism meant only self-interest and inefficiency. In his defensive 1915 article, Pritchett criticized his critics, describing their aspersions as "well calculated to arouse all our latent patriotism for what Professor Royce calls 'provincial independence in education.'"[43] His foil was Josiah Royce, a famous Harvard philosopher, who had recently responded to the CFAT's 1914 study of education in Vermont, which included the attack on the state's normal schools that I discussed in chapter four.

The Vermont study was not purely an instance of elite reformers swooping in on an unsuspecting locality. The state's own legislature had set it in motion in 1912, with a resolution that was right up the academic engineers' alley—calling for a commission to report on the "rights, duties, and obligations" of Vermont's four colleges and universities, "with such recommendations as will prevent unnecessary duplication and consequent financial waste." They also asked for suggestions for the reorganization of "the entire educational system of the state, as will promote the ends of unity, harmony, economy, and efficiency." The commission, which included the CFAT trustee Nicholas Murray Butler, immediately hired the CFAT to do the work. The ensuing report had three principal authors—professors from Harvard, Columbia, and Wisconsin—and five secondary authors, none of them from Vermont.[44]

Royce's response, published as a pamphlet in 1914 and a 1915 article in *School and Society*, focused on the CFAT report's insistence that Vermont stop its long-standing practice of paying a subsidy to Middlebury College.[45] Instead, the report's authors had argued, the state should give aid only to institutions that it wholly controlled—namely, the University of Vermont at the top of the higher education pyramid and the normal schools at the bottom. The private baccalaureate college in the middle should be left to fend for itself.

Middlebury was only an example, though, as Royce made clear: "I do not ask you to think of those fortunes of Middlebury College, by and for themselves, at all." Royce was using the case to build an argument against the academic engineers' vision of top-down control. He contrasted this with his own alma mater, the University of California, which by 1915 had developed a high degree of autonomy despite its public status. In this process, Royce explained, "the University gradually became more and more representative of its community, more and more plastic to local influences." The end result, he said, was "a distinctly Provincial Self-Expression."[46] Louis Brandeis would have been pleased.

But, Royce went on, something stood in the way of this pluralism: academic engineering. "Nothing is more hopeless for helping people to understand the real conditions of the educational life of a province than the disposition to 'standardize' methods of education and modes of institutional control,—a disposition for which, I am sorry to say, the Carnegie Foundation, at present, especially stands. . . . It is a foundation fond of 'clear cut' formulas; that is to say, of hastily chosen abstractions."[47]

The professor then nailed the academic engineers for their much-trumpeted outsider status: "Beware the advice which expresses the habits of those who persistently dwell upon the fact that they are 'outsiders' and therefore 'unprejudiced.'"[48] This type of impartiality was not an asset, he argued, but a deficit that blinded the reformers to the local knowledge of practitioners and those with a nuanced understanding of local conditions—a version of what James Scott has called "metis."[49] Royce sounded almost religious when he described such on-the-ground know-how and adaptability as virtuous, especially in contrast to the alternative: "standardization is in general, and especially at the present time in this country, a tendency to something that is evil."[50]

Royce finished by invoking a dear friend and fellow Harvard philosopher. The position of the academic engineers

is, in William James' favorite phrase, "a vicious abstraction,—a barren piece of intellectualism." I add in my own name the objection which I now repeat: "This formula of the Carnegie Foundation is a very natural but unconsciously misleading expression of a spirit of officialism, and of standardization, which today forms one of the dangers that dwell in the higher regions of American educational life." I hope that we may still return in some respects to the freedom of the province. I hope that we may keep alive our own provincial institutions and memories, with the wise but not too systematic, and not hopelessly fettered, independence in the adaption of means to ends.[51]

Although Royce took care to speak of "provinces," which could be interpreted multiple ways, the American political system dictated that individual states were the logical locus of "provincial independence," a position echoed by Brandeis.[52] Stakeholders in many states relied on that logic to lash out at the academic engineers, like a Regent of the state board of education in Colorado who launched what a local informant called an ad hominem "vicious assault" on Andrew Carnegie while the legislature considered participating in the CFAT pension plan.[53] In Nebraska, William Jennings Bryan led a successful campaign in the state legislature to reject CFAT pensions, which he called "the most insidious poison that now threatens our nation."[54]

Other states saw more protracted battles for local control. In Montana, the academic engineer Edwin Craighead arrived in 1912 hell-bent on consolidating the state's four colleges and universities but faced furious resistance, as Jules Karlin describes. The state's newspapers were fiercely against his plan, with one indicting the academic engineering movement: "the supporters of the consolidation scheme, for scheme it is, seem to represent the educational cult." Politicians attacked him, including the governor and legislators from both parties. Craighead didn't help himself on the University of Montana campus, where he proved himself to be "an arrogant, dictatorial administrator." The state Board of Education fired him in 1915.[55] The Montana story closely follows Iowa's, where the "educational cult" found some initial success. The state's legislature appointed a commission to grade the state's colleges and universities, public and private, into three tiers, and its Board of Education hired an academic engineer to lead their flagship university—John Bowman, a completely unqualified CFAT staffer. Even there, though, the tide turned against the reformers. Like Craighead, Bowman got canned after just three years. And the state turned against the CFAT's attempts to dictate its higher education policy, as a contemporary critic happily described: "Iowa seemed to offer [the reformers] the best opportunity for triumph because a combination of circumstances made it possible for the Foundation to advise all sorts of upheavals. . . . [But] the legislature with practical unanimity rejected every important suggestion of the Foundation." The critic went on to predict that these defeats would be seen as "tame as compared with what will be coming to the Carnegie Foundation when the people realize the possibility of danger lurking in the administration of these millions."[56]

The critics of reform often described their state governments and educational bureaus as agents of accountability who were themselves accountable to the citizenry—in pointed contrast to the unaccountable big foundations. In addition to his religious-themed attack, Chancellor Day of Syracuse invoked state control, writing to Pritchett, "We have a Department of Education in this State which acts under the authority of the State in such matters. It is responsible. . . . Why should you therefore demand the right or privilege of an inspection for such publication as you have been sending out to the colleges of the country?"[57]

His fellow New Yorker Thomas Churchill, chairman of the City College Board of Trustees, leaned even harder on republican ideology in a slashing attack on the academic engineers: "American government, if it is anything at all, is representative of the will of the people and accountable to it. But in education, a service to all men, a service in essence universal, this effort to control by the offer of money a large number of collegiate institutions and through them the public school system which furnishes their students, this self-instituted machine, this *imperium in imperio*, is unutterably vicious and evil."[58]

And in 1914, years after he had been at the center of his state's controversy, the president of Ohio University was still railing against the CFAT and insisting that his own elected officials were the ones who should be in charge, not third-sector bureaucrats in New York City: "The dictatorial manner in which that organization, through its President, speaks to legislative authority in Ohio regarding the manner in which higher educational interests are to be combined, regardless of local conditions and chartered rights, is a high-handed attempt to dictate and control, which has thus far, through the good sense of our lawmakers, proved abortive."[59]

ACADEMICS AGAINST ACADEMIC ENGINEERING

Josiah Royce was not just a random critic; he was a famous Harvard professor. But it was his criticism, more than his status, that made him the featured speaker at the inaugural meeting of the American Association of University Professors, in January 1915. Royce's words there summed up a type of grassroots resistance to the academic engineers' reform agenda—if distinguished professors can be classified as "grassroots":

An association like ours is strongly interested in the proper "limits of standardization." We do not want our institutions reduced to a dead level, or required, by "external pressure," to conform to rules and habits. . . . Standardization is at the present time very much vaunted as essentially scientific in its nature. It is not scientific. . . . It is militaristic. Perhaps every great and warlike nation needs to have its military preparations directed by the general staff. Academic education should not be so directed. When such direction goes beyond due bounds, it disgraces and degrades educational life.[60]

The AAUP, which I will address more extensively in the next chapter, quickly became known for its defense of "academic freedom," the principle that professors should have the right to express ideas and to conduct their teaching and research according to their own methods, without interference from internal administrators or external overseers. The academic engineers never openly opposed academic freedom—in many cases, they conspicuously praised it. But by 1915, the founders of the AAUP pinpointed their vision of top-down control as antithetical to it.

Also in attendance at that inaugural meeting was James Cattell, a professor of psychology at Columbia, who was best known as the longtime editor of both *Science* and *Popular Science*.[61] Cattell was evidence that not everyone who fit the profile of an academic engineer became one. He held a German PhD, dabbled in eugenics, and was affiliated with an elite research university. But his path led elsewhere.

In his editorials, Cattell had long scorned the CFAT as enabling the repression of academic freedom. In 1909, he critiqued the very idea of professorial pensions: "The withholding of part of a professor's salary to be paid ultimately after good behavior in the form of an annuity will tend to increase the autocracy of university administration and to limit not only the freedom of action but also the freedom of speech of the professor."[62] Later, he slammed Morris Cooke's CFAT report, "Academic and Industrial Efficiency," for its application of business logic, including top-heavy administrative structures, to universities. He accused the reformers of promoting "department-store methods" in vain attempts to increase efficiency as they applied things like "cost per unit hour" to a field in which they made no sense. In sponsoring such outrageous reports, he wrote, the CFAT was both "inquisitorial" and "dictatorial."[63] He also published his bitter correspondence with foundation officials like Thwing and Pritchett in *Science*, including his accusation that "beneficiaries of the foundation may not criticize its conduct or the educational schemes it promotes."[64]

Then, in 1913, Cattell published a thundering attack on "the autocratic system of administration which has developed in our universities," in the form of a 484-page book called *University Control*.[65] In addition to his introductory essay and several from like-minded peers, the book included 299 anonymous letters from professors, attesting to the sorry state of affairs that higher education reform was producing.

Cattell heaped praise on the medieval university, which he called "extraordinarily unhierarchical, democratic, anarchic, in its organization." This stood in stark contrast to the tight control of American universities and even of German ones, which Cattell saw as fading from their onetime greatness because of the interference of the national government. The primary culprit, he explained with a multitude of metaphors, was the modern university's leader:

> In the academic jungle the president is my black beast. . . . The trouble in the case of the university president is that he is not a leader, but a boss. . . . No one believes that a city should be owned by a small self-perpetuating board of trustees who would appoint a dictator to run it, to decide what people live there, what work they must do and what incomes they should have. Why should a university be conducted in that way?[66]

His criticism was primarily directed at the internal dynamics of universities and not at external reformers. That said, the leaders he was criticizing—like Nicholas Murray Butler, who was both president of Cattell's own Columbia and a member of the CFAT executive committee for decades—*were* academic engineers, imposing their ethos of control on their own institutions. And he blamed them for ruining those institutions: "Johns Hopkins, Clark, Stanford, and Chicago were founded one after the other with promise of higher things, and each has relapsed into the common mediocrity." As for Columbia, it had devolved into "vastness and crudeness."[67]

The connection to the foundations and their ethos was made directly by other authors in *University Control*. These included Joseph Jastrow, a professor at Wisconsin who in 1908 had predicted an anti-reform wave in academia: "The literature of protest is growing."[68] In Cattell's volume, Jastrow warned of "the danger of externalism" and accused the CFAT, "which is ostensibly devoted 'to the Advancement of Teaching' (yet is governed by a board of college presidents with no representative of the teaching profession)," of trying to hasten "the destruction of the academic freedom and initiative that is necessary to the advancement of human intelligence, and to promote that kind of organization which under the guise of uniformity and system effectively suppresses progress."[69]

Columbia's board of trustees fired Cattell in 1917, ostensibly for political reasons: he had opposed the draft in the lead-up to the First World War. However, as Hans-Joerg Tiede explains, the board had tried to dismiss the professor at least twice before, including shortly after the publication of *University Control*. His overt criticism of Butler, reported in the New York newspapers, had infuriated the administrators, but it was only when the draft issue came up that a Columbia trustee was able to state, "We have got the rascal this time and must leave him no loophole."[70]

A week after Cattell's dismissal, the famous historian Charles Beard resigned from the Columbia faculty in protest. No one could accuse him of disloyalty; unlike the academic engineers, who generally harbored affection for Germany up until the United States entered the hostilities, Beard had been agitating for war since 1914.[71] His resignation letter, addressed to Butler, was mostly civil toward the president whom Cattell had so flagrantly antagonized. Beard reserved his scorn for the "few obscure and wilful trustees who now dominate the university and terrorize the young instructors."[72] The target was shifted a bit, but the idea was the same: elite administrators with their eyes on control inevitably stifled academic freedom.

A few months later, Beard did the exact thing that would have pissed off the academic engineers the most: he started a new university. In early 1918, he dreamed up a new institution to compete against existing elite schools, in collaboration with fellow academics, civic leaders in New York, and the young heiress Dorothy Straight, who bankrolled the project. They published a pamphlet declaring the launch of a "new school" that would be "as powerful in modern life as some of the great universities were in the Middle Ages" and take on the role that Johns Hopkins had in the late nineteenth century as "the center of the best thought in America." Furthermore, the institution would "lead in emancipating learning from the narrow trammels of lay boards of trustees."[73] The result was the New School for Social Research, a unique competitor to Columbia and its peers, whose founders believed that its democratic form of administration would be just as important as its boundary-pushing research. As Peter Rutkoff and William Scott describe, the founders "saw themselves as advocates of a cosmopolitan and progressive humanism that contrasted profoundly with Butler's defense of the American status quo."[74]

Alongside Beard in creating the New School and serving on its founding faculty was Thorstein Veblen, an economist who had been on faculty at

Chicago and Stanford and was best known for his identification of "conspicuous consumption" in his 1899 book, *The Theory of the Leisure Class*. His more recent book, published in 1918 but mostly written prior to 1916, was more to the point.[75] Its title—*The Higher Learning in America*—was bland, but the subtitle told the whole story: *A Memorandum on the Conduct of Universities by Business Men.*[76]

As Richard Teichgraeber shows, the book owed a huge debt to the "literature of protest" that had already emerged from the ranks of academia, especially Cattell's 1913 book, which Veblen acknowledged had served "'as ground and material' for much of its argument."[77] His argument, put one way, was that the business logic of the wealthy men who funded the reformist foundations and sat on university boards contaminated institutions and the higher education system itself by flowing down through presidents and other administrators and then stifling the lowly professors. Put another way, a fish rots from its head.

In American higher education, Veblen found "an unreflecting deferential concession to the usages of corporate organization and control, such as have been found advantageous for the pursuit of private gain by businessmen." This was driven by a "naive faith that business success 'answereth all things,'" which was particularly problematic given that these businessmen typically knew nothing about higher education. In a thinly veiled reference to Carnegie, Veblen noted that "more than one of the greater businessmen have spoken, advisedly and with emphasis, to the effect that the higher learning is rather a hindrance than a help to any aspirant for business success." Such hostility at the top of the administrative hierarchy, he argued, meant grave trouble for the faculty.[78]

That trouble took the form of menacing presidents, including men like Butler and William Rainey Harper, whom Veblen singled out in anonymized but obvious references.[79] He called them "captains of erudition," a play on the common term "captains of industry," and noted that they were "a picked body of men, endowed with a particular bent."[80] The captains of erudition were the academic engineers by another name, of course. Veblen's critique focused on them as autocratic institutional leaders rather than external reformers. This is largely because he simply didn't care about the institutions on which the academic engineers aimed their most draconian reforms—small denominational colleges, normal schools, schools for minoritized students, and other institutions that he plainly admitted do "not call for particular notice here, since these schools lie outside the university field, and so outside the scope of this inquiry."[81]

That said, Veblen did devote an entire chapter of critique to the concept of "vocational training," which had "no connection with the higher learn-ing," despite the current vogue for it among higher education leaders. He gleefully trashed many of the academic engineers' efforts to extend practi-cal forms of postsecondary education to the masses:

> [They] deal with matters foreign to the academic interest—fitting schools, high-schools, technological, manual and other training schools for me-chanical, engineering and other industrial pursuits, professional schools of diverse kinds, music schools, art schools, schools of "domestic sci-ence," "domestic economy," "home economics" (in short, house-keeping), schools for the special training of secondary-school teachers, and even schools that are avowedly of primary grade; while a variety of "university extension" bureaus have also been installed, to comfort and edify the unlearned with lyceum lectures, to dispense erudition by mail-order, and to maintain some putative contact with amateur scholars and dilettanti beyond the pale.[82]

But the academic engineers could wreak havoc on elite research universi-ties themselves as well, and the source of their ethos was unmistakable: "The fact is that businessmen hold the plenary discretion, and that busi-ness principles guide them in their management of the higher learning." The result was that in choosing a president, university boards would in-evitably "select a candidate who shall measure up to their standard of business-like efficiency in a field of activity that has substantially nothing in common with that business traffic in which their preconceptions of efficiency have been formed."[83]

Finally, he argued, "such businesslike standardization and bureaucratic efficiency," along with "aimless utilitarian management," meant the "di-sastrous" destruction not just of academic freedom but of the academic ideal itself.[84] The only solution was the complete removal of higher educa-tion's "centralized and arbitrary government" and the "dissolution of this 'trust'-like university coalition."[85]

Veblen wrote much of *The Higher Learning in America* during the cru-cible of reform, when the academic engineers were ascendant. By 1918, however, when the book actually made it into print and Veblen helped launch the New School, his proposed counter-reformation had lost much of its urgency. Notably, 1918 was also the year that the CFAT abandoned its pension scheme, as I will discuss in this book's last chapter. And the New School, created in direct opposition to the reformer's ethos of control, began to fade almost as soon as it had started. Within four years, most of its founders had wandered away.[86] These included John Dewey, who had momentously left Columbia to join the New School but returned to Butler's domain two years later.[87] The battle had not been won, per se. By 1922, it was just increasingly moot.

JOURNALISTS

The professoriate was an obvious source of resistance. It was the ultimate "insider" group to counter the "outsider" academic engineers. But as Zachary Haberler argues, to make their counter-reform case professors often relied on a sector that was certainly outside the higher education sphere: the press. Both before and after the formation of the AAUP, they savvily used mass media to press their case for autonomy while staving off their "radical" public image.[88]

Journalists turned out to be great allies. The 1908 editorials with which I opened this chapter indicate the deep hostility that much of the press had toward top-down reform. As James Wallace shows, "liberal journalists" were vocal participants in the debates over both K–12 schooling and higher education.[89] A landmark of their contribution was the 1914 founding of the *New Republic*, which, like the New School, was financially backed by Dorothy Straight. The magazine served as a rebuttal to the establishment periodicals in which the academic engineers published, and Wallace calls its early approach to higher education "Veblenesque."[90] But this was ultimately a case of prominent Manhattanites debating other prominent Manhattanites. For the most impressive display of journalistic resistance to reform, we have to look to California.

Upton Sinclair showed up to the party late, but as usual he entered with plenty of theatrics. The most famous of the muckraking journalists had made his name with attacks on big industry in books like *The Jungle*, but in the second decade of his career he turned to higher education.

His 1923 book, *The Goose-Step*, was five hundred pages of unrelenting attacks on the academic engineers and their allies in universities across the country. He heaped plenty of scorn on the GEB and the CFAT as organizations in a chapter called "The Foundations of Fraud," but he dedicated plenty of his text to ad hominem takedowns of individual academic engineers and the elite universities they led. The first in line was Columbia, which Sinclair had briefly attended. He despised Butler ("sitting in his high watch-tower and keeping guard over his empire of education"[91]) and the businessmen who sat on the university's board ("in Columbia you have plutocracy, perfect, complete and final"[92]). He especially scorned the university's prosecution of top-down control beyond its campus: "Columbia's educational experts take charge of the school and college systems of the country, and the production of plutocratic ideas becomes an industry as thoroughly established, as completely systematized and standardized as the production of automobiles or sausages."[93]

As the book's title suggested, Sinclair indicted the academic engineers for their love of German-style control, which they gave up only at the onset of the First World War. He traced this to their own educations: "a curious fact which I note about one after another of these academic drill-sergeants . . . every one of them learned the Goose-step under the Kaiser!"[94] The president of the University of California came in for a typical harangue: "Benjamin Ide Wheeler, ex-professor to the German Kaiser, and tireless singer of the Kaiser's praises, holder of a Heidelberg degree, and of honorary degrees from all the great Eastern centers of the interlocking directorate."[95]

When it came to the foundations, Sinclair was equally acerbic. The CFAT was "an endowment to certain privileged universities, with a highly autocratic control accompanying the gift" and dismissed its pension plan as a "shrewd device for the enslavement of college professors." As for its president, who had "a stranglehold over American institutions of learning," "Dr. Pritchett goes about like an Indian war-chief with scalps at his belt." The GEB, Sinclair argued, "holds over the head of every college and university president a perpetual bribe to sell out the interests of the people."[96] Together, he claimed, the foundations had successfully executed a plan to capture the nation's higher education institutions and turn them into a tightly controlled system run by elites in New York and Washington. He was right, of course, about their intentions but gave them too much credit when it came to the success part.

By the time *The Goose-Step* came out, academic engineering was already fading. But other journalists had been battling the movement for more than a decade. In 1909, an editorial in the *Charlotte News* argued, "If the educational arc lights of the Carnegie Foundation are permitted to have their way, higher education will be turned into a sort of autocracy . . . [that aims to] either intimidate small colleges into accepting dictation, or wipe them from the face of the earth."[97] The *Raleigh News & Observer* agreed, calling the academic engineers "a precious class of Know-It-Alls" who "rush about over the country in palace cars, stop a little while at a college town, look over its way of running its affairs, and then rush back to New York to tell the world how poorly they are managed."[98] The *Springfield Republican* wrote in 1910 that "the pretensions of Dr. Pritchett at present suggest that he would soon develop an educational primacy and authority in effect scarcely inferior to that of the minister of education in the Kingdom of Prussia" and that the CFAT's power was "as vicious as it is ridiculous."[99] Predictably, the *Burlington Free-Press* was incensed in the aftermath of the 1914 CFAT report on Vermont, editorializing that the state was "the victim of the project to establish an 'educational trust'" and declaring that "the Foundations are menacing academic freedom."[100]

By the 1910s, journalists were usually college graduates, which gave them an interest in the autonomy of their alma maters. And in the heyday of muckraking they had an inclination to attack concentrations of wealth and power. As Merle Curti describes, an alumnus of the University of Wisconsin kicked off a torrent of criticism in the press with a 1909 *Collier's* article attacking that university's leaders for stifling academic freedom and promoting business interests.[101] In 1913, Oswald Garrison Villard, the editor of the *New York Evening Post* and a Harvard alumnus, penned a furious editorial condemning that university's new academic engineer president, A. Lawrence Lowell, for pushing an "efficiency nostrum": "And what shall it profit the university to have gained countless student-hours and experiment-units and to have lost what is highest and best in it?"[102] In 1915, he attacked the general idea of outside control of higher education, with particular animus toward the supposedly objective surveys that the academic engineers loved: "The very idea of a survey of this nature is repugnant to the idea of a university. . . . [It is] a childish and mischievous futility."[103]

But some journalists tried a gentler approach, like John Palmer Gavit, a veteran newspaperman who authored the first version of the Associated Press *Stylebook*.[104] Commissioned by Villard, Gavit visited thirty colleges and universities for up to five weeks at a time, resulting in a series of *Evening Post* articles and a book he described as a compromise: "not a technical study by an expert in education, not a muck-raking by a reformer of any sort."[105] His radical intervention was to examine schools through the undergraduate student's lens. This would have been unthinkable to the academic engineers, who saw only the institutional point of view, or to their faculty foes, who saw only their own. Gavit was dogmatically humanistic in his analysis, insisting that it made little sense to think of colleges as mere organizations, since they were also "centers of Personality, of happy and inspiring *personal* relationships with definite human beings, known by name and loved for what they are and for what that enabled them to give."[106]

Gavit also celebrated the extracurriculum, which was a shared annoyance for the academic engineers and their critics in academia. The reformers' standpoint was best summed up by Woodrow Wilson's famous 1909 quip that "so far as the colleges go, the sideshows have swallowed up the circus, and we in the main tent do not know what is going on."[107] They were joined by their antagonist Veblen, who mocked "the extensive range of extra-scholastic traffic known as 'student activities'" and claimed they existed only for "the elaboration of the puerile irregularities of adolescence."[108] Gavit insisted, on the contrary, that activities like athletics, fraternities, and student government were just as important as the formal curriculum in preparing college students for future life. This was in terms of both fostering "the essentials of character" and giving students organizational spaces to practice democracy and leadership.[109]

Other people who bought ink by the barrel saw value in the undergraduate experience and had the resources to back it up with more than just words. Phoebe Apperson Hearst, who partnered with her son William Randolph Hearst in building a newspaper empire, donated lavishly to the University of California and became its first female regent. Her gifts were aimed at students, not systems, including what Alexandra Nickliss identifies as the first need-based scholarships in the United States, which were targeted at "young women from regions 'of the state remote from the seat of the university.' The recipients were known as 'Phoebes.'"[110] She also funded a student center for women, which included a gym and meeting spaces for extracurricular organizations.[111] In Southern California, Ellen Browning Scripps did her one better by founding a new small women's college. Scripps was a journalist who became wealthy by founding and running a nationwide chain of newspapers. Her 1925 gift to start the school came with ideas about leadership opportunities for undergraduate women as well as a mandate that would have pleased Veblen: "Scripps College shall illustrate what we hear spoken of as 'Academic Freedom'; that there shall be no clamp put on the search for truth in whatever direction it may be found."[112]

It is important to note that some journalists had a vision of higher education that was fully in sync with the academic engineers. Chief among them was Edwin Slosson, who wrote a series of institutional profiles for the *Independent*. They were reprinted in 1910 as the book *Great American Universities*, which helped to cement the vision of the higher education pyramid. Slosson focused on fourteen institutions, selected because they "stand at the head of the list prepared by the Carnegie Foundation for the Advancement of Teaching."[113] He celebrated "bigness," championed the "utilitarianism" of institutions like Wisconsin, and attacked professors whose "methods of instruction are much the same as those used in the universities of the thirteenth century."[114] Slosson also slammed the "ritualism" of colleges, like academic regalia, as an inefficient and aristocratic distraction from their proper work: "a dozen mortar boards on the campus are more of a menace to democracy than a million-dollar endowment from a trust magnate."[115] He had even harsher words for intercollegiate athletics: "they attract an undesirable set of students," "cultivate the mob mind," and "divert the attention of the students from their proper work and pervert the aims of education."[116] In their place, he suggested "intercollegiate contests in intellectualism" in which "the Association of American Universities [will] prescribe the rules and the Carnegie Foundation and General Education Board offer the prizes."[117]

But Slosson was an exception to the general trend of his profession, perhaps in part because before becoming a journalist he had earned a PhD at Chicago when William Rainey Harper was at the height of his influence. He was also writing in 1910, the height of academic engineering. A decade later, his stance was eclipsed by anti-reform writers like Gavit and Albert Jay Nock, a writer for *The Nation* and the founder of *The Freeman*, which provided a venue for Veblen, Beard, and other critics of the academic engineers. Nock was a proto-libertarian, and he applied his political ethos to higher education. In a 1921 editorial, he allowed himself to dream of a university in complete opposition to the strictures of top-down control:

> with only the loosest and most formal organization, with little property, no examinations, no arbitrary gradations, no money-grubbing president, no ignorant and meddlesome trustees! A university that would not hold out the slightest inducement to any but those who really wanted to be put in the way of learning something . . . a university that imposed no condition but absolute freedom.[118]

Like the New School, Nock's imagined university was much more than a place that offered intellectual freedom to professors. Nock wasn't a professor, and his dream wasn't really about professors—or any other individuals. Like the academic engineers, Nock was focusing on *institutions*, and in his vision the institutions themselves were the ones that would be free.

IN DEFENSE OF THE SMALL COLLEGE

In 1906, less than a year after his $10 million gift to launch the CFAT, Andrew Carnegie received an unsolicited handwritten letter from someone named Daniel K. Pearsons, who described a completely divergent type of higher education philanthropy: "I have watched your grand work with great interest. My plans have been along a different line, that of Endowment to small colleges where the poorer classes are educated."[119]

Wealthy from real estate speculation, the childless Pearsons was determined to meet Carnegie's "Gospel of Wealth" challenge and give away all of his money before he died. Although he had not gone to college, he had decided that small liberal arts schools would be his primary beneficiaries. His deeply sentimental description of them was completely antithetical to the academic engineers' disdain: "No father was ever more proud of or took greater joy in his children than I do in my colleges. They are good and growing children and are my crown and joy."[120] In his letter, Pearsons reported that he had thus far donated $4 million in unrestricted endowment funds to small colleges scattered across the country, most of which he had never visited.

His biography, published by the Daniel K. Pearsons Publishing Co. and written by Daniel Pearsons (his namesake nephew, although presumably the man himself collaborated), described him as "the greatest and most far-reaching philanthropist of the age" and pronounced in a tortured metaphor that "from his giddy height of unselfishness and benevolence for humanity, he put his finger unerringly upon the spots in our fair country where his money would do the most good and strengthen deserving institutions about to die, or linger along as invalids for lack of his reviving oxygen tank."[121]

This strategy was a blatant slap at the academic engineers, who certainly would have preferred that the oxygen be withheld. Pearson's values turned the GEB's geography-informed scheme of winners and losers on its head. He *deliberately* chose to support isolated schools in the nation's interior, as he explained in a speech defending the "freshwater college": "These are the only schools of higher education within the reach of a very large and a very representative class of young men and women—those who make up the moral backbone of this nation."[122] He often spoke of this "representative class" and their needs in uncomfortably personal terms: "I've got the smartest set of boys in the world. Flaxen-haired boys from the sod houses of the mountains and the prairies. . . . They can't go down east to college and I am trying to build up colleges where they can go."[123] And he was more than happy to support denominational institutions: "When a man comes in and tells me in bland and soothing tones that his college is non-sectarian and all that kind of thing, I don't want to have anything to do with him. It is all humbug. . . . No, we want Christian, not rationalistic schools; and we must try to keep the country rooted and grounded in the old religious convictions."[124]

Pearsons was a kook, but it turned out that he was hardly unique in being a partisan of the small colleges. Many smaller-scale philanthropists and boosters stepped up to support these institutions during the crucible of reform, and while some small schools did indeed die, their mortality rate was nowhere near what the academic engineers had predicted. These backers did not claim that they were practicing efficiency. Their support came from a place of affection.

That affection was often, like Pearsons's, almost familial—"alma mater," of course, means "our mother." This maddened the reformers. Harper sarcastically noted in *The Prospects of the Small College* that "the love of an alumnus for his alma mater is something sacred and very tender. Does the true son think less of his natural mother because she is, perhaps, poor and weak, or even sick and deformed?" Pritchett was more forthright in a 1910 speech that criticized collegiate alumni for their affection: "the loyalty which they have exhibited has in nearly all cases been a loyalty of sentiment, not a loyalty of deep thinking."[125]

Notably, many of the harshest critics of the academic engineers were alumni of small liberal arts schools: Veblen had gone to Carleton, Beard to DePauw, and Cattell to Lafayette (where his father was the president). Their counter-reform platform rested primarily on the idea of faculty control, but alumni control was also on the table. Another fierce critic, Du Bois, made the case in the speech that brought down Fayette McKenzie: "the alumni of Fisk University are and of right ought to be the ultimate source of authority in the policy and government of this institution."[126] Nock, who attended St. Stephens College (now Bard), went a step further and argued that the *current students* should be in control.[127]

The reformers partially had themselves to blame for the rising influence of alumni. The biggest effect of their campaign to get institutions to break their denominational ties was that the schools no longer required their trustees to be members of a denomination—typically, clergymen. As the reverends and ministers left college boards, a new class of leaders replaced them. Members of this new class had money to donate.[128] The nationwide trend was unmistakable: a 1917 study found that 38 percent of trustees at US colleges and universities were "business men" and only 14 percent were clergy, a dramatic reversal from the situation in the nineteenth century. In the small colleges, the trend was even more pronounced. Among nondenominational private institutions with less than 1,000 students, 44 percent of trustees were in the business category, and just 10 percent were clergy.[129]

The academic engineers recognized this as a mixed blessing; a CFAT report criticized the "so-called 'practical business man'" who was appointed to a board despite having "neither the experience nor the time to attend to the duties of a trustee."[130] But there was a yet bigger problem: since the small colleges lacked the brand names necessary to draw nationally prominent business leaders, these new trustees were overwhelmingly graduates of the schools themselves.

As one example of the shift, in 1890 Trinity College in Connecticut was governed by a board of visitors that comprised seven reverends and no one else, and a corporate board with eleven reverends out of twenty-four total members.[131] In 1920, the visitors were gone and the corporate board had just three reverends left—but now included an astounding nineteen alumni among its twenty-three members (the exceptions were the clergymen and a local bank president).[132] In the intervening years, Trinity had severed its ties with the Episcopal Church in response to the CFAT mandate. But we can even see the trend at schools that had been nondenominational since their founding, like Lehigh. The decline in clergymen on its board between 1890 and 1915 was not terribly dramatic—from two to one. But the growth in alumni members was—from zero in 1890 (the school was founded in 1865) to nine in 1915, out of a total of fourteen.[133] Perhaps the most telling example, however, was Vassar, then a women's college. In 1885, the college's all-male board of trustees included thirteen ministers out of its twenty-six members. In 1920, the board was down to four ministers, but it now included seven women, all of them Vassar alumnae.

A good number of these trustees occupied board seats that had specifically been set aside for alumni. A scholar who surveyed 180 independent liberal arts colleges in 1931 found that fully 50 percent of them had dedicated alumni seats on their boards.[134] However, this was hardly the whole story—in 1920, Trinity had three such dedicated seats, but these were dwarfed by the sixteen other alumni who occupied regular board seats. Public institutions, though, rarely had such provisions, and given their political standing they were generally more protected from alumni influence. In one extreme example, in 1913 the legislature in Idaho (a state where the ethos of centralized control was especially strong) voted to ban alumni from the state university's board of regents, on the theory that they could not be trusted to govern it with cold-blooded efficiency.[135] At least one *New Republic* writer, however, was skeptical in 1915 that "the cautious admission, in recent years, of alumni trustees" would accomplish much of anything: "Self-perpetuating boards will always propagate their own kind, and even if alumni trustees were ever inclined to be anything but docile, their minority representation would always be ineffective for democracy."[136]

The affection for small colleges eventually spilled over from alumni into the academic engineering circle—including people who had no affiliation with the schools they were supporting. On the same day that the Pearsons letter arrived, Andrew Carnegie also received a note from his close friend Andrew D. White, who was asking the industrialist to support Illinois College, a school of 254 students. He stressed that his interest was still primarily in "leading universities" like Cornell, which he had helmed for twenty years. But he did see some use for small liberal arts colleges, "so long as they do the intermediate collegiate work for which they are fitted, and do not attempt to delude the general public into the belief that they are doing the university work for which their endowment and equipment does not fit them."[137] Even Frank Vanderlip sheepishly wrote to Carnegie on behalf of "Rio Grande College in southern Ohio, a very small institution. It is in a sort of back woods district, but is doing a noble work and is hampered by the want of a small addition to its funds."[138]

Carnegie opened his personal checkbook to both of these small colleges, along with a growing number of others after 1906.[139] This generated consternation from other academic engineers, as his personal secretary explained in a worried letter to Pritchett: "Mr. Carnegie was frankly told at a meeting of the General Education Board recently that he had given too much. You have no doubt discovered the fact, as I have, that any and all kinds of pressure put upon Mr. Carnegie to make a gift, by parties outside, however influential and well-informed in their own line, result in wrong action in ninety-nine cases out of a hundred."[140] In a 1910 GEB memo, Gates added to the scorn, blaming lousy colleges in the western United States for preying on softening philanthropists: "The new college president goes east, stopping at Chicago for an interview with our excellent friend, Dr. D. K. Pearson [sic], finding his way in time to the office of Mr. Carnegie and then to a group of generous New England capitalists whose names will be found connected with almost every such college in the west." In 1914, Pritchett criticized his benefactor without naming him: "It has been assumed that any college was necessarily a good thing to help. The business man has had no means of scrutinizing these efforts. He gives as the Lord sends his rain, to the just and to the unjust."[141]

One reason that people like the "generous New England capitalists" were so friendly to colleges with which they had no connection may have been that the schools were increasingly savvy about sharing what William Clark calls "academic charisma."[142] Mortarboards, gowns, and honorary degrees—the ritualistic baubles that Slosson had belittled—offered a form of honor even better than the pride of autodidactism. The author of a study on the "use and abuse" of honorary degrees found that the number handed out by colleges did not grow significantly between 1890 and 1916 but that the recipients had changed: degrees given to "representatives of organized religion" plummeted and were replaced by ones given to "representatives of business and industry." The idea, of course, was not to honor these men's brains—just their pocketbooks: "Few of the business men honored had scholarly inclinations or achievements. . . . Their financial power and monetary contributions to universities were probably the real reasons for the degrees bestowed upon them."[143] Between 1906 and 1915, Carnegie accepted a number of honorary degrees from small colleges like Kenyon, Lehigh, Hamilton, Allegheny, and Queen's College in Ontario. To mark the occasion, Lehigh declared April 28 Carnegie Day, which the college marked by suspending classes and regaling the honoree with a schedule of festivities.[144]

The colleges also got better at making a case for themselves, not in spite of their smallness but because of it. This was a marked shift. In a 1909 book, the president of Ohio's Miami University, who had clashed fiercely with Pritchett, disavowed the "small college" moniker and tried to rebrand schools that were doing "big things" despite a modest enrollment as "the real college."[145] In 1918, however, the longtime president of Haverford College published an unapologetic defense of small liberal arts colleges like his own, which had just 186 students and never renounced its Quaker affiliation. He summed up the academic engineers' attack on the institutions: "There are too many of them, most should be eliminated. . . . As in business the small house falls before the trust or the wealthy consolidation, so the small college will gradually disappear by survival of the fittest."[146] And yet, these supposedly "unfit" schools were surviving. The author credited this to the small college's commitment to "general training and close comradeship," which stood in contrast to the impersonal, vocation-oriented model pushed by the academic engineers. Small colleges, he wrote, stood for "the cultural as against the technical idea in education. . . . For if the man is broadly and thoroughly trained he is capable of anything."[147]

The next year, the president of St. Stephens echoed him, declaring that "the day of the small college, far from being over, is just commencing. New ones must be founded and old ones properly equipped for their work." The reason was that the large university was failing the undergraduate student. The small college, he wrote, was a far better choice: "It furnishes him that life of intimate comradeships which his soul at this period of life rightly desires. It furnishes discipline in habits of study, regularity of life, and that enthusiasm for knowledge which only close personal touch between instructors and pupils can impart."[148]

The rhetoric seems to have paid off, literally, when it came to fundraising. In the 1915–16 academic year, Bowdoin took in more donations than Johns Hopkins. Haverford received more than Cornell. And Wellesley raked in over a million dollars, two-thirds of what Harvard raised.[149] These were not schools that were disappearing anytime soon.

IN DEFENSE OF THE BLACK COLLEGE

Nearly all of the forces I have described so far in this chapter were in play when it came to defending Black colleges and universities from the forces of reform: loyal alumni, crusading journalists, reactionary academics, and those who loved small colleges that emphasized comradeship and liberal learning. Their work came largely after 1915, in part because as long as Booker T. Washington was alive, dissent was pointless. And by that time, they had one more force for the academic engineers and their allies to reckon with: empowered and aggrieved students. Together, despite the long odds, these groups managed to preserve the autonomy and status of the schools we now call historically Black colleges and universities.

W. E. B. Du Bois was the most visible member of this resistance but certainly not the only one. Institutional leaders were very much part of it, including George Johnson, an administrator at Lincoln University in Pennsylvania. Writing in *The Nation*, Johnson slammed a 1915 GEB report that encouraged more vocational education at Black colleges: "It means the closing of the door of opportunity to all but the favored few among negro youth." Furthermore, he pointed out, obeying the command to vocationalize their curricula would put the institutions in a catch-22 situation with the academic engineers: "If [the Black college] deviates from the standard college in subjects taught and time given and preparation required, it is *ipso facto* excluded from the benefits of the Carnegie Foundation the Advancement of Teaching; the General Education Board and the other benevolent foundations can only help it by breaking their own rules; the educational departments of the various States must at once withhold from it and its degrees all legal recognition."[150]

Another voice against reform came from John Hope, a Brown graduate who had been a professor of classics before becoming president of Morehouse. At a 1915 conference convened by the GEB, Hope pushed back on the survival-of-the-fittest ethos as well as the idea that college enrollments should remain low: "When we realize how big a population we are going to have . . . it is a serious question in my mind whether we ought to think about getting rid of those schools." He also strongly defended the role of Protestant denominations in supporting Black colleges.[151] However, as Leroy Davis shows, Hope's onetime "radicalism" faded as his career went on. He grew increasingly cozy with academic engineers like Wallace Buttrick and Thomas Jesse Jones, earning him the suspicion of other Black leaders.[152] This was especially true in the run-up to the GEB-backed Atlanta University consortium project, which made him the most prominent Black educator in the country.

Journalists were also leaders in the defense of Black colleges. Many of them were alumni of the schools. One was Harrison Pinkett, a Howard graduate who usually published under a pen name—an unsurprising choice in an era when Washington controlled much of the Black press. In 1907, writing as P. S. Twister in the *Chicago Conservator*, he railed against the changes at his alma mater, especially the newly installed president Thirkfield's "attempt to industrialize Howard University."[153] The *Conservator* was also a leading voice against Washington, who variously tried to run it out of business and purchase it.[154] The paper's part-owner was the pioneering journalist Ida B. Wells, who had attended Shaw University (now Rust College) in Mississippi. As Mia Bay describes, Wells staked much of her late career on challenging Washington on both educational and political grounds, as did her ally William Monroe Trotter, the outspoken editor of the *Boston Guardian*.[155] These journalists were definite outliers in the Black press, but their independence from the Tuskegee Machine allowed them to attack it.

Another prominent critic came from the white press: Oswald Garrison Villard, a member of a journalistic family that included his grandfather, the abolitionist newspaperman William Lloyd Garrison. As the owner and editor of the *New York Evening Post*, Villard attempted to echo his famous relative as a powerful white voice defending Black Americans. He was generally conciliatory toward Washington, but his backing of the Association of Negro Industrial and Secondary Schools was an attempt to subvert the Tuskegee Machine by supporting small Black colleges across the South.[156] Villard was also instrumental in creating the NAACP, which Washington boycotted, and fought Woodrow Wilson on his policy of segregation in the federal government, which Washington refused to publicly oppose.[157]

Du Bois, though, was the clear leader of the counter-reform movement in many of the critical categories. He pushed back as an academic, especially in the updated 1910 version of his sociological landmark *The College*

Bred Negro-American, which went further than the 1900 version in making the case for expanding liberal college training to many more Black students.[158] After leaving academia, he continued his mission as a journalist. Du Bois founded *The Crisis* in 1910, along with Villard and others, and served as its editor for more than two decades. He published an annual "Education Number" that reliably denounced the academic engineers. A 1915 editorial was typical, not naming the GEB outright but describing an "insidious attempt" to keep Black people "in ignorance far below the average standard of this nation. . . . This is true not by accident but by design, and by the design not so much of the laboring white masses of the nation but rather by the design of rich and intelligent people, and particularly those who masquerade as the Negroes' 'friends.'"[159] In 1918, he argued that the "great educational boards . . . have ideas with regard to the education of Negroes with which thinking Negroes do not agree" before prominently featuring Black students who had recently earned graduate degrees.[160] The next year, he directly attacked Hampton, which "with its millions of endowment" was working "to perpetuate the American Negro as a docile peasant and peon, without political rights or social standing." Its many "promising and brilliant students," he went on, "go out as half-educated, partially trained men. . . . Small wonder that educated Negroes resent this and demand that Hampton cease to bury talent and deflect genius."[161]

And Du Bois's alumnus status gave him a platform for attacks on the white leaders of Fisk. Just weeks after his public denunciation of Fayette McKenzie, he began gathering contact information for his fellow alumni, to whom he then mailed out one thousand copies of his speech.[162] In January 1925, he brought together 150 "Fiskites" in New York to form a new alumni association distinct from the university-sanctioned one, with the aim to "see that Fisk is freed of its present incubus."[163] (He even invited Washington's widow, a Fisk alumna, who declined to attend in a deeply ambivalent letter.[164]) The group revived the *Fisk Herald,* the banned student newspaper, as their own organ—edited, of course, by Du Bois, who wrote in it, "Fisk University has fallen on evil days; it has gotten money and lost the Spirit."[165]

But as Raymond Wolters shows, it wasn't Du Bois, or the massed alumni, who brought down McKenzie. It was the Fisk students. In November of 1924, one hundred of them picketed a board of trustees meeting in Nashville, chanting, "Down with the tyrant!" and "Away with the czar!"—a particularly potent cry just six years after the execution of Nicholas II.[166] In February of the next year, a larger group demonstrated late into the night, smashing windows and threatening the school's administration.

McKenzie called the police, and fifty white officers arrived to break up the crowd—a hegemonic display of force that incensed Black leaders across the country.[167] The students went on strike, with at least half of the entire college boycotting classes for over a month. This broke the trustees' confidence in the president, and he resigned in April over the fury of one of his "staunchest supporters on the board": Thomas Jesse Jones.[168] In contrast, Paul Cravath, the board chair, wrote to Wallace Buttrick that it would have been "futile" for McKenzie to remain. (He also, characteristically, asked the GEB leader to suggest Fisk's next president.)[169]

Student activists were not unique to Fisk. Black students had been protesting administrative decisions at Talladega College in Alabama for decades, including a 1906 walkout after the president chose a white man to fill a staff position that was traditionally given to Black men. The Talladega students even directly petitioned the school's backers in New York and won some concessions from the president.[170] Another student group took the lead in a controversy at Florida A&M, an 1890 land-grant school. As Antonio Holland explains, its president, Nathan B. Young, was a Black former Tuskegee instructor who believed that he could merge a vocational mission for his Black students with genuine academic study. He secured a Carnegie library for the school in 1908 and the next year won the moniker "college" for an institution that had previously been known as Colored Normal School.[171] However, the federal Bureau of Education refused to classify it as a college. The bureau's Higher Education Division director, the academic engineer Kendric Babcock, explained to Young that A&M should stick to practical, sub-baccalaureate fields: "At the time of my visit to Tallahassee last year I got the impression that you were very wisely and properly emphasizing the mechanical arts, agriculture, household science, and normal courses."[172] Young pushed forward and inaugurated a bachelor of science degree but also continued to prioritize vocational training and indulged other interests of the academic engineers, including hosting Florida's Negro Extension Division.[173]

Still, Young's attempt to maintain a place for academic study at A&M earned him the scorn of the openly racist State Board of Control. Arguing that the "needs of the Negro youth of the state are largely in the fields of agriculture, industry, and home making," in 1921 the board required the school to make each student pick a vocational trade that would be the center of his or her course of study. In a miserably cruel act, they also demanded that Young expel any student who was more than one month behind on housing fees. And then, when he balked at that, they fired him.[174]

The A&M students were incensed, particularly by the fact that Young's board-appointed successor was the college's dean of vocational studies, who did not hold a bachelor's degree. They went on strike, boycotting classes, and nearly a third of the student body actually withdrew their enrollments that fall. Far more ominously, in October campus buildings began bursting into flames, including what Wolters calls "the hated Mechanical Arts building," which burned to the ground. Although no one was ever criminally charged in the arsons (which did not cause any deaths or injuries), "it was common knowledge on the campus that rebellious students had been responsible."[175] The new president expelled fourteen students for their role in organizing the strike and another three for suspected connections to the fire. Still, even the Board of Control knew that his position was untenable, and in 1924 they fired him, too. The A&M students—a deeply marginalized group—had stood up to power.

An even more surprising backlash came in 1927 at the very institution Du Bois had found so odious: Hampton Institute. There, stunned administrators described students who were "possibly unique in the annals of student strikes, demanding as they did more and better education."[176] James Gregg, the institution's leader, had, like Young, attempted to assimilate academic and vocational studies since he had taken over after the orthodox academic engineer Hollis Frissell died in 1917. Gregg introduced bachelor's degree programs for the first time in Hampton's history but emphasized that they were purely utilitarian, in line with the reformers' wishes. Hampton was "not a liberal arts college and should never seek to be," he announced, only a "technical and professional college."[177] This was as far as he could push the institution, given the restrictionist views of his trustees, including George Foster Peabody, who wrote that the "so-called academic education was the true weakness of the Negro educational system."[178]

Gregg's timidity continued in 1926 when the Virginia legislature, in echoes of the Kentucky Day law, passed a mandatory faculty segregation law that was directly targeted at Hampton, which had an integrated teaching staff for its all-Black student body. Though some thought that the law could be easily challenged in court, Gregg refused to do so, with the backing of board members like William Howard Taft and James Dillard, a longtime leader of both the GEB and the Phelps-Stokes Fund.[179]

This was an indignity for the Hampton students, as was a stringent code of conduct that treated them like children. But their most resonant complaints were about academic issues. Since the early '20s, they had raised objections, sometimes through formal student council petitions, that their instructors were unqualified and that academic classes and entire programs listed in the school's catalog were not actually offered.[180] Their long-simmering dissatisfaction came to a head in October 1927, with a series of actions that sound more like late-'60s student activism. The student body organized a twenty-one-member Student Protest Committee, which marched into Gregg's office and presented him with a list of seventeen demands, covering both loosened discipline and strengthened academic standards. When he held firm, they went on strike. Even an official administrative report acknowledged that the students were not just troublemakers: "The leaders attempted and in a measure succeeded in turning their effort into a seeming 'holy war' for the ultimate good of the Institute. . . . The strike was therefore, perhaps in the minds of many students, *for* Hampton, not *against* their school."[181]

Gregg counterpunched, shutting down the entire institution for two weeks, expelling four students, and suspending nearly seventy more. The Hampton alumni association was torn and tried to play a conciliatory role, publicly supporting Gregg but also calling for a "readjustment of the relations existing between faculty and students in order to keep up that mutual understanding and respect necessary for the smooth and efficient running of the educational machinery."[182]

Although the student strike did not resume when Hampton reopened, according to Wolters, resentment continued to simmer until early 1929, when the campus was "on the verge of anarchy." The situation was exacerbated by an exodus of academic faculty, many of whom wanted the school to "become a real center of higher education." Finally, the alumni stepped into the fray, sponsoring a visitation committee that reported to the board that Gregg had lost control of both students and instructors, and backing up the students' complaint that some of those instructors were "wholly unfit as teachers in an educational institution." The board accepted Gregg's resignation in May. His successor, according to Wolters, "forthrightly took pride in the development of advanced students and thus legitimized the collegiate curriculum."[183] The next year, the trustees changed his title from principal to president—the first in Hampton's history.

OUTSIDERS AND INSIDERS

The dramatic roles of students, alumni, and professors in pushing back on the academic engineering agenda is fundamentally about jealous insiders fighting off the impositions of outsiders. Yes, often their foes were also insiders—namely, the presidents of the institutions where they taught and learned—but those foes were always intertwined with a far larger movement that was emanating from the big foundations in New York and their allies in Washington.

The same can be said for the advocates of religious institutions and small colleges (which were, of course, often the same). They were fiercely defending their precious redoubts against an external menace. In doing so, they echoed less Daniel Webster's famously meek quip about Dartmouth— telling the Supreme Court that "there are those who love it"—and more his overlooked thundering closing statement: "when I see my alma mater surrounded, like Caesar in the senate house, by those who are reiterating stab upon stab, I would not, for this right hand, have her turn to me and say, *et tu quoque me fili!—and thou too, my son!*"[184]

This dynamic would not have surprised the academic engineers at the start of the crucible of reform. They fully expected insiders to defend their institutions, but they did not expect them to do it so effectively.

The insiders I have described here, it is important to note, were almost always working independently. They may have gotten solace from reports of resistance at another college or from a rallying newspaper editorial, but they ultimately were on their own. In the next chapter, I will discuss organizations that formed, mostly starting around 1915, as a result of insiders reaching beyond their campuses and forming coalitions that competed for authority with the academic engineers. But well before those groups came together, something resembling a nationwide movement had already begun out of the actions of thousands of individuals at hundreds of colleges, universities, and institutes, all insisting that they could determine their own affairs much better than the outside "experts" ever could.

7: ORGANIZED RESISTANCE

The academic engineers were nothing if not organized. With their boards, committees, associations, and conferences, they wielded the full power of the bureaucratic apparatus that was increasingly dominating American policymaking in the early twentieth century.[1]

For people who feared and hated the academic engineers, ad hoc resistance had its place. As we saw in the previous chapter, forceful editorials, pamphlets, and protests certainly helped to change public opinion, bringing the crucible of reform to an end and removing the impunity with which the reformers operated up to that point.

But it turned out that the best way to fight organization was with organization. Individual voices could push back on academic engineering, but they could never *replace* it. Replacement required the work of coalitions that could rival the GEB, the CFAT, and their allies in elite universities. These coalitions, which arose suddenly and almost simultaneously around 1915, rarely directly attacked the power of the reformers. Instead, they worked to destabilize and subvert that power and eventually claim it for themselves. This had to be a team effort, argued a speaker at the first meeting of the Association of American Colleges, one of the key groups leading the counter-reformation: the colleges had to accept "that this is an age of organization." Together, they could imitate the academic engineers by harnessing "the influence and inspiration of the kind of organization which has made colossal world enterprises of certain businesses. . . . We cannot afford longer to be without it."[2]

The coalitions that sprung up around 1915 had two transparent goals, neither of which was the outright abolition of academic engineering. The first was to secure a seat at the table of reform so that they could speak up for themselves in real time instead of reacting to already-issued edicts handed down from New York. The second was self-governance. The counter-reformers didn't demand the abandonment of standards; they demanded that they be allowed to set and enforce *their own* standards.

A third goal, never stated directly, was to capture power and then do nothing with it. Self-control meant letting colleges and universities alone.

In nearly every case, once the coalitions had claimed the mantle of self-governance, they drifted toward broad standards of inclusion and ensuring institutional autonomy. This wasn't a dereliction—it was the whole point.

But "nothing" ultimately turned out to be something. The many associations created in opposition to academic engineering almost all still exist today, doing work that includes expanding college access to marginalized or isolated communities, protecting academic freedom, and ensuring mutual accountability through the accreditation process. These are fundamental assumptions of our modern higher education system, each of them forged in the crucible of reform.

ASSOCIATIONS AS A TOOL OF THE REFORMERS

The institutional associations that anchored the counter-reformation had examples to follow. The creation of two notable reformist organizations bookended the heyday of the academic engineers and served as their vehicles: the Association of American Universities (AAU) and the American Council on Education (ACE). Like the GEB and the CFAT, these organizations had bland names and generic missions but were dominated by reformers with an activist agenda. However, neither had much impact in their early years, and the development of the ACE is an excellent window into the rapid transformation of reform post-1915.

The AAU has a seemingly inclusive name, but it has actually always been the most exclusive club in American higher education. As of 2022, it had only sixty-six members, and at its 1900 founding it had just fourteen. While the eliteness of the original list was largely predictable—Harvard, Yale, Princeton, Stanford, etc.—its brand of exclusivity was different from the categorical exclusions that the academic engineers would later lay down. The AAU allowed two types of institutions that were conspicuously excluded from the early CFAT accepted lists. Public institutions were welcome and were originally represented by Michigan, Wisconsin, and California. So were religious ones. Of course, they were recently founded ones with grand aspirations: the University of Chicago and the Catholic University of America, each of which styled itself as the apex of a denominational pyramid. And size didn't matter: Clark University, with just eleven faculty members and thirty-six students (all at the graduate level), had a seat at the table.[3]

The AAU's founding mission statement had three goals, each of which presaged a plank of the academic engineering platform. The first was standardization: in this case, of graduate education. The second was groveling over the Germans: to "raise the opinion entertained abroad of our own Doctor's degree." And the third was the reform of low-status institutions: to "raise the standard of our own weaker institutions."[4] The AAU members certainly did not expect to accomplish the third goal by adding "weaker" schools to its ranks so that they might improve by osmosis. In its first six years of existence, the association admitted exactly one new member: the University of Virginia.

The AAU was unquestionably a club for academic engineers. Many of the most prominent ones were there at the association's first meeting, hosted by William Rainey Harper on the Chicago campus, including Nicholas Murray Butler, David Starr Jordan, Benjamin Wheeler, and William Torrey Harris. The CFAT founding board, put together five years later, featured the presidents of eight out of the eleven private universities on the AAU list. In 1907, the association voted to offer a permanent invitation to "the President of the Carnegie Foundation for the Advancement of Teaching" to participate in all AAU meetings, which was made especially easy because the group started meeting regularly in the CFAT office in New York.[5] Pritchett, characteristically, participated fully and even took the group to task, writing in a 1907 report that it had not lived up to its third founding goal: "The association has done nothing to raise standards. It has in fact quite ignored the question of standards."[6]

The next year, the AAU got its act together, on Pritchett's terms. It created "a committee for the standardizing of American colleges . . . [with] the cooperation of the president of the Carnegie Foundation, who, in the name of the Association, should be officially invited to join in the undertaking."[7] The goal was to publish an accepted list, just like the CFAT was doing, in this case for colleges that met the AAU's criteria for preparing students for graduate school. In 1913, they added another star member to the committee: Kendric Babcock, who had recently departed the federal Bureau of Education after the scandal concerning his own ranked list of colleges and universities.[8] The association marked his arrival by directly petitioning the newly sworn-in US president, Woodrow Wilson, to release Babcock's report.[9]

After six years, the members of the standardization committee found that their work was "not the simple task" that they had anticipated. So they came up with a shortcut. The AAU's stamp of approval would be automatically given to three groups: the AAU members themselves, the schools on the CFAT's annual accepted list, and schools that would be on the CFAT list had they not been religiously affiliated ("such a list has readily been furnished by the Carnegie Foundation").[10] As Hawkins describes, though, the

AAU later got more directly involved in enforcing standardization through its Committee on Classification, which received a large Carnegie Corporation grant in the 1920s to conduct in-person inspections of colleges, "with the understanding that the AAU was continuing the classification program begun by the CFAT."[11]

Criticism, not surprisingly, came quickly. Shortly after the AAU was formed, New York University's chancellor applied for admission for his institution. Twenty-three NYU professors publicly protested the move by denouncing the association, questioning its moral authority, and accusing it of operating like "the commercial combines of our day."[12] The chancellor withdrew his request. The comparison to the industrial trusts had sticking power, however, even before Carnegie and Rockefeller personally invested in higher education reform in 1905. According to Hawkins, "analogies with cartelization in industry were readily made," and newspapers began deriding the AAU as "the Ph.D. Trust."[13]

The association also drew the wrath of a different group: the National Association of State Universities. The vast majority of its members were excluded from the AAU, which only redoubled their frustration at being denied recognition by the CFAT. At a 1907 meeting, the president of the University of Illinois asked "whether we shall suffer anything in this Association from any action in the work of standardizing, taken by the so-called Association of American Universities . . . the 14 institutions that have connected themselves together and given themselves that name, and declined to set up any standard of admission, simply excluding everybody else."[14] The NASU did not object to the project, just its origin. The head of the University of Kansas proposed that the association develop its own "scheme of standardization," arguing that "it is time for State Universities to come to the front and claim the authority and importance that belong to them, and that it will be very decidedly against their interests if they allow the work of standardizing to fall too much into the hands of other authorities."[15] Opponents of the academic engineers loved this counterattack, including an Iowa newspaper that celebrated its state university president's NASU participation with antitrust imagery: he "has found a new trust to 'bust,' . . . wielding the 'big stick' over the octopus. . . . The present 'Ph.D. trust' will think that it has had a jolt from the White House and another Iowan will have the credit of putting one more monopoly out of business."[16]

The AAU never lived up to the eminence of its membership list. Hawkins argues that its always-questionable impact faded even more between the world wars, with the association's work dwindling to holding annual meetings and maintaining the classification project. Part of this fade reflected the decline of academic engineering itself, but it also stemmed from the sudden prominence of a new organization: the American Council on Education.

The ACE, founded in 1918, was far more inclusive than the AAU. It was intended as an association of associations, including the AAU and others that I will discuss later in the chapter, but it admitted individual institutions as well. It did not closely guard its membership, and its name even suggested it would encompass all of American education—although it never really attempted to extend beyond the higher education realm.

Then, as now, the ACE was primarily a Washington-based lobbying group. Its founding cause was to push for student draft deferments, but it grew in purpose after World War One ended. It quickly turned to lobbying for the creation of a cabinet-level Department of Education, which would help fulfill the academic engineers' hopes for federal control of the educational system. The ACE saw the proposed department's work as "giving conscious recognition to education as one of the supreme interests of the nation" and coordinating the hodgepodge of national efforts to shape education ("much duplication of work inevitably results . . . without system and without centralized responsibility"). The association also revived long-standing academic engineering passions like the Wisconsin Idea ("the guidance of experts in the formulation of governmental policies") and the national university ("a great super-graduate school can be maintained at the capital, manned by the best that the Nation possesses").[17]

The first permanent head of the ACE fit the classic academic engineering profile: Samuel Capen, who had done graduate study at Leipzig and taught at Clark before succeeding Babcock as the Bureau of Education's higher education specialist. But Capen was more suspicious of top-down control than his peers. He argued in 1919 at Knox College that while he was in favor of a "nationalized educational scheme" directed from Washington, it should revolve around the normative control of "intellectual leadership" rather than the coercive control of "subsidies granted to institutions which meet governmentally prescribed standards." This was, of course, a repudiation of the CFAT's and GEB's theory of action. He continued the theme in setting parameters for the proposed Department of Education: "Congress should recognize that the power to give or withhold financial support constitutes a very real menace to the department's genuine capacity for leadership." And then he further denounced the academic engineering idea: "Suppose it established arbitrary and ironclad standards which must be met by colleges seeking national recognition for their degrees, standards made in the serene seclusion of Washington without reference to an infinite variety of local conditions, standards promulgated with papal finality, subject neither to discussion nor appeal. Many a worthy and vital independent college would find itself gripped as between the clashing rocks that menaced the Argonauts."[18]

Unlike the leaders of the AAU, Capen ran an organization that represented all of American higher education, not just its most elite tier. He could hardly denigrate the base of the pyramid. Furthermore, the reformism of 1919 was vastly different from that of 1900 or 1905; the type of social control advanced by the academic engineers in their heyday had become unacceptable. Still, the ACE was a top-down affair. For the entirety of Capen's three-year tenure at its helm, the organization's rotating chairmanship was held by the president of an AAU university. And when Capen resigned in 1922, he was replaced by someone with an unimpeachable academic engineering pedigree: Charles R. Mann, a Chicago professor with a PhD from Berlin. Mann had been on the CFAT payroll from 1914 to 1918, when he was conducting a Flexner-style survey of engineering education in the United States. Not surprisingly, while Flexner had trashed most medical schools, Mann's report was full of praise for engineering as a field and celebrated the "deeper public recognition of the importance of the engineer's function in national life."[19]

Hawkins shows that under Mann's leadership, the ACE became more bureaucratic and interconnected with the business community, including extending membership to trade groups like the US Chamber of Commerce.[20] David Noble explains that Mann also believed that colleges and universities should be much more focused on vocational preparation and worked with Pritchett and others toward that goal, through projects sponsored by the National Research Council and bankrolled by the GEB.[21] Mann continued to praise the engineering ethos, and while he never advocated the coercive control of earlier years, he always believed that a "central agency" led by disinterested experts should shape the course of higher education. But as the '20s turned into the '30s, he was increasingly marginalized. Influential players, including a new generation of foundation leaders who believed in much broader, unqualified support for colleges and universities, helped shift the ACE in a new direction and he was eased out of his leadership in 1934.[22] His successor, George Zook, whom I will describe in the next chapter, represented a completely new kind of educational leader.

The ACE and the AAU were ultimately bit players in the academic engineering movement. They came too early and too late, respectively, but more importantly voluntary associations were simply not effective vehicles for advancing reform. They were much better suited to blocking it.

THE LITTLE GUYS STRIKE BACK: THE ASSOCIATION OF AMERICAN COLLEGES

The academic engineers had plenty of criticism for all aspects of higher education, but no institutions bore the brunt of their complaints more than small colleges—especially small religious colleges. So it is appropriate to mark the end of the crucible of reform with the January 1915 gathering of a group of small religious colleges: the first annual meeting of the Association of American Colleges.

The AAC's name signaled open defiance of the AAU, as did the motto it adopted: "inclusiveness and interhelpfulness rather than of exclusiveness." Presenters at the conference spoke of extending membership to "all the colleges of the American continent," and its founding president explained that "advance is made as we socialize larger and larger groups; and the fundamental purpose, perhaps, of this organization is that we shall become a social solidarity."[23] At the end of its first year of existence, the association had 190 dues-paying institutional members.

The AAC's origins date to 1911, with the formation of the Council of Church Boards of Education, which brought together six Protestant denominations in the interest of reckoning with the increasingly perilous position of Christian colleges. At first, they played nice with the academic engineers. Buttrick attended their second conference, and they described their goals in friendly terms: "a better geographical distribution of denominational colleges . . . a proper standardization of institutions . . . appropriations to weak but high grade schools for a limited period until they could meet the requirement of larger foundations, such as the General Education [Rockefeller] Board."[24]

But when the CCBE became the AAC in 1915, things changed dramatically. The theme of the association's first two annual meetings was defense. Nearly every speaker referenced the CFAT, the GEB, or the Bureau of Education, often describing their joint program of reform as an existential threat. The president of Upper Iowa University warned about a topdown "program outlined for the educational development of America. . . . It excludes any satisfactory consideration of the American college, and looks finally toward the elimination of everything strictly collegiate."[25] The president of Allegheny College noted that already "some denominational colleges have been crushed out of existence by the new order."[26] The president of Earlham College argued that the college "is being savagely attacked. . . . A certain type of businessman would point out the futility of college education as judged by the helplessness of the college product. The vocational expert would storm the centres of American culture with a pitchfork and a monkeywrench. And worse than all this, certain builders of educational systems would actually ignore the college and go on about their business as though the college did not exist."[27] In a different address, he paraphrased Benjamin Franklin's warning at the signing of the Declaration of Independence: "if the American colleges do not hang together, they are likely to hang separately."[28]

Some speakers criticized the academic engineers' efficiency obsession. The president of Grinnell lamented that the cultural side of college was being overlooked: "education involves more than training, more than wage-earning capacity, more than efficiency. . . . Efficiency too often is understood to be the ability to manage a machine, or to make a machine, or to get a job. These are all noble ends. No one wishes to object to them. But they should not preoccupy the educational field. They ought not to put out of business the present-day college."[29] A Presbyterian Church leader argued for a broader definition of the word in his criticism of the quantitative studies that the academic engineers loved: "some of the things which make for the efficiency of a college cannot be reduced to statistics, however sanctified the statistician. History, tradition, ideals, great personalities are all of the essential substance of college efficiency, but they may not be reduced to percentages or presented in tabular form."[30] Others built on the Grinnell president's renunciation of the reformers' interest in socially efficient vocational study for low-status students. The president of Goucher College proudly claimed that at top women's colleges like his own, "The so-called vocational or utilitarian subjects are ignored. The nearest any of these institutions comes to household economics or domestic science, so far as I have been able to observe, is represented by a few courses in applied chemistry or micro-biology."[31]

Another theme was the imminent threat of the institutional hierarchy that the academic engineers helped build. The president of Whitman College explained it with a potent metaphor: "the American college will find its life ground out between the nether millstone of high school development and the upper millstone of a Teutonic conception of higher education."[32] More so than the high school, though, the junior college was the problem. The president of Colorado College declared that "I have no patience with so-called 'junior colleges,'" and the president of Lake Forest College echoed his skepticism about the new institution: "I think it is unfair that young people should be given the impression that they are actually going to college when they are merely doing under high school conditions two years of such work as is done by the freshmen and sophomores of a college."[33] At the inaugural meeting, someone moved that the term "junior college" be banned from all AAC publications and that the schools be deemed "institutes."[34] The motion was tabled, but the point was made.

Some speakers took a more triumphal tone. The president of James Millikin University claimed that the existential threat was over: "That is finished. It is established. The colleges are not to be killed off. They have grown more vigorously and powerfully ever since President Harper's first investigation and pronouncement on that subject."[35] Robert L. Kelly, who became the AAC's first permanent director, declared that "the chief watchword of this Association is not preparedness against its foes. The colleges of America are not frightened. They are not building a fortification behind which they may hide from their enemies."[36]

Kelly would go on to lead the AAC for almost two decades, and his confidence set the tone. In fact, the organization reached out to the academic engineers from the start. They invited Philander Claxton, the US commissioner of education, to the first meeting, but he was "unavoidably detained in Washington."[37] The next year they invited Pritchett, who was a no-show due to "a serious business conflict."[38] One of his CFAT deputies had laughed at the AAC when its first conference was announced, writing to him, "I have seen four of these schools and am chiefly impressed with the general ignorance, even on their own part, of what they are really doing. A mere comparative array of the real facts would, if generally understood, be the death blow of several of them."[39] Claxton did finally show up at a meeting, in 1916, and delivered an address that directly insulted the assembled representatives, bragging about the pyramidal system he was designing, "capped by a great National University" and fortified with low-status schools in the form that William Rainey Harper had called for: "two hundred or more of the smaller colleges should, I believe, become Junior Colleges."[40]

These types of insults were hardly a surprise; they were the reason the AAC came together in the first place. But they did not dissuade Kelly and his fellow leaders from a policy of rapprochement with the academic engineers. In a particularly clever move, at their second meeting they elected Henry King as the association's president. Not only was King the president of a nondenominational college (Oberlin), he also sat on the CFAT board. And in Claxton's stead, the AAC welcomed Samuel Capen to the first meeting, in his role as the Bureau of Education's higher education specialist. He previewed the moderate stance he would take when he ran the ACE, noting the problematic nature of classification schemes: "however successful they may appear to the classifiers, the classified sometimes have had a different opinion." Capen defended the rankings of organizations like the bureau, the AAU, and the CFAT as important but conceded that they were designed as narrow studies that looked at only a few factors; "there are numerous other admirable and worthy ends which a college may pursue."[41]

Most momentously, Capen invited the AAC to send a representative to Washington to participate in a bureau-organized Committee on Higher Education Statistics. The small colleges would finally have a seat at the table, alongside the academic engineer–dominated organizations like the AAU. They chose Donald Cowling, the president of Carleton College, to attend; three years later he would work closely with Capen to launch the ACE, ensuring that the colleges would have a seat at that table, too.

Ultimately, those seats were all that the AAC members wanted. For a decade, they had been the subjects of reform. Banding together meant they could demand to be part of the reform conversation. The Upper Iowa president argued that policies "ought to come from this body. . . . The colleges must act where the colleges are concerned."[42] The Whitman president said that while standards were important, "self-standardization" should be the AAC's objective. "I think that an important distinction needs to be made between a standardization which is a conforming to the measure of standards set up by outward conformity, and a voluntary self-initiated standardization which springs from the earnest attempt to attain one's own ideals."[43] Kelly continued the theme, noting that colleges had been injured "by straining to meet some demand of standardization imposed from above or at least from without."[44]

Cowling returned from Washington with good news. The joint committee had decided that "no attempt should be made to divide institutions into classes such as Class I, Class II, or Class A, Class B, etc."[45] This was a victory for sure, because such classifications had always served to denigrate or exclude small colleges. A few years later, Hawkins writes, "the AAC turned the tables on the AAU when a committee presented ratings of graduate departments in universities as judged by college professors."[46] The association talked about the importance of self-study but balked at actually carrying one out. In 1924, when a member proposed that the AAC launch its own critical examination of liberal arts colleges, the proposal was blocked by a group that included Capen, who by then was a full-fledged AAC member representing the University of Buffalo.[47]

In the mid-'20s, the rapprochement project picked up steam, especially after 1923, when the AAC voted to allow the undergraduate divisions of large research universities to join the association. Very soon, most AAU members were also AAC members. In 1925, the AAC received a grant from the Carnegie Corporation and, astoundingly, began holding meetings in the foundation's New York headquarters—exactly as the AAU had met in the CFAT offices two decades earlier.[48] Even more astoundingly, in 1928 the AAC elected as its president someone who had never run a college: Trevor Arnett, the protégé of William Rainey Harper, who had just been named as the new president of the GEB.

These developments are reminiscent of the last scene in *Animal Farm*, when the pigs dine with the farmers, and "it was impossible to say which was which."[49] But in making the comparison, we need to remember who is who. The AAC had not turned into a reformist organization. The philanthropists were the ones who had turned. *They* were Orwell's pigs: erstwhile revolutionaries turning into the reactionaries they had once fought. As I will explain in the next chapter, by the late '20s the big foundations and their allies in government were coming around to a vision of higher education that was far more decentralized and self-governed than the system they had yearned for in 1905.

The very existence of the AAC spurred on that process. As one speaker had pointed out at its 1915 meeting, "It is trite to say that this is an age of organization. It is only by organization nowadays that we can accomplish great results."[50] Of course, the "great results" of the AAC were actually the lack of results elsewhere. The association showed that the reformers were not the only ones who could organize around an idea; the colleges could do it, too. And their idea was especially simple. As the president of Colorado College noted at that first meeting, the small college had no demands, "except that it shall be untrammeled."[51]

ORGANIZED ACADEMICS: THE AMERICAN ASSOCIATION OF UNIVERSITY PROFESSORS

The small college was not alone in wanting to be untrammeled. In January 1915, the same month that the AAC came together in Chicago, a group of academics met in New York to form the American Association of University Professors.

The AAUP is invariably associated with the defense of academic freedom, especially in the form of investigating the firings of professors. Academic freedom, however, was not the association's raison d'etre in 1915. John Dewey, one of its founding leaders, explained at that first meeting that while these firings were worrisome, "such cases are too rare to demand or even suggest the formation of an association like this."[52]

Instead, as Hans-Joerg Tiede shows, the AAUP formed in order to directly challenge the academic engineers: "the association was founded to serve as a national body to speak for the profession as a whole in response to efforts to organize and standardize American higher education. . . . The professoriate, if it wished to influence these efforts, required an organized voice with which to respond."[53] The committee of Johns Hopkins professors who came up with the initial idea for the group described their goals in 1913: "to create means for the authoritative expression of the public opinion of the profession; and to make possible collective action, on occasions when such action seems called for."[54] This action, presumably, would include responding to violations of academic freedom but would certainly not be limited to it.

It was not even urgent to oppose the academic engineers on the issue. Many of the reformers had studied in Germany and happily paid lip service to *Lehrfreiheit*, the scholar's freedom of inquiry and teaching. Pritchett claimed that his foundation advocated for allowing "the widest freedom to professors" but also brushed aside actual academic freedom cases, noting "the extraordinary egotism" of the dismissed professors who sometimes wrote him asking for help.[55]

The keynote speaker at the New York meeting was Josiah Royce, who offered a reprise of the punishing attack on the CFAT that he had published the previous year. It was an old theme for the assembled academics. Five years earlier, Arthur Lovejoy, the professor most responsible for the AAUP's existence, had called for a veritable takeover of the foundation: "It is time for the rank and file of the teaching body to demand that the management of the Carnegie Foundation shall be altered in whatever manner is necessary in order to protect them against the sort of deception and the sort of indignity to which they have been subjected in the recent administration of this potentially beneficent institution."[56] And the attacks continued well after 1915, with another influential AAUP leader, Joseph Jastrow, writing four years later about the numerous "failings and failures of the Carnegie Foundation," which included "the Prussian-like superiority associated with the belief that authority makes right" and its "external non-academic control over the souls of American university teachers."[57] Elsewhere, Jastrow attacked Pritchett directly and issued a call to arms: "it is now or never for the professor to indicate that he is vertebrate."[58] Scott Nearing, a former Penn professor who became active in the AAUP after his highly publicized firing, broadened the criticism by attacking "plutocratized education," meaning "the idea of an educational system owned and largely supported by the people but dominated by the business world."[59]

Not all academics agreed with these militant stances, including a group of Cornell professors who balked at joining the association because they did not want to be seen as "attacking the existing condition of affairs in any destructive or antagonistic spirit."[60] And while Tiede describes the AAUP's original primary "principle" as "clearly aimed at the movements for standardization in which the Carnegie Foundation, the AAU, and the Bureau of Education were already engaged," its wording was nonconfrontational: "that, in the working out of a national policy of higher education and research, the general body of university teachers shall exercise an effectual influence." In short, like the small colleges, the professors wanted a seat at the table.

That said, in one important way they were much more like the AAU than the AAC: exclusiveness. Even the AAUP's name was exclusive, since it seemingly warned away mere *college* professors. Some of the founding members wanted to organize around institutional membership rather than individual memberships so that simply teaching at an "approved" university would guarantee entry to the association. The idea fell apart, however, when they realized that the only ready-made list of high-quality institutions was the one maintained by the CFAT.[61]

Individual membership still offered plenty of exclusivity, however. The association initially limited itself to professors "who have won distinction" and required an elaborate nomination and vetting process. As a result, of the initial 867 members, two-thirds came from AAU universities.[62] The AAUP's leadership, predictably, was also dominated by elite schools. The situation became particularly glaring when the association dispatched investigative committees to non-elite institutions. The team that investigated the far-off University of Utah over an important academic freedom case consisted of seven professors: two from Princeton, two from Columbia, and one each from Penn, Johns Hopkins, and Harvard.[63]

Even when academic freedom was the focus, as it increasingly became, the AAUP in its early years dug in mostly on cases where larger issues of governance were at play. The Nearing case, as described by Hawkins, was a prime example. Nearing was seemingly fired because of his liberal economic views, including opposition to child labor. This was particularly problematic because he was on the faculty of Penn's Wharton School of Finance and Commerce, which had both a conservative reputation to uphold and a long-standing notion that donors, going back to Joseph Wharton himself, were entitled to "dictate what was to be taught." Furthermore, the Wharton alumni were vocal, but not in the way that most alumni behaved; they loudly attacked academic freedom, which they described as the promotion of "bizarre and radical theories," and stridently supported the Penn administration.[64]

This was an excellent place for the AAUP to flex its muscles, with Lovejoy describing the offense as being "not directed solely or most significantly, against the individual teacher affected; it is directed also against the local faculty as a body, and against the academic profession at large." The charges against Penn, as summarized by a sympathetic report in the *New Republic*, were that "the governing power is in the hands of a close corporation of men financially interested in the perpetuation of certain economic doctrines, who have the power of appointment, promotion and dismissal over teachers of economics without trial, without hearing, and without public notice." Lovejoy focused on the outsider status of the alumni and trustees who were meddling in academic affairs: "it is an instance of lay intervention in what is essentially a professional question." The AAUP's investigation and action were ultimately successful, extracting concessions from Penn's board that included a stronger tenure policy and rights of due process for dismissed professors.[65]

When it came to the big picture of professorial autonomy, the AAUP found opposition from many corners. Tiede reports that its first major document, the 1915 General Declaration of Principles, was largely ignored by the CFAT, although Van Hise, one of the foundation's most influential board members, opposed it because it was "written wholly from the point of the professors" and did not take into account "the public interest."[66] The declaration, indeed, built on Lovejoy's criticism of outsiders, alienating the academic engineers with its warning that universities were being threatened by "the opinions or prejudices of men who have not been set apart or expressly trained for the scholar's duties."[67] AAU types sneered at the association, like the president of Ohio State, who compared it to a common trade union: "The professor desires to set his own standards of service and to measure the time he shall give as well as to evaluate his own service. This is essentially the contention of the coal miners who insist upon a five-and-a-half-day week."[68] And while an observer noted that most newspapers supported the declaration, the editorial board of the *New York Times*, an establishment standard-bearer closely aligned with Nicholas Murray Butler, trashed it: "It would be well for the Professors' union to understand that the screeching, the shallowness, and the pretense of too many Professors are bringing on the vocation a certain discredit."[69]

The AAUP also found itself at odds with the AAC over the declaration.

Timothy Cain explains that some leaders of small colleges were exasperated with the association, including the president of Amherst, who denounced it as a "professorial oligarchy" and criticized the declaration for holding institutional leaders to a different standard than the faculty. The AAC formed its own Committee on Academic Freedom, which issued a 1917 report that again attacked the declaration. The crux of the dispute was the locus of freedom. The AAC represented colleges, not individuals, and therefore "argued for institutional, not professorial, academic freedom."[70] Small college presidents bristled at top-down control when it came for them but not so much when they were dispensing it.

Furthermore, although both organizations were founded in opposition to the overbearing power of academic engineering, they had different ideas of who the "little guy" was. The AAUP saw themselves as a group of disenfranchised individuals being mistreated by institutional presidents and trustees, plus reformers and standardizers in the big foundations and government. The AAC, meanwhile, recognized the AAUP as an organization run by star academics from elite universities who did not seriously challenge the right of those institutions and the foundations to dominate a national higher education system. They were right; John Wigmore, the AAUP's second president, defended the CFAT's work "to eliminate the educational weeds" and "to influence institutional improvement by a system of rewards."[71] The professors just thought that they should be the ones doing the dominating, by being in charge of the big universities, like Veblen and Cattell had demanded—and even being in charge of the big foundations, too.

On that note, in 1919 Cattell published a scathing attack on the CFAT that called for a takeover of the foundation: "The first step should be to discard those responsible for the existing situation; then the teachers should come into control of a foundation established for their benefit." While he obsequiously noted that "Mr. Carnegie and Mr. Rockefeller have had the best of intentions in making their large endowments," he ominously noted that in a democracy, citizens cannot "leave it to the king and his lords to care for them."[72] His report celebrated the AAUP, which he had helped to launch, and made clear that the association had the high ground in its latest feud with the academic engineers.

That feud revolved around the old idea of pensions, which had faded from public view as the CFAT dramatically expanded its ambitions after 1905. Critics, however, had never forgotten that the pension program allowed the foundation to exert coercive control over institutions, and Cattell himself had applied a similar claim to individual professors, complaining in 1909 that deferring some compensation until retirement—specifically, after 20 years of employment at the same institution—would automatically limit academic freedom, by cowing faculty members into "good behavior" in order to keep their pensions.[73] The issue rose again, ironically, when the CFAT moved to end the program.

In 1916, Pritchett set in motion a plan to convert its old system of pensioning into a new organization called the Teachers Insurance and Annuity Association (TIAA, which still exists today). It would be a contributory annuity program, with institutions and individual professors paying in after a founding subsidy from the CFAT coffers. The move incensed the AAUP, which demanded that the foundation halt the plan and that the association be allowed to name trustees to the CFAT board. Tiede notes that their demand for representation had merit; a contributory retirement program was presumably a mutual insurance company, which by law was governed by its policyholders. This gave the professors an opening to stake a larger claim: "thus, the disagreement was as much about the diverging views of the AAUP and the Carnegie Foundation over principles of governance generally as it was about the organization of TIAA specifically."[74]

Even some CFAT board members had doubts about the new plan and expressed them to Pritchett. Some lamented that giving up the pensions would diminish the foundation's capacity for control; David Starr Jordan shared his reformist colleague Elwood Cubberly's opinion that the change "would ruin the usefulness of the Foundation. What up to now has promised to become a great national undertaking, would probably drop to the ranks of a small and somewhat exclusive affair."[75] Van Hise warned that his trustees were suspicious and that "this action will result in deepseated distrust in the good faith of the Foundation."[76] Jacob Schurman of Cornell argued that "every effort should be made" to win over the AAUP: "the Teachers Insurance and Annuity Association will be hurt very much at the outset if it does not enjoy the confidence of the teaching profession, and that confidence would be greatly impaired by an adverse vote of the Professors Association."[77]

Pritchett dug in, however, writing in a "confidential" pamphlet to professors that "the free pension system is not in the interest of the teacher." It was never a "permanent solution," he argued, and "has served its purpose." He ended the pamphlet with an extended, cherry-picked quotation about the CFAT from Wigmore's presidential report at the 1916 AAUP convention, including his meaningless platitude that "the founder's idea was a noble and unique one; himself and his trustees are entitled to our heartiest gratitude and cordial sympathy." Pritchett, conveniently, forgot to include Wigmore's strong opposition to the TIAA plan; the professor called it "radical" and "a fundamental error . . . going down to the roots of our educational system."[78]

The CFAT offered some concessions, starting with the establishment in 1917 of a Commission on Insurance and Annuities that offered seats at the table to the AAUP, the AAU, the AAC, and the NASU. The biggest change came when Pritchett promised to organize the TIAA independently, with its own board, and to ensure that the seed funding for the new company would come from the Carnegie Corporation, not the CFAT. He got the last laugh, however. The AAUP's leaders were appalled to learn that half of the new TIAA trustees were also CFAT trustees, and the new association's president was . . . Henry Pritchett.[79] As for the supposed benefit of switching funding to the Carnegie Corporation, by 1921 Pritchett had become the president of that as well.

Eventually, however, the AAUP reached a rapprochement with the academic engineers. They shared a mutual interest in diminishing the role of trustees, especially those who governed public universities, who were often unqualified political appointees. Combined opposition inspired those trustees and regents to form their own defensive organization, the Association of Governing Boards of State Universities and Allied Institutions, in 1923. The AAUP and the foundations also both sought to raise the salaries of professors, which had not kept up with inflation, falling by a third in adjusted dollars between 1914 and 1920.[80] In 1920, the GEB began distributing a $50 million fund to bolster those salaries. That was possible, Raymond Fosdick argues, only because Fred Gates had left his leadership role and a "more humane" generation of reformers had taken over.[81] Similarly, the AAUP reconciled with the CFAT—after Pritchett retired. The two organizations collaborated on two major studies in the 1930s, and the new CFAT president often sought the professors' counsel.[82]

Rapprochement with the AAC was even more momentous, however. Tiede reports that in the early 1920s, the AAUP sought to collaborate with institutional associations on academic freedom standards "so as to increase the likelihood that institutions would adopt such standards."[83] According to Cain, they first approached the AAU for that collaboration, but the elite association "demurred." Samuel Capen, in his role as ACE president, encouraged the professors to work with the AAC instead.[84] The partnership worked; the two organizations cosponsored an important conference on the topic in 1925 and continued collaborating up to their coauthorship of the landmark 1940 document *Statement of Principles on Academic Freedom and Tenure*, which still guides institutional policies today.

Seats at the table, won by the "little guys" as academic engineering sputtered, eventually turned into real influence.

ORGANIZING AT THE MARGINS

Neither the presidents of the small colleges in the AAC nor the professors in the AAUP were actually little guys, of course. They were, with almost no exceptions, white men with access to power. Even though they didn't always get their way, when they spoke, people listened—including the academic engineers.

Most of the institutions that I described in chapters four and five lacked that voice. Since they served marginalized populations, by design they were easy to ignore. They also lacked the material resources needed to quickly organize themselves—and for them organization was of even more importance.

The normal schools were exhibit A. By 1914, they had endured years of hearing the academic engineers demean them, demand that they trim their sails, and even call for their outright closure. They did not yet have a formal organization, but they did have a division within the National Education Association. Normally a sleepy backwater, the division occasionally made a splash, as in 1908 when it resolved that its members should drop the word "normal" and call themselves colleges as well as establish "departments of research work."[85] The splash it made at the 1914 NEA convention was more of a cannonball. The division passed a resolution that praised "the effort of normal schools to resist undue standardization" and directly attacked the CFAT and the GEB:

> We view with alarm the activity of the Carnegie and Rockefeller foundations, agencies not in any way responsible to the people, in their efforts to control the policies of our state educational institutions, to fashion after their conception and to standardize our courses of study, and to surround the institutions with conditions which menace true academic freedom and defeat the primary purpose of democracy as heretofore preserved inviolate in our common schools, normal schools, and universities.[86]

Newspapers across the country reported the story with headlines like "Call Foundations Menace."[87] Albert Winship, a sympathetic journalist, endorsed the attack and noted that it reflected "larger, broader, deeper" nationwide antipathy toward the academic engineers felt by "friends of the normal schools" as well as other critics. Among the complaints he listed was the CFAT's reliance on outsider appraisal of the schools: "The Foundation has selected men with no appreciable ability for the work assigned to them. The only weight that can be attached to the opinion of the men criticizing normal schools is that they have the Carnegie millions behind them."[88]

There was a clear gender dynamic to this fight. One of the leaders of the NEA division was Margaret Haley, a prominent teachers union organizer. She especially bristled at the idea of the all-male CFAT board dictating policy for normal schools, which served an overwhelmingly female population.[89] In a private letter to a deputy, Pritchett demanded to know who was behind the NEA resolution, speculating that they were people "connected with the Churchill outbreak."[90] He was referring to an uproar the previous fall, in response to an attempt to oust the president of the New York City school board, led by Nicholas Murray Butler and backed by Flexner and other prominent academic engineers. Thomas Churchill, that president, also chaired the board of trustees of Hunter College, a former normal school well on its way to becoming a full-fledged public college. A well-organized coalition of female teachers rose to defend Churchill, who kept his job, including Bridgett Peixotto, an icon of first-wave feminism.[91]

Pritchett still managed to scoff at the criticism. He found it "rather amusing" that despite the attitude of the normal school division, at the same convention David Starr Jordan had been elected president of the NEA, ensuring that the academic engineers would continue to run the show.[92] And he was right. The NEA of 1914 was certainly an emblem of top-down hierarchy, with powerful men lording authority over low-status institutions and educators. Their vision certainly included the idea, in Winship's words, that "at any cost there must be a stop put to all normal school aspirations."[93]

Three years later, the normal schools finally managed to come together in an independent organization. Actually, there were two: the National Council of State Normal School Presidents and the American Association of Teachers Colleges, each of which met for the first time in 1917. Each served a collection of institutions that included both normals and colleges, and in 1923 they accepted the inevitable and merged under the AATC name. The combined association became an ACE member, and in 1925 it also merged with the NEA's normal school division, which was then elevated to a full department within the association, "with complete autonomy."[94]

One person was a leader in each of the three associations: Homer Seerley, who had been the president of the Iowa State Teachers College since 1886. Seerley had run afoul of the academic engineers earlier in the decade, following his successful effort to drop his institution's "normal school" moniker. Ironically, he did so with the express intent of securing a spot on the CFAT accepted list.[95] The CFAT, which was already meddling in Iowa affairs through its placement of John Bowman as the University of Iowa's president, urged the state to review the school's status, leading to a recommendation to limit it to a two-year institution without the ability to grant the bachelor's degree. When Seerley opposed the plan, the foundation launched what Winship called a "petty and petulant attack" on him, hoping "to make a horrible example of the Iowa State Teachers College" and "seeking to discredit" the president personally.[96]

It was no wonder that Seerley led the push for the associations. Before they formed, he had to defend his own institution and reputation solo, on his own turf. But with his new platform, he was able to go on the offensive. In 1920, speaking as president of the AATC and as the National Council's delegate to ACE, he harshly criticized a CFAT study of normal schools in Missouri. He called the report "uncalled for meddling" and "a discredit to American scholarship," warning that "the American public always resents and overlordship or assumed domination such as the foundation undertakes to reach in this report. . . . Normal schools are institutions founded by the American common people and are not the creations of experts of wealthy foundations."[97]

Seerley also encouraged the constituent schools of the National Council to examine themselves before the academic engineers did so for them. He presented his own institution's self-study at the council's second meeting, prefacing it as a retort to the reformers "who assumed for themselves the dictatorship of educational public policy" and who advocated the "degrading" and "suppression" of teachers colleges.[98] Predictably, the academic engineers sneered at Seerley's ideas, including Butler, who described the Iowa report as "compiled in a spirit of protest" and completely devoid of "recommendations for change." He noted that "it is utterly impossible for the inside surveyor in most cases, in the light of his own familiarity with them, to see things differently from what they are."[99] Butler's hostility was well placed; self-study would soon become one of the most effective guards against the top-down designs of the academic engineers.

The gender dynamics under the surface of the normal school controversies were on full display when it came to the defense of higher education for women, and they played out in surprising ways. The first and most prominent group in that domain was not an association of institutions (the Women's College Coalition dates only to 1972) but one of former students, including those from coeducational schools: the Association of Collegiate Alumnae. Even more notably, its forays into self-standardization predated not just the counter-reformation but the crucible of reform itself. Starting in 1886, the ACA had a formal approval procedure to admit groups of alumnae from specific colleges into its ranks, which had initially represented just eight institutions. Thus, even though it was an individual membership association, the association was in effect publishing an accepted list of schools. In 1891, one ACA leader acknowledged that the group had to choose "between a broad and generous spirit of fellowship and a policy of rigid discrimination" and noted that the latter would hold "the standard of collegiate education for women so high that the influence of the Association may be felt not only by all college women, whether within the Association or not, but by all collegiate interests in the country."[100]

In 1904, one step ahead of the CFAT, the ACA's approval process became much more quantitatively rigid in its assessments of colleges and universities, with minimum marks for faculty size, endowment, and degree requirements.[101] Marion Talbot and Lois Rosenberry suggest that the foundation drew inspiration from the women's group but also that its dominance of higher education reform soon eclipsed the older association; in 1909, the ACA moved to adopt the CFAT's standards as its own. In 1912, they also incorporated the Bureau of Education's Class I rank of women's colleges as "the academic standard of admission" for the association. But this intertwining with the academic engineers came to a sudden halt in that pivotal year—1915—when the ACA voted to drop their links to other standards and "to leave the [approval] committee entirely free in its study of academic ratings."[102]

A parallel organization, the Southern Association of College Women, also dallied with the academic engineering but ended up asserting its own standards and views. From 1912 to 1916, the group conducted a wide-ranging study of women's colleges in the South. The group proudly sent its final report, which ranked the institutions into categories that included "imitation and nominal colleges," to both the CFAT and the GEB.[103] In another area, however, the SACW took a definite stance against the anti-liberal tide of the reformers. As Joan Marie Johnson shows, in 1905 the association formally opposed "practical education" like home economics and semiskilled vocational training. Throughout the following years, they defended the traditional liberal arts curriculum, including Latin, at women's colleges across the South. The group also worked to dispel the notion that higher education for women was incompatible with contemporary ideas of femininity; as one leader put it, "college women are no longer freaks in appearance, manner, or point of view."[104] Their efforts resulted in a growing acceptance of the appropriateness and importance of true higher education for women in the region perhaps most hostile to it. In 1921, the SACW merged with the ACA to form the American Association of University Women, which still exists today.

The junior colleges also struggled with questions of status and "practicality." Like the normal schools, they had long been a plaything of elite reformers, but their position was even weaker, since they were a direct creation of the academic engineers. As such, they were the last major group of institutions to associate, coming together as the American Association of Junior Colleges in 1920. They lacked the fighting spirit of the normal school groups and the AAC. Still, like those organizations, the point of the AAJC was to take back control from outsiders. One of its founding leaders described its original motivation as "defending this child which appeared to be greatly in need of defense."[105]

James M. Wood, the association's leading organizer and the president of Stephens Junior College in Missouri, set the tone with his keynote address at the 1920 meeting. He argued that junior colleges should be four-year institutions, serving students from age sixteen to twenty, and should issue the bachelor's degree. He also called for a huge expansion in the number of the institutions so that a junior college was within close reach of the majority of American students. Wood's vision was the antithesis of the restrictive policy of the academic engineers; he argued that his plan would "make it possible for additional hundreds and thousands of boys and girls to get an A. B. fully equal to that granted at the present time. . . . The larger the number of such graduates we have in a country like ours, the better off we are as a nation."[106]

While the bachelor's degree proposal was heartily debated at the meeting, the assembled junior college leaders were united in the idea that their institutions should grow in purpose and reach. Another theme was high standards. David MacKenzie of Detroit Junior College, who was elected as the association's first president, argued that the schools should hire only instructors with master's degrees, with a preference for PhD holders. He also made the case for making junior colleges resemble traditional colleges as much as possible, including offering a robust array of extracurricular activities.[107]

The academic engineers' point of view was represented at the meeting by Philander Claxton, the US commissioner of education. He rejected Wood's proposal, arguing that the junior colleges must be two-year schools only, but was conciliatory on other points. He agreed that high standards were paramount and heartily endorsed the transfer function of the institutions. They must hire highly trained instructors, he argued, who would promote "interest in college life." This would bring genuine college education to "tens of thousands" of students unable to enter traditional institutions as freshmen.[108]

What was most notable in Claxton's remarks was that despite his elite position, he made no mention of the two most derogatory functions proposed for the junior college: as a dumping ground for undesirable students and as a primarily vocational institution.[109] These concessions did not last, however, even within the AAJC. As Steven Brint and Jerome Karable argue, as the '20s went on, the association changed dramatically. Whereas at first the junior college presidents had been running the show, within a few years a new group of leaders, dominated by professors of education at AAU institutions (especially Stanford and Chicago) had taken over. They were "academic men attuned to the interests of the universities and skeptical of the free play of student choice." Their main focus was limiting the aspirations of junior colleges and pushing a "vocational counterideology [that] celebrated 'practicality' and 'realism.'"[110] In short, the ideas of the academic engineers, redux.

Of course, these institutions—today's community colleges—have largely remained two-year institutions, and many of them are both primarily vocational and subservient to higher authorities. The AAJC story is an important reminder that organization, by itself, was not enough to gain autonomy and status. Institutions at the margins of higher education still needed to fight.

If there was a group of schools that needed to fight more than anyone else, it was the Black colleges. As we have seen, more than any others these institutions experienced the strictures of top-down control, lack of academic freedom, and delimited aspirations. It is no surprise that the nation's first faculty labor union—a level of organization well beyond the professors' guild of the AAUP—formed at Howard University in 1918.[111]

But a group of colleges had already come together in a defensive organization in 1913. This was not the association of industrial schools that I described in chapter five (the ANISS), which also came together in 1913 to subvert Booker T. Washington's Tuskegee Machine. By contrast, the Association of Colleges for Negro Youth represented only true colleges and universities that offered the bachelor's degree. Seven schools showed up to the first meeting, including Howard and Fisk. Notably, those "flagships" of Black higher education were not represented by their white presidents but by Black professors. Howard sent George M. Lightfoot, whose expertise as a scholar of Latin was a quiet rebuttal to the academic engineers, especially Washington, who loved to bash the classics. Fisk's representative was even more revealing: George E. Haynes, a sociologist, cofounder of the Urban League, and a disciple of W. E. B. Du Bois. Just as his mentor had been the first Black person to earn a PhD from Harvard, Haynes accomplished the same distinction at Columbia. In addition to his service on the faculty, Haynes had a secret role in Fisk history. In 1908, he had convinced Du Bois to give the incendiary speech that brought down President James Merrill, imploring him, "You must help save Fisk. She is surrendering to industrialism."[112]

As Michelle Dalton shows, Haynes was the driving force behind the ACNY, but the association elected two white men as its founding president and vice president. In 1913, Black higher education itself was riven between the idea of promoting leaders of color or tapping white people to be the face of a movement that desperately needed money and status from elites. To that end, at the first meeting the assembled colleges also voted to hold themselves to an externally imposed standard—the CFAT definition of a college, even though none of them would be recognized by the foundation for years.[113]

This dance grew less delicate over time, and by 1919 the ACNY had elected its first Black president (a Morehouse professor) and was borrowing increasingly bold rhetoric from the AAC about defending the small college from reformers who saw value only in big universities and sub-baccalaureate institutes.[114] The association rallied after Thomas Jesse Jones's study of Black education came out in 1917, which openly denigrated every ACNY member besides Howard and Fisk.

The members' opportunity to speak truth to power came at their 1919 meeting, their first after a period of suspended operations during the war. Haynes had left Fisk the previous year, and the institution's controversial white president, Fayette McKenzie, sent himself as representative, along with one of the Fisk trustees: Jones. Although there is no transcription of the discussion, Dalton reports that the two academic engineers walked into a buzzsaw. The members criticized Jones's report to his face, particularly his suggestion that most of them become junior colleges. He never showed up at an ACNY meeting again.[115]

Around 1919, the association became increasingly focused on becoming the authority on Black colleges so that their own recognition would be internally determined, rather than waiting for bigots to pass judgment on them. This was particularly urgent when it became clear that elite universities were relying on Jones's report to deny admission to graduate programs to the alumni of Black colleges besides Howard and Fisk. At first, they had to work surreptitiously. The association landed a small grant ($500) from the GEB in 1919 for a proposed effort toward better relations with high schools. However, when it turned out that they had actually used the money to fund visits to evaluate nonmember colleges, a subsequent proposal to the GEB was personally turned down by Flexner in 1920.[116]

By 1928, the ACNY felt bold enough to present itself to the ACE as a national accrediting agency for Black colleges. Leo Favrot, a GEB officer, caught wind of the proposal and urgently petitioned the Southern Association of Colleges and School (SACS) to begin accrediting Black schools, which it had previously ignored. He took pains to promise that the Southern Association could "rate Negro colleges as such without in any sense admitting these colleges to membership." Favrot was also able to sweeten the deal with a $35,000 grant from the GEB.[117] The foundation then took the opportunity to deny a proposal from Du Bois to support a study of Black colleges and tell him that "you may be interested to know" that they had funded the SACS effort, to be headed by a white Dartmouth professor.[118]

The ACNY knew it was powerless to stop this development and focused its energy on influencing the accreditation team, which Dalton argues it was able to do. But the results were mostly unsatisfactory. Paraphrasing the CFAT's terminology, in 1930 the SACS published an "Approved List" that comprised just seven schools. Six were in Class B, and just one was in Class A (Fisk; Howard was not located in the SACS region).[119] Seven was better than the two named in Jones's report, but the hard-fought process showed how full recognition for Black colleges was still a dream, even as their once-marginalized white peer institutions were achieving it.

SELF-CONTROL: REGIONAL ACCREDITATION BODIES

It was not inevitable that the SACS would be tapped to accredit Black colleges in 1930. After all, the association had only started accrediting white institutions in 1919. And in fact, no voluntary associations of colleges and universities were involved in accreditation until March 1913, when the North Central Association of Colleges and Secondary Schools issued a list of seventy-three "approved" institutions across fifteen states.[120]

The North Central's list was a very different animal than the CFAT, AAU, and Bureau of Education lists. It had small colleges, denominational colleges, women's colleges, public universities, and technical schools. It had ten of the much-maligned Iowa colleges. Was it completely inclusive? No. Many institutions were left off, including all normal schools and teachers colleges, plus the handful of Black colleges in the Midwest. But the fact that schools like Lake Forest College and Olivet College were on the same, undifferentiated approved list as the Universities of Chicago and Michigan meant that a new day was dawning.

The regional voluntary associations that continue to do the work of accreditation today are different from the AAC (now AACU), AAUP, and other groups that were formed in direct opposition to academic engineering. This is because for the most part, they already existed long before the academic engineers came to prominence. However, in their early decades they had few functions. It was only under the shadow of academic engineering that these once sleepy bodies began the work that defines their existence today. Between 1913 and 1919, four regional bodies covering the vast majority of the country began accrediting colleges and universities: the North Central Association, the Southern Association, the Middle States and Maryland Association, and the Northwest Association. (The New England Association maintained that its exclusive membership list was a sufficient form of gatekeeping and did not take on a formal accreditation role until 1952.)[121]

This is a good place to consider that there were four possible answers to the question of control in higher education. The first was the laissez-faire situation that had given the academic engineers the impetus for reform. By 1913, no one wanted this to come back. The second was the system that had prevailed in Britain: a handful of elite institutions that tightly held the power of degree-granting, meaning that smaller institutions had to affiliate with them and play by their rules. But this could never be replicated in the United States; the legacies of the 1819 Dartmouth College decision and the ensuing laissez-faire era meant that charters to incorporate and issue degrees were both freely given and irrevocable. The third solution was another pipe dream in the context of the United States: control by a national ministry of education, as in France or Germany. The federal Bureau of Education had a bully pulpit but almost no actual powers, and there was very little appetite in Congress to change that.

The only answer left was the idea of associational control, which is what the academic engineers settled on. They recognized the power of collected groups of institutions and influential individuals and believed that by channeling that power to create and then run a national higher education system, they could reach their holy grail of efficiency. And yet, associational control escaped them.

The reason why is that they had wagered all their chips on *elite* associations. The foundation boards, the AAU, and the ACE were all dominated by elites from the higher education world or the private sector. But in a nation in which the right to assembly is enshrined in the Constitution, other associations were inevitable. In this chapter, we have seen how groups of small colleges, teachers colleges, Black colleges, and professors formed and managed to sap the academic engineers' power in just a few short years around 1915. That said, none of those groups managed to wrest away true control from the academic engineers.

The regional associations were the ones who pulled it off. No one anticipated this, but in hindsight these groups had a number of distinct advantages over the others. First, they were under the radar. In January 1915, the AAC and AAUP launched with guns blazing against the academic engineers, who were already on the defensive. Everyone understood that they were partisans, primed for battle but not for governance. By contrast, the regionals never staked an anti-reform claim or indicated that they were seeking control. They were also very specifically institutional associations of colleges and universities, unlike the foundation boards or the AAU, meaning that influential reformers like Henry Pritchett, Fred Gates, and Philander Claxton had no seats at their tables. While they did have seats for the academic engineers who happened to run elite universities, the fact that the regionals were *regional* meant that the usual suspects were divided and conquered. The presidents of Stanford, Chicago, Columbia, and Yale sat together on the CFAT board, but they were split up when it came to the regional associations, where they had they had the same vote as leaders from far humbler schools.

And to that end, because the regionals had so little power at their outsets they were fundamentally democratic groups. All types of institutions were allowed to join, and they were frequently represented not by their presidents but by deans or professors. When the Middle States Association launched its accreditation work in 1917, its twelve elected officers included only two representatives of AAU institutions—professors from Penn and Columbia. The other institutions represented in the officer ranks included Dickinson, Pittsburgh, and Stevens Institute. They were joined by two women, a Vassar professor and a Barnard dean.[122]

The academic engineers did recognize that the regional associations had some power but not in terms of controlling colleges. Instead, the aim was control further down the ladder, which was natural because the regionals included high schools as members. The year 1906 marked the founding of the National Conference Committee on Standards of Colleges and Secondary Schools, a group that included four regionals and the NASU. It also included the CFAT as a member—and in fact routinely convened in the CFAT offices, where its work mainly involved enforcing the Carnegie Unit standard when it came to college admissions. Notably, this committee lasted only until 1923, when it became clear that the regional bodies had become much more than an apparatus of the reformers.[123]

As Scott Gelber argues, the early history of accreditation was marked by the triumph of "academic insiders." And while they never claimed that they were returning to the laissez-faire era, the approval process was very generous. "Instead of providing a vehicle for external scrutiny, accreditors adopted a highly deferential and permissive approach . . . a procedure that reinforced the culture of academia while defusing outsider pressures."[124] Furthermore, he notes that the regionals quickly shifted evaluation processes away from the quantitative metrics favored by the academic engineers and even away from studying outcomes at all. The North Central Association initially asked institutions for evidence that their students were being prepared for graduate school but dropped the question by 1915.[125]

The hallmark of the deferential approach became the self-survey, which is still the centerpiece of the accreditation process, under the name of self-study. The technique had actually been pioneered by the normal schools, especially in the aftermath of a top-down survey of eight normals in Wisconsin in 1911. That critical report generated predictable backlash, but as one participant described, the schools "chose to cooperate, agree, and build rather than to controvert," and both administrators and faculty participated in a new 1914 survey after they were reassured that "insiders' intimate knowledge of the conditions" were to be highly valued.[126] Homer Seerley followed up with an "Inside Survey" of the Iowa State Teachers College in 1917, which he described as a retort to "high-sounding investigations" made by "self-appointed" reformers who approached their work with axes to grind.[127] The first book on the subject came out in 1917, strongly criticizing notions of efficiency and arguing that the most important goal of evaluation should be helping schools live up to their own expectations: "Little good can come from asking colleges to place their standards higher. What colleges need most is to fill up the gaps between what they have already undertaken and what they are getting done."[128] In short, the idea was to let institutions set their own goals and then self-assess whether they had met their goals.

In addition to self-study, the fundamental democracy of regional accreditation lives on today. The practice of campus visits by teams of external accreditors, which started in the 1920s, is emblematic. The team members are not professional evaluators but rather professors and administrators at peer institutions. Even more to the point, through the decades most teams have included representatives from institutions that are not even peers. In its most recent evaluation, the University of Chicago's evaluation team included a representative from Creighton University; Dartmouth's included a representative from Drexel University, and Stanford's included a representative from the University of Hawaii.

Accreditation by the regional associations triumphed by the middle of the '20s, as we can see from the changes in the Bureau of Education's accreditation roundup, a pamphlet that came out roughly every four years starting in 1917. The first edition listed five voluntary associations that were undertaking accreditation work: the AAU, the AAC, the CFAT, the North Central Association, and the Southern Association (which had not yet issued a list).[129] In 1922, the bureau added the Middle States Association and the Catholic Educational Association, which had accredited seventy-one institutions as "standard colleges."[130] In 1926, the Northwest Association and the New England Association appeared, as did the Teachers Colleges and Junior Colleges associations. But the CFAT was off the list.[131]

Perhaps the surest sign that the regionals were winning the battle for control was that they started to be the objects of criticism. This became clear by 1921, with an internal controversy in the Middle States Association. At that year's meeting, when the accreditation committee was ready to report on its first approved list, an organized group of nine small colleges protested to block the release of the list. The former president of Lehigh urged the association to think about the schools that did not make the cut: "Once listed as inefficient, it will be practically impossible to undo the harm that has been done." The president of Wilson College argued that autonomy was more important than standards: "There is something subtler and more gracious in the purpose to be free to grow than any standardization plan can ever measure." A member of the accreditation committee acknowledged that there would be some losers in the process but reminded the group that its homegrown list was still superior to external rankings, as it was far more inclusive and had been constructed with "greater thoroughness than similar work by other educational bodies." The association voted to release the list but on a very slim margin: seventy-three members in favor and sixty-two against. As a concession, in addition to its list of fifty-nine fully accredited schools, the committee added an additional eleven that it deemed as being on the cusp of approval, including several of the ones that had protested.[132]

Resentment against the accreditation process continued to build until it reached a head in 1939. That head came when a prominent speaker at an ACE conference delivered a fiery speech titled "Seven Devils in Ex-change for One," in which he insisted that the regional bodies that had assumed the work of "voluntary standardization" were no better than the heavy-handed nationwide control envisioned by the academic engineers. He acknowledged that the early years of standardization had been neces-sary, in the sense of forming "vigilance committees" to guard against the "dishonesty" and "educational malpractice" that had marked the laissez-faire era. That said, he argued that it was now time to end the use of "en-gineering standards" ("they are certainly not educational standards"), whether conducted by the big foundations, the federal government, or the regional associations:

> I am against standardizing, any standardizing whatever, and against all accrediting. I am persuaded that it would be better for the future of higher education if you [members of accreditation committees] were all to disap-pear as of tomorrow and if your places were left permanently vacant. The necessary job of vigilance committees—and I freely admit that it was once necessary—has been done. The crooks are under lock and key, or they have already tasted hemp and are no more. . . . The American universities gave the standardizing agencies license to live. Whenever the leaders of the universities are ready to unite in the decision that these agencies shall live no longer, they will disappear. I think that day approaches.[133]

THE WORM IS TURNING

That speaker at the ACE conference was Samuel Capen, who had fully com-pleted his transformation from reformist leader to counter-reformation hero. In so many ways he emblemized the shift in attitudes that followed the crucible of reform. The Leipzig-trained expert in "educational admin-istration" had left Clark University for the Bureau of Education in 1914, ready to follow Kendric Babcock in the work of whipping the nation's col-leges and universities into shape. But by 1939 he was a vicious opponent of federal authority over higher education, stating that local control was far preferable: "Even if it also remains a sprawling amorphous organism, afflicted with waste and duplication and inco-ordination, it will still be more vital and more flexible than if it should fall under the inevitably ill-informed and opinionated direction of a Federal bureaucracy."[134] This, from a former federal bureaucrat.

As David Noble explains, in the mid-1910s Capen had been a close col-laborator with Pritchett, and both were leading members of the Society for the Promotion of Engineering Education, an organization that perfectly espoused the academic engineering ethos. And yet, by the '30s he was a critic of "engineering standards" and top-down control. Noble also describes him as an exemplar of "class prejudice," citing a 1907 incident in which he carelessly injured a poor immigrant and then mocked him.[135] But at his 1922 inauguration as chancellor of the University of Buffalo, he denounced "those who would limit the number of college students on the basis of any distinction of race or sex or creed or social standing."[136]

In 1919, he became the founding director of the ACE, where he endorsed a "nationalized educational scheme" but then welcomed the AAUP, the AAC, and the regional associations to the table, learning from their grievances and demands for autonomy. His evolution continued when he left ACE to lead Buffalo, a modest private institution, and became closely involved with the AAC. In his inaugural address, he warned about "agencies built up to enforce a mechanical standardization" and committed the institution to an educational "long experiment" that needed autonomy to work.[137] He echoed that language in the next decade and tied it to both Enlightenment and American values: "There are two ways to effect educational reform. One is by decree. The other is by investigation and experiment. One is the authoritarian way. The other way is the way of science. The latter is consonant with the principles of democracy."[138]

Perhaps most remarkable about Capen's evolution is the platform from which he began speaking. In 1935, the renounced reformer added another distinction to his long list: CFAT board member. He would eventually become the board's chairman.

Capen had changed, but so had the CFAT—and the entire apparatus of higher education reform in the United States. By 1935, Pritchett had finally relinquished control of the foundation, and a genuinely new era had dawned. Of course, many legacies of the academic engineering era would persist into the '30s and indeed to the present day—including the accreditation process, which certainly did not "disappear" as Capen had predicted. But the counter-reformation had progressed enough that this new foundation official could state at the end of the decade that colleges and universities across the country "are tired of having the educational and financial policies of their institutions dictated by a horde of irresponsible outsiders." He went on, "For the first time since the beginning of my long voyage under letters of marque and reprisal I am filled with hope . . . because at long last the worm is turning."[139]

8: A NEW CONSENSUS
AND A NEW ETHOS

By the mid-1930s, it was all over. The individual voices, social movements, and organized associations had done their work. Although their impact was still very much around, the academic engineers themselves were gone. They had not been defeated in an outright battle. Rather, they disappeared by attenuation. Their opponents chipped away at the reformers' authority, sapped their power, subverted their plans. They watched as the social-political mood of the nation increasingly rejected their ethos. And in many cases, the academic engineers simply failed all by themselves.

To understand the collapse of this once-powerful movement, it is helpful to turn once again to presidential politics. In 1912, the American people had elected an academic engineer to the White House: Woodrow Wilson. Sixteen years later, they elected an *actual* engineer as president: Herbert Hoover. Both were political outsiders—Wilson had less than two years of elected office at his election, and Hoover had none. And both had close ties to elite universities.[1] Wilson's leadership of Princeton was his sole claim to national fame. Hoover's ties to Stanford were profound. He had been a member of the university's first graduating class, had served as a trustee since 1912, and maintained close ties to David Starr Jordan.[2]

Hoover, in 1928, was the embodiment of the still-potent academic engineering profile. William Leuchtenberg writes that his "talisman was 'efficiency.'"[3] He had applied his skills as an engineer first to getting rich through mining and then to performing public service, most famously as an enormously successful coordinator of food aid in Europe during World War One, and then as US secretary of commerce. He was, more than any other person elected president, a technocrat. In his speech accepting the Republican nomination—delivered at Stanford Stadium—he trumpeted the "increased national efficiency" that his party had created as well as the "business system" and "our magnificent educational system" that had emerged in recent years.[4]

We know how Hoover's presidency ends: the Great Depression, Hoovervilles, a punishing electoral defeat in 1932, and the dawn of a new era of generous, experimental government ushered in by Franklin Roosevelt—

guided in part by a "Brains Trust" of college professors.[5] But Hoover's stupendous failure had nothing to do with incompetence, as is sometimes reported. If anything, he was *too* competent. Leuchtenberg argues that he could not turn off his engineering mind and approach the Depression as a human problem. He quotes Hoover as extolling the value of "the cold and uninspiring microscope of fact, statistics, and performance" over imagination, quotes a close associate describing him as "too much a machine," and quotes journalists calling him "'a glutton for statistics' obsessed with 'the elimination of waste.'"[6] At his inauguration, Hoover had been hailed as "The Great Engineer."[7] When Roosevelt crushed him in 1932, winning forty-two states, he was still an engineer. But no one wanted engineers anymore.[8]

So it went with the academic engineers. By the 1930s, they had worn out their welcome many times over. A new vision eclipsed the technocracy of reform, emphasizing institutional autonomy, student access, and experimentation. These values, which signaled a thoroughly new era in American higher education, still inform the sector today.

That said, important aspects of the academic engineers' vision persist as well. Ultimately, the full story of academic engineering takes a dialectical form, with a novel synthesis emerging in the '20s and '30s that merged aspects of the foundations' program of reform and the counter-reformation that answered it. A new generation of leaders who could speak the language of reform both drifted away from academic engineering and helped steer it toward a consensus with its opponents.

That consensus maintained the reformers' esteem for research as well as their social engineering vision, focused on "the practical life": that post-secondary education should imbue students with economic and social value. But it presented a new pathway to those objectives. Control and efficiency were out. Autonomy and aspiration were in. By the mid-1930s, in theory at least, anyone—students and institutions alike—could reach for the bachelor's degree and beyond.

AN ATTACK ON THE NEW CONSENSUS

Before examining how the new consensus was built, it is useful to look backward from a point in time. Many things mark 1936 as the symbolic end of the era of academic engineering. Quotations are an easy place to start, like this one from March of that year, published in the Association of American Colleges *Bulletin*:

Standardizing agencies and inspecting staffs have had tremendous influence in persuading the public to a belief in measurable "standards," and in getting such standards regarded as essential to first-class education. It is hard to exaggerate the coercive pressures of these voluntary inspectors upon the schools themselves.[9]

Skepticism about "standardizing agencies" was not remarkable for the AAC crowd. What is remarkable about the quotation is its source—Walter A. Jessup, the new president of the CFAT. Here's another 1936 quotation, from a speech delivered at Johns Hopkins. The speaker noted huge spikes in college enrollment over the past four decades (up 287% nationwide since 1890) and explained:

This state of things arouses the friends of the few. They want drastic reforms. They insist on merciless selection. They demand an educational pyramid, not a gently tapering column. . . . Let us have done with spoon-feeding, nursing of lame ducks, etc., etc. Against this seemingly cruel and unfeeling policy the defenders of the many make outraged protest. They declare that true Americanism calls for equality of educational opportunity, its extension to the largest possible number, preparation for civic and community life, a sharing of the great tradition of knowledge, skill, beauty and the higher pleasures of the mind with the many, instead of having this as in the past a monopoly of a privileged class.[10]

This time, the speaker was George E. Vincent, president of the Rockefeller Foundation and a GEB board member. He went on to state that the proper course was in the middle of these two paths, but he saved his harshest language for "the friends of the few" and their "educational pyramid." In short, the stances of the big foundations had shifted so much that their leaders felt free to openly criticize the academic engineers who had launched them.

Specific turning points also marked the importance of 1936 across the spectrum of colleges and universities. The year was Harvard's tercentenary, presided over by the institution's egalitarian president James Conant, who had taken over from the staunch academic engineer A. Lawrence Lowell three years earlier. Franklin Roosevelt gave the keynote address, calling on Harvard to return to its roots of "tolerance" and "self-restraint," to leave behind "the tumult and the shouting" and march forward "under the old banner of freedom."[11] February marked the death of John Hope, who had turned Atlanta University into a true research university. The president of the GEB eulogized him at his funeral, praising him for the "extraordinary development" of the university, which he proudly noted offered a graduate education comparable to any other institution.[12] And at the bottom of the academic pecking order, 1936 also saw the closure of Seth Low Junior College in Brooklyn, Nicholas Murray Butler's dumping ground for Jewish applicants to Columbia, which was the last remnant of the hierarchical affiliation schemes for private universities initiated by William Rainey Harper. Many of its alumni, as well as Brooklyn political leaders, protested the closure—not because they wanted it to continue in its subservient state but because they wanted it to become a true four-year college under the Columbia umbrella. Butler, clinging to the university's presidency in his thirty-fourth year, shut down the campus rather than allow that to happen.[13]

More than anything, though, 1936 was marked by the publication of a book. It was a deeply critical book, written by the president of the University of Chicago. Such a book is a fitting end point for this saga, which had its origins in two other deeply critical texts by Chicago leaders: Fred Gates's 1888 *Need for a Baptist University in Chicago*, which established both the logic and the style of academic engineering, and Harper's 1900 *Prospects of the Small College*, which locked in restriction, subordination, and top-down control as the movement's key tenets.

The book's author was Robert Maynard Hutchins, the thirty-seven-year-old boy wonder of American higher education. He had been nationally prominent since age twenty-nine, when he became the dean of the Yale Law School. Hutchins's "young man in a hurry" reputation echoed that of academic engineers like Harper, and he shared many of the reformers' ideas, including a "bigger is better" philosophy that led him to attempt a merger between Chicago and Northwestern in 1933.[14] He had a curious pedigree as well that gave him insight into the struggles of the 1910s and '20s: his father was the president of Berea College. The elder Hutchins had brought Berea back from an extreme focus on "the practical life" and reestablished it as a real baccalaureate college.

Hutchins's *The Higher Learning in America*, which conspicuously stole the exact title of Thorstein Veblen's 1917 attack on academic engineering, has been reprinted dozens of times since 1936, including major new editions in 1962 and 1995. It is widely regarded as a timeless book. But while some of its themes indeed have staying power, it is also a very distinct product of 1936.

In some ways, Hutchins was simpatico with the academic engineers.

He despised the elective system and despised the extracurriculum even more (he notoriously shut down Chicago's storied football team in 1939, the same year that the "last academic engineer," John Bowman, gutted the University of Pittsburgh's). He trashed collegiate alumni, calling them a "reactionary element" who played "a weird and oftentimes a terrifying role" in colleges and universities.[15] He had a circumspect view of academic freedom, and he saw tightly controlled higher education institutions as the pathway to "a society rationally ordered"—the final four words of his book.[16] According to Frederick Rudolph, Hutchins's notion of control was profoundly shortsighted: "a rejection of the climate of freedom which, while capable of creating great chaos, had also built the University of Chicago."[17]

In other ways, though, Hutchins came out swinging against the academic engineers. He attacked "the service-station conception of a university," meaning one that was responsive to students and society, and held special scorn for the extension movement. He decried "the American system of educational measurement" and directly attacked the Carnegie Unit conception of marking student attainment.[18] Mary Ann Dzuback argues that he echoed Veblen in more than title, in his stance that "business values should not dictate educational or administrative policy in universities."[19] And he claimed that many of the problems he identified could be traced to the role of philanthropic largesse, asking, "How much of the current confusion in universities would have been eliminated if boards of trustees had declined gifts which merely reflected the passing whims of wealthy men?"[20]

Ultimately, Hutchins was railing against neither the academic engineers nor their opponents. His equal-opportunity attack was directed squarely at the *consensus* that developed out of the two platforms between 1915 and 1936. Above all, he hated the "practical" vocationalism of modern higher education—the notion that college should prepare students for jobs. He claimed this had its origins in the Darwinian logic that animated the reformers of thirty years prior, because it led students and institutions alike to focus only on adaptation to social and economic conditions.[21] This, in turn, led to anti-intellectualism and a gutting of higher education's founding values: "If you set out to prepare a boy for a trade there are and can be no limits to the triviality to which you will descend."[22] He defamed institutional autonomy and prescribed a narrowly designed, standard undergraduate curriculum for all institutions, from junior colleges to universities. And he also attacked the generous access that the new consensus offered, writing that it came from a "confused notion of democracy. . . . According to this notion a student may stay in public education as long as he likes, may study what he likes, and may claim any degree whose alphabetical arrangement appeals to him."[23]

The Higher Learning in America wasn't all grievance; the book also gave momentum to innovations that would inform the new era, most notably the "general education" movement that would have a deep impact in the mid-twentieth century. But for our purposes, it is important because it proves the existence of a new era—precisely because Hutchins had so much to criticize about it.[24]

THE MIDDLE PATH

Despite the tidy dialectical story I've set up, in reality the new consensus was not inevitable. Its emergence came from the efforts—subtle, not overt—of a new generation of higher education leaders who emerged after 1915. These individuals could speak the language of reform, but they had a fundamentally different set of values and, more importantly, a radically different approach than the academic engineers.

Instead of 1936, we could also pinpoint the dawn of a new era to September 18, 1933, when—improbably—a portrait of George Zook graced the cover of *Time* magazine.[25] Zook appeared there in his capacity as Roosevelt's first Commissioner of Education, holding a post once occupied by stalwarts of academic engineering like Elmer Brown and Philander Claxton. He couldn't have been more different from those reformers.

First of all, Zook was far from an engineer—real or pretend. He was a historian. When he was the thirty-four-year-old chair of the Penn State history department, he was tapped to succeed Samuel Capen as the chief of the Bureau of Education's Higher Education Division, on the strength of his assistance to the war effort through the federal Committee on Public Information.[26] Zook began making an impact just three months into the job, when he organized the conference of junior colleges that gave birth to the AAJC. In his opening remarks, he signaled that the era of academic engineering was over. He called for more colleges, not fewer: "The country probably had at one time a surplus of colleges and universities, but to my mind the time has come when we can say truthfully that the country has a real need for every kind of institution of learning in existence."[27] A few months before his first stint in the bureau ended, in 1925, he made the same case at an AAC conference in his proud presentation of a report that deftly co-opted the style of the academic engineers to push the expansion of higher education opportunity. As Hawkins writes, it was "a quintessential Zookian enterprise, offering precise data, with a careful drawing of progressive, pro-education conclusions. The report was a harbinger of change. In it, Zook reversed a generation of attacks on overproliferation of colleges."[28]

That was a theme that Zook maintained for his entire career, including when he left Washington to run the upstart University of Akron for eight years, then when he returned as commissioner, and finally when he soon left that job to become the director of the ACE, from 1934 to 1950. Throughout his career, he preached the new consensus doctrine, including in a 1938 speech that served up most of what Hutchins had railed against. Zook defended the "service-station" model of responsive higher education, arguing that "changes in national economic circumstances and modifications of popular social philosophy play an unending tattoo on all social institutions, including our colleges and universities." He insisted that external control of institutions should be abandoned in favor of "a very large measure of self-government," with voluntary accreditation associations serving as the only agents of accountability. Even those, Zook said, should strenuously avoid anything approximating standardization and should instead promote innovation: "there is nothing more stimulating and profitable to an institution than the intelligent selection and pursuit of its own objectives."[29] Zook's foremost push in favor of the new consensus came a decade later, when he was the primary author of the landmark Truman Commission report, *Higher Education for American Democracy*, which informed the purported "golden age" of higher education: decades of generous federal policy toward colleges and students alike, coupled with the dismantling of old barriers to higher education based on gender, race, and religion.

Zook's youth made him part of a generation that came to prominence after the crucible of reform had ended. However, other people who helped create the new consensus were active during that period—and in fact worked side by side with the reformers themselves. One of these was Capen, whose views shifted radically after he left the bureau to lead the ACE, and then to run a low-status university. But others never made such a dramatic shift. Some even held on to their positions and leveraged them to temper the excesses of reform.

In this book, I have painted the GEB and CFAT as pure instruments of academic engineering, but in fact their boards always included individuals who saw a middle path. The most prominent of these was Charles Eliot, the aged president of Harvard, who was on both the CFAT and GEB boards from their early years but was frequently out of step with his peers. He opposed both the junior college idea and the national university idea. (Madsen credits him with single-handedly spiking the latter on multiple occasions, against majority sentiment.[30]) And Eliot was, after all, the creator of the elective system, which had instantiated the spirit of laissez-faire in the college curriculum. Flexner directly attacked him for this work in the pages of *Science* in 1909, saying that he had torn down the nineteenth-century old-time college but had failed to build anything up in its place.[31] Gates piled on in a memo the next year, describing Eliot's generous attitude toward philanthropy as undermining the whole academic engineering movement. [32] M. Carey Thomas, the leading woman academic engineer, launched multiple attacks on him.[33] And when he left the CFAT board, Andrew Carnegie wrote to Pritchett, "Very sorry indeed to hear of President Eliot's resignation, but he does not know how clearly we regard him as an exception. . . . I think we need not be in a hurry to fill his place."[34]

But Eliot was far too prominent to sideline, and even though his votes in CFAT and GEB deliberations were frequently in the minority, his voice resonated well beyond the foundation boardrooms. Eliot's positions were in some ways a throwback, but they also set the stage for the new consensus vision that educational institutions should be widespread and well funded, that they should respond to societal needs, and that they should not shy away from preparing students for jobs.[35]

He also was not the only exception on the CFAT board. Jacob Schurman, the president of Cornell, was certainly another. Although it was a privately endowed AAU university, Cornell was also a land-grant institution. Thus, in 1908, Schurman found himself as president of the National Association of State Universities, at whose conference he delivered a barely veiled attack on the academic engineers next to whom he sat at CFAT board meetings. He opened by praising the American "genius for compromise" and included a radical call for free tuition at all public colleges and universities. But the address was most notable for his attack on the reformist foundations, including the one on whose board he had served since day one: "I make no exception even of the Carnegie Foundation." These foundations, he argued, "create a new and dangerous situation":

It is no longer the case of a rich man giving his money, going his way (eventually dying), and leaving the university free to manage its own affairs. The purse strings are now controlled by an immortal power, which makes it its business to investigate and supervise and which lays down conditions that the university must accept if it is to receive grants of money. An irresponsible, self-perpetuating board, whose business is to

dispense money, necessarily tends to look at every question from the pecuniary point of view; it wants its money's worth; it demands immediate
and tangible results. Will not its large powers and enormous influence in
relation to the institutions dependent upon it tend to develop in it an attitude of patronage and a habit of meddling? The very ambition of such a
corporation to reform educational abuses is itself a source of danger. Men
are not constituted educational reformers by having millions to spend.[36]

Schurman remained on the CFAT board for fifteen years, serving as a check
on Pritchett and the other true believers. The foundation's first in-house
historian, Howard Savage, wrote to Bowman in 1950 that after his review
of board meeting minutes, "Schurman appears from every point of view
as a conceited recalcitrant and trouble-maker."[37] The Cornell president
probably would have enjoyed the description.

Other leaders drifted away from academic engineering, taking their
weight with them. One of the most prominent of these was Anson Phelps
Stokes, the powerful secretary of Yale, who was second in command to the
university's president and oversaw a staff of forty.[38] He was a member of
the GEB board 1912 to 1932 and, according to Fosdick, was often a voice
of moderation, opposing Gates's policy of tight control of grant recipients
and directly reproaching Flexner for trying to dictate curricular choices.[39]
Stokes was also a philanthropist in his own right as the director of the
Phelps-Stokes Fund, his wealthy family's private foundation. The fund had
underwritten Thomas Jesse Jones's *Negro Education*, that emblem of the
subordination of Black colleges, but Stokes soon moved away from that
restrictionist model. By 1925, he defied Jones by arguing that Fisk's problematic president, Fayette McKenzie, had to go, and he was in favor of
replacing him with a Black person.[40] Speaking of presidencies of Black institutions, Stokes turned down an invitation to lead Hampton in 1917. His
given reason indicated the emerging new consensus: he wanted to remain
in his current job so he could "do my bit towards the firm establishment of
Yale as a University equally given to culture, research, and public service,
and more adapted in organization, in the system of instruction, and in the
ideals for which it stands to the needs of a modern democracy."[41] In his
declining letter, he also noted his dream of a more "spiritual atmosphere"
in academia. This presaged a surprising second act for the devout Epis-
copalian after he retired from his Yale post (to be replaced as secretary by
the twenty-three-year-old Robert Maynard Hutchins). He moved to Washington, DC—not to join the Bureau of Education or the ACE but to become
the canon of the National Cathedral.

Sometimes a second act was not a choice. Lilian Wyckoff Johnson was a budding academic engineer when she became the president of Ohio's Western College for Women in 1904. She had done graduate study at Leipzig, earned a PhD from Cornell, and was a close ally of Philander Claxton. She gushed over the establishment of the GEB: "It is only by some such disinterested body with sufficient means at its command that a system truly related in all its parts can be evolved. . . . Not only ten million dollars, but hundreds of millions should be entrusted to it for this great work."[42] After three years, however, she left Western under unclear circumstances and was replaced by a man. She next became the driving force behind the creation of the West Tennessee Normal School (today's University of Memphis) but was denied the presidency and her desired faculty appointment when the school opened—again, the jobs went to men (who did not hold PhDs), even though the school overwhelmingly served women. According to M. Sharon Herbers, at that point she permanently removed herself from the higher education sector and devoted herself to "democratic and Christian principles," becoming a progressive farmer in rural Tennessee and helping run an integrated community school.[43]

Discrimination likely chased Johnson away from academic engineering, but Robert Moton managed to outrun it. Moton should have been the obvious choice to succeed Hollis Frissell as president of Hampton, where he was a top administrator, but word came to him that the job would never go to a Black man. (That remained true until 1949.) Becoming principal of Tuskegee after Washington died was his consolation prize.[44] Moton did break through a different color barrier in 1920, when he became the first Black person named to the GEB board. In his own quiet way, he steadily worked to elevate the cause of true Black higher education. He stayed involved with Hampton, urging a trustee in a strictly confidential note ("destroy this letter, for reasons obvious") to reject a candidate for the school's open presidency "who is out of sympathy with the colored people, that is who might feel that the Negro should stay in his place."[45] Moton was nationally prominent (he was the only speaker at the 1922 dedication of the Lincoln Memorial who was not a current or former US president), but he did his most important work behind the scenes. This included his below-the-radar work to turn Tuskegee into a real college. He first opened a junior college division, and then in 1929, Tuskegee—for all time identified with its academic engineer founder, who swore that it had no ambitions beyond industrial training—began offering the bachelor's degree.[46]

Another campus revolution, less quiet, was happening in Minneapolis. The University of Minnesota and its president, George Vincent, had once been pioneers of the "don't come to us, we'll come to you" idea of extension. By the early '30s, Lotus Coffman had replaced Vincent (who left to run the Carnegie Corporation) as president. As his signature accomplishment, Coffman completely flipped the extension idea on its head. In 1933, he opened a new undergraduate division: the General College, which he described as an "experiment, an adventure in the field of higher education."[47] "General" signified both a general (well-rounded) education and open access to the general population. Its founding dean, the former journalist Malcolm MacLean, half-jokingly referred to the program, which had essentially no admissions requirements, as the "great slag heap of academic discards."[48] The General College curriculum combined lightly vocational courses, "overview" surveys of academic disciplines and topics, and "euthenics" courses on the appreciation of art and culture. Students could earn an associate's degree in the program and were welcome to seek a bachelor's degree as well, if they could meet the regular admissions standards of the university.[49] In short, the General College was serving the student masses but in a very different way than the academic engineers had envisioned. Instead of studying far away—at distant junior colleges, in extension classrooms, or through a packet that arrived in the mail—these students were now welcomed to fully share in the campus, social life, and academic brand of an AAU university.

The General College was no fluke, either. Many other institutions established similar schools or colleges in the '30s and '40s, some of which live on, including at Columbia, Boston University, and Pittsburgh. And the program earned the admiration of a new generation that had taken the reins from the academic engineers. Will Learned, who had been on the CFAT staff since he was a young man, was particularly impressed by the experiment and helped promote it.[50] The GEB helped bankroll it.[51] Coffman was offered the presidency of the CFAT, which he turned down in order to stay at Minnesota.[52] And MacLean, remarkably, became the president of Hampton in 1940, despite having no background in Black higher education.[53]

To restate the point from the beginning of this section, none of these individuals did battle with the academic engineers or actively sought to usurp their thrones. They didn't need to, since the reformers' power and eminence had been under attack by others since 1908. Thus, MacLean, Coffman, Moton, Stokes and many others who helped formulate and spread the ideas undergirding the new consensus could do their work by playing nice with the academic engineers and then, without fanfare, taking over their foundations and their schools.

WHAT HAPPENED TO THE FOUNDATIONS?

Both of the major foundations associated with the academic engineers still existed in 1936, but they were vastly different organizations than they had been just a decade earlier.

Fred Gates remained a trustee of the GEB board until the last day of 1928; five weeks later, he was dead. But his dominance of the foundation had already ended after he handed over its management to Wallace Buttrick in 1917. Buttrick had been part of the organization since its very beginning, and while he was firmly in the academic engineering camp, Fosdick writes that he also worked to steer its programs away from "Gates' rather artificial formulas."[54] Most notably, he took a stand for institutional autonomy; when Pritchett wrote him in 1920 with an idea for a tightly controlled system of gifting Rockefeller's latest $50 million donation to the GEB, Buttrick rejected it: "We ascertain to the best of our knowledge and judgment whether the administration of a college is in safe hands and then give them money to use as they please. . . . We ought not to bring direct pressure to bear on the policy of the institution."[55] By 1923, however, Buttrick was in poor health, and it was time to transfer power once more.

Most everyone assumed that Flexner would be the GEB's new leader. He was by far its most famous staffer and in many ways had been the face of the organization since 1917. But when it came time to vote, the board chose Wickliffe Rose, a Rockefeller Foundation trustee best known for leading the massive effort to eradicate hookworm in the South. Fosdick, who knew both men personally, writes that Rose was "far more of an administrator than Flexner, far less impulsive, and perhaps with better poise and balance." Rose abandoned Gates's mission to shape a national higher education system, instead focusing on "the *quality* of education." Flexner hung on at the GEB until 1928, spending his final years steering big grants to elite research universities, including Princeton—which tapped him to be the founding leader of its new affiliate, the Institute for Advanced Study.[56]

Rose also left the GEB in 1928, and with those departures, the GEB stopped being a force in higher education reform. From that point on, the foundation focused on improving primary and secondary education for Black children in the South. That goal had always been of much greater interest to John D. Rockefeller Jr., who by this point had taken over his family's philanthropic work. But even that work faded. After a spend-down period, the GEB and the younger Rockefeller both died in 1960, when the board's few remaining programs and assets were absorbed into the Rockefeller Foundation.

The CFAT still exists and has never fully abandoned its focus on higher education. (It reemerged as a ranking agency in 1970 with the inauguration of the Carnegie Classification of Institutions of Higher Education.) But like the GEB, the CFAT had moved away from its reformist mission by 1936.

In 1918, the foundation dropped a bombshell: it was dismantling its pension program, claiming that it was no longer financially sustainable.[57] In reality, as Arthur Lovejoy had pointed out in 1913, the program had *never* been sustainable and had always been arbitrarily administered according to Pritchett's whims.[58] Nevertheless, the CFAT spun it off as the supposedly independent TIAA (Pritchett still controlled it), boosted by a million-dollar gift from the Carnegie Corporation.

In doing so, the organization abandoned its primary "carrot" used for extracting compliance from colleges and universities in its standardization push. Pritchett's motivation for this shift is not fully clear; he certainly relished the fact that the TIAA plan annoyed the leaders of the AAUP, but he also had apparently changed his mind about how to best promote reform. Writing to a trustee in 1917 about his plans, he explained: "As I look back over the whole history of our pension administration the most serious mistake seems to me to have been the assumption that a free pension was in the interest of the college teacher and of the college. This was a fundamental mistake. . . . When one has started on the wrong track there seems to me no other thing possible except to turn about and get on the right road."[59]

The "right road," for the 1920s, meant a renewed emphasis on research and surveys, an attempt to double down on the success of the Flexner Report. Over the decade, the CFAT published major reports on teacher education, legal education, education in Pennsylvania, Canadian education, European education, dental education, pensions for K–12 teachers, intercollegiate athletics, and college admissions.[60]

Pritchett announced his retirement in 1930, his twenty-fifth year as CFAT president. At age seventy-three, he was simply old, but he was also now running an organization that had shifted away from him. We can learn as much by looking at how he was replaced. His first successor was no surprise—Henry Suzzallo, a first-generation reformer and a protégé of Butler who had been installed as president of the University of Washington due to meddling by Pritchett and other academic engineers and then forced out by a populist governor (the university's faculty, notably, made no protest).[61] Pritchett had also tried to install him as president of the University of California in 1919.[62] But Suzzallo died unexpectedly in 1933. He would be the last academic engineer to lead the CFAT.

In the first round of nominations for a new president, four trustees picked Coffman of Minnesota, who was offered the job but declined it.[63] The runner-up was George Zook, who represented a clean break from academic engineering. Frank Aydelotte, president of Swarthmore (and by then a CFAT trustee) also got a nomination. And other trustees pushed other candidates associated with small colleges; the president of Hamilton College recommended someone by saying, "I like the fact that he was graduated from a small college for it seems to me that the new president of the Foundation should be someone who includes liberal arts institutions in his thinking."[64]

In the end, the board picked Walter Jessup, a man who had decried the "coercive pressures" of earlier incarnations of the educational foundations. He was a graduate of Earlham, a small Quaker college. In 1916 Jessup had succeeded John Bowman as the president of the University of Iowa, where he then spent two decades repairing Bowman's damage and promoting harmony among the state's "sister institutions."[65] Furthermore, Jessup sat on the board of education of the Methodist Church.[66] He made it clear early on that his leadership of the CFAT would de-center coastal elitism; for at least two years after he became the foundation's president, he continued living in Iowa City, traveling to New York only for official business.[67]

Jessup also inaugurated the most important change in the foundation's mission. The CFAT would continue to sponsor studies about higher education, but, he indicated in 1936, it would now take a very different approach: "Certainly every change that has been made in standards has been introduced on the assumption that, as the institution attains new standards, the institution will improve, and that the product will improve with the institution. Why do we not transfer our administrative attention from THE INSTITUTION, with its four-year straight-jacket and its external standards, to the students themselves? The students are the integrating factor of the system."[68]

Students! The president of the CFAT was expressing an interest in students. A new day had truly dawned.

WHAT HAPPENED TO THE COLLEGES?

One notable thing did *not* happen to the non-elite "other people's colleges" between 1905 and 1936. They did not disappear by attrition, consolidation, or demotion. Quite the opposite happened. Every year, some schools closed their doors, but far more opened. In 1905, the Bureau of Education counted 901 institutions of higher education, including normal schools and technical schools. In 1936, it counted 1,695. What's even more impressive is the rapid pace of change in the '30s; 30 percent of that growth happened in the final three years of the period. And even more impressive than that was the growth in bachelor's degrees awarded: from 15,556 in 1905 to 143,125 in 1936—an 820 percent increase. [69]

Instead of disappearing, the schools had learned two things. The first was that they didn't need to depend on the big foundations for approval and funds. The second was that they *did* need to depend on someone else for approval and funds. Like Walter Jessup, the colleges discovered students.

These two things were related. Money had to come from somewhere, and increasingly the pipeline of Carnegie and Rockefeller largesse was either drying up or becoming inaccessible; in 1925, for example, Wisconsin's board of regents forbade the university from accepting any money from the CFAT or GEB.[70] As an alternative, undergraduate students became the financial pipeline. At private institutions, this meant tuition hikes—as Thelin has shown, independent colleges began raising their price tags dramatically after 1920.[71] A 1937 article by a Mount Holyoke professor noted this and added with alarm that enrollments at liberal arts institutions had been flat over the past fifteen years, while public enrollments had exploded. His takeaway was that, especially since these hikes were taking place during the Great Depression, the privates were increasingly becoming bastions of socioeconomic privilege.[72] He was right, of course. But at the same time, the math was there for all to behold: much higher tuition, with a stable number of enrollments, meant a lot more revenue.

At the publics, the math was less direct but still student-driven. Claudia Goldin and Laurence Katz demonstrate that in the '20s and '30s, a virtuous cycle took place in public institutions in the Midwest and West: increasing state support (doled out in annual appropriations from legislatures) led to increased college enrollment, which then reinforced the public's willingness to keep funding higher education.[73] Just as the high school had experienced a similar cycle of support a generation earlier, many Americans now saw college as something worth taxing themselves for, with the understanding that the colleges would have a spot for them or their children.

During the crucible of reform, most colleges and universities had tried to prove that they had something of value to offer *the academic engineers* and their notions of an efficient society. Not so by 1936; now, they were trying to prove that they had something of value for *students*. And students valued one thing above any other: bachelor's degrees.

This meant that the reformers' dream of convincing middling four-year institutions to turn into junior colleges was officially dead by the '30s. William Rainey Harper's scheme had never enticed more than a half dozen schools to decapitate themselves and affiliate with Chicago, and that was the best offer on the table. In 1936, the Bureau of Education calculated that just forty-one four-year schools had dropped to junior college status since 1900, with the vast majority of those transitions coming before 1920. Meanwhile, since 1930 alone, at least forty had done the opposite, converting to baccalaureate colleges. The bureau quoted a state official on the trend: "the expansion of established junior colleges into 4-year degree-granting institutions . . . is 'what the parents want, what the children want, and what the social system wants.'"[74]

At the same time, brand-new two-year schools were suddenly sprouting literally everywhere, but they served a vastly different function than the dumping ground that the academic engineers had envisioned. At the height of the Depression, in 1934, Roosevelt's Federal Emergency Relief Administration began directing money to states for the purpose of establishing "emergency colleges" meant to educate out-of-work young people. Hundreds popped up almost immediately, many of them in affiliation with public universities (Michigan called its dozens of schools "community colleges" decades before that term came into common use[75]). These two-year institutions were not designed to redirect students away from universities but instead to draw new entrants into the higher education system in the first place. And those students were welcomed to stick around; the University of Michigan built a "barracks" on campus in anticipation of a flood of transfers.[76] The emergency college idea—to use college education as a way to accommodate and improve the lives of a vast mass of at-risk young people (and, conveniently, to keep them out of the labor market)—set the stage for the landmark higher education event at the other end of Roosevelt's presidency: the GI Bill.

Normal schools, too, were defying the will of the academic engineers. A CFAT staffer visiting Virginia in 1921 denigrated the state's four public normal schools as "pretty poor," owing to the legislature's "mistake" of giving them their own administrative board. The state would soon take them over and whip them into shape "within five years," he predicted.[77] He was dead wrong. It took only three years for the legislature to not only affirm the autonomy of the board but also allow the normal schools to rename themselves as "teachers colleges" and offer the bachelor's degree. Why? Because doing so was immensely popular. The Richmond *Times Dispatch* reported on the local reaction that met the president of Fredericksburg

State Normal School (today's University of Mary Washington), who had been the lead lobbyist for the effort: "the faculty in a body met President Chandler at the station upon his return from Richmond and escorted him to the school, conducted him to the assembly hall, where the students had assembled. The students rendered him an ovation."[78]

And the Virginia schools were certainly not alone. A 1936 study found a nationwide trend: between 1900 and 1933, the number of normal schools had decreased from 286 to 101, while the number of teachers colleges increased from two to 175. All of the newly christened colleges were offering the bachelor's degree, and 29 of them were offering the master's. And many of them were soon dropping the word "teacher" from their names as well; it, too, was pejorative. Three decades later, Alden Dunham reported that no new teachers colleges had been founded after 1929. He calculated that 166 former public normals or teachers colleges had become full-fledged colleges or "regional universities" by 1967. Only one remained.[79]

An equally dramatic progression happened even faster with the technical schools. Carnegie Tech, in Pittsburgh, is a perfect example. When Andrew Carnegie established it in 1900, it was unquestionably a sub-baccalaureate institution, offering strictly vocational classes to working students, mostly in the evenings. Within a decade, however, a vocal interest group began agitating for change: the alumni, who were losing out on jobs and even membership in vocational societies because they lacked a degree. In 1912, the administration successfully petitioned the Pennsylvania legislature for the right to offer the bachelor's degree, which they promptly began doing. Two years later, they started conferring master's degrees. This kicked off an explosion in enrollment, more than doubling by the end of the decade; in 1915, the school built its first dormitories. In 1921, a survey commissioned by the Carnegie Corporation and headed by Samuel Capen declared the tech school to be a university.[80] And by the mid-'30s, the school increasingly looked like any other college, with a liberal curriculum (including required "cultural courses"), athletics teams, and no less than forty-one fraternities and sororities.[81]

Carnegie Tech had the blessings of association, of course—in 1914, it became the first technical school to make it onto the CFAT accepted list—but it was not an outlier. Drexel Institute, across the state in Philadelphia, had also been founded as a purely vocational school. A speaker at its opening ceremony, whom I quoted in chapter four, defined its intended students as "the vast army which must live by labor." In 1905, its trustees debated a proposal to begin offering degrees but voted it down. In 1914, however, they finally relented and gained the legislature's approval to offer the bachelor's.[82] And the same story played out at Georgia Tech, a public technical school. At its opening ceremony, its founder insisted that the school would not offer academic degrees and vowed never to compete with the University of Georgia: "The head is in Athens; the hands are here." The school was legally allowed to offer the bachelor's but did so only for engineering until 1908, when it added a degree in architecture.[83] The real watershed was in 1915, when Georgia Tech students were allowed to earn a degree in "commerce"; many other nontechnical disciplines followed shortly. Or perhaps the watershed actually came the next year, when its suddenly prominent football team won the most lopsided game in history, defeating Cumberland College 222–0 (Tech's coach was John Heisman, the future namesake of the Heisman Trophy).[84]

Institutions of higher education that served Black students were also quickly moving toward collegiate status by the '20s, trailing the normal schools by a few years. Tuskegee was offering the bachelor's degree by 1929. The same year, the embattled white leader of Hampton declared that his school "is now a college."[85] Public Black institutions were doing the same thing. Lincoln Institute, Missouri's 1890 land-grant institution, had degenerated to what Antonio Holland calls "a secondary industrial and normal school" during the 1910s, when racist state officials sought to constrain its ambitions. In 1920, however, progressive Republicans took over the state capitol, and the next year they acknowledged the importance of their Black constituency by renaming the school Lincoln University. In 1923, Nathan Young, who had been fired from Florida A & M for his attempts to advance its mission, was named president, vowing to make Lincoln "a standard, fully accredited liberal arts college." In 1929, it awarded eighteen bachelor's degrees and, more importantly, received an unprecedented appropriation of $650,000 from the state legislature. And in 1934, it got the biggest prize of all: full accreditation from the North Central Association.[86]

The foundations were also coming around to the idea of true Black higher education. Even Du Bois admitted as much in 1929, writing that "with considerable reluctance but inevitable logic," the GEB was now supporting the liberal arts mission of Black colleges. He couldn't help but note that "it was not until several [GEB board] members, including Dr. Buttrick, died" that the change could happen."[87] In 1934, the twenty-year history of the Association of Colleges for Negro Youth ended, largely because the Southern Association had agreed to accredit Black baccalaureate colleges under the same terms as white colleges (although the white-dominated organization did not extend full membership to the Black schools until 1957).[88]

Perhaps most surprising is what happened to many of the small bac-calaureate colleges that had been in the crosshairs of the academic engi-neers. Instead of disappearing, they became the centers of innovation for American higher education.

In 1916, Robert Kelly of the AAC declared at the group's second an-nual meeting that "excellence is not inconsistent with variety."[89] The small colleges had organized themselves in order to oppose standardization; heterogeneity would therefore be their watchword. David Riesman has described the '20s and '30s as an era of "rebellious and experimental out-look" for colleges, and the trend was certainly noticed by its contemporary observers.[90]

In 1932, the National Society for the Study of Education described the era in a book-length report on "changes and experiments in liberal-arts education." The opening chapter explained that the colleges had survived academic engineering and were ready to flourish; "they [have] passed through the initial stage of destructive criticism and are well advanced in a period of change resulting from constructive criticism."[91] The report included descriptions of 128 distinct innovations happening on campuses across the country. Many of them offered first glimpses at features that we now take for granted as part of college education, among them hon-ors programs (begun at Swarthmore), independent study classes (Reed), cross-registration (Pomona and Scripps), interdisciplinary majors (Sweet Briar), pre-matriculation advising (Carleton), junior year abroad (Smith), and student psychological services (Southern Methodist).[92]

The honors program, pioneered at tiny Swarthmore, is, of course, an enduring idea, but it also introduced an even more impactful one, closely related to Minnesota's General College. Honors opened the door to the notion that colleges could unabashedly serve advanced students and me-diocre ones at the same time. It was the former part that captivated some of the academic engineers—Flexner praised it effusively[93]—but the general idea pleased other elitists, like the *New York Times* editor who described "the experiment of allowing students of exceptional mental endowment to get all they can out of college unhampered by the dead weight of those less brilliant."[94] Snottiness aside, the very existence of an honors program was excellent marketing. It offered a signal to all students, even the mediocre ones who were destined for the regular curriculum, that the college was taking a new approach to undergraduate education: in Frederick Rudolph's words, "the return of the student to the teaching-learning experience."[95]

One of the most visible examples of the "return of the student" was not at a liberal arts institution but at an AAU powerhouse: Wisconsin. To be fair, the small handful of students (never more than two hundred at a time) in the university's Experimental College that operated between 1927 and 1932 were only nominally part of the larger institution, not least because those students shared fully in the autonomous college's governance. The program's founder, Alexander Meiklejohn, had plenty of liberal arts bona fides given his decade of service as the president of Amherst College. There, as Adam Nelson explains, he had transformed a "staunchly traditional school" into one where the curriculum was centered on detached critical examinations of twentieth-century problems.[96] Meiklejohn had also excelled at provoking the academic engineers and their wealthy backers. He invited Veblen to campus to speak, and in 1920, he launched a subversive version of extension, with Amherst-sponsored "worker's classes" that featured readings from Marx and Lenin.[97] In other ways, though, he resembled the academic engineers. Nelson calls his administrative style "dictatorial" (journalists compared him to Woodrow Wilson), he fetishized European higher education, and Flexner admired his commitment to intellectual purity. Whatever Meiklejohn was, the Amherst trustees grew tired of it. In 1923 they fired him, over angry student protests.[98] After turning down an offer to join the leadership of the New School, he ended up in Madison in 1925 with the chance to start an innovative liberal arts program within a research university.

The year 1925 also marked the Wisconsin regents' ban on accepting gifts from "incorporated educational endowments" and the university's inauguration of Glenn Frank, a progressive journalist with no administrative experience, as its new president.[99] Thus, the Experimental College was born in a spirit of defiance against the waning influence of the academic engineers. Frank gave Meiklejohn free rein for his program. The design that launched in 1927 featured a single mandatory curriculum that somehow combined ancient Greek philosophy with the study of American social problems. The college was housed in a brand-new building on the periphery of the university, and its all-male students (many of whom were gay, Jewish, or other minoritized identities) were famously aloof from their peers on the main campus.[100] The experiment ended in 1932, when the university shut it down amid dwindling enrollment numbers, but its very existence showed that radical innovations from the liberal arts world might have lasting currency in the nation's great universities. A far more durable effort began at the University of Texas in 1935, with the launch of the still-extant Plan II baccalaureate program. Its founding director described it as a rebuttal to the typical practice of "putting the competent man through a mill," instead aiming "to fill in and round out the culture of the individual student."[101]

Experimentation could also revive liberal arts colleges that were on the ropes, or even create new ones. Since 1925, Meiklejohn had served as a consultant to St. John's College in Maryland, an ancient (1784) institution that faced declining endowment and enrollment and then finally lost its accreditation in 1936. It promptly relaunched itself completely, with a mandatory curriculum that was radicalism masquerading as conservatism: a Great Books program that began with the Greeks, whom Meiklejohn revered, and reached modern texts only in a student's senior year.[102] In the previous decade, the journalist Hamilton Holt took over and reorganized tiny Rollins College in Florida as a school based on "human contact between teacher and student." Holt's Conference Plan banned lectures and exams, replacing them with casual seminars. Like Meiklejohn, however, Holt proved to be an autocratic leader and ran afoul of the AAUP in 1933 for firing professors without due process.[103] Faculty and student exiles from Rollins continued the trend, though, heading to North Carolina to found Black Mountain College that same year. Black Mountain had two key ideals: truly democratic governance (it had no president, no deans, and no trustees) and a belief that the creative arts should hold the same academic status as the sciences or humanities.[104]

That latter value was also a founding principle of all-women's Bennington College, which opened in 1932.[105] Its founding Sponsors' Committee included middle path purveyors like Samuel Capen, Anson Phelps Stokes, and John H. Finley, the former president of City College who left the higher education sector to become a journalist.[106] "The Bennington Idea" put students at the center of the college, basing the curriculum on "teach[ing] individuals, recognizing their wholeness, their diversity, and complexity."[107] Rudolph notes that Bennington embraced the academic engineers' old foe, the extracurriculum: "making work and play . . . one undifferentiated experience."[108] And yet, Bennington was supported at its start with a large grant from the GEB.

New combinations of work, play, and learning took on even more importance at Antioch College in Ohio. In 1920, the school inaugurated a new president, Arthur Morgan, who was a civil engineer (his expertise was in flood control, and in 1933 he left Antioch to run FDR's Tennessee Valley Authority). Morgan instituted a radical new curriculum that instantiated the new consensus; every student had to undertake a "co-operative" placement in a work site (typically in nearby Dayton) to gain on-the-job experience while still enrolled in the college's liberal arts courses.[109] In many ways, Morgan was the academic engineers' ideal: an actual engineer, an outsider (he lacked even a bachelor's degree), and a proponent of practical, vocationally oriented education. But when he reached out to reformers like Flexner, Pritchett, and Angell, they ignored him, and the GEB declined his requests for grants.[110]

The problem was that Morgan was trying to introduce practicality while retaining the baccalaureate college model. As Stephen Herr has shown, Antioch's new program was directly influenced by Tuskegee and Berea, those darlings of Northern philanthropists, and the nearby University of Cincinnati, which had inaugurated a co-operative program of its own in 1907.[111] But those forebears were very different. Tuskegee and Berea based their versions of industrial education on the premise that they were offering "uplift" to "backward" racial and ethnic groups. Furthermore, their version of industry was plainly blue-collar, whereas Morgan bragged that "Antioch will train primarily for proprietorship and management, not for subordinate employment."[112] Cincinnati, meanwhile, had restricted its co-operative curriculum to engineering students, who were already immersed in practicality. Antioch, by contrast, was an all-white, middle-class baccalaureate college with a traditional residential campus that was mandating pseudo-apprenticeships for all students, even the ones studying the arts and humanities. This was a bridge too far for the academic engineers. But, it turned out, it was exactly the type of bridge between the liberal and the practical that defined the new consensus.

Antioch quickly became famous, spreading the co-operative idea around the country; at least 137 colleges were employing some version of it by the end of the '20s.[113] The idea was completely radical in 1920: that students might earn credit toward a bachelor's degree by doing work in a manufacturing plant or in a business office. But while the full co-op model is rare today, there is absolutely nothing radical about its underlying notion anymore.[114] We simply call it an internship.

Once the academic engineers were no longer leading them, the foundations eventually came around to the idea that small colleges could be centers of innovation. The GEB finally contributed to Antioch in 1933 and spent much of its diminishing higher education appropriations supporting other small schools. (The foundation also made large gifts to Bennington, Minnesota's General College, and even Stephens College, the influential junior college that had rebranded itself as an experimental baccalaureate institution.[115]) At the CFAT, Walter Jessup fully embraced the small colleges' role in innovation. He explained in a 1934 speech that they were leading the way in vanquishing the evils of standardization: "Indeed, were a catalogue made of present experiments in higher education, it would be apparent that the colleges are among the liveliest spots in the whole educational field. The desire to break down the mechanical standards of education that have been assumed to be essential is seen in all of these experimental projects."[116] The next year, a deputy excitedly wrote to him from California, praising the spirit of innovation he had seen at Redlands, Scripps, Pomona, and Mills, all of which "really amazed me with their readiness to consider serious changes of the most revolutionary sort." This was in stark contrast to what he had found in Berkeley: "So far as I can see the U. of C. is simply standing pat and doing nothing actually to solve the real puzzle. . . . [They] consider themselves helpless in the grip of the general credit machine."[117]

Praising small colleges for their autonomy and novelty while lambasting an elite research university for acting like a machine: again, this was not Henry Pritchett's CFAT. And Jessup went even further in a 1936 speech, by invoking the gospel of Matthew's "mint and anise" critique of "hypocrites" who follow the letter of the law but neglect justice and mercy. The small colleges, he went on, were the ones who had successfully defied the academic engineers' efforts to impose conformity. "To carry the biblical analogy somewhat further, most of us like to think of the liberal arts college as the Keeper of the Ark of the Covenant."[118]

A NEW ETHOS: UPLIFT

The fact that by the mid-'30s, foundation leaders thought that big universities had something to learn from small colleges indicated that the academic engineers' status hierarchy had not held. The reformers certainly never contemplated that colleges like Middlebury, Wesleyan, and Swarthmore would remain more prestigious—more *elite*—than their respective states' flagship public universities.

But institutions once intended for the bottom of the pecking order had something else to contribute to the 1936 consensus besides innovative ideas and a challenge to an engineered system. The small colleges and, perhaps even more so, institutions designed for marginalized students contributed a new ethos to replace the academic engineers' fixation on efficiency.

Like the internship-for-credit idea, the new ethos was radical in the '30s but is mundane today. Simply put, it said that college education could significantly elevate a student's place in society. That elevation partially came from the fact that by 1920, the college graduate was widely understood to have an advantage in the labor market, which had not been the case a generation prior.[119] But the idea of "uplift"—the heart of the new ethos— had meaning beyond employment prospects.

Uplift harkened back to a conception of the world in which religious salvation, earned through piety, could elevate human beings to a higher plateau: the "amazing grace" that saved the "wretch" in a famous 1779 hymn. That type of human progress was nowhere in the brutal logic of social Darwinism, which underlaid the plans of the academic engineers. To them, talent and potential were innate; while they could be nurtured, it was ultimately survival of the fittest that would sort out the worthy from the mediocre masses. And from there stemmed their vision of a strati-fied educational system: a handful of celestial institutions that featured pure academics and research, twinkling above a vast base of second-class schools that offered earthly training to earthy students. Could a wretched student climb up from the bottom, as the junior college idea promised? Yes, in theory, but not if he was *actually* a wretch. He had to be exceptional, in every sense of the word, in order to secure one of the limited spots at the top. He had to *climb*. Uplift was not on offer.

The new ethos resurrected the idea that a true wretch might be saved. Not through church. Through college.

The small colleges, so many of which had religious origins, were a ma-jor source of this idea. Earle Ross, a historian of the old guard, sneered in 1942 about the "vague and ill-directed desire for uplift and betterment" that permeated the nineteenth-century college and blamed Christian de-nominations for promising "supposed material advantage and 'cultural' uplift," resulting in a proliferation of small colleges that "tended invariably to lower standards and to foster ruinous competition."[120] Ross, of course, was echoing the academic engineers and trying to extol what he imagined to be the virtues of the "practical" land-grant university.

Ross was wrong in many ways, as Sorber and others have pointed out, including for not realizing that the land grants were hardly exemplars of practicality. He also totally missed the consensus that had built in the prior two decades. Contrast his dismissal with a 1925 speech by the presi-dent of Rutgers: "A truly cultural education is practical. On the other hand, an education which may be described as thoroughly practical is also cul-tural; that is, it promotes growth and development."[121] And Ross also didn't realize how much the small college's innovatively repackaged offer of sal-vation had filtered up into the university itself. In the early '30s, the leader of St. Stephen's College advertised his school as an "experimental station" that would "help find out how to take the typical product of our secondary schools and transform him into a man reasonably prepared for intellectual activity and for happiness and for usefulness in living."[122] St. Stephens was not a random small college; in 1928, it had become a division of Columbia.

But student "growth and development" had never been the exclusive franchise of the liberal arts colleges. It also came from the nontraditional schools that I described in chapters four and five. The most obvious among them were the land-grant colleges (of which Rutgers was one). Unlike either research universities or liberal arts colleges, the land grants were created specifically for "the liberal and practical education of the industrial classes." This founding mission became especially important when states applied their land-grant funds to their flagship research universities—as at California, Wisconsin, and others—to the delight of the reformers, who abhorred duplication. Thus, the dogma of the efficiency ethos allowed the uplift ethos to quietly infiltrate the top of the pyramid.

The most potent fonts of uplift were not the land grants, though. Instead, they were the institutions that served racially or culturally distinct populations. Tuskegee and Berea introduced the idea that higher education could lift up not just individuals but entire groups of "benighted" people. Booker T. Washington's book-length advertisement for Tuskegee (masquerading as autobiography) had the idea right in its title: *Up from Slavery*. The education Washington got at Hampton and was now giving others in Alabama had the power to raise young people out of their marginal lives and elevate them into respectable, if second-class, citizens— therefore lifting up the entire Black community. At Spelman Seminary, closely associated with the Rockefellers, an administrator specifically applied the ethos to the higher education of Black women, who would be "a new and uplifting force, to supply the public schools with competent teachers, and to enrich the whole life of the Negro race, industrial, social, religious, political, with higher ideals, improved methods and trained and qualified leaders."[123]

Crucially, prior to 1920 these types of institutions did not encroach on the ivory tower portion of higher education, for two reasons: first because they served clearly "othered" people (i.e., Black, indigenous, and "mountaineer"), and second because their programs were primarily sub-baccalaureate. Thus, they were safe schools for the academic engineers to back. Furthermore, they could openly aspire to rapid growth, as Berea did in a 1909 fundraising appeal: *"our success depends upon reaching a large number of young people,* so as to extend our influence as widely as possible without delay."[124] A traditional baccalaureate college could certainly make no such proposal without getting smacked down.

Uplift through higher education was such a powerful concept that some people thought it could go beyond elevating individuals and demographic groups into entire regions or nations. Berea touted itself as a proponent of "mountain uplift": bringing Appalachia up to modern societal standards while maintaining its unique identity.[125] Some saw the entire South as a region in need of this type of help; a 1909 brochure for the three hundred–student Trinity College (which later became Duke) brochure praised the school's potential: "no institution in the South of this kind is better equipped for the moral and intellectual uplift of our people."[126] The idea could even be extended to the entire nation of China, where a group of Yale alumni including Anson Phelps Stokes opened an American-style baccalaureate institution called Yali College in 1914. They believed that the school would offer "moral uplift" to students who would, in turn, enter public service and make China a modern democracy.[127]

So, in some ways, the uplift ethos meant that college was not just for privileged white people anymore. Or, more specifically, not just for white men anymore, since by the '20s the rapid development of normal schools into full-fledged colleges was opening new opportunities to hundreds of thousands of women. However, the most telling application of the uplift ethos happened when the concept developed at low-status schools migrated to the most elite ones of all.

Between 1928 and 1930, Harvard and Yale received a combined $25 million in donations to build a series of "houses" that would provide living and social spaces for the universities' undergraduates, many of whom had been living off campus, either in cheap apartments or in fancy clubhouses that resembled fraternities. All of the money came from one man: Edward Harkness, who sat on the boards of eight different railroads and was the scion of a family made fabulously wealthy by early investments in John Rockefeller's business empire.[128] Two decades prior, a Rockefeller-connected industrial philanthropist presumably would have directed his higher education money to a cause much more aligned with academic engineering, perhaps one that sought to "fix" or eliminate small colleges. But in 1928, Harkness saw tremendous value in those schools; as the *Boston Globe* reported, "Mr. Harkness believes it is desirable to break the larger college up into smaller social units so that a university like Harvard may combine the advantages of both the large and small institution."[129]

Samuel Morison reports that the "house" idea originated in both a general push to "decentralize Harvard" and a 1926 proposal to create a Swarthmore-like "experimental house for honors students." The university applied for a GEB grant to fund it and got denied, but Harkness supplied the necessary funds two years later—and extended it to the entire undergraduate body. Surprisingly, many students hated the idea, from across the status spectrum. The establishment-linked Harvard *Crimson* denounced it because "clubmen did not like being herded with the majority."[130] Meanwhile, a radical Yale publication run by disaffected students who wanted academic purity offered the opposite take, slamming the houses as antithetical to the intellectual spirit of the university by "pandering to the unfit and immature."[131]

And there, in that mutual disgust from both patricians and iconoclasts, was the proof that the new ethos and the new consensus had made it to the top of the higher education pyramid. The sides would have to meet in the middle. Although Harvard and Yale remained exclusive for generations (the former was still being run by the academic engineer A. Lawrence Lowell, a notorious anti-Semite and racist who banned Black students from the new houses), their campuses now had physical manifestations of the idea that college was a place where all kinds of students—even the "unfit"— could benefit and grow. And the definition of "unfit" took at least two forms: low-income students who had previously been excluded from the social life of college and unintellectual students who were showing up at college precisely *for* that social life. They might grumble about each other, but both would now live under the same roof, in the same "college within a college."[132]

And once it was at the top of the pyramid, the uplift ethos was everywhere. Throughout the '30s, the ACE conducted studies of the rapidly growing "student personnel" field, meaning higher education professionals who worked directly with undergraduates but were not academic instructors. This work culminated in a 1937 ACE conference, presided over by George Zook, and a subsequent report that is considered the foundational text of student development theory.[133] The report introduced the concept of "the whole student" and argued that it was higher education's duty "to assist the student in developing to the limits of his potentialities." The authors also pointed out that the concept was not a new one but rather one that had been the center of the nineteenth-century college before being trampled during the heyday of academic engineering: in the good old days, they wrote, "interest in the whole student dominated the thinking of the great majority of the leaders and faculty members of American colleges."[134] Nor was the connection vague between the new "student personnel" profession and the old religious order; David Levine argues that before 1920, campus branches of the YMCA (then an explicitly Christian organization) "served as the de facto student affairs office at most universities."[135]

"Student development" was an updated, more objective version of uplift. As such, it was not confined to schools that offered moral enlightenment or proposed to transform marginalized communities. It was for every student at every college, from Tuskegee to Swarthmore to Yale. And, reflexively, the fact that by 1937 the ACE and so many others embraced it as the primary objective of higher education meant that anyone could be a college student, because anyone could benefit from student development.

This radical conclusion set the stage for the position of American colleges and universities in the mid-twentieth century. That period, widely known as the "golden age" of higher education, was bookended by two events. Each would have been unthinkable to the academic engineers. In 1944, the US Congress passed the GI Bill, designed to "readjust" returning veterans, isolated and shocked by war, to American society. It did so by *sending them to college*. And then, twenty-one years later, the Congress passed the Higher Education Act, which committed the federal government to making college affordable for all Americans. When Lyndon Johnson signed the bill (at his alma mater, a normal school that became a university), he described college not as a gathering place for the gifted, or a hub of knowledge production, or any sort of problem to be solved. It was, instead, a solution to poverty, a bulwark of freedom, and, for individual Americans, not a destination but the journey itself: "the path to achievement and fulfillment."[136]

Fifty years before Johnson's speech, at the end of the crucible of reform, John Finley had already set the stage for the new consensus and the golden age. Finley, the recently appointed president of the University of the State of New York, defined "the ideal college" as a place in which practical and cultural pedagogies are fused in order to lead young people "into the race mind," by which he meant the knowledge and ideals of the human race. The college student, he wrote, should go "out into the bush as the Australian youth with the sage of his tribe," and also to struggle personally like the wretches in Dante's purgatory: "They are not simply doing things, pursuing purgatorial and infernal vocations; they are working out their soul's salvation." This was the uplifting education that would be broadly offered under the new consensus. The academic engineers were right about the potential societal benefits of higher education, but they were dead wrong about limiting its privileges. Finley continued: if the college "is to continue to be *for the many* what it has been, thank God, *for the few*, if it is to be *for all the fit*, a place of understanding, of rebirth, of entering the race mind, then is our American college to be the ideal college."[137]

CONCLUSION

Four Legacies

Academic engineering is the ghost in the machine of the American higher education system. It is, after all, the reason that we even speak of such a "system."

The reformers left behind four enduring legacies. Three of them I have covered extensively in this book and will only briefly reiterate here: the logic of reform, infrastructural developments, and the counter-reform toolbox that emerged from the reaction to academic engineering. The fourth is more speculative, stemming from the new consensus of the 1930s: the uniquely American phenomenon of covert status hierarchy.

The enduring logic of reform begins with the academic engineers' fundamental premise that higher education is a problem to be solved. They saw potential in the sector, but that was a secondary observation. Primarily, they saw waste, inefficiency, and a vague "demoralization" in American colleges and universities. There were too many institutions, and they were mostly acting in their own parochial interests rather than for the greater social good. Lousy colleges were giving lousy degrees to lousy students. And none of them were working together in a rational, coordinated system. American higher education, they insisted, had to get its act together.

Some of the academic engineers' specific complaints are impolitic today. It is rare (though not impossible) to find a critic who demands that fewer students go to college. But we are certainly familiar with the get-your-act-together refrain directed at institutions. Importantly, the logic of reform extends to all parts of the ideological spectrum. Take the bedrock principle of efficiency. Conservatives want higher education to get its costs under control to save taxpayer dollars; progressives want the same thing to reduce student debt. Both camps identify administrative "bloat" as a key vice—that's new, but the efficiency ethos is not. Or, take high-level curricular questions. Business leaders are annoyed by the endurance of liberal arts programs that don't sound like jobs; the creative class is inversely worried that colleges are churning out vocation-focused automatons. In both cases, fault lies with the schools (not with students, or communities, or the labor market), and those schools are ordered to change.

The narrative that higher education is the problem has not always been the dominant one. During the three decades following 1936, especially during the purported "golden age" that followed World War II, policymakers and other elites largely saw college as a solution to social problems. The 1944 GI Bill proposed college as a "readjustment" for millions of dissociated veterans, and the 1965 Higher Education Act proposed it as a remedy for socioeconomic inequality. In between, the 1947 Truman Commission (chaired by George Zook) reported that higher education was the way to preserve and spread democracy itself. These years in which college was the solution were accompanied by generous government and foundation support. But by the 1970s they were over, giving way to an ongoing "accountability era" in which the academic engineers' doctrines of efficiency and utility came roaring back. That is the world we live in today.

The reformers also left an infrastructural legacy. When Fred Gates borrowed the word "system" from engineering and called it "the pivot of the whole conception," he wasn't just doing a thought experiment. Although American higher education is much more loosely coupled and dynamic than the reformers envisioned—it is a "complex adaptive system"[1]—it is a system nonetheless, and we can credit the academic engineers for its formation.[2]

One aspect of building systemic infrastructure was the creation of new institutions—most notably junior colleges, which as today's community colleges now actively enroll over 40 percent of all American undergraduates (a statistic that does not count students at four-year institutions who previously transferred from community colleges) and are geographically dispersed so that the vast majority of Americans live within close proximity to at least one.[3] At the other end of the spectrum, the academic engineers also created the flagship public university. They didn't actually launch schools like Michigan, Indiana, or Berkeley, but they enshrined them as alpha institutions that maintained their status even when Michigan State, Purdue, and UCLA became elite research universities; elsewhere, they made sure that schools like Ohio State and the University of Florida were recognized as alpha institutions even above older public universities within their states. One academic engineer in 1906 anticipated the expansionary phase of American higher education by calling for "a continued growth at the top and a lopping off at the bottom" for the flagship university, with the vast majority of undergraduate students "scattered over the state at fifty other institutions."[4]

This type of arrangement—an elite flagship and dispersed broad-access schools—became the hallmark of the hierarchical public systems that the reformers promoted within each state. Today, these state systems are much more tightly coupled than the national system. The textbook case is California, which in 1960 established its "Master Plan" that enshrined three distinct tiers of higher education. The plan assigned each tier its own legislatively ordered mission, degree offerings, governance structure, and admissions quotas. Predictably, the system was a pyramid, with the broadest, lowest tier consisting of community colleges that were ordered to educate two-thirds of the state's undergraduates and legally forbidden from offering the bachelor's degree. For the most part the Master Plan codified existing practice and was largely equivalent to what Benjamin Wheeler and other academic engineers tried to instate in the 1910s (with the main difference being that the top-tier University of California now had multiple campuses). The plan also established a statutory "coordinating council" that was exactly the same as the state boards that the academic engineers had championed in places like Iowa.

The academic engineers also left an infrastructural legacy through their efforts to delegitimize private baccalaureate colleges. The institutions that we now call liberal arts colleges still exist, of course, and in the midcentury they were recognized as important experiment stations, especially for practices related to student development. Although some are prestigious today, they educate a very small percentage of students and are certainly no longer the center of American higher education, as they were in the nineteenth century. They now find themselves trading on "distinctiveness" to maintain their enrollments and endowments.[5] The small colleges did not simply fade from the scene; the academic engineers knocked them out of it.

But even with a diminished role, they did survive, and the strategies they developed to do so became part of the counter-reform toolbox that is the academic engineers' third legacy. The toolbox also emerged from the efforts of technical schools, normal schools, and historically Black schools to become full-fledged colleges in defiance of the reformers' designs. Some of the strategies were rhetorical: touting the cherished American tradition of local control, wielding the interstitial powers of the press and the pulpit, and expanding the notion of academic freedom to include institutional autonomy. Others were associational; the inter-institution groups that formed around after 1915 gave marginalized colleges a forum for pushing back on the big foundations and for advancing ideas and innovations that could counter top-down reform. Most of these still exist, including the regional accreditation bodies that emblemize the loose coupling of the national higher education system. The most successful parts of the toolbox are not outright refusals of reform but rather more subtle approaches that *assimilate* reform and tame it. The accreditation bodies style themselves as accountability agencies, after all. The best weapon against regulation is self-regulation.

The heart of the counter-reform toolbox is not a strategy but an idea: the uplift ethos. Academic engineering focused on restricting ambition. The reformers tried to restrict the ambitions of institutions, which inevitably restricted the ambitions of students. Touting the uplift ethos—the idea that going to college can improve human beings—allows institutions to flip the script. If college can foster social mobility and democratic citizenship, then who can argue for restricting college access? And, therefore, who can argue for placing limits on institutions that want to grow, offer more degrees, and reach for higher rungs on the status ladder?

That status ladder is central to the final legacy of the academic engineers: the college-based American status hierarchy. Like the new consensus, it emerged dialectically out of the struggle between the reformers and their many detractors.

College-going in the nineteenth century was binary. You either went to college or you didn't. Yes, some institutions were older and more famous than others, but there wasn't much that a Columbia education afforded a nineteenth-century student that he couldn't have obtained at NYU or at City College. (Social capital was one thing, but it was not legible to the planners who intended to organize society.) Institutional privilege was also binary. Because of the tradition of corporate autonomy that went back to the 1819 Dartmouth College Decision, any school with an easily obtained state charter could offer everything that Harvard did.

The academic engineers hated these situations. They hated that any student—even one without a high school diploma—could show up at Gale College in Galesville, Wisconsin, and claim a PhD. The reformers wanted a socially efficient society in which labor was rationally divided (along with the status and prerogatives that followed various forms of labor), and they believed that the higher education sector could help create that society. But not under the laissez-faire model.

This is what undergirded their drive to differentiate institutions. It was a reflection of their interest in formally differentiating American social roles. And because those roles were inevitably going to be stratified, so were postsecondary institutions. Hence, the academic engineers' hoped-for institutional pyramid. At its tapered peak would be a handful of research universities in optimal locations. Its broad base would consist of junior colleges, distributed far more liberally, and "practical" sub-baccalaureate schools that focused on vocational training, including normal schools. Below the base would be a well-buried foundation of high schools.

The wrinkle the reformers never fully ironed out lay in the middle of their intended system. There, they placed a motley group of institutions: land-grant schools, teachers colleges, superior technical institutes, and the small percentage of liberal arts colleges (including Black and women's colleges) that weren't slated for demotion or disappearance. Even at the height of the crucible of reform, it was clear that these schools would become or remain as real colleges. Despite their love of restrictions, the academic engineers knew they had to stop restricting at some point. In some cases, their hesitation was personal: was Henry Pritchett really going to block MIT from becoming a university (or, for that matter, Carnegie Tech)? In other cases, hesitation came when one reformist value clashed against another: was the geography-obsessed Fred Gates really going to join Benjamin Wheeler in trying to block a normal school from becoming a university in Los Angeles, one of the nation's fastest-growing cities? And in yet others, the hesitation was out of a sense of equity: was John D. Rockefeller Jr. really going to countenance Thomas Jesse Jones's plan to deny the right to issue the bachelor's degree to all but five Black colleges?

Of course, it's not just that the reformers blinked. There was also a limit to their power. They had money and a mandate, but ultimately they could only coerce and cajole, not dictate. That was especially true for the institutions that they had designated as losers. Those colleges, told to retreat or die, had nothing to lose from defying the academic engineers.

When resistance came, it did not claim a democratic or egalitarian mantle. Its claim was autonomy, either of the little guy against the big guy (why should a wealthy New York foundation, accountable to no one, tell Gale College what to do?) or of local control (why should that foundation tell the state of Ohio how to run its public colleges?). The resistance did not emphasize the fact that allowing colleges to survive and grow would create opportunities for countless students. It simply rejected the idea of a formal hierarchy imposed by New York or Washington.

As the dream of formal stratification died, another type of hierarchy was developing without drawing loud complaints. This one was semiformal, based on membership in certain clubs. Predictably, it began at the top, with the formation of the AAU. The club of research universities allowed a separation of the truly elite from the merely prestigious. Amherst College, distinguished though it was, could not join the AAU. But a club with a somewhat less restricted membership turned out to be the best instance of this phenomenon: the CFAT accepted list. The list was conceived as an instrument of reform; colleges that complied with the foundation's standards could receive the blessing of free pensions for its professors. But very quickly, it turned out that the pension program wasn't the real blessing—merely appearing on the list was. After all, even after it spun off TIAA and stopped issuing pensions, the CFAT kept publishing lists, and colleges kept clamoring to get on them. To be on the accepted list was to join a very privileged club.

The colleges also formed their own clubs. The AAC, the AATC, the ACNY, and their peer associations were protective, but they were also places for colleges to find their identity. In the process of joining together and collectively advocating for themselves, they also formulated shared senses of mission and identity. Today, we instantly understand what it means to call a school an HBCU, or a land-grant institution, or a liberal arts college—but those identities were constructed, largely through the associations.

That said, to lean on Orwell once more, while all associations were created equal, some were more equal than others. Everyone who understood the higher landscape knew that it was better to be in the AAU than the AAC and that it was better to be a flagship university than a stand-alone land-grant. This undoubtedly fulfilled some of the academic engineers' hopes of an institutional status hierarchy, even if it was only semiformal. And since it wasn't created by edict, the semiformal hierarchy was less of a threat to low-status institutions. Most importantly, it was *fluid*. The low-status schools accepted the ladder with the understanding that they could climb it. And while it's rare, it happens: today's AAU includes a former small denominational college (Duke, which joined in 1938), a former normal school (UCLA, 1974), and a former sub-baccalaureate tech school (Carnegie Mellon, 1982), plus five non-flagship land-grant institutions.

Inevitably, the sorting out of institutions led to the sorting out of students. David Levine shows how the uplift message of the new consensus (which he calls the "culture of aspiration") attracted huge numbers of new college students in the '20s and '30s. But at the same time, he argues, an anti-meritocratic sorting led the new entrants into low-status colleges: "ethnic and poor students often surpassed their more affluent peers in academic ability and drive, but more often than not they were channeled into less acclaimed schools." Meanwhile, elite institutions developed baroque admissions processes that served to "preserve the hegemony of the white Anglo-Saxon Protestant upper middle class."[6]

So, a status hierarchy did emerge for both colleges and students. Compared to the pyramids dreamed up by the academic engineers, it engendered little protest. That was because it was opaque to the uninitiated.

Beyond their own failures of execution, there was another reason that the academic engineers' formal stratification never came to be. It was *un-American*. The reformers pined for German-style social engineering, but the United States' traditions of democracy and pluralism meant that it would never come to their side of the Atlantic. Whether from the institutional standpoint (the Dartmouth College decision was settled case law) or from the individual (this was a nation that glorified "self-made men," not least of them Carnegie and Rockefeller), Americans would not tolerate a transparent effort to delimit opportunity.

Therefore, if there was going to be a status hierarchy, it had to be opaque. The academic engineers, at times, acknowledged this. When they championed a new type of postsecondary school that was explicitly designed to divert institutions and students away from the bachelor's degree, they still called it a college. Yes, it was "junior," but the reformers allowed even the supposedly inferior students destined for these second-class schools to claim that they were "going to college." The democracy of nomenclature has only grown (despite the reformers' early gripes about the liberal use of "university") and has only made the status hierarchy more opaque. How is a naive student supposed to differentiate between the University of California, Los Angeles and the California State University, Los Angeles?

Of course, most students aren't naive at all. They know the difference. And for that reason, the status hierarchy has turned out to be not just opaque but *covert*. When I use that term, I don't mean that the informal tiers of higher education are hidden from American students; I mean that they are hidden from the American system of values. The same goes for the hidden tiers of American society itself.

The academic engineers didn't create the elite notion that society should be stratified. That's an old one. But they did create the idea that colleges and universities should be the primary guide to the strata. It's not hard to imagine a different system. What if Carnegie, Rockefeller, and the technocrats they empowered had committed themselves to a status differentiation based on a national testing regime? You could go to Harvard and prep there for the big test, but you still might get beaten by an autodidact and miss out on the best jobs and privileges.

Instead, the reformers chose college. Despite their litany of complaints, they saw the tremendous potential of colleges and universities to covertly sort out social tiers. This was an errand that was distinct from other functions like knowledge production. Research, in fact, was a signifier of elite status, in addition to being an end in itself. So was the presence of graduate schools for esteemed professions, which is why the academic engineers were so hostile to lower-tier institutions that maintained law or medical schools. And that concept allowed them to envision sprawling schools at the top of the pyramid that cut against their first principles. Was it *efficient* to have a university that featured undergraduate education, doctoral training, professional schools, research, and extension services—and also run a publishing press and a museum, accredit a state's high schools, and advise its legislature? Surely not. That wasn't vertical integration in the model of the trusts; it was a leviathan. But maintaining such a university served a different version of efficiency, in which society was best structured when certain institutions, and the people associated with them, were dominant.

The same logic explains why the reformers were so pleased with the sub-baccalaureate "institutes" designed to offer vocational training to the masses. Was it *efficient* to teach carpentry or steamfitting to students in a handsomely endowed school with a college-style campus? Again, surely not. But instead of backing an apprenticeship model that would have made a lot more sense, they saw larger social and political benefits in directing students to institutions that offered a taste of "higher" learning without conferring any real status.

Today, the higher education pyramid still exists. In a conflation that would certainly please the academic engineers, the community college is now the location of most "practical" postsecondary education. It is the ideal institution to populate the base of the pyramid—not least because, as some scholars argue, it serves a diversionary function in "cooling out" students who arrive intending to earn a bachelor's degree but end up in a vocational track.[7] Above them, the middle of the pyramid is populated, ironically, by the very institutions that the academic engineers feared would emerge: the overgrown teachers colleges and denominational schools that we now call "comprehensive" or "regional" universities, both public and private. These schools are the most formally democratic part of the covert status hierarchy: broad-access institutions that award degrees that are legally identical to those of the elite universities at the top of the pyramid, even if everyone knows they're not really the same.

The system works because of its opacity and fluidity but also because the "uplift" ethos that emerged by the '30s is still with us. Students, faculty, administrators, and policymakers all agree that college really can transform people. So even though the system is obviously stratified, an ambitious community college student can transfer to a four-year school and then perhaps go to graduate school at an elite university. The fact that most don't do that is immaterial. The system can legitimately offer access and exclusivity at the same time, as long as the route to the top of the pyramid—no matter how steep—is well-lit.

The same prospect of uplift that applies to students also applies to institutions, which were the reformers' focus all along. Not only did it become possible to climb up to the exclusive groups at the top of the hierarchy, low-status colleges and universities can actively better themselves because of their newfound ability to mingle with elite universities. Some of this mingling happens in egalitarian associations like the accreditation bodies or the ACE, and some of it happens on a more personal level, like when low-status institutions hire the graduates of elite doctoral programs as their faculty. With the notable exception of community colleges—which are typically forbidden by state laws from offering the bachelor's degree or sponsoring research—any institution can hang out in the broader club of higher education in the hopes of one day getting invited into one of its private rooms.

This was not the system that the academic engineers set out to create in 1905. But, amazingly, it was a system that nevertheless fulfilled their long-term goals. They envisioned a United States where society was stratified by occupational status, where power would accumulate in New York and Washington, and where the nation's economic, military, and technological sectors, among others, would become the envy of the world. And above all they were sure that higher education would become the flywheel for that process—a process in which American higher education itself would *also* become the envy of the world. Each of those things happened. What they got wrong was that a tightly coupled system, dictated by "experts" in a foundation office, was never going to deliver all of that.

The academic engineers thought that they really were engineers. They tried their damnedest to make that tightly coupled system, and then they dealt with the outrage, resistance, and compromise that followed their failure to do so. But out of their failure emerged a loosely coupled system—rife with ambiguities and inefficiencies—that triumphed beyond anyone's imagination.

ACKNOWLEDGMENTS

I am indebted to a number of scholars who saw promise in me and told me to keep going. The list includes Ellis Turner, Seth Rockman, Tom Gleason, Leah Gordon, Larry Cuban, Woody Powell, Mitchell Stevens, Anthony Antonio, Jon Zimmerman, and Harold Wechsler. At the head of the class is David Labaree, who has been a tremendous mentor, role model, cheerleader, and friend.

Many, many friends contributed support, ideas, feedback, and criticism to this book as it developed. I am especially grateful to Jeremy Jimenez, Eliza Evans, Victoria Rodriguez, Cristina Lash, Matt Kelly, Ethan Hutt, Cristina Groeger, and Cynthia Alcantar. Extra appreciation goes to David Johnson, a world-class colleague and comrade.

This book was made possible by generous research fellowships from the National Endowment for the Humanities and the Stanford Center on Philanthropy and Civil Society. (Any views, findings, conclusions, or recommendations expressed in this book do not necessarily represent those of the National Endowment for the Humanities.) Additional financial support came from many divisions within Stanford University and the University of Nevada, Reno. I benefited from the excellent work of research assistants who gathered documents in collections I was unable to visit, including Christopher Collins at Berea College, Danyelle Valentine at Fisk University, and Edith Powell at Tuskegee University. I am also grateful to a list too long to name of remarkable archivists and librarians across the United States.

I am deeply indebted to the fantastic staff and anonymous reviewers of the University of Chicago Press, especially Mollie McFee and Elizabeth Branch Dyson, who has been the best editor I could possibly imagine.

Finally, I am forever grateful for the love and support of my parents and brother, my brain trust of friends from high school and college, my extended family and fan club, and my children, Max and Del, whose own books I can't wait to read. Above all, I owe everything to my lovely and talented wife, Liana, whose various roles as research assistant, project manager, and editor vastly improved the book, and whose love, patience, and encouragement made it all possible.

———

Portions of chapters 1, 2, and 3 have been previously published in the following peer-reviewed journal articles:

Ris, Ethan W. "The Education of Andrew Carnegie: Strategic Philanthropy in Higher Education, 1880–1919." *Journal of Higher Education* 88, no. 3 (2017): 401–429. Reproduced by permission of Taylor and Francis Group, LLC, a division of Informa plc.

Ris, Ethan W. "The Origins of Systemic Reform in American Higher Education, 1895–1920." *Teachers College Record* 120, no. 10 (2018): 1–42. Reproduced by permission of Teachers College, Columbia University. Original article: https://www.tcrecord.org/content.asp?contentid=22250.

Ris, Ethan W. "The Academic Engineers: Understanding a Cohort of Higher Education Reformers." *Perspectives on the History of Higher Education* 33, no. 1 (2020): 18–48. Reproduced by permission of Taylor and Francis Group, LLC, a division of Informa plc.

APPENDIX

A Partial List of the Academic Engineers

† *Formal Affiliation with the Carnegie Foundation for the Advancement of Teaching*

* *Formal Affiliation with the General Education Board*

Elisha Benjamin Andrews*
James Rowland Angell†
Trevor Arnett*
William H. Baldwin, Jr.*
Kendric Babcock
John G. Bowman†
Elmer Brown
William Lowe Bryan†
Nicholas Murray Butler†
Wallace Buttrick†
Edwin B. Craighead†
William Henry Crawford†
Abraham Flexner†*
William Trufant Foster
Hollis Frissell*
William Goodell Frost
Clyde Furst†
Frederick Gates*
Arthur Twining Hadley†
William Rainey Harper†*
William Torrey Harris
Abram Hewitt
Ernest O. Holland
Alexander Humphreys†
Edmund J. James
Morris K. Jesup*
Thomas Jesse Jones*

David Starr Jordan†
Henry Churchill King†
James Kirkland†
Alexis Lange
A. Lawrence Lowell†
Samuel Black McCormick†
Fayette McKenzie
Robert C. Ogden*
George Foster Peabody*
Henry S. Pritchett†
Louis Reber
Rush Rhees†
L. Clark Seelye†
Edward O. Sisson
Edgar Fahs Smith†
William F. Slocum†
Henry Suzzallo†
M. Carey Thomas
Charles F. Thwing†
Charles Van Hise†
Frank Vanderlip†
George E. Vincent*
Booker T. Washington
Benjamin Wheeler
Ray Lyman Wilbur
Woodrow Wilson†

NOTES

INTRODUCTION

1. W. Richard Scott, "Unpacking Institutional Arguments," in *The New Institutionalism in Organizational Analysis*, ed. Paul J. DiMaggio and Walter W. Powell (Chicago: University of Chicago Press, 1991), 164–82.

2. Much scholarship explores the Gilded Age, its key personalities, and its implications. For arguments that it was a fundamentally transformational period in American history, see the essays in Charles W. Calhoun, ed., *The Gilded Age: Perspectives on the Origins of Modern America* (Lanham, MD: Rowman & Littlefield, 2007); and Leon Fink, *The Long Gilded Age: American Capitalism and the Lessons of a New World Order* (Philadelphia: University of Pennsylvania Press, 2015).

3. For more on the impact of engineering on American ideas, see David F. Noble, *America by Design: Science, Technology, and the Rise of Corporate Capitalism* (New York: Oxford University Press, 1979). The classic text on the impact of social Darwinism on American ideas is Richard Hofstadter, *Social Darwinism in American Thought, 1860–1915* (Philadelphia: University of Pennsylvania Press, 1944).

4. Michael D. Cohen, James G. March, and Johan P. Olsen, "A Garbage Can Model of Organizational Choice," *Administrative Science Quarterly* 17, 1 (1972): 1–25. Much of this famous article concerns the application of the authors' proposed model to colleges and universities, including the "small, poor colleges" that were a primary focus of the academic engineers' reform efforts.

5. For the nineteenth-century success of the high school, see William J. Reese, *The Origins of the American High School* (New Haven, CT: Yale University Press, 1995).

6. I have previously described this group in two articles that inform the first three chapters of this book: Ethan W. Ris, "The Origins of Systemic Reform in American Higher Education, 1895–1920," *Teachers College Record* 120, 10 (2018): 1–42; Ethan W. Ris, "The Academic Engineers: Understanding a Cohort of Higher Education Reformers," *Perspectives on the History of Higher Education* 33, 1 (2020): 18–48.

7. Laurence R. Veysey, *The Emergence of the American University* (University of Chicago Press, 1965); Roger L. Geiger, *To Advance Knowledge: The Growth of American Research Universities, 1900–1940* (New York: Oxford University Press, 1986); Julie R. Reuben, *The Making of the Modern University: Intellectual Transformation and the Marginalization of Morality* (Chicago: University of Chicago Press, 1996).

8. John R. Thelin, *A History of American Higher Education, Third Edition* (Baltimore, MD: Johns Hopkins University Press, 2019), 234.

9. P. A. Hutcheson, "Reconsidering the Community College," *History of Education Quarterly* 39, 3 (1999): 320.

10. The closest analogue to my focus here is David O. Levine, *The American College and the Culture of Aspiration, 1915–1940* (Ithaca, NY: Cornell University Press, 1986).

11. Of course, there is a huge volume of scholarship on these non-elite institutions. But almost all of this scholarship looks at individual schools or groups of similar schools in isolation. As I will argue throughout the book, the academic engineers were at the center of the debates over Black colleges, liberal arts colleges, community colleges, etc.—simultaneously. While the categories are real and important, this book's narrative of reform encompasses them all.

12. John R. Thelin, "Horizontal History and Higher Education," in *The History of U.S. Higher Education: Methods for Understanding the Past*, ed. M. Gasman (New York: Routledge, 2010), 71–83. Thelin describes philanthropic pursuits as an example of horizontal history: "it allowed philanthropists the effective option to pursue broad goals as distinguished from being confined exclusively to building and funding 'vertical' institutions."

13. David O. Levine, *The American College*, 13.

14. Thelin, *History of American Higher Education*, gives the foundations twelve pages of analysis; Roger Geiger gives them ten (R. Geiger, *The History of American Higher Education: Learning and Culture from the Founding to World War II* [Princeton, NJ: Princeton University Press, 2015]); and there are only passing mentions in David Labaree's survey (D. F. Labaree, *A Perfect Mess: The Unlikely Ascendancy of American Higher Education* [Chicago: University of Chicago Press, 2017]). Two generations earlier, Frederick Rudolph acknowledged that "both the Carnegie Foundation and the General Education Board tried to weaken further and kill off the weaker denominational colleges, underestimating the vitality of these institutions" but gave only three pages to the foundations (F. Rudolph, *The American College and University: A History* [Athens, GA: University of Georgia Press, 1962/1990], 431–34). Brubacher and Rudy grossly miscategorize the CFAT's reformist agenda as a "byproduct" of its "main purpose," which was to distribute pensions (J. S. Brubacher and W. R. Rudy, *Higher Education in Transition: A History of American Colleges and Universities* [New Brunswick., NJ: Transaction, 1958/2008], 358).

15. Lee Shulman, president of the CFAT from 1997 to 2008, once told me that whenever he encounters a "house history" of a college or university, he plays a game of checking the book's index to see if the CFAT is there. It always is.

16. Geiger, *To Advance Knowledge*; H. D. Graham and N. Diamond, *The Rise of American Research Universities: Elites and Challengers in the Postwar Era* (Baltimore MD: Johns Hopkins University Press, 1997); L. Cuban, *How Scholars Trumped Teachers: Change without Reform in University Curriculum, Teaching, and Research, 1890–1990* (New York: Teachers College Press, 1999). The one widely recognized "triumph" attributed to the academic engineers was about professional education: the 1910 Flexner Report, sponsored by the CFAT, which spurred dramatic reforms in medical schools and the demise of many institutions.

17. Ellen Condliffe Lagemann, *Private Power for the Public Good. A History of the*

Carnegie Foundation for the Advancement of Teaching (Middletown, CT: Wesleyan University Press, 1983).

18. Clyde W. Barrow, *Universities and the Capitalist State: Corporate Liberalism and the Reconstruction of American Higher Education, 1894–1928* (Madison: University of Wisconsin Press, 1990).

19. This is an inversion of Andrea Walton's astute argument that "philanthropy was the most powerful force in the formative years of the university in the U.S." Walton also argues that "philanthropy's role in higher education remains understudied," pointing to a gap that I hope to help fill with this book (A. Walton, "The History of Philanthropy in Higher Education: A Distinctively Discontinuous Literature," in *Higher Education: Handbook of Theory and Research, Vol. 34* [New York: Springer International, 2019], 479.) Other "foundations" existed prior to the GEB's 1902 establishment, but they lacked the full-time staff and permanent endowments that defined 20th-century foundations.

20. Olivier Zunz gives due credit to these foundational foundations in his survey of American philanthropy but moves quickly past them (O. Zunz, *Philanthropy in America: A History* [Princeton, NJ: Princeton University Press, 2014]).

21. Joan Malczewski has demonstrated the role of philanthropic foundations as agents of reform in K–12 schooling in the South (J. Malczewski, *Building a New Educational State: Foundations, Schools, and the American South* [Chicago: University of Chicago Press, 2016]).

22. For example, A. Giridharadas, *Winners Take All: The Elite Charade of Changing the World* (New York: Vintage, 2019); R. Reich, *Just Giving: Why Philanthropy Is Failing Democracy and How It Can Do Better* (Princeton, NJ: Princeton University Press, 2018); D. Callahan, *The Givers: Wealth, Power, and Philanthropy in a New Gilded Age* (New York: Vintage, 2017).

23. K. Orren and S. Skowronek, "Institutions and Intercurrence: Theory Building in the Fullness of Time," *Nomos* 38 (1996): 111–46.

24. Mitchell L. Stevens and B. Gebre-Medhin, "Association, Service, Market: Higher Education in American Political Development," *Annual Review of Sociology* 42 (2016): 121–42.

25. James Axtell, ed., *The Educational Legacy of Woodrow Wilson: From College to Nation* (Charlottesville, VA: University of Virginia Press, 2012).

26. Tracy L. Steffes, *School, Society, and State: A New Education to Govern Modern America, 1890–1940* (Chicago: University of Chicago Press, 2012).

27. Christopher P. Loss, *Between Citizens and the State: The Politics of American Higher Education in the 20th Century* (Princeton, NJ: Princeton University Press, 2012).

28. J. F. Padgett and C. K. Ansell, "Robust Action and the Rise of the Medici, 1400-1434," *American Journal of Sociology* 98, 6 (1993): 1259–1319.

29. Stevens and Gebre-Medhin, "Association, Service, Market," describe Harvard president Charles Eliot as the quintessential practitioner of robust action in American higher education. The example has merit—he was certainly a member

of the powerful elite—but Eliot always had a public, goal-oriented agenda. Padgett and Arnell's archetype is the sphinxlike Cosimo de Medici; a better analogue for his robust action is the John D. Rockefellers, Senior and Junior, who quietly amassed enormous financial capital, political connections, and patronage powers and brought them to bear on the higher education sector in fluid and often surprising ways.

30. The 350,000 square foot Education and Social Economy building at the World's Fair was directly adjacent to the Germany pavilion. (Pharus, *Pharus-map World's Fair St. Louis* [S.l, 1904] Map, https://www.loc.gov/item/99466762.)

31. R. Zemsky, *Making Reform Work: The Case for Transforming American Higher Education* (New Brunswick, NJ: Rutgers University Press, 2009); K. Carey, *The End of College: Creating the Future of Learning and the University of Everywhere* (New York: Riverhead, 2015); R. Craig, *College Disrupted: The Great Unbundling of Higher Education* (New York: Palgrave Macmillan, 2015); S. Goldrick-Rab, *Paying the Price: College Costs, Financial Aid, and the Betrayal of the American Dream* (Chicago: University of Chicago Press, 2016).

32. Labaree, *A Perfect Mess*; P. G. Altbach, P. J. Gumport, and D. B. Johnstone, *In Defense of American Higher Education* (Baltimore, MD: Johns Hopkins University Press, 2001).

33. F. Zakaria, *In Defense of a Liberal Education* (New York: W.W. Norton & Company, 2015); M. Edmundson, *Why Teach? In Defense of a Real Education* (New York: Bloomsbury USA, 2014).

34. D. Bok, *Universities in the Marketplace: The Commercialization of Higher Education* (Princeton, NJ: Princeton University Press, 2009); D. L. Kirp, *Shakespeare, Einstein, and the Bottom Line: The Marketing of Higher Education* (Cambridge, MA: Harvard University Press, 2009); M. S. Roth, *Beyond the University: Why Liberal Education Matters* (New Haven, CT: Yale University Press, 2014).

CHAPTER 1

1. Upton Sinclair, *The Goose-Step: A Study of American Education* (Pasadena, CA: self-published, 1923), 18. Sinclair borrowed the term "interlocking directorate" from the 1912–1913 federal Pujo Committee investigation into the Wall Street "money trust" of banking executives. The reformers would not have disagreed with the characterization, and they did not view their social relations negatively. One of them joked in 1910 about his recent appointment to the board of an institution whose president sat on his own board: "It seemed to me that if I became one of his trustees, I should be able to retaliate upon him for any disciplinary measures which he might adopt with me. For example, if he should introduce a resolution into the board of trustees of the Carnegie Foundation, cutting down my modest compensation as President, I might retaliate by a similar reduction in the enormous salary which is paid him as President of Stevens Institute" (H. S. Pritchett, "Address of Dr. Pritchett at Stevens Institute Alumni Dinner," *Stevens Institute Indicator*, February 12, 1910, 169).

2. M. E. McGerr, *A Fierce Discontent: The Rise and Fall of the Progressive Movement in America, 1870–1920* (New York: Free Press, 2003).

3. McGerr, *A Fierce Discontent*, xiv.

4. David B. Tyack, *The One Best System: A History of American Urban Education* (Cambridge, MA: Harvard University Press, 1974).

5. Raymond E. Callahan, *Education and the Cult of Efficiency* (Chicago: University of Chicago Press, 1962). For the best description of the "efficiency craze" that emerged from Taylorism, see Samuel Haber, *Efficiency and Uplift: Scientific Management in the Progressive Era* (Chicago: University of Chicago Press, 1965), 51–74.

6. David F. Labaree, *Someone Has to Fail: The Zero-Sum Game of Public Schooling* (Cambridge, MA: Harvard University Press, 2010), 116.

7. Tyack, *The One Best System*, 126–29.

8. This was especially true when it came to the academic engineers who ran elite universities. Columbia's Nicholas Murray Butler, Harvard's Charles Eliot, and Chicago's William Rainey Harper were all leaders in the project to centralize and modernize urban school systems. The presidents of the University of Illinois, the University of Iowa, and Brown University all served terms as superintendents of major city systems during this era, and many other college and university presidents sat on school boards. (Tyack, *The One Best System*, 127.)

9. Emily J. Levine, "Baltimore Teaches, Göttingen Learns: Cooperation, Competition, and the Research University," *American Historical Review*, June 2016, 780–823.

10. Sinclair, *The Goose-Step*, 115.

11. W. H. G. Armytage, *A Social History of Engineering* (Cambridge, MA: MIT Press, 1961 [2003]), 168–184.

12. "System" is another word directly borrowed from engineering (A. S. Paul, "Defining 'System'—an Engineering Point of View," *INCOSE International Symposium* 7, 1 (1997): 364–70.

13. James McKeen Cattell, *Carnegie Pensions* (New York: Science Press, 1919), 12–13.

14. A. Flexner, *I Remember: The Autobiography of Abraham Flexner* (New York: Simon and Schuster, 1940), 111.

15. J. Christie, *Morris Llewellyn Cooke: Progressive Engineer* (Taylor & Francis, 1983), 2–3

16. J. White, "Andrew Carnegie and Herbert Spencer: A Special Relationship," *Journal of American Studies* 13, 1 (1979): 57–71.

17. Christie, *Morris Llewellyn Cooke*, 6–11.

18. Henry Pritchett, "Shall Engineering Belong to the Liberal Professions?" in *Inauguration: President Charles Sumner Howe, Case School of Applied Science* (Cleveland: Imperial Press, 1904), 27–32.

19. C. W. Barrow, *Universities and the Capitalist State: Corporate Liberalism and the Reconstruction of American Higher Education, 1894–1928* (Madison: University of Wisconsin Press, 1990), 67.

20. H. S. Pritchett, "Preface," in M. L. Cooke, *Academic and Industrial Efficiency:*

A Report to the Carnegie Foundation for the Advancement of Teaching (Boston: Merrymount, 1910), v.

21. Cooke, *Academic and Industrial Efficiency*, 5.

22. Cooke, 6–7.

23. Cooke, 22–23.

24. C. F. Birdseye, "Analyzing the College Business," *The American College* 1, 1 (1909), 85–102.

25. W. Kent, "Academic Efficiency," in *A Symposium on Scientific Management and Efficiency in College* (Lancaster, PA: New Era, 1913), 147.

26. G. H. Shephard, "Efficiency in Engineering Education" in *A Symposium on Scientific Management and Efficiency in College* (Lancaster, PA: New Era, 1913), 190.

27. H. Münsterberg, *Vocation and Learning, Vol. IV* (St. Louis, MO: Lewis Publishing, 1910), 190.

28. H. S. Pritchett, "Some Tendencies of the College of Technology," speech delivered at Clarkson School of Technology, 1906, Box 11, Henry Smith Pritchett Papers (HSPP), Library of Congress Manuscript Division, Washington, DC.

29. Cooke, *Academic and Industrial Efficiency*, 8.

30. Many historians of philanthropy identify the Peabody Education Fund (established in 1867, thirty-five years before the GEB) as the first foundation. However, it was designed to expire after thirty years, as opposed to the permanent foundations established by Carnegie and Rockefeller and many philanthropists thereafter.

31. These were in addition to the degree-granting institutions endowed with large founding gifts by Rockefeller and Carnegie: respectively, the University of Chicago (1890) and the Carnegie Institutes of Technology (1900; now Carnegie Mellon University).

32. Zunz, *Philanthropy in America.* J. Sealander, *Private Wealth and Public Life: Foundation Philanthropy and the Reshaping of American Social Policy from the Progressive Era to the New Deal* (Baltimore, MD: Johns Hopkins University Press, 1997).

33. Zunz, *Philanthropy in America,* 2.

34. Judith Sealander, "Curing Evils at Their Source: The Arrival of Scientific Giving," in L. J. Friedman and M. D. McGarvie, *Charity, Philanthropy, and Civility in American History* (New York: Cambridge University Press, 2003), 217–39.

35. R. Chernow, *Titan: The Life of John D. Rockefeller* (New York: Random House, 2004), 44–46.

36. Chernow, *Titan,* 556; US Bureau of Labor Statistics, "CPI Inflation Calculator," https://www.bls.gov/data/inflation_calculator.htm, accessed on March 1, 2021.

37. Ida M. Tarbell, *History of the Standard Oil Company, Volume One* (New York: McClure, Phillips, & Co., 1904), 29, 292.

38. Kenneth W. Rose, "Why a University for Chicago and Not Cleveland? Religion and John D. Rockefeller's Early Philanthropy, 1855–1900," *From All Sides: Philanthropy in the Western Reserve* (Cleveland, OH: Case Western Reserve University, 1995), 3.

39. Chernow, *Titan,* 302–03.

40. Chernow, 303-06.

41. Joseph M. Gould, *The Chautauqua Movement: An Episode in the Continuing American Revolution* (Albany, NY: SUNY Press, 1961), 39-54.

42. J. W. Boyer, *The University of Chicago: A History* (Chicago: University of Chicago Press, 2015), 70.

43. Rose, "Why a University for Chicago," 10-12.

44. Chernow, *Titan*, 308.

45. Chernow, 314.

46. Chernow, 328.

47. For more on the shift away from charity, see Sealander, "Curing Evils."

48. M. B. Katz, "Public Education as Welfare," *Dissent* 57, 3 (2010): 52-56.

49. R. B. Fosdick, *Adventure in Giving: The Story of the General Education Board, a Foundation Established by John D. Rockefeller* (New York: Harper & Row, 1962), 6.

50. A historiographical quirk is partly to blame for the misunderstanding. The definitive text on the GEB is Raymond Fosdick's *Adventure in Giving*, an in-house postmortem written two years after the foundation ceased operations. Fosdick devotes only thirteen pages to the GEB's general higher education reform work prior to the '20s, dwelling instead on its impact (both positive and negative) on the education of African Americans. This is understandable for a book published in 1962, just eight years after *Brown v. Board* and in the thick of the civil rights era. Despite his choice of emphasis, Fosdick acknowledges that the foundation's early grants for Southern K-12 education were "small, experimental, and exploratory" and that one might fairly question whether that work "was carried through with the same vigor and thoroughness which characterized its activity in other areas. Larger and more dramatic programs, particularly in the fields of college, university, and medical education seem in retrospect to have cut across the simpler urgencies that attracted the trustees in the beginning" (Fosdick, *Adventure in Giving*, 21, 77). Joan Malczewski has shown that in its early years, the GEB bankrolled K-12-focused projects in the South but left most of the actual work to its subsidiary, the Southern Education Board (J. Malczewski, *Building a New Educational State: Foundations, Schools, and the American South* [Chicago: University of Chicago Press, 2016], 37-39).

51. Gates explicitly spelled this out to his fellow GEB trustees shortly after the gift: "[Rockefeller's] letter holds our aim strictly to the higher education, that is, to colleges and to universities or to schools having similar educational compass and rank. Other people may give us other funds for other objects. This fund is for higher education exclusively" (F. T. Gates, "The Purpose of the Rockefeller Foundation with Suggestions as to the Policy of Administration," 1906, Box 19, Office of the Messrs. Rockefeller Records, Series O [OMRO], Rockefeller Archive Center, Sleepy Hollow, NY).

52. J. F. Wall, *Andrew Carnegie* (New York: Oxford University Press, 1970), 82.

53. Ethan W. Ris, "The Education of Andrew Carnegie: Strategic Philanthropy in American Higher Education, 1880-1919," *Journal of Higher Education* 88, 3 (2017): 401-29.

54. A. Carnegie, *Dedication of the Carnegie Library at the Edgar Thomson Steel Rail Works, Braddocks* [sic]: *Address to the Workmen* (Pittsburgh, PA: n.p., 1889), 20–21.

55. A. Carnegie, *Address to the Students of the Curry Commercial College, Delivered by Andrew Carnegie, June 23d, 1885* (Pittsburgh, PA: n.p., 1885).

56. Wall, *Andrew Carnegie*, 835.

57. Laurence R. Veysey, *The Emergence of the American University* (Chicago: University of Chicago Press, 1965), 14.

58. Ethan W. Ris, "Hierarchy as a Theme in the US College, 1880–1920," *History of Education* 45, 1 (2016): 57–78.

59. P. Mickelson, "American Society and the Public Library in the Thought of Andrew Carnegie," *Journal of Library History* 10, 1 (1975): 117–38.

60. A. A. Van Slyck, *Free to All: Carnegie Libraries & American Culture, 1890–1920* (Chicago: University of Chicago Press, 1995), 13.

61. A. Carnegie, Letter to J.B. Corey, November 18, 1896, Box 39, Andrew Carnegie Papers (ACP), Library of Congress Manuscripts Division, Washington, DC.

62. G. Atherton, Letter to A. Carnegie, October 27, 1895, Box 33, ACP, emphasis original.

63. W. J. Holland, Letter to A. Carnegie, May 2, 1896, Box 37, ACP.

64. W. J. Holland, "A New African Saturnid," *Entomological News* 7 (1896), 133–35.

65. M. Bishop, *A History of Cornell* (Ithaca, NY: Cornell University Press, 1962), 29.

66. A. Carnegie, Letter to Andrew D. White, November 27, 1891, Box 13, ACP.

67. D. Madsen, *The National University: Enduring Dream of the USA* (Detroit: Wayne State University Press, 1966).

68. A. Carnegie, Letter to Andrew D. White, April 26, 1901, Box 82, ACP.

69. A. Carnegie, Letter to Theodore Roosevelt, November 28, 1901, Box 85, ACP.

70. A. S. Hewitt, Letter to A. Carnegie, December 6, 1901, Box 85, ACP.

71. In the twentieth century, both Carnegie Tech (now Carnegie Mellon University) and Cooper Union would become not only true colleges but two of the nation's most prestigious engineering schools. I will address technical schools like these at length in chapter 4.

72. Howard J. Savage, *Fruit of an Impulse: Forty-Five Years of the Carnegie Foundation, 1905–1950* (New York, NY: Harcourt, Brace and Company, 1953).

73. Ellen C. Lagemann describes this concern for professors as dating to Carnegie's early days as a Cornell trustee, citing Wall and stating that "this has been the standard explanation for Carnegie's establishment of the CFAT" (Lagemann, *Private Power,* 48, 213 n. 29). Wall, in turn, cites Lester, who tells the same story, dated to 1890, without any citation or attribution (Wall, *Andrew Carnegie*, 870; R. M. Lester, *Forty Years of Carnegie Giving* [New York, NY: Charles Scribner's Sons, 1941], 45). Even in the unlikely event that this sympathy was genuine, the fact that Carnegie waited fifteen years before acting on it raises serious questions about his commitment to the cause.

74. In a salient example, just a few months after announcing the CFAT gift, he summarily declined to aid the family of a Cornell professor who had died prema-

turely, leaving behind an impoverished widow and a disabled child (J. Bertram, Letter to Jacob Schurman, August 8, 1905, Box 119, ACP).

75. A. Carnegie, "Halifax Technical School," typescript, September 26, 1900, Box 249, ACP.

76. J. Bertram, Letter to A. B. Kittredge, December 6, 1905, Box 122, ACP.

77. A. D. White, Letter to A. Carnegie, January 25, 1904, Box 102, ACP.

78. J. Schurman, Letter to A. Carnegie, telegram, April 18, 1905, Box 115, ACP.

79. W. R. Harper, Letter to A. Carnegie, April 21, 1905, Box 115, ACP. W. R. Harper, Letter to A. Carnegie, November 11, 1905, Box 121, ACP.

80. R. J. Storr, *Harper's University: The Beginnings* (Chicago: University of Chicago Press, 1966), 331.

81. William R. Harper, *The President's Report* (Chicago: University of Chicago Press, 1903), lxx–lxxi.

82. Most Carnegie biographies devote little attention to his interest in higher education, except for mentions of his late-in-life gifts and his endowment of what is now Carnegie Mellon University. Wall, *Andrew Carnegie*, gives a more balanced overview of the philanthropist's agency in this period, although it is largely anecdotal and decontextualized from the larger history of American higher education. David Nasaw, *Andrew Carnegie* (New York: Penguin, 2007), almost entirely ignores Carnegie's higher education philanthropy.

83. Veysey, *Emergence*. Shortly after Veysey's book came out, James Axtell described it as "fundamentally 'house history,' the story of what goes on inside academia" (J. Axtell, "The Death of the Liberal Arts College," *History of Education Quarterly* 11, 4 [1971]: 349).

84. Sealander, "Curing Evils," 217.

85. Chernow, *Titan*, 310.

86. Boyer, *University of Chicago*, 42.

87. Fosdick, *Adventure in Giving*, 6–16.

88. F. T. Gates, *Chapters in My Life* (New York: Free Press, 1977), 46–53.

89. Gates, *Chapters*, 55.

90. Fosdick, *Adventure in Giving*, 14.

91. Gates, *Chapters*, 58.

92. Quoted in Boyer, *University of Chicago*, 44.

93. Quoted in Chernow, *Titan*, 310.

94. Chernow, *Titan*, 311.

95. Gates, *Chapters*, 215. The charter was secured by Senator Nelson Aldrich of Rhode Island, a powerful Republican whose daughter had recently married John D. Rockefeller Jr.

96. Gates, *Chapters*, 217.

97. T. Arnett and W. W. Brierly, "Introductory Letter," in General Education Board, *Annual Report of the General Education Board, 1928–1929* (New York: n.p., 1930).

98. F. T. Gates, "Memo. by Mr. Gates," 1910, Box 19, OMRO, 7.

99. Gates, *Chapters*, 217–18.

100. A. Flexner, *Henry S. Pritchett: A Biography* (New York: Columbia University Press, 1943); Savage, *Fruit of an Impulse*; Lagemann, *Private Power.*

101. The best of these is by Steven Kanter ("Henry Pritchett and His Introduction to the Flexner Report of 1910," *Academic Medicine: Journal of the Association of American Medical Colleges* 85, 11 [2010]: 1777–83.] Paul Mattingly incorporates Pritchett into his analysis of leaders who shaped the idea that higher education had "social responsibilities" but portrays him as a thoughtful steward of Carnegie's largesse rather than a hard-charging reformer; he then pivots to the Flexner Report. (P. H. Mattingly, *American Academic Cultures: A History of Higher Education* [Chicago: University of Chicago Press, 2017], 216–18.)

102. Lagemann, *Private Power*, 22.

103. Flexner, *Henry S. Pritchett*, 198.

104. Flexner, 20; Lagemann, *Private Power*, 23; H. S. Pritchett, "The Chronicles of Henry Smith" (unpublished memoir), HSPP, Box 1.

105. Flexner, *Henry S. Pritchett*, 29–49.

106. For more on MIT's low-status early days, see Samuel C. Prescott, *When M.I.T. Was 'Boston Tech,' 1861–1916* (Cambridge, MA: MIT Press, 1954).

107. A. Carnegie, Letter to Henry L. Higginson, November 26, 1904, Box 109, ACP.

108. W. Frew, Letter to A. Carnegie, November 29, 1904, Box 109, ACP.

109. H. S. Pritchett, Letter to A. Carnegie, July 19, 1905, Box 118, ACP; Bruce Sinclair, "Mergers and Acquisitions," in *Becoming MIT: Moments of Decision*, ed. David Kaiser (Cambridge, MA: MIT Press, 2010), 37–58.

110. H. S. Pritchett, *Massachusetts Institute of Technology Annual Report of the President and Treasurer, December 9, 1903* (Boston: n.p., 1904).

111. C. F. Thwing, "A Pension Fund for College Professors," *The North American Review* 181, 588 (1905): 722–30; H. S. Pritchett, Letter to A. Carnegie, February 6, 1905, Box 111, ACP.

112. H. S. Pritchett, Letter to A. Carnegie, February 6, 1905, Box 111, ACP.

113. H. S. Pritchett, "Mr. Carnegie's Gift to the Teachers," *The Outlook* 83 (May 1906): 123.

114. H. S. Pritchett, "A National System of Education" (typescript, extended version of "The Organization of Higher Education," *Atlantic Monthly*, December 1908, Box 7, HSPP.

115. Flexner, *Henry S. Pritchett*, 129.

116. F. A. Vanderlip and B. Sparkes, *From Farm Boy to Financier* (New York: D. Appleton-Century Company, 1935), 77.

117. F. A. Vanderlip, "The Co-ordination of Higher Education," in *Business and Education* (New York: Duffield and Company, 1907), 5.

118. F. A. Vanderlip, "The Young Man's Future: An Address Delivered before the American Institute of Bank Clerks, St. Paul, 1906," in *Business and Education*, 51.

119. Vanderlip, "The Co-ordination of Higher Education," 3.

120. Vanderlip, 10.

121. Vanderlip, 10–12.

122. Henry H. Klein, *Standard Oil or the People: The End of Corporate Control in America* (New York: self-published, 1914), 31–32.

123. Flexner, *I Remember*, 13. Thomas Henry Huxley was an English biologist who championed Darwin and coined the word "agnostic."

124. Flexner, 52.

125. Flexner, 56.

126. Flexner, 62.

127. T. N. Bonner, *Iconoclast: Abraham Flexner and a Life in Learning* (Baltimore, MD: Johns Hopkins University Press, 2002), 32–47.

128. Flexner, *I Remember*, 88–101.

129. A. Flexner, *The American College: A Criticism* (New York: The Century Co., 1908), 11.

130. Flexner, *The American College*, 15.

131. Flexner, 145.

132. Flexner, 12.

133. Flexner, *I Remember*, 111.

134. Flexner proudly had little experience with medical education, but he certainly was familiar with the medical world—and with the world of New York–based strategic philanthropy. His older brother, Simon, had been the president of the Rockefeller Institute for Medical Research (now Rockefeller University) since its 1901 founding.

135. Flexner, *I Remember*, 121.

136. A. Flexner, *Medical Education in the United States and Canada: A Report to the Carnegie Foundation for the Advancement of Teaching* (CFAT Bulletin No. 4) (Boston: Merrymount Press, 1910), 178. In the course of his study, Flexner got into considerable hot water. Pritchett had to apologize to a member of the Harvard Medical School faculty for "friction" that occurred during his visit there. (HSP to William T. Councilman, January 22, 1909, Box 8, HSPP.) The same day, Pritchett wrote to a mutual friend, expressing concern that "a good many criticisms have come to me concerning him, somewhat to the effect that he is erratic and hard to get along with and somewhat uncertain in his judgment" (HSP to Cyrus Adler, January 22, 1909, Box 8, HSPP).

137. J. R. Thelin, *A History of American Higher Education* 149. The medical education community continues to see the report's publication as the seminal moment in its history, for better or for worse; see, for example, the twenty-seven articles on Flexner published in a special edition of *Academic Medicine* (85 [2]) marking the report's centenary in 2010.

138. E. H. Harley, "The Forgotten History of Defunct Black Medical Schools in the 19th and 20th Centuries and the Impact of the Flexner Report," *Journal of the National Medical Association* 98, 9 (2006): 1425–29.

139. A. Carnegie, Letter to Charles W. Eliot, June 16, 1910, Box 32, Carnegie Foundation for the Advancement of Teaching Records, 1905–1979 (CFATR), Columbia University Rare Book and Manuscript Library, New York, NY.

140. A. Flexner, "The Usefulness of Useless Knowledge," *Harper's* 179, October 1939, 544–52.

141. Clark Kerr, "Introduction to the Transaction Edition: Remembering Flexner," in Abraham Flexner, *Universities: American, English, German* (New Brunswick, NJ: Transaction, 1994/1930), ix–xxxii.

142. See, for example, Christian Anderson, "Building an Icon: The Rise and Fall of John G. Bowman, Chancellor of the University of Pittsburgh, 1921-1945," *Perspectives on the History of Higher Education* 28, 1 (2011): 137–59.

143. Columbia University in the City of New York, *Catalogue and General Announcement 1906–1907*(New York: Columbia University Press), 15.

144. John G. Bowman, Letter to Charles T. Burnett, November 4, 1907, Box 45, CFATR.

145. S. Persons, *The University of Iowa in the Twentieth Century: An Institutional History* (Iowa City, IA: University of Iowa Press, 1990), 57.

146. Quoted in Persons, *The University of Iowa,* 57.

147. C. Furst, Letter to William Learned, April 28, 1914, Box 38, CFATP.

148. Anderson, "Building an Icon," 141–50.

149. "Boot for Bowman," *Time Magazine,* October 2, 1939.

150. The CFAT's main contribution to intercollegiate athletics reform came well after its influence had waned, with the 1929 Savage Report: Howard J. Savage, *American College Athletics* (New York: Carnegie Foundation for the Advancement of Teaching, 1929).

151. Anderson, "Building an Icon," 150–54.

152. A. P. Stokes, *A Brief Biography of Booker Washington* (Hampton, VA: Hampton Institute Press, 1936), 28.

153. M. Bay, *To Tell the Truth Freely: The Life of Ida B. Wells* (New York: Macmillan, 2009), 245.

154. Louis Harlan, *Booker T. Washington, Volume 2: The Wizard of Tuskegee, 1901–1915* (New York: Oxford University Press, 1983), 322.

155. *Up from Slavery* was only partially an autobiography; it was also a running advertisement for donations to Tuskegee. The text was first serialized in *The Outlook,* a highbrow New York newsmagazine that served as an outlet for many academic engineers.

156. B. T. Washington, *Up from Slavery: An Autobiography* (New York: Burt Company, 1901), 55–57.

157. James D. Anderson, *The Education of Blacks in the South, 1860-1935* (Chapel Hill: University of North Carolina Press, 1988), 34.

158. Ris, "The Education of Andrew Carnegie," 414.

159. Manhattan was also the setting for the most troubling episode of Washington's life, when he was viciously assaulted by a white man while visiting an apartment building on the Upper West Side. (Harlan, *Booker T. Washington,* 379-404.

160. Stokes, *A Brief Biography,* 21.

161. W. E. B. Du Bois, *Dusk of Dawn: An Essay toward an Autobiography of a Race Concept* (New York: Harcourt, Brace & World, 1940), 71.

162. Harlan, *Booker T. Washington*, viii. The octopus was a metaphor commonly employed by contemporary critics of Gilded Age industrial conglomerates; see Rebecca Solnit, "The Octopus and Its Grandchildren," *Harper's*, August 2014, 5-7.

163. Arnold Cooper, "The Tuskegee Machine in Action: Booker T. Washington's Influence on Utica Institute, 1903-1915," *Journal of Mississippi History* 48 (November 1986): 283-95.

164. Quoted in Harlan, *Booker T. Washington*, 199-200

CHAPTER 2

1. F. T. Gates, "The Purpose of the Rockefeller Foundation with Suggestions as to the Policy of Administration," 1906, Box 19, OMRO.

2. In his historiographical essay on the Progressive Era, Daniel Rodgers explains, "It was the merger of the prestige of science with the prestige of the well-organized business firm and factory that gave the metaphor of system its tremendous twentieth-century potency—and it was presumably for this reason that that metaphor flourished more exuberantly in the United States, along with industrial capitalism itself, than anywhere else." (D. T. Rodgers, "In Search of Progressivism," *Reviews in American History* 10, 4 [1982]: 113-32.)

3. H. S. Pritchett, "The Organization of Higher Education," *Atlantic Monthly* 102, December 1908, 783-89. Pritchett was making a classic reformist claim: true "freedom" would come from giving up autonomy and submitting to the will of the planners. This rationale, in many ways, was the defining elite American ideology for the first half of the twentieth century, from William McKinley's imperialism to Robert Moses's urban planning. It was also, of course, the claim of the hegemonic regimes that ravaged much of the globe in the 1930s and '40s. The academic engineers were a very long way from *arbeit macht frei*, but even so we must recognize the inseparable links between the dream of efficiency and the nightmare of totalitarianism.

4. J. K. Galbraith, *The Economics of Innocent Fraud: Truth for Our Time* (Houghton Mifflin Harcourt, 2004), 7.

5. Chernow, *Titan*, 150-51.

6. Quoted in "Educational Trust a Menace to Religion," *The Irish Standard* 26, 36 (1911): 1-2. I will return to this critic, the Catholic leader Thomas Brosnahan, in chapter six.

7. H. U. Faulkner, *The Decline of Laissez Faire, 1897-1917* (New York: Holt, Rinehart, and Winston, 1951), 366.

8. For an extended analysis of this logic, in full force during a "merger movement" that lasted from 1895 to 1904 and spurred the rapid development of the trusts, see Neil Fligstein, *The Transformation of Corporate Control* (Cambridge, MA: Harvard University Press, 1990).

9. A. Flexner, *The American College*, 153.

10. Ross is also known as one of the causes célèbres of the early "academic freedom" movement, due to his dismissal from the Stanford faculty on political

grounds. See H. J. Tiede, *University Reform: The Founding of the American Association of University Professors* (Baltimore, MD: Johns Hopkins University Press, 2015), 35–37.

11. E. A. Ross, *Social Control: A Survey of the Foundations of Order* (New York: Macmillan, 1901), 59.

12. For the role of eugenics in Progressive Era reform, see Thomas Leonard, *Illiberal Reformers: Race, Eugenics, and American Economics in the Progressive Era* (Princeton University Press, 2016).

13. D. Blackbourn, *The Long Nineteenth Century: A History of Germany, 1780–1918* (New York: Oxford University Press, 1998).

14. H. S. Pritchett, "A National System of Education" (typescript, extended version of "The Organization of Higher Education"), 1908, Box 7, HSPP.

15. H. S. Pritchett, Letter to Theodore Roosevelt, August 29, 1906, Box 3, HSPP.

16. H. S. Pritchett, Letter to A. Carnegie, October 19, 1911, Box 31, CFATR.

17. H. S. Pritchett, "The Organization of Higher Education," *Atlantic Monthly*, December 1908, 783–89.

18. Gates, "The Purpose of the Rockefeller Foundation,." 2–3.

19. Upton Sinclair (*The Goose-Step*) loudly made this claim in a book I will discuss at length in chapter six. More recently, his line of attack has been picked up by Clyde Barrow (*Universities and the Capitalist State*), whose Marxist interpretations of higher education philanthropy frame the foundations' work as hegemonic.

20. A. Carnegie, "Copy of Letter from Mr. Andrew Carnegie" (typescript), 1905, Box 114, ACP.

21. W. Peterson, Letter to A. Carnegie, April 19, 1905, Box 115, ACP.

22. F. T. Gates, "Memo. by Mr. Gates," 1910, Box 19, OMRO.

23. F. A. Vanderlip, "The Co-ordination of Higher Education," 9.

24. J. Schneider, Letter to Charles Eliot, May 22, 1905, Box 79, Records of the President of Harvard University, Harvard University Archives.

25. O. G. Willard, Letter to A. Carnegie, November 11, 1910. Box 31, CFATR.

26. A. Carnegie, Letter to Charles W. Eliot, August 22, 1905, Box 119, ACP.

27. For more on the Carnegie Unit's controversial status, see Elena Silva and Taylor White, "The Carnegie Unit: Past, Present, and Future," *Change: The Magazine of Higher Learning* 47, 2 (2015): 68–72

28. H. S. Pritchett, "Mr. Carnegie's Gift to the Teachers," *The Outlook*, May 1906, 120–125.

29. C. Furst, "The Problem of the Financial Support of Higher Education," *Education* 36, 5 (1916): 277.

30. Ross, *Social Control*, 60.

31. Gates, "The Purpose of the Rockefeller Foundation," emphasis original.

32. H. S. Pritchett, Letter to Frank Vanderlip, 1905, Box 18, CFATR.

33. C. Furst, "The Educational Utility of the Great Foundations," *Educational Review* 62, 2 (1923): 98–106.

34. C. Furst, "Tests of College Efficiency (Address at Meeting of Harvard Teachers' Association, March 9, 1912)," 1912, Box 36, CFATR.

35. Carnegie Foundation for the Advancement of Teaching, *Second Annual Report of the President and Treasurer*, (New York: self-published, 1907), 65.

36. "The Carnegie Foundation (Confidential) April 9th, 1906," 1906, Box 18, CFATR Papers.

37. H. Hawkins, *Banding Together: The Rise of National Associations in American Higher Education, 1887-1950* (Baltimore, MD: Johns Hopkins University Press, 1992), 10–15.

38. Association of American Universities, *Journal of Proceedings and Addresses* (Chicago: self-published, 1901), 11.

39. "Association of American Universities: Committee on Aim and Scope" (minutes), November 17, 1908, Box 45, CFATR.

40. C. Furst, Letter to William S. Learned, April 28, 1914, Box 38, CFATR.

41. Quoted in "Mr. Rockefeller's Educational Trust," *Current Literature* 42, 3 (March 1907): 254.

42. A. Flexner, *The General Education Board: An Account of Its Activities, 1902–1914* (New York: self-published, 1915).

43. "How J.D. Rockefeller's Vast Gift Will Reach American Students," *The Brooklyn Citizen*, March 3, 1907, 13.

44. Gates, "Memo. by Mr. Gates," 2–3.

45. Gates, 7.

46. H. S. Pritchett, "Address to Alumni of the Massachusetts Institute of Technology at the Reunion Banquet," *Technology Review* 6, 3 (1904): 8.

47. The academic engineers liked to criticize Midwestern states for their overabundant colleges, but the Eastern Seaboard, especially Boston, was just as inundated with institutions. In 1906, Carnegie's personal secretary forwarded a request for money from Boston University to Pritchett, writing, "Mr. Carnegie does not see why Boston should have two universities" (J. Bertram, Letter to Henry S. Pritchett, May 15, 1906, Box 2, HSPP).

48. H. S. Pritchett, "Meeting of the M.I.T. Alumni at Huntington Hall, May 4, 1905" (news clipping), 1905, Box 38, CFATR.

49. C. W. Eliot, Letter to Henry S. Pritchett, July 22, 1904, Box 3, HSPP.

50. N. M. Butler, Letter to Henry S. Pritchett, April 28, 1905, Box 2, HSPP.

51. Vanderlip, "The Co-ordination of Higher Education."

52. H. S. Pritchett, "Shall Engineering Belong to the Liberal Professions?" In *Inauguration: President Charles Sumner Howe, Case School of Applied Science* (Cleveland: The Imperial Press, 1904), 27–32.

53. H. S. Pritchett, Letter to A. Carnegie, April 28, 1910, Box 31, CFATR.

54. These mergers are detailed in Alice H. Songe, *American Universities and Colleges: A Dictionary of Name Changes* (Metuchen, NJ: The Scarecrow Press, 1978).

55. For example, J. Martin et al., *Consolidating Colleges and Merging Universities: New Strategies for Higher Education Leaders* (Baltimore, MD: Johns Hopkins University Press, 2017); Ricardo Azziz et. al., *Strategic Mergers in Higher Education* (Baltimore, MD: Johns Hopkins University Press, 2019).

56. "Mr. Rockefeller's Educational Trust," *Current Literature* 42, 3 (March 1907): 254.

57. H. S. Pritchett, "Confidential Memorandum for Mr. Carnegie," 1906, Box 31, CFATR.

58. Allen E. Ragan, *A History of Tusculum College, 1794-1944* (Bristol, TN: The King Printing Company, 1945), 100-04.

59. Pritchett, "Confidential Memorandum for Mr. Carnegie." All four institutions still exist.

60. H. S. Pritchett, "The Relations of Christian Denominations to Colleges" (typescript of address to Conference on Education of the Methodist Episcopal Church, South, May 20, 1908), Box 11, HSPP.

61. H. S. Pritchett, "The Organization of Higher Education," *Atlantic Monthly* 102, December 1908, 783-89.

62. H. S. Pritchett, "The Spirit of the State Universities," *Atlantic Monthly* 105, June 1910, 741-53.

63. Flexner, *The American College*, 5; H.S. Pritchett, "The Relations of Christian Denominations."

64. Pritchett, "The Spirit of the State Universities," 749.

65. "Mr. Rockefeller's Gift to Education," *The University Review* 4, 1 (1905): 416.

66. W. F. Slocum, "The Present Status and Probable Future of the College in the West," in *The American College: A Series of Papers Setting Forth the Program, Achievements, Present Status, and Probable Future of the American College* (New York: Henry Holt and Co., 1915), 131-46.

67. H. S. Pritchett, Letter to Wallace Buttrick, February 3, 1910, Box 52, CFATR.

68. C. Furst, "Tests of College Efficiency," *The School Review* 20, 5 (1912): 323.

69. W. S. Learned, Letter to Henry S. Pritchett, March 19, 1914, Box 38, CFATR.

70. Pritchett, "Confidential Memorandum for Mr. Carnegie."

71. Classics of this genre include B. R. Clark, "The 'Cooling-Out" Function in Higher Education," *American Journal of Sociology* 65, 6 (1960): 569-76; S. Brint and J. Karabel, *The Diverted Dream: Community Colleges and the Promise of Educational Opportunity in America, 1900-1985* (New York: Oxford University Press, 1989). For a synthesis of the community college's role in stratifying the higher education sector, see D. F. Labaree, "From Comprehensive High School to Community College: Politics, Markets, and the Evolution of Educational Opportunity," *Research in Sociology of Education and Socialization* 9 (1990): 203-40.

72. At least one scholar disagrees; James Ratcliff argues that the institutional form was actually created two years before Harper took it up, by J. M. Carroll of Baylor University (J. L. Ratcliff, "Seven Streams in the Historical Development of the Modern American Community College," in G. A. Baker, *A Handbook on the Community College in America: Its History, Mission, and Management* [Westport, CT: Greenwood Press, 1994], 3-16). Notably, like Harper, Carroll was also attempting to subordinate small Baptist colleges and bring them into the orbit of his university.

73. W. R. Harper, *The Prospects of the Small College* (Chicago: University of Chicago Press, 1900), 9.

74. Harper, 31.

75. Harper, 35–37.

76. N. M. Butler, "Shall There Be a Two Years' College Course?" *The Review of Reviews* 26, 1 (1902): 589–94.

77. C. Furst, "Ideals of Women's Colleges" (transcript of address at Annual Meeting of the Southern Association of College Women, Atlanta, April 22, 1915), Box 36, CFATR.

78. J. L. Wattenbarger and A. A. Witt, "Origins of the California System: How the Junior College Movement Came to California," *Community College Review* 22, 4 (1995): 17–25.

79. C. L. McLane, "The Junior College, or Upward Extension of the High School," *The School Review* 21, vol. 3 (1913): 161–70.

80. D. S. Jordan, Letter to H. S. Pritchett, April 15, 1908, Box 32, CFATR.

81. L. V. Koos, *The Junior-College Movement* (Boston: Ginn & Co., 1925), 10.

82. Only seven colleges agreed to the affiliation plan, which collapsed after Harper's death in 1905 (Storr, *Harper's University*, 211–22). I will return to the Chicago affiliation scheme in chapter three.

83. Seth Low College, which I will return to in chapter five, was a bigoted attempt by Butler to confine Jewish students to a lesser institution far from Morningside Heights. See R. A. McCaughey, *Stand, Columbia: A History of Columbia University in the City of New York* (New York: Columbia University Press, 2003), 270–71.

84. Brint and Karabel, *The Diverted Dream*.

85. I. H. Reynolds, "The Junior College," *The Methodist Review* 99, 1 (1916): 100–02.

86. Koos, *The Junior-College Movement*, 317–38.

87. C. W. Eliot, Letter to Henry S. Pritchett, March 16, 1908, Box 32, CFATR.

88. R. P. Pedersen, "The Origins and Development of the Early Public Junior College: 1900–1940" (PhD diss., Columbia University, 2000).

89. R. P. Pederson, "Value Conflict on the Community College Campus: An Examination of Its Historical Origins," in L. F. Goodchild and H. S. Wechsler, *The History of Higher Education: Second Edition* (Needham, MA: Simon & Schuster, 1997), 502.

90. F. A. Vanderlip and H. S. Pritchett, "Preliminary Report of the Statistics Gathered for the Trustees of the Carnegie Foundation," 1905, Box 18, CFATR.

91. F. T. Gates, Letter to W. R. Harper, January 26, 1898, Box 8, WRH Papers.

92. F. T. Gates, "Memorandum on Educational Conditions and Prospects in the State of Nebraska," 1906, Record Group III 26, Box 19, OMRO, 7.

93. Gates, 12.

94. H. S. Pritchett, "The Relations of Christian Denominations."

95. Gates, "The Purpose of the Rockefeller Foundation," 4–5.

96. Gates, 5.

97. A. Carnegie, "St. Andrew's University Proposed Rectorial Address by Andrew Carnegie," 1902, Box 248, ACP, 7.

98. J. White, "Andrew Carnegie and Herbert Spencer: A Special Relationship," *Journal of American Studies* 13, 01 (1979).

99. Harper, *The Prospects*, 21–22.

100. Carnegie, "Copy of Letter from Mr. Andrew Carnegie." This language strongly echoed, perhaps inadvertently, the 1871 British law known as the Universities Tests Act, which opened up fellowships at Oxford and Cambridge to non-Anglicans for the first time.

101. A. Carnegie, Letter to A. C. Harris, March 16, 1909, Box 266, ACP.

102. Statistics on colleges and universities that dropped religious affiliations are based on a comparison of data in the annual reports of the office of the US Commissioner of Education, which collected self-reports from institutions on their religious affiliations. The data are incomplete, so 37 is the minimum number of institutions that became nonsectarian during the period. The commissioner's report for 1904–05 listed 320 denominational schools (including Black-serving institutions). Other institutions diminished the control of denominational orders over their boards and policies but still maintained official affiliation; these are not reflected in the federal data. The CFAT stipulation was likely not the only factor in the severance of denominational ties during this period; as Julie R. Reuben (*The Making of the Modern University*) demonstrates, a wide variety of forces promoted secularization in colleges and universities. CFAT approval was often a forcing function that enabled institutional leaders to convince boards to sever ties, a long-sought goal.

103. H. S. Pritchett, Letter to Andrew Carnegie, January 30, 1907, Box 2, HSPP.

104. It is important to note that "progressive" Americans in the early twentieth century typically used the word "Christian" as an adjective and not as a noun (as is typical today). They used it to describe behavior, individuals, and institutions to signify that they were acting in the manner and spirit of Jesus Christ, rather than fulfilling a particular theological profile. Pritchett explained this usage in a 1910 *Atlantic* article: "When one thinks of Christianity as a system of morals founded upon those virtues which Christ himself taught—gentleness, meekness, unselfishness, patience, justice, love—he recognizes that the system of Christian morals receives at the hands of science the strongest possible support" (Pritchett, "The Spirit of the State Universities").

105. Pritchett, "The Relations of Christian Denominations."

106. W. J. Bryan, "Resigns His Trusteeship," in *The Commoner Condensed: Vol VI.* (Chicago: The Henneberry Company, 1907), 2.

107. For more on this theme, see G. M. Marsden, *The Soul of the American University: From Protestant Establishment to Established Nonbelief* (Oxford University Press, 1994). As Marsden relates, in the 1920s Bryan took his anti-evolution crusade to a series of college campuses, railing against "the evil influence of these Materialistic, Atheistic or Agnostic professors" (319–21).

108. H. S. Pritchett, Letter to Frank Vanderlip, July 20, 1905, Box 18, CFATR.

109. George A. Gates, Letter to Henry Pritchett, July 13, 1905, Box 49, CFATR.

110. Arthur J. May, *History of the University of Rochester*, University of Rochester Library, http://rbscp.lib.rochester.edu/2347, accessed on November 3, 2019.

111. G. L. Collis, Letter to Henry Pritchett, April 15, 1907, Box 46, CFATR.

112. H. A. Buchtel, Letter to Henry S. Pritchett, April 22, 1910, Box 50, CFATR.

113. H. A. Buchtel, Letter to Henry S. Pritchett, November 20, 1908, Box 50, CFATR.

114. H. A. Buchtel, Letter to John Bowman, October 22, 1909, Box 50, CFATR.

115. H. A. Buchtel, Letter to John Bowman, March 7, 1909, Box 50, CFATR. Until 2020, the Methodist Church still had nominal control over the board of trustees of the University of Denver (whose legal name was Colorado Seminary until that year). See http://www.du.edu/media/documents/pdf/bylaws_of_the_colorado_seminary_2014_06_06.pdf.

116. W. W. Smith, Letter to Henry S. Pritchett, November 12, 1907, Box 49, CFATR.

117. Details on the Coe presidents are from the college's website: http://www.public.coe.edu/historyweb/presidents.htm. Pritchett made life difficult for Smith's successor, withholding pension funds until the board removed language from Coe's charter mandating that the college simply report the results of its trustee elections to the Presbyterian Synod (*Fourth Annual Report of the President and the Treasurer* (New York: CFAT), 19.)

118. W. H. Crawford, Letter to HSP, April 4, 1908, Box 32, CFATR.

119. J. Schurman, Letter to HSP, December 2, 1905, Box 18, CFATR.

120. W. D. Hyde, *The College Man and the College Woman* (Boston: Houghton Mifflin, 1906), 278-80.

121. H. S. Pritchett, Letter to William D. Hyde, July 25, 1906, Box 45, CFATR.

122. H. S. Pritchett, Letter to Thomas H. Hubbard, June 20, 1907, Box 45, CFATR.

123. W. W. Hyde, Letter to HSP, June 26, 1907, Box 45, CFATR.

124. Hyde, Letter to HSP.

125. T. H. Hubbard, Letter to HSP, January 4, 1908, Box 45, CFATR.

126. H. S. Pritchett, Letter to Andrew Carnegie, December 28, 1907, Box 31, CFATR.

127. W. D. Hyde, Letter to Andrew Carnegie, January 21, 1908, Box 45, CFATR.

128. W. D. Hyde, Letter to HSP, January 21, 1908, Box 45, CFATR.

129. Gates's fear was directed at a diffuse group that Scott Gelber has called "academic Populists," who exerted major influence in public universities in North Carolina, Nebraska, and Kansas between 1890 and 1905 (S. M. Gelber, *The University and the People: Envisioning American Higher Education in an Era of Populist Protest* [Madison, WI: University of Wisconsin Press, 2011]).

130. Gates, The Purpose of the Rockefeller Foundation," 14.

131. Carnegie Foundation for the Advancement of Teaching, *Annual Report of the President and Treasurer, Vol. 3* (Boston: Merrymount Press, 1908), 80.

132. *Report of the Commissioner of Education for the Year Ending June 30, 1905* (Washington, DC: Government Printing Office, 1907).

133. D. A. Jordan, Letter to HSP, April 15, 1908, Box 32, CFATR.

134. E. B. Craighead, Letter to HSP, February 6, 1913, Box 32, CFATR.

135. "State Board Recommends Consolidation of Schools," *The Missoulian*, December 24, 1912, 3.

136. E. B. Chennette, *The Montana State Board of Education: A Study of Higher Education in Conflict, 1884-1959* (PhD diss., University of Montana, 1972), 197–236.

137. J. P. Dyer, *Tulane: The Biography of a University, 1834-1965* (New York: Harper & Row, 1966), 120–23.

138. J. H. Gardiner, *Harvard* (New York: Oxford University Press, 1914); H. B. Adams, "The State and Higher Education," in *Proceedings of the Department of Superintendence of the National Educational Association at Its Meeting in Washington, March 6-8, 1889* (Washington, DC: Government Printing Office, 1889), 262–78.

139. C. A. Bacote, *The Story of Atlanta University: A Century of Service, 1865-1965* (Atlanta, GA: Atlanta University Press, 1969), 121–22. The Atlanta subsidy was a small recompense for the state of Georgia's failure to offer any public opportunities for Black students to attend college with its federal land grant resources.

140. J. G. Schurman, *Grounds of an Appeal to the State for Aid to Cornell University: Being the Address Delivered on Friday, the Eleventh of November, 1892, Upon His Inauguration as President* (Ithaca, NY: Cornell University Press, 1892), 29, 81.

141. A. C. Carnegie, Letter to Andrew D. White, November 27, 1892, Box 17, ACP.

142. A. Carnegie, Letter to Charles W. Eliot, August 22, 1905, Box 119, ACP.

143. G. Crothers, Letter to Andrew Carnegie, June 7, 1905, Box 117, ACP.

144. These statistics are from *Report of the Commissioner of Education for the Year Ending June 30, 1905* (Washington, DC: Government Printing Office, 1907).

145. F. A. Vanderlip, Letter to HSP, June 27, 1905, Box 18, CFATR.

146. Boyer, University of Chicago, 127–29.

147. E. B. Andrews, Letter to Andrew Carnegie, August 1, 1905, Box 118, ACP.

148. H. S. Pritchett, "Shall the University Become a Business Corporation?" *Atlantic Monthly* 96 (3), 1905, 289–99.

149. H. S. Pritchett, Letter to Charles W. Eliot, May 18, 1906, Box 60, Charles Eliot Papers, Harvard University Archives.

150. CFAT *Bulletin of the Carnegie Foundation for the Advancement of Teaching: Papers Relating to the Admission of State Institutions to the System of Retiring Allowances of the Carnegie Foundation* (New York: self-published, 1907).

151. H. S. Pritchett, Letter to "Trustees, with the exception of President Hadley," January 2, 1908, Box 32, CFATR.

152. A. Carnegie, Letter to CFAT Trustees, March 31, 1908, Box 150, ACP.

153. R. E. Knoll, *Prairie University: A History of the University of Nebraska* (Lincoln, NE: University of Nebraska Press, 1995), 54.

154. A. Carnegie, Letter to HSP, May 9, 1908, Box 31, CFATR.

155. H. S. Pritchett, Letter to Andrew Carnegie, June 7, 1910, Box 177, ACP.

156. A. Carnegie, "Memo," January 11, 1911, Box 31, CFATR.

157. H. S. Pritchett, Letter to Andrew Carnegie, November 25, 1911, Box 31, CFATR.

CHAPTER 3

1. R. H. Wiebe, *The Search for Order, 1877-1920* (New York: Macmillan, 1967).

2. D. T. Rodgers, "In Search of Progressivism," *Reviews in American History* 10, 4 (1982): 118.

3. F. T. Gates, "The Country School of To-Morrow," *General Education Board Occasional Papers* 1 (1913): 15.

4. H. S. Pritchett, "The Large Number of Institutions in the United States and Canada Bearing the Name College or University," in *Carnegie Foundation for the Advancement of Teaching: Second Annual Report of the President and Treasurer* (New York: self-published, 1907), 77.

5. For more on track standardization, see D. J. Puffert, "The Standardization of Track Gauge on North American Railways, 1830-1890," *The Journal of Economic History* 60, 4 (December 2000): 933–60.

6. Pritchett, "The Large Number of Institutions," 77. In addition to being a triumph of efficiency, the development of railroads in "undeveloped country" was a triumph of settler colonialism that exploited immigrant labor and trampled on the sovereignty of indigenous nations (see M. Karuka, *Empire's Tracks: Indigenous Nations, Chinese Workers, and the Transcontinental Railroad* [Berkeley: University of California Press, 2019]. For reflections on US universities' historical and ongoing technologies of colonization, especially in the context of railroad-driven western expansion and the land-grant movement, see la paperson, *A Third University Is Possible* [Minneapolis: University of Minnesota Press, 2017].)

7. A. D. Chandler, *The Visible Hand: The Managerial Revolution in American Business* (Cambridge, MA: Harvard University Press, 1977), 79.

8. Chandler, *The Visible Hand*, 145.

9. This differentiation of managerial roles also informs Chandler's description of "managerial hierarchies," a phenomenon already identified contemporaneously by Max Weber, who showed that "a clearly established system of super- and subordination in which there is a supervision of the lower offices by the higher ones" was the hallmark of the modern bureaucratic organization (M. Weber, *Economy and Society: An Outline of Interpretive Sociology* [Berkeley: University of California Press, 1922/1978], 957.)

10. In chapter six, I will describe Louis Brandeis's attacks on "bigness" as ideological fodder for the broad resistance that ended the crucible of reform in the 1910s.

11. Chandler, *The Visible Hand*, 347.

12. D. F. Labaree, *The Making of an American High School: The Credentials Market and the Central High School of Philadelphia, 1838-1939* (New Haven, CT: Yale University Press, 1988,) 109–10.

13. The term "people's college" originated in 1839, coined by an advocate of the common school movement who was arguing for increased public appropriations to public secondary schools. See William J. Reese, *The Origins of the American High School* (New Haven, CT: Yale University Press, 1995), 28.

14. Marc VanOverbeke, *The Standardization of American Schooling: Linking Secondary and Higher Education, 1870–1910* (New York: Palgrave Macmillan, 2008), 11–12.

15. Carnegie Foundation for the Advancement of Teaching, *Second Annual Report of the President and Treasurer* (New York: self-published, 1907), 79.

16. The author of an 1894 text titled *History of Higher Education in Rhode Island* declared it "difficult to say which were the institutions for higher education. Some with no more pretentious title than 'school,' 'academy,' or 'seminary,' gave instruction in their advanced classes in some of the studies pursued in the freshman class in college," and went on to give ample description of secondary schools offering "higher education" (W. H. Tolman, *History of Higher Education in Rhode Island* [Washington, DC: Government Printing Office, 1894].)

17. Diane Ravitch, for example, credits the reform of secondary education to individuals like David Snedden, the commissioner of public education in Massachusetts. Snedden, a devotee of Herbert Spencer and a student of Edward Ross, certainly advocated separating the work of the high school from that of the college. Specifically, he urged high schools to move toward vocational education for all but a very small number of students, leaving no doubt about which institution was superior. But Snedden, who spent his career focused on K–12 education, was actually the exception to the rule about reformers in the 1890s and 1900s (Diane Ravitch, *Left Back: A Century of Failed School Reforms* (New York: Simon & Schuster, 2000), 81–86).

18. *Report of the Committee on Secondary School Studies, Appointed at the Meeting of the National Educational Association July 9, 1892, With the Reports of the Conferences* (Washington, DC: Government Printing Office, 1892).

19. H. S. Wechsler, *The Qualified Student: A History of Selective College Admission in America* (New York: John Wiley & Sons, 1977), 40–59.

20. Carnegie Foundation for the Advancement of Teaching, *Second Annual Report*, 65.

21. D. Tyack and L. Cuban, *Tinkering toward Utopia: A Century of Public School Reform* (Harvard University Press, 1995), 91–93.

22. S. B. McCormick, "Discussion of Questions Submitted to Trustees of the Carnegie Foundation," December 1, 1905, Box 18, CFATR.

23. H. S. Pritchett, Letter to J. A. Marquis, December 30, 1909, Box 49, CFATR.

24. H. S. Pritchett, Letter to Charles Van Hise, December 27, 1909, Box 45, CFATR.

25. *Twenty-Sixth Report of the Board of Trustees of the University of Illinois* (Springfield, IL: Illinois State Journal Co., 1912), 34–35. While the Illinois board took the symbolically important step of formally killing off the preparatory school, they also simultaneously created a new institution in the name of educational research: "a training and experimental school of secondary grade for the School of Education." Thus, they had their cake and ate it, too.

26. Carnegie Foundation for the Advancement of Teaching, *Second Annual Report*, 75

27. A. D. White, *Advanced Education: The Relations of the National and State Governments to Advanced Education* (Boston: Office of Old and New, 1874), 476–77

28. D. H. R. Dawson, "Letter," in F. W. Blackmar, *The History of Federal and State Aid to Higher Education in the United States* (Washington, DC: Government Printing Office, 1890). For more on Dawson, see K. R. Johnson, "N. H. R. Dawson: United States Commissioner of Education," *History of Education Quarterly* 11, 2 (1971): 174–83. Dawson is important to the historiography of higher education, since one of his few decisive actions as the bureau's leader was commissioning a book-length history of each state's higher education sector.

29. H. B. Adams, "The State and Higher Education," *Proceedings of the Department of Superintendence of the National Educational Association at Its Meeting in Washington, March 6–8, 1889* (Washington, DC: Government Printing Office, 1889), 262–78. A cabinet-level Department of Education did not become a reality until 1980.

30. H. R. Evans, "William Torrey Harris: An Appreciation," in *William Torrey Harris, 1835–1935* (Chicago: Open Court, 1936), 1–14.

31. W. T. Harris, *Report of the Commissioner of Education for the Year 1888–89* (Washington, DC: Government Printing Office, 1891), xix.

32. W. T. Harris, Letter to N. E. Ailes, February 15, 1905, Box 18, CFATR.

33. Evans, "William Torrey Harris," 7.

34. "The National Council of Education," in *National Educational Association: Fiftieth Anniversary Volume, 1857–1906* (Chicago: University of Chicago Press, 1907), 607–18.

35. S. P. Capen, "College 'Lists' and Surveys Published by the Bureau of Education," *School and Society* 6 (July 14, 1917): 38.

36. H. S. Pritchett, "Should the Carnegie Foundation Be Suppressed?" *North American Review* (April 1914): 13.

37. K. Babcock, *A Classification of Universities and Colleges with Reference to Bachelor's Degrees* (Washington, DC: Government Printing Office, 1911), 4.

38. K. Babcock, "Higher Education in the United States," in *Report of the Commissioner of Education for the Fiscal Year Ended June 30, 1911, Vol. 1* (Washington, DC: Government Printing Office, 1912), 43–44.

39. Babcock, *A Classification of Universities*, 5. For more on the Babcock report, see D. S. Webster, "The Bureau of Education's Suppressed Rating of Colleges, 1911-1912," *History of Education Quarterly* 24, 4 (1984): 499–511, but with a grain of salt. Webster makes serious errors in describing some features of the report, including the categorizations of institutions like Northwestern University and Clark University.

40. M. J. O'Connor, "Classification of Colleges," *America* 7, 26 (1912): 621–22.

41. Reprinted in R. W. Lykes, *Higher Education and the United States Office of Education (1867–1953)* (Washington, DC: Government Printing Office, 1975), 48–49.

42. Capen, "College 'Lists' and Surveys," 39.

43. Lykes, *Higher Education*, 51.

44. Thelin, *A History of American Higher Education*, 79.

45. *Hearings Before the Committee on Education, House of Representatives, Sixty-Third Congress, Second Session, on H. R. 11749, A Bill to Create a National University at the Seat of the Federal Government* (Washington, DC: Government Printing Office, 1914), 135.

46. *Hearings Before the Committee on Education*, 286.

47. David Madsen, *The National University: Enduring Dream of the USA* (Detroit: Wayne State University Press, 1966), 67–103.

48. *University of the United States: March 10, 1896, Submitted by Mr. Kyle, from the Committee to Establish the University of the United States, to Accompany S. 1202* (Washington, DC: Government Printing Office, 1896), 67–110.

49. Madsen, *The National University*, 104–06.

50. *Hearings Before the Committee on Education*, 378

51. "National Association of State Universities," in *Report of the Commissioner of Education, 1907–1908*, vol. 1 (Washington, DC: Government Printing Office, 1909), 67.

52. *Hearings Before the Committee on Education*, 135–36.

53. A. Carnegie, Letter to Andrew D. White, April 26, 1901, Box 82, ACP.

54. A. S. Hewitt, Letter to Andrew Carnegie, December 6, 1901, Box 85, ACP.

55. C. Jencks and D. Riesman, *The Academic Revolution* (Garden City, NY: Doubleday, 1968); Roger L. Geiger, *To Advance Knowledge: The Growth of American Research Universities, 1900–1940* (Oxford University Press, 1986); Julie R. Reuben, *The Making of the Modern University*, etc.

56. The one honest attempt to create a research university without undergraduates was Clark University of Massachusetts, founded under the leadership of G. Stanley Hall in 1881. The experiment lasted less than twenty years; the university opened an undergraduate division in 1900.

57. W. James, "The Ph.D. Octopus," *Harvard Monthly* (March 1903): 1–9.

58. "Stevens Institute Gets Castle Point," *New York Times*, June 6, 1909.

59. H. S. Pritchett, "Address of Dr. Pritchett at Stevens Institute Alumni Dinner," February 12, 1910, Box 39, CFATR.

60. H. S. Pritchett, "The College of Discipline and the College of Freedom," *The Atlantic*, November 1908, 603–10

61. *Annual Report of the Commissioner of Education*, 1898-99, vol. 1 (Washington, DC: Government Printing Office, 1899), 1564–65.

62. Carnegie Foundation for the Advancement of Teaching, *Second Annual Report*, 80

63. H. Bumstead, Letter to HSP, July 12, 1907, Box 46, CFATR.

64. Joseph M. Gould, "The Baptist Dream of a Super-University," in *The Chautauqua Movement: An Episode in the Continuing American Revolution* (Albany: SUNY Press, 1961), 41.

65. Storr, *Harper's University*, 14

66. Storr, *Harper's University*, 17

67. Rose, "Why a University for Chicago and Not Cleveland?", 10.

68. Storr, *Harper's University*, 24.

69. Storr, 211.

70. Storr, 77.

71. Storr, 214.

72. Storr, 215.

73. Storr, 216.

74. W. R. Harper, *The President's Report: 1892–1902* (Chicago: University of Chicago Press, 1903), lxvi–lxvii.

75. W. R. Harper, *The Prospects of the Small College* (Chicago: University of Chicago Press, 1900).

76. Wechsler, *The Qualified Student*, 189.

77. "The Catalogue," *Baylor University Bulletin* 16, 3 (1913): 12.

78. J. L. Wattenbarger and A. A. Witt, "Origins of the California System: How the Junior College Movement Came to California," *Community College Review* 22, 4 (1995): 17–25.

79. J. Hope, "Our Atlanta Schools," *The Voice of the Negro* 1, 1 (January 1904): 10–16.

80. Gates, "The Purpose of the Rockefeller Foundation," 4.

81. H. S. Pritchett, "Education and the Nation," *Atlantic Monthly* 109, April 1912, 543–53.

82. F. T. Gates, "Minute on Higher Education in South Dakota and the Newer States, Anent the Application of Yankton College," 1909, OMRO, Group III 26, Box 19.

83. *Report of the Commissioner of Education, 1907–1908*, 672. These states were Arkansas, Delaware, Florida, Idaho, Maine, Nevada, Vermont, West Virginia, and Wyoming, plus the territories of Arizona and New Mexico. I count the 1862 Land Grant institutions as having a claim to university status, even if their names did not yet reflect that. As I will explain in chapter four, by 1909 these institutions were much more than agricultural schools.

84. S. Sherwood, *The University of the State of New York: History of Higher Education in the State of New York* (Washington, DC: Government Printing Office, 1900), 44–56.

85. *Statement of the Commissioner of Education to the Secretary of the Interior for the Fiscal Year Ended June 30 1898* (Washington, DC: Government Printing Office, 1898).

86. Carnegie Foundation for the Advancement of Teaching, *First Annual Report*, 44. Not all of the academic engineers agreed about lifting the New York definition wholesale. Butler, who knew the work of the University of the State of New York very well, expressed doubt to Pritchett: "As to educational standard: Will it be wise to follow the New York definition quite so closely? That definition was the product of the activity of Mr. Melvil Dewey, who was very much given to a quantitative method of determining matters essentially qualitative" (N. M. Butler, Letter to HSP, February 13, 1906, Box 32, CFATR.) Dewey, a New York educator famous today for his system of library cataloging, was perhaps the most ardent efficiency fiend in an era full of them.

87. Carnegie Foundation for the Advancement of Teaching, *Third Annual Report*, 150.

88. W. Reid, Letter to Andrew Carnegie, December 26, 1902, Box 93, ACP.

89. S. Sherwood, *The University of the State of New York: History of Higher Education in the State of New York* (Washington, DC: Government Printing Office, 1900), 37–39.

90. "Dr. Draper Will Accept; to Be Elected Commissioner of Education Thursday—the Regent Slate," *New York Times*, March 8, 1904.

91. Sherwood, *The University of the State of New York*, 40–44.

92. Harper, *The Prospects*, 28.

93. H. S. Pritchett, "Shall the University Become a Business Corporation?" *The Atlantic* 96, September 1905, 289–99.

94. G. E. MacLean, "The Promise and Potency of Educational Unity in the United States," *University of the State of New York Regents Bulletin No. 61*, 1903, 224–40.

95. Nathan M. Sorber, *Land-Grant Colleges and Popular Revolt: The Origins of the Morrill Act and the Reform of Higher Education* (Ithaca, NY: Cornell University Press, 2018), 60–79.

96. CFAT, *Third Annual Report*, 81.

97. Hawkins, *Banding Together*, 81.

98. H. S. Pritchett, "The Spirit of the State Universities," 747.

99. M. M. Connerly, *The Effects of Isomorphism on the American State Normal School: The Case of the Institution in Cedar Falls, Iowa from 1890 to 1915* (PhD diss., University of Kansas, 2013).

100. Scott M. Gelber, *The University and the People: Envisioning American Higher Education in an Era of Populist Protest* (Madison: University of Wisconsin Press, 2011).

101. M. McGiffert, *The Higher Learning in Colorado: An Historical Study, 1860–1940* (Denver: Allan Swallow, 1964); D. G. Sansing, *Making Haste Slowly: The Troubled History of Higher Education in Mississippi* (Jackson, MS: University Press of Mississippi, 1990).

102. Lois A. Fisher, "The Role of Politics in the Organization and Development of Public Higher Education in Idaho and Washington," *History of Higher Education Annual 1985* (1985): 111–33. Fisher chalks up some of the differences to ideology but describes that ideology as part of the general Progressive positions of politicians rather than any reform movement that specifically targeted the higher education sector.

103. D. S. Jordan, Letter to HSP, April 15, 1908, Box 32, CFATR.

104. Sansing, *Making Haste Slowly*, 78–84.

105. D. G. Sansing, *The University of Mississippi: A Sesquicentennial History* (Jackson, MS: University Press of Mississippi, 1999), 200.

106. "Mass Meeting on University Topic Called," *Jackson Daily News*, January 23, 1920.

107. J. B. Young and J. M. Ewing, *The Mississippi Public Junior College Story: The First Fifty Years, 1922–1972* (Mississippi Junior College Association, 1978).

108. Pritchett, "The Spirit," 747–748.

109. T. N. Hoover, *The History of Ohio University* (Ohio University Press, 1954), 176.

110. Hoover, *The History of Ohio University*, 189.

111. E. Orton, "The Lybarger Bill," Ohio State University Alumni Association, http://babel.hathitrust.org/cgi/pt?id=osu.32435014961981, accessed on March 1, 2018.

112. Hoover, *The History of Ohio University*, 187-90.

113. Cited in "The Carnegie Foundation and the Pritchett Bomb," *The Ohio Teacher* 30, 1 (1909): 7-13.

114. "The Carnegie Foundation and the Pritchett Bomb," emphasis original.

115. "The Dictation of Swollen Wealth," *Columbus Evening Dispatch*, June 17, 1909.

116. Pritchett, "The Spirit," 747.

117. Nobel Media AB. "Nomination Archive." NobelPrize.org. Accessed on October 6, 2020. https://www.nobelprize.org/nomination/archive/show.php?id=8363, accessed on April 1, 2020.

118. B. Wheeler, "The American State University," *Educational Review* 51, 1 (1916): 34.

119. "Vocational Bills Passed by Senate," *Sacramento Bee*, April 23, 1915.

120. M. Dundjerski, *UCLA: The First Century* (Third Millennium Publishing, 2011), 15.

121. B. I. Wheeler, Letter to E. A. Dickson, February 16, 1916, Box 18, Edward A. Dickson Papers (EADP), UCLA Library Special Collections, Los Angeles, CA.

122. B. I. Wheeler, Letter to E. A. Dickson, September 15, 1916, Box 18, EADP.

123. E. C. Moore, Letter to E. A. Dickson, June 6, 1918, Box 18, EADP.

124. A. P. Fleming, Letter to E. A. Dickson, March 1, 1919, EADP.

125. "Annual Report of the President of the University," *University of California Bulletin* 13, 7 (1920): 260.

126. D. P. Barrows, Letter to E. A. Dickson, April 25, 1921, EADP.

127. Los Angeles Chamber of Commerce, "Resolution," September 29, 1921, Box 18, EADP; V. Randall, Letter to E. A. Dickson, January 15, 1923, Box 18, EADP.

128. R. G. Sproul, Letter to E. A. Dickson, March 26, 1923, Box 18, EADP.

129. R. G. Sproul, Letter to E. A. Dickson, May 11, 1923, Box 18, EADP.

130. M. A. Young, Letter to E. A. Dickson, June 1, 1925, Box 18, EADP.

131. S. Persons, *The University of Iowa in the Twentieth Century: An Institutional History* (Iowa City: University of Iowa Press, 1990), 34-42.

132. Persons, *The University of Iowa*, 50.

133. Connerly, *The Effects of Isomorphism*, 122-31.

134. Persons, *The University of Iowa*, 51.

135. Persons, 54-57.

136. Persons, 60.

137. W. S. Learned, Letter to Clyde Furst, March 26, 1914, Box 38, CFATR.

138. Learned, Letter to Clyde Furst, March 26, 1914.

139. W. S. Learned, Letter to Clyde Furst, March 31, 1914, Box 38, CFATR.

140. W. S. Learned, Letter to Clyde Furst, March 26, 1914, Box 38, CFATR.

141. W. S. Learned, Letter to Clyde Furst, April 4, 1914, Box 38, CFATR.

142. Ravitch, *Left Back*, 81–86.

143. W. S. Learned, Letter to Clyde Furst, April 4, 1914, Box 38, CFATR. Learned added a postscript to this letter: "By the way I'm having a rattling good time out here."

144. C. Furst, Letter to William S. Learned, April 28, 1914, Box 38, CFATR.

145. "Boot for Bowman." *Time*, October 2, 1939.

CHAPTER 4

1. Thomas D. Snyder, ed., *120 Years of American Education: A Statistical Portrait* (Washington, DC: National Center for Education Statistics, 1993), 64–65.

2. W. J. Reese, *The Origins of the American High School* (New Haven: Yale University Press, 1999), 257.

3. "Illinois Heads list of Accredited Schools," *Chicago Tribune*, March 21, 1914.

4. "Dr. Ernest Martin Hopkins Dies," *New York Times*, August 14, 1964; "Too Many Men in College," *The Journal of the National Education Association*, vol. 11 (1922): 390.

5. Harold Ramis, dir., *Caddyshack*, Orion Pictures, 1989.

6. A. Carnegie, "Pennsylvania State College Address," 1904, Box 252, ACP.

7. A. Carnegie, *Dedication of the Carnegie Library at the Edgar Thomson Steel Rail Works, Braddocks [sic]: Address to the Workmen* (Pittsburgh: n.p., 1889).

8. A. Flexner, *The American College: A Criticism* (New York: The Century Co., 1908), 15.

9. F. Vanderlip, "The Co-ordination of Higher Education," in *Business and Education* (New York: Duffield and Company, 1907), 5. This type of anti-intellectualism certainly had a long history in post-Enlightenment America, going back at least to Ralph Waldo Emerson's scathing "American Scholar" address to Harvard's Phi Beta Kappa chapter: "Meek young men grow up in libraries, believing it their duty to accept the views which Cicero, which Locke, which Bacon, have given; forgetful that Cicero, Locke and Bacon were only young men in libraries when they wrote these books" (R. W. Emerson, *The American Scholar* (New York: Laurentian Press, 1901).

10. F. T. Gates, "The Colleges and Rural Life: Confidential to Members of the Board," 1910, Group III 26, Box 19, OMRO.

11. H. M. Kliebard, *Schooled to Work: Vocationalism and the American Curriculum, 1876–1946* (Teachers College Press, 1999), 1–25.

12. J. F. Wall, *Andrew Carnegie* (New York: Oxford University Press, 1970), 21.

13. B. T. Washington, "Industrial Education for the Negro," in *The Negro Problem: A Series of Articles by Representative American Negroes of To-Day* (New York: James Pott & Co., 1903), 12–13

14. Kliebard, *Schooled to Work*, 25.

15. "Mr. Huntington's Address," *Sacramento Record-Union*, May 17, 1899, 7.

16. Jane Addams, "The Subjective Necessity for Social Settlements," in *The Ameri-*

can City: A Sourcebook of Urban Imagery, ed. Anslem L. Strauss (Routledge, 2017), 211–12.

17. Woodrow Wilson, "Princeton for the Nation's Service: An Address Delivered on the Occasion of His Inauguration as President of Princeton University," in *The Public Papers of Woodrow Wilson: College and State* (New York: Harper & Brothers, 1925), 448.

18. C. F. Thwing, *College Training and the Business Man* (New York: D. Appleton & Co., 1904), 71.

19. Thwing, *College Training*, 31.

20. University of Illinois, "Installation of Edmund Janes James, PH.D., LL.D., as President of the University," (Urbana, IL: n.p., 1906), 448.

21. Wilson, for example, took a very different stance than James when it came to the purpose of baccalaureate study: "The college should seek to make the men whom it receives something more than excellent servants of a trade or skilled practitioners of a profession." (Wilson, *Princeton for the Nation's Service*, 450.)

22. H. S. Pritchett, "The Place of Industrial and Technical Training in Popular Education," *Technology Review* 4, 1 (1902): 15.

23. L. Veysey, *The Emergence of the American University* (Chicago: University of Chicago Press, 1965), 72–73.

24. "An Act Donating Public Lands to the Several States and Territories Which May Provide Colleges for the Benefit of Agriculture and Mechanic Arts," http://www. ourdocuments.gov/doc.php?doc=33&page=transcript, accessed on March 1, 2020.

25. N. M. Sorber, "Introduction," *Perspectives on the History of Higher Education* 30, 1 (2013): 3. Sorber cites several authors who make this assumption, including Edward Eddy. However, even the foreword to Eddy's 1956 book, penned by the head of the American Association of Land-Grant Colleges, declares that the purpose of the Morrill Act was not vocational education but rather "a system of colleges and universities in which the search for new knowledge in neglected fields of fundamental importance to the American people (and the application of this knowledge in practice) would have an honored place, though not to the exclusion of other traditional disciplines." Without the parenthetical, the description sounds simply like the academic engineers' vision for the topmost stratum of the higher education pyramid (Russell I. Thackery, "Foreword," in Edward Danforth Eddy Jr., *Colleges for Our Land and Time* [New York: Harper & Brothers, 1956], x.).

26. Eldon L. Johnson, "Misconceptions about the Early Land-Grant Colleges," *Journal of Higher Education* 52, 4 (1981): 341.

27. William T. Foster, *Administration of the College Curriculum* (Boston: Houghton Mifflin, 1911), 166.

28. Sorber, *Land-Grant Colleges*, 90–99, 127–29.

29. CFAT *Fifth Annual Report of the President and Treasurer* (Boston: Merrymount Press, 1910), 16, 23–26. The CFAT's determination that they were a single university was based on a letter sent by Purdue's president stating that "the two institutions do not complete or duplicate, but supplement each other to the end that

the state possesses in the two the various departments which in many states are combined in a single state university."

30. Connerly, *The Effects of Isomorphism*, 115.

31. "Eighth Biennial Report of the Board of Control of State Institutions of Iowa" (Des Moines: Emory H. English, 1912), 65–66.

32. "Eighth Biennial Report," 70–71.

33. Joe Corry and James Gooch, "The Wisconsin Idea: Extending the Boundaries of a University," *History of Education Quarterly* 46, 4 (1992): 305–20. See also J. David Hoeveler, *John Bascom and the Origins of the Wisconsin Idea* (Madison: University of Wisconsin Press, 2016).

34. F. T. Gates, "The Colleges and Rural Life," 24.

35. State Board of Public Affairs *Report Upon the Survey of the University of Wisconsin* (Madison: State Printer, 1914), 13, 24. The report's primary author asked the CFAT for assistance, but Pritchett ordered a deputy to ignore him because he was incompetent (H. S. Pritchett, Letter to W. S. Learned, July 14, 1914, Box 38, CFATR.).

36. State Board of Public Affairs, *Report Upon the Survey*, 199.

37. C. A. Ogren, *The American State Normal School: An Instrument of Great Good* (New York: Palgrave Macmillan, 2005), 65.

38. Ogren, *The American State Normal School*, 56.

39. E. Orton, J. A. Bownocker, and P. Jones, *The Lybarger Bill* (Columbus, OH: n.p., 1906), emphasis original.

40. Connerly, *The Effects of Isomorphism*, 134–42.

41. Ogren, *The American State Normal School*, 204.

42. Ogren, 203.

43. Charles A. Harper, *A Century of Public Teacher Education* (Washington, DC: National Education Association of the United States, 1939), 138–39.

44. H. S. Pritchett, Letter to W. Buttrick, January 11, 1911, Box 52, CFATR.

45. W. Issel, "The Politics of Public School Reform in Pennsylvania, 1880-1911," *The Pennsylvania Magazine of History and Biography* 102, 1 (1978): 90.

46. E. O. Holland, *The Pennsylvania State Normal Schools and Public School System* (PhD diss., Columbia University, 1912), 91–94.

47. Holland, *The Pennsylvania State Normal Schools*, 94.

48. Holland, 3.

49. PASSHE has the word "state" in its title while the system that includes Penn State, Temple, and the University of Pittsburgh is known as the Commonwealth System of Higher Education. This is significant because Pennsylvania is technically a commonwealth and not a state. The elite institutions get to use the real name, and the low-status ones do not. Virginia is also a commonwealth; VCU is a research university while Virginia State University is a historically Black college. Kentucky State University, in another commonwealth, is also a historically Black institution.

50. Fisher, "The Role of Politics," 115–16.

51. Fisher, "The Role of Politics," 121–22.

52. J. S. Brown, "Normal Schools and Junior Colleges," in *National Conference of Junior Colleges, 1920*, ed. G. F. Zook (Washington, DC: Government Printing Office, 1922), 59.

53. Ogren, *The American State Normal School*, 65.

54. E. Alden. Dunham, *Colleges of the Forgotten Americans* (New York: McGraw-Hill Book Co., 1969), 27-37. Dunham's book was partially sponsored by the CFAT.

55. Three years later, Carnegie gave another gift to Cooper Union: a small parcel of land at the corner of Forty-Second Street and Lexington Avenue. For more than one hundred years, the rent on that parcel allowed every Cooper student to attend college tuition-free; its tenant is the Chrysler Building (Ris, "The Education of Andrew Carnegie," 407.).

56. C. M. Depew, "Oration," in *Drexel of Art, Science, and Industry: Dedication Ceremonies* (Philadelphia: n.p., 1893), 21-22.

57. A. Carnegie, Letter to William McConway, January 19, 1902, Box 87, ACP.

58. Depew, "Oration," 24.

59. A. C. Carnegie, *The Education of the Negro: A National Interest* (Tuskegee, AL: Tuskegee Institute Steam Print, 1906), 5.

60. Clyde Furst, "Recent Educational Progress: An Address before the Educational Society of Johns Hopkins University," 1916, Box 36, CFATR.

61. J. D. Watkinson, *Educating the Million: Education, Institutions, and the Working Class, 1787-1920* (PhD diss., University of Virginia, 1995), 220.

62. Pritchett, "The Place of Industrial and Technical Training," 4.

63. H. S. Pritchett, Letter to A. Carnegie, September 24, 1904, Box 2, HSPP.

64. "Thank Carnegie: Franklin Fund Board Act on His Offer," *Boston Globe*, December 21, 1904.

65. "Thank Carnegie."

66. Edward O. Sisson, "The First Years," in *Bradley Polytechnic Institute: The First Decade, 1897-1907* (Peoria, IN: n.p., 1907), 48-57.

67. B. Sinclair, "Mergers and Acquisitions," in *Becoming MIT: Moments of Decision*, ed. D. Kaiser (MIT Press, 2010), 44.

68. These and other editorials were reprinted in an MIT periodical: "The Proposed Harvard-Technology 'Merger,'" *Technology Review* 6 (1905): 183-99.

69. Sinclair, "Mergers and Acquisitions," 54.

70. C. R. Richards, Memo to GEB, 1922, Box 641, General Education Board Records (GEBR), Rockefeller Archive Center, Sleepy Hollow, NY.

71. E. E. Hewitt, Letter to "Mr. Cutting," May 25, 1922, Box 641, GEBR.

72. Judith Goodstein, "History of Caltech," last modified 29 June 1998, https://www.nobelprize.org/prizes/themes/history-of-caltech, accessed on April 1, 2020.

73. The school is now called the Benjamin Franklin Institute of Technology.

74. C. F. Thwing, "Address on Behalf of the Universities and Colleges," *Stevens Institute Indicator* 20, 2 (1903): 153.

75. F. A. Vanderlip, "A New College Degree," in *Bulletin No. 3.*, New York State Education Department (Albany: n.p., 1906), 74.

76. Quoted in S. Brint and J. Karabel, *The Diverted Dream: Community Colleges and*

the Promise of Educational Opportunity in America, 1900–1985 (Oxford University Press, 1989), 24.

77. Quoted in William DeGenaro, "Class Consciousness and the Junior College Movement: Creating a Docile Workforce," *JAC* 21, 3 (2001): 499–520.

78. L. V. Koos, *The Junior-College Movement* (Boston: Ginn & Co., 1925), 19.

79. Brint and Karabel, *The Diverted Dream*, 27.

80. Quoted in Brint and Karabel, *The Diverted Dream*, 35.

81. University of California, Berkeley, Committee on Courses of Instruction, *The Junior College in California: A Circular* (Berkeley: University of California Press, 1915), 17.

82. W. C. Eells, *The Junior College* (Boston: Houghton Mifflin, 1931), 63.

83. Brint and Karabel, *The Diverted Dream*, 38–41.

84. Quoted in W. J. Cooper, "The Junior-College Movement in California," *The School Review* 36, no. 6 (1928): 421.

85. B. R. Clark, "The 'Cooling-Out' Function in Higher Education," *American Journal of Sociology* 65, 6 (1960): 569–76.

86. G. M. Woytanowitz, *University Extension: The Early Years in the United States, 1885–1915* (Washington, DC: National University Extension Association, 1974), 23–25.

87. Gates, "The Colleges and Rural Life," 22.

88. Woytanowitz, *University Extension*, 71.

89. Louis. E. Reber, "University Extension and the State University," *Science*, vol. 34, no. 885 (December 15, 1911): 825–33.

90. "University Extension Experiment," *The Journal of Education*, vol. 65, no. 16 (April 18, 1907): 427.

91. Michael Shinagel, *"The Gates Unbarred": A History of University Extension at Harvard, 1910–2009* (Cambridge, MA: Harvard University Press, 2009), 19.

92. For its first three years, all Harvard Extension courses were held in the city of Boston (Shinagel, *"The Gates Unbarred,"* 32).

93. Eells, *The Junior College*, 98

94. J. A. Moyer, "University Extension," *The Journal of Education* 97, 14 (1923): 374–76.

95. Shinagel, *"The Gates Unbarred,"* 45. Harvard Extension completely abandoned the associate's degree in 1933, replacing it with something called the adjunct in arts degree (W. C. Eells, *Academic Degrees* [Washington, DC: US Dept. of Health, Education, and Welfare, 1960], 98.).

96. The line was actually the product of the university's public relations staff. J. Corry and J. Gooch, "The Wisconsin Idea: Extending the Boundaries of a University," *Higher Education Quarterly* 46, 4 (1992): 306.

97. J. D. Hoeveler, "The University and the Social Gospel: The Intellectual Origins of the 'Wisconsin Idea,'" *The Wisconsin Magazine of History* 59, 4 (1976): 282–98.

98. Shinagel, *"The Gates Unbarred,"* 43.

99. C. Van Hise, "The University Extension Function in the Modern University,"

in *Proceedings of the First National University Extension Conference* (Madison, WI: n.p., 1915), 17.

100. R. R. Price, "Minnesota's University Weeks," in *Proceedings of the First National University Extension Conference*, 163–64.

101. A. C. Rieser, *The Chautauqua Moment: Protestants, Progressives, and the Culture of Modern Liberalism* (New York: Columbia University Press, 2003), 99.

102. Rieser, *The Chautauqua Moment*, 104.

103. Rieser, 210.

104. Woytanowitz, *University Extension*, 24.

105. Rieser, *The Chautauqua Moment*, 207.

106. J. F. Kett, *The Pursuit of Knowledge under Difficulties: From Self-Improvement to Adult Education in America, 1750-1990* (Stanford, CA: Stanford University Press, 1994), 187.

107. Richard R. Price, "The General Extension Division, *Bulletin of the University of Minnesota* 18 (November 1915), 152–154.

108. George E. Vincent, "The Few or the Many," in *Adult Education in Action*, ed. Mary L. Ely (New York: George Grady, 1936).

109. Van Hise, "The University Extension Function," 21.

CHAPTER 5

1. C. V. Woodward, *The Strange Career of Jim Crow: A Commemorative Edition* (New York: Oxford University Press, 2002).

2. Although the second decade of the century was capped by the passage of the Nineteenth Amendment, guaranteeing women the right to vote, the movement had largely been stymied until a sudden flurry of progress in 1918–20 (E. F. Weiss, *The Woman's Hour: The Great Fight to Win the Vote* [New York: Viking, 2018.]).

3. H. S. Wechsler, *The Qualified Student: A History of Selective College Admission in America* (New York: John Wiley & Sons, 1977); J. Karabel, *The Chosen: The Hidden History of Admission and Exclusion at Harvard, Yale, and Princeton* (New York: Mariner Books, 2006); M. Synnott, "The Admission and Assimilation of Minority Students at Harvard, Yale, and Princeton, 1900-1970," *History of Education Quarterly* 19, 3 (1979): 285–304., L. T. Ulrich, ed., *Yards and Gates: Gender in Harvard and Radcliffe History* (New York: Palgrave, 2004).

4. *Brown v. Board of Education of Topeka* 347 U.S. 483 (1954).

5. D. B. Potts, *Wesleyan University, 1831–1910: Collegiate Enterprise in New England* (Middletown, CT: Wesleyan University Press, 1999), 210–18.

6. L. D. Gordon, *Gender and Higher Education in the Progressive Era* (New Haven, CT: Yale University Press, 1990), 17–18; "G. Stanley Hall: Male Chauvinist Educator," *The Journal of Educational Thought* 10 (3): 194–200.

7. T. G. Dyer, *Theodore Roosevelt and the Idea of Race* (Baton Rouge: Louisiana State University Press, 1980), 143–67.

8. H. S. Wechsler, "An Academic Gresham's Law: Group Repulsion as a Theme in American Higher Education," *Teachers College Record* 82, 4 (1981): 567–88.

9. Sam Scott, "Why Jane Stanford Limited Women's Enrollment to 500," *Stanford Magazine*, September 2018; Gordon, *Gender and Higher Education*, 43; R. Bordin, *Women at Michigan: The Dangerous Experiment, 1870s to the Present* (Ann Arbor: University of Michigan Press, 2001), 20.

10. V. B. Brown, "Conservative among Progressives: Woodrow Wilson in the Golden Age of American Women's Higher Education," in *The Educational Legacy of Woodrow Wilson: From College to Nation*, ed. J. Axtell (University of Virginia Press, 2012).

11. May, *History of the University of Rochester*, Chapter 13.

12. Gordon, *Gender and Higher Education*, 45–46.

13. Amy Thompson McCandless, *The Past in the Present: Women's Higher Education in the Twentieth-Century American South* (Tuscaloosa: University of Alabama Press, 1999), 97.

14. W. R. Harper, *The President's Report* (Chicago: University of Chicago Press, 1903), cxi–cxiii; Gordon, *Gender and Higher Education*, 112–117.

15. Mary Louise Wright, "Moss-Grown Traditions Shunned by Man Who Plans to Build an Ideal College." *New York Evening Mail* (1910).

16. Edwin W. Slosson, "Educational Tendencies in the West," *Book News Monthly*, September 1913, 99.

17. M. Nerad, *The Academic Kitchen: A Social History of Gender Stratification at the University of California, Berkeley* (Albany: SUNY Press, 1999), 18–19.

18. H. S. Pritchett, "A Woman's Opportunity in Business and the Industries," 1907, Box 11, HSPP.

19. Pritchett, "A Woman's Opportunity."

20. Kathleen Dunn, "The Impact of Higher Education upon Career and Family Choices: Simmons College Alumnae, 1906-1926," in *Changing Education: Women as Radicals and Conservators*, ed. Joyce Antler and Sari Knopp Biklen (SUNY Press, 1990), 157–59.

21. W. R. Harper, *The Prospects of the Small College* (University of Chicago Press, 1900), 26.

22. J. S. Mulder, *Woodrow Wilson: The Years of Preparation* (Princeton, NJ: Princeton University Press, 1978), 92.

23. D. S. Webster, "The Bureau of Education's Suppressed Rating of Colleges, 1911-1912," *History of Education Quarterly* 24, 4 (1984) 500–01.

24. Statistics gathered from *Report of the Commissioner of Education* (1908), 722–734.

25. Clyde Furst, "Ideals of Women's Colleges" (transcript of address at Annual Meeting of the Southern Association of College Women, Atlanta, April 1915), Box 36, CFATR.

26. Gordon, *Gender and Higher Education*, 71. See also Barbara M. Solomon, *In the Company of Educated Women: A History of Women and Higher Education in America* (New Haven, CT: Yale University Press, 1985), 59.

27. Eells, *The Junior College*, 29.

28. E. A. Colton, "Report of the Committee on the Junior College Problem," *Pro-*

ceedings of the Twentieth Annual Meeting of the Association of Colleges and Secondary Schools of the Southern States (Nashville, TN: Publishing House of the Methodist Episcopal Church, South, 1914), 46.

29. "Royal Holloway College Conference," *The Journal of Education* 342 (1898): 72–73.

30. Solomon, *In the Company of Educated Women*, 134.

31. Solomon, 134.

32. Helen Leftkowitz Horowitz, *The Power and Passion of M. Carey Thomas* (New York: Knopf, 1994 158.

33. M. Carey Thomas, *Education of Women* (Albany, NY: J. B. Lyon Co., 1899), 17.

34. Horowitz, *The Power and Passion*, 340–43, 381–83; Oliver B. Pollak, "Antisemitism, the Harvard Plan, and the Roots of Reverse Discrimination," *Jewish Social Studies* 45, 2 (1983): 113–22.

35. Horowitz, *The Power and Passion*, 330.

36. Wechsler, *The Qualified Student*, 134.

37. *Catholic Directory, Almanac, and Clergy List* 12, 1 (1905): passim.

38. P. Gleason, *Contending with Modernity: Catholic Higher Education in the Twentieth Century* (New York: Oxford University Press, 1995), 49.

39. Pope Leo XIII blessed the university with an encyclical declaring that the institution would be one-of-a-kind and urging it to affiliate with Catholic colleges across the United States (Leo XIII, *Magnis Nobis Encyclical on the Catholic University of America*, http://www.vatican.va/content/leo-xiii/en/encyclicals/documents/hf_l-xiii_enc_07031889_magni-nobis.html, accessed on February 1, 2020.

40. H. S. Pritchett, Letter to A. Carnegie, July 20, 1911, Box 31, CFATR.

41. *Pierce v. Society of Sisters of the Holy Names of Jesus and Mary* 268 U.S. 510 (1925).

42. "Reports of the Proceedings and Addresses of the Seventh Annual Meeting," *Catholic Educational Association Bulletin* 7, 1 (1910): 142.

43. "Reports of the Proceedings and Addresses of the Eighth Annual Meeting," *Catholic Educational Association Bulletin* 8, 1 (1911): 140–56.

44. "Reports of the Proceedings and Addresses of the Tenth Annual Meeting," *Catholic Educational Association Bulletin* 10, 1 (1913): 183.

45. T. E. Shields, "Survey of the Field: The Control of Educational Agencies," *Catholic Educational Review* 8 (1914): 312.

46. "Reports of the Proceedings and Addresses of the Ninth Annual Meeting," *Catholic Educational Association Bulletin* 9, 1 (1912): 137. "*Vae victis*" means "woe to the vanquished" in Latin and was commonly uttered after a Roman military conquest to mean something akin to "to the victors go the spoils."

47. Of course, the Catholic institutions didn't go anywhere. As David Levine shows, their enrollments exploded after 1916 (Levine, *The American College*, 77).

48. N. Ignatiev, *How the Irish Became White* (New York: Routledge, 1995).

49. M. G. Synott, *The Half-Opened Door: Discrimination and Admissions at Harvard, Yale, and Princeton, 1900-1970* (Westport, CT: Greenwood Press, 1979); Karabel, *The Chosen*.

50. Levine, *The American College*, 148–57; Z. Eleff, "'The Envy of the World and the Pride of the Jews': Debating the American Jewish University in the Twenties," *Modern Judaism* 31, 2 (2011): 230.

51. M. Fishberg, *The Jews: A Study of Race and Environment* (New York: Charles Scribner's Sons, 1911), 376.

52. *Annual Report of the Hebrew Technical Institute for the Year 1909* (New York: n.p., 1910).

53. L. I. Newman, *A Jewish University in America?* (New York: Bloch Publishing Co., 1923), 68.

54. Eleff, "'The Envy of the World,'" 235–39.

55. Wechsler, *The Qualified Student*, 145–68.

56. Quoted in Levine, *The American College*, 147.

57. R. A. McCaughey, *Stand, Columbia: A History of Columbia University in the City of New York* (New York: Columbia University Press, 2003), 270–71; L. Hirt, "Columbia for Jews? The Untold Story of Seth Low Junior College," *Columbia Current* (fall 2016).

58. W. E. B. Du Bois, *The College-Bred Negro: A Report of a Social Study Made Under the Direction of Atlanta University* (Atlanta: Atlanta University Press, 1900), 106.

59. Du Bois, *The College-Bred Negro*, 106.

60. Harlan, *Booker T. Washington,* 138.

61. Eric Anderson and Alfred A. Moss, *Dangerous Donations: Northern Philanthropy and Southern Black Education, 1902-1930* (Columbia, MO: University of Missouri Press, 1999), 51.

62. Anderson and Moss, *Dangerous Donations*, 69.

63. Du Bois, *The College-Bred Negro*, 105.

64. Woodrow Wilson, *A History of the American People, Vol. 5* (New York: Harper & Bros., 1902), 60–64.

65. J. Malczewski, *Building a New Educational State: Foundations, Schools, and the American South* (Chicago: University of Chicago Press, 2016), 13.

66. N. J. Ring, "The 'New Race Question': The Problem of Poor Whites and the Color Line," in *The Folly of Jim Crow: Rethinking the Segregated South*, ed. S. Cole and N. J. Ring (College Station: Texas A & M Press, 2012), 101.

67. Anderson and Moss, *Dangerous Donations*, 43.

68. Anderson, *The Education of Blacks,* 259.

69. T. Savit, "Abraham Flexner and the Black Medical Schools," *Journal of the National Medical Association* 98, 9 (2006): 1415–24.

70. Thomas Jesse Jones, *Negro Education: A Study of the Private and Higher Schools for Colored People in the United States (Bureau of Education Bulletin No. 38)* (Washington, DC: Government Printing Office, 1917), 58–65. By 1917, this argument was an old one, although Jones may have been especially parsimonious. Even Du Bois wrote in 1900 that a total of twelve Black colleges and universities "would amply supply the legitimate demand for the higher training of Negroes for a generation or more. This would mean that the college departments of 22 institutions

be closed and that the college work be concentrated" (Du Bois, *The College-Bred Negro*, 112.).

71. Harlan, *Booker T. Washington*, 200.

72. Anderson and Moss, *Dangerous Donations*, 16, 11.

73. Anderson, *The Education of Blacks*; J. D. Anderson, *Education for Servitude: The Social Purposes of Schooling in the Black South, 1870–1930* (PhD diss., University of Illinois, 1973).

74. Ris, "The Education of Andrew Carnegie", 408–09.

75. Anderson and Moss, *Dangerous Donations*, 85.

76. "The Exhibits: Historical, Sociological, and Educational," *The Tuskegee Student* 18, 15 (April 28, 1906).

77. "Annual Catalog Edition 1915–16," *The Tuskegee Institute Bulletin* 10, 2 (1916).

78. Roscoe C. Bruce, "The Academic Aims," in *Tuskegee & Its People: Their Ideals and Achievements* (New York: D. Appleton and Co., 1905), 56–57. Bruce was the son of Blanche Bruce, a Black US senator from Mississippi during the Reconstruction Era.

79. Charles W. Eliot, "The Value During Education of the Life-Career Motive," *The American College* 2, 5 (1910): 357.

80. Anderson, *The Education of Blacks*, 34.

81. Bruce, "The Academic Aims," 61.

82. Anderson, *The Education of Blacks*, 34.

83. "The Tuskegee Idea" *New York Times*, December 2, 1899.

84. H. S. Enck, "Tuskegee Institute and Northern White Philanthropy: A Case Study in Fund Raising, 1900–1915," *The Journal of Negro History* 65, 4 (1980): 336–48. Inflation calculation is from the Bureau of Labor Statistics (https://data.bls.gov/cgi-bin/cpicalc.pl).

85. Endowment statistics are from the previous year: "Property, Fellowships and Scholarships, Fees," *Report of the Commissioner of Education for the Year Ended June 30, 1914* (Washington, DC: Government Printing Office, 1915), 264–76.

86. Enck, "Tuskegee Institute," 338.

87. L. R. Harlan, ed., *The Booker T. Washington Papers, Volume 3* (Champaign, IL: University of Illinois Press, 1974), 583–87. Although Washington delivered the address in Atlanta, his words were meant to go far beyond the local audience, as he indicated with his gratitude for "the constant help that has come to our educational life, not only from the Southern states, but especially from Northern philanthropists, who have made their gifts a constant stream of blessing and encouragement."

88. B. T. Washington, "President Washington's Address," *The Tuskegee Student* 8, 15 (1906).

89. B. T. Washington, "General Introduction," in *Tuskegee & Its People: Their Ideals and Achievements* (New York: D. Appleton and Co., 1905), 7.

90. B. T. Washington, "The Fruits of Industrial Training," *The Atlantic*, October 1903. Washington's disdain for baccalaureate institutions was still on full display

in his private letters, however. In 1910, he complained to a Hampton administrator that commentary by an editor at the *Independent* "puts me in rather an awkward position, that is, in the position of defending higher education. I meant to do no such thing. I meant to tell a simple story of the work that Fisk is doing. This matter of defending and explaining these so-called higher institutions makes me tired." The offending comment had noted "how mistaken is the idea that he is concerned only in the industrial training which will fit the race to support themselves in a humble station of life" (B. T. Washington to R. M. Moton, March 24, 1910, in L. R. Harlan, *The Booker T. Washington Papers Collection, Vol. 10.* (Champaign, IL: University of Illinois Press, 1972) 283, 291.

91. Anderson, *The Education of Blacks*, 255.

92. Quoted in Anderson, *The Education of Blacks*, 260.

93. H. Bumstead, "Secondary and Higher Education in the South for Whites and Negroes," *Publications of the National Association for the Advancement of Colored People* 2, 1 (1910): 5.

94. Harlan, *Booker T. Washington, Volume 2*, 177.

95. R. W. Logan, *Howard University: The First Hundred Years, 1867–1967* (New York: New York University Press, 1969), 154–56.

96. Harlan, *Booker T. Washington, Volume 2*, 177.

97. J. M. Richardson, *A History of Fisk University, 1865–1946* (Tuscaloosa: University of Alabama Press, 1980), 67.

98. Harlan, *Booker T. Washington,*, 180.

99. According to a newspaper report, the Howard trustees seriously considered choosing a Black man as the new president ("Who Will Be New President of Howard?" *The Afro-American Ledger* [Baltimore], June 1, 1912.).

100. Richardson, *A History of Fisk University*, 25–33.

101. Richardson, 80.

102. The Slater Fund also used its philanthropic largesse to push industrial education at Spelman Seminary, which served Black women, during the same time period. However, as Johnetta Cross Brazzell argues, the Spelman administrators "were able to manipulate the curriculum in such a way as to receive the sorely needed external funds but also keep the curriculum on a steady course that was firmly grounded in the classical/literary education arena" (J. C. Brazzell, "Brick without Straw: Missionary-Sponsored Black Higher Education in the Post-Emancipation Era," *The Journal of Higher Education* 63, 1 [1992]: 44.).

103. W. T. B. Williams, Letter to J. G. Merrill, November 7, 1906, Box 137, GEBP.

104. W. E. B. Du Bois, "Galileo Galilei," 1908, reprinted with Du Bois's commentary in W. E. B. Du Bois, *The Education of Black People: Ten Critiques, 1906-1908* (Amherst: University of Massachusetts Press, 1973), 17–30.

105. Richardson, *A History of Fisk University*, 63. Richardson primarily cites the fundraising difficulties, but Du Bois gives himself credit for Merrill's exit, writing, "President Merrill resigned in the summer. I was sorry for that. I did not mean this for a personal attack. I was attacking a system and a tendency" (Du Bois, *The Education of Black People*, 30.)

106. G. A. Gates, Letter to W. Buttrick, December 20, 1909, Box 137, GEBP.

107. W. Buttrick, Letter to P. D. Cravath, February 3, 1910, Box 137, GEBP; W. Buttrick, Letter to G. A. Gates, January 27, 1911, Box 137, GEBP.

108. H. S. Pritchett, Letter to W. G. Waterman, January 28, 1909, Box 52, CFATR.

109. G. A. Gates, Letter to B. T. Washington, *BTW Papers,* vol. 10, 1910, 313.

110. C. A. Bacote, *The Story of Atlanta University: A Century of Service, 1865-1965* (Atlanta: Atlanta University Press, 1969), 153-56.

111. G. F. Peabody, Letter to H. L. Simmons, December 18, 1911, Box 137, GEBP.

112. W. Buttrick, Letter to G. F. Peabody, December 19, 1911, Box 137, GEBP.

113. Bacote, *The Story of Atlanta University*, 155.

114. "Confidential to Dr. Buttrick," 1913, Box 137, GEBP.

115. Richardson, *A History of Fisk University*, 67. Gates was keen to point out that Washington had sent his son, Booker Jr., to Fisk (*BTW Papers*, vol. 10, 313.).

116. Harlan, *Booker T. Washington*, 186.

117. C. K. Beyer, "The Connection of Samuel Chapman Armstrong as Both Borrower and Architect of Education in Hawai'i," *History of Education Quarterly* 47, 1 (2007): 23-48.

118. D. F. Lindsey, *Indians at Hampton Institute, 1877-1923* (Champaign, IL: University of Illinois Press, 1995), 188.

119. Christopher Nicholson, *To Advance a Race: A Historical Analysis of the Intersection of Personal Belief, Industrial Philanthropy and Black Liberal Arts Higher Education in Fayette McKenzie's Presidency at Fisk University, 1915-1925* (PhD diss., Loyola University of Chicago, 2011), 59-60.

120. L. K. Neuman, *Indian Play: Indigenous Identities at Bacone College* (Lincoln: University of Nebraska Press, 2014), 39-56. Higher education reform hurt indigenous Americans in more ways than the push for vocationalism at Hampton and Indian University. As Margaret Nash argues, in both symbolic and literal ways the land-grant movement served as a "state-sponsored system of Native dispossession" (M. Nash, "Entangled Pasts: Land-Grant Colleges and American Indian Dispossession," *History of Education Quarterly* 59, 4 [2019]: 437-67.

121. Nicholson, *To Advance a Race*, 59-60.

122. Anderson, *The Education of Blacks*, 264.

123. F. McKenzie, Letter to J. Rosenwald, December 31, 1919, Box 17, Fayette A. McKenzie Papers (FAMP), Fisk University Archives.

124. F. McKenzie, Letter to W. C. Graves, June 25, 1917, Box 17, FAMP.

125. Fosdick, *Adventure in Giving*, 190.

126. Anderson, *The Education of Blacks*, 266

127. R. Wolters, *The New Negro on Campus: Black College Rebellions of the 1920s* (Princeton University Press, 1975), 33-34.

128. Quoted in Anderson, *The Education of Blacks*, 266.

129. Richardson, 84-91.

130. Du Bois claimed that the president was personally booking singing engagements, including one that featured only female students: McKenzie "carried them downtown at night to a white men's club, took them down an alley and admitted

them through the servants' entrance and had them sing in a basement to Southern white men, while these men smoked and laughed and talked. If Erasmus
Cravath, the first president of this institution, knew that a thing like that had
happened at Fisk University he would, if it were in any way possible, rise from
the grave and protest against this disgrace and sacrilege" (Du Bois, *The Education
of Black People*, 56–57.)

131. Du Bois, *The Education of Black People*, 41.

132. W. E. B. Du Bois, "Diuturni Silenti," in Du Bois, *The Education of Black People*,
42–59.

133. Wolters, *The New Negro on Campus*, 62–63.

134. W. E. B. Du Bois, *The Souls of Black Folk: Essays and Sketches* (Chicago: A. C.
McClurg & Co., 1903), 3.

135. Jones, *Negro Education*, 55–60.

136. Despite Young's lifelong association with Washington, as Antonio Holland
shows, he sometimes clashed with his mentor over educational philosophy and
ended up as an advocate for liberal education for African Americans, both at
Florida A&M and at Lincoln University in Missouri, where he ended his career
(A. F. Holland, *Nathan B. Young and the Struggle over Black Higher Education* [Co-
lumbia, MO: University of Missouri Press, 2006.]).

137. W. E. B. Du Bois and A. G. Dill, *The College-Bred Negro American: Report of a
Social Study Made by Atlanta University under the Patronage of the Trustees of the
John F. Slater Fund* (Atlanta: Atlanta University Press, 1910), 7, 12.

138. Du Bois, *The College-Bred Negro*, 112.

139. Anderson and Moss, *Dangerous Donations*, 85.

140. The Black newspaper *New York Age* reported in 1906 that Washington had
in fact come up with the idea for the GEB but had been refused a trusteeship:
"There are no Afro-Americans on the Board, the insulting assumption . . . being
that the Afro-American is a good subject for charity, but is no good as an advisor
or co-equal laborer in disbursing the moneys given for his education." The article
accused the other foundations of similar prejudice, which extended even to their
staffs: "In none of the offices of these boards are employed any Afro-Americans,
except as messengers" ("What Is the Matter with the General Education Board?"
New York Age, December 6, 1906.).

141. W. E. B. Du Bois, *Dusk of Dawn: An Essay Toward an Autobiography of a Race
Concept* (New York: Harcourt, Brace and Company, 1940).

142. H. S. Enck, "Black Self-Help in the Progressive Era: The 'Northern Campaigns' of Smaller Southern Black Industrial Schools, 1900-1915," *The Journal of
Negro History* 61, 1 (1976): 79.

143. B. G. Brawley, *A Short History of the American Negro* (New York: The Macmillan Co., 1913), 153.

144. Arnold Cooper, "The Tuskegee Machine in Action: Booker T. Washington's
Influence on Utica Institute, 1903-1915," *The Journal of Mississippi History* 48
(1986): 283–95.

145. "The Work and Plans of The Association of Negro Industrial and Sec-

ondary Schools," HathiTrust Digital Library, https://hdl.handle.net/2027/uiuc.2878998_001, accessed on May 15, 2020.

146. E. M. Rudwick, "Booker T. Washington's Relations with the National Association for the Advancement of Colored People," *The Journal of Negro Education* 29, 2 (1960): 134–44.

147. "Work and Plans," 11.

148. O. G. Villard, Letter to B. T. Washington, May 21, 1914, *BTW Papers*, vol. 13, 27.

149. Enck, "Black Self-Help," 86.

150. Cooper, "The Tuskegee Machine," 291–95.

151. B. T. Washington, Letter to T. J. Jones, March 6, 1915, *BTW Papers*, vol. 13, 250. Taylor was a graduate of MIT and worked hard to associate Tuskegee with his alma mater.

152. B. T. Washington, Letter to A. P. Stokes, November 9, 1912, *BTW Papers*, vol. 12, 52.

153. B. T. Washington, Letter to A. P. Stokes, November 1, 1912, *BTW Papers*, vol. 12, 44.

154. A. P. Stokes, "Introduction," in Jones, *Negro Education*, xi–xii.

155. Stokes, "Introduction," xiii

156. C. G. Woodson, "Thomas Jesse Jones," *The Journal of Negro History* 35, 1 (1950): 107–09.

157. Woodson, "Thomas Jesse Jones," 107. Woodson and others have strongly criticized Jones for his work on spreading industrial education in Africa in the 1920s. However, Andrew Zimmerman demonstrates how this project was in fact begun by Washington himself, in collaboration with officials from imperial Germany (Andrew Zimmerman, *Alabama in Africa: Booker T. Washington, the German Empire, and the Globalization of the New South* [Princeton, NJ: Princeton University Press, 2010].).

158. W. E. B. Du Bois, "The General Education Board," 1929, W. E. B. Du Bois Papers (WEBDBP), Special Collections and University Archives, University of Massachusetts Amherst Libraries (online repository).

159. Quoted in "Notes and Announcements," *Bulletin of the American Association of University Professors* 16, 6 (1930): 436.

160. Bacote, *The Story of Atlanta University*, 262.

161. V. L. Avery, *Philanthropy in Black Higher Education: A Fateful Hour Creating the Atlanta University System* (New York: Palgrave Macmillan, 2013), 137.

162. Bacote, *The Story of Atlanta University*, 261.

163. B. Brawley, *History of Morehouse College* (College Park, MD: McGrath, 1970), 106.

164. Bacote, *The Story of Atlanta University*, 264–65.

165. Avery, *Philanthropy in Black Higher Education*, 112–13.

166. Avery, 116.

167. Avery, 120, xix.

168. Avery, 129.

169. *Guide to the Trevor Arnett Papers*, University of Chicago Library, https://www .lib.uchicago.edu/e/scrc/findingaids/view.php?eadid=ICU.SPCL.ARNETT, accessed on July 15, 2019.

170. Avery, *Philanthropy in Black Higher Education*, 130.

171. Fosdick, *Adventure in Giving*, 200–203.

172. Avery, *Philanthropy in Black Higher Education*, 144.

173. Avery, 146.

174. Avery, 161.

175. Avery, 165–67.

176. M. P. Douglass, *Phoenix in Academe: The Birth and Early Development of the Claremont Graduate University, 1925–1952* (Bloomington, IN: Xlibris, 2010).

177. Elisabeth S. Peck, *Berea's First 125 Years: 1855-1980* (Lexington: University Press of Kentucky, 1982), 46.

178. Peck, *Berea's First 125 Years*, 68–69, 47–48.

179. B. T. Washington, Letter to W. G. Frost, February 12, 1903, Box 7, William G. Frost Papers (WGFP), Berea College Archives, Berea, KY.

180. As Ogden warned Frost in 1905, persistent rumors were circulating that "while outwardly opposing the Day law you were secretly in favor of it" (R. C. Ogden, Letter to W. G. Frost, December 1, 1905, Box 8, WGFP.).

181. *Berea College v. Kentucky*, 211 US 45 (1908).

182. W. G. Frost, "The Attitude of Berea College," *Louisville Courier-Journal*, April 3, 1904.

183. Du Bois, *The College-Bred Negro*, 36. In fact, Hopkins did not admit a Black undergraduate until 1945 (K. Pearce, "In Memoriam: Frederick Scott," *Johns Hopkins University Hub*, last modified July 20, 2017, https://hub.jhu.edu/2017/07/20/frederick-scott-johns-hopkins/).

184. Peck, *Berea's First 125 Years*, 53.

185. W. H. Wilson et al., Letter to W. G. Frost, March 28, 1904, Box 23, WGFP; Peck, *Berea's First 125 Years*, 54.

186. W. G. Frost, Confidential Memo to Trustees, March 17, 1904, Box 23, WGFP.

187. W. G. Frost, Letter to A. Carnegie, April 19, 1905, Box 8, WGFP.

188. "Race Separation at Berea; A Ringing Protest Against It from William Lloyd Garrison," *New York Age*, March 7, 1907.

189. "Berea College's 'Jim Crow' Annex," *New York Age*, December 6, 1906.

190. W. Isom, dir., *The Swift Story*, East Tennessee PBS, 2015.

191. Peck, *Berea's First 125 Years*, 56–57.

192. "40 Students Leave Lincoln Institute," *Paducah News-Democrat*, October 31, 1925.

193. "Randle Bond Truett Elected President of Lincoln Institute," *Louisville Courier-Journal*, October 4, 1932.

194. "A Southern White Man's Impression of Tuskegee," *Connecticut School Journal* 7, 40 (1902): 12.

195. "White Illiteracy in the South," *Colored American* (Washington, DC), March 29, 1902, 8.

196. Peck, *Berea's First 125 Years*, 68–69.

197. Frost's reference to the "lost" western frontier was a direct reference to the historian Frederick Jackson Turner's "frontier thesis," posed two years earlier, which held that the constant existence of a frontier had shaped American society in virtuous ways but had now been obliterated by the westward expansion of white Americans.

198. H. D. Shapiro, *Appalachia on Our Mind: The Southern Mountains and Mountaineers in the American Consciousness, 1870–1920* (Chapel Hill: University of North Carolina Press, 1978), 119–22.

199. M. Carson, *Settlement Folk: Social Thought and the American Settlement Movement, 1885–1930* (Chicago: University of Chicago Press, 1990).

200. N. S. Shaler, Letter to W. G. Frost, February 15, 1985, Box 5, WGFP; D. N. Livingston, "Science and Society: Nathaniel S. Shaler and Racial Ideology," *Transactions of the Institute of British Geographers* 9, 2 (1984): 181–210.

201. W. G. Frost, "Our Contemporary Ancestors in the Southern Mountains," *Atlantic Monthly*, March 1899.

202. W. G. Frost, Letter to J. W. Lloyd, May 4, 1899, Box 5, WGFP.

203. W. G. Frost, Letter to A. Carnegie, February 6, 1903, Box 7, WGFP; W. G. Frost, Letter to A. Carnegie, May 2, 1912, Box 10, WGFP.

204. "Berea College Meeting at the Old South Church," pamphlet, Box 15, William J. Hutchins Papers (WJHP), Berea College Archives, Berea, KY.

205. "Address of Frost and W.J. Hutchins, Inauguration," 1920, Box 15, WJHP.

206. W. G. Frost, "The Southern Mountaineer: Our Kindred of the Boone and Lincoln Type," *American Monthly Review of Reviews* 21, 3 (1900): 307.

207. Peck, *Berea's First 125 Years*, 79; W. G. Frost, *For the Mountains: An Autobiography* (New York: Fleming H. Revell Co., 1937), 295.

208. Frost, *For the Mountains*, 143.

209. R. C. Ogden, Letter to W. G. Frost, April 30, 1906, Box 8, WGFP.

210. B. P Washington, Letter to W. G. Frost, May 24, 1907, Box 9, WGFP.

211. Peck, *Berea's First 125 Years*, 92.

212. "What You Will See at Berea," *The Berea Quarterly* 18, 4 (1915): 25.

213. Peck, *Berea's First 125 Years*, 98; W. G. Frost, "An Educational Institution to Fit: Convocation Address—January 1920," Box 15, WGFP.

214. *Berea College General Catalog, 1917–1918* (Berea, KY: n.p., 1918), 4.

215. "Carnegie Hall Audience Hears of Berea's Needs," *Brooklyn Daily Eagle*, February 11, 1911.

216. "Few in the Audience Had Seen Lincoln; Appeals for Berea College," *New York Times*, February 11, 1911.

217. W. Wilson, "Berea and the Nation," pamphlet, excerpted from *The Outlook*, March 4, 1911, Box 10, WGFP.

218. Wilson, "Princeton for the Nation's Service."

219. W. Wilson, Letter to W. G. Frost, December 27, 1899, Box 5, WGFP.

220. W. Wilson, Letter to A. Carnegie, May 18, 1914, Box 223, ACP.

221. A. Carnegie, Letter to W. Wilson, May 21, 1914, Box 224, ACP.

222. H. S. Pritchett, Letter to W. Wilson, 1914, Box 45, CFATR.

223. Frost, *For the Mountains*, 291.

224. W. G. Frost, Letter to H. S. Pritchett, July 9, 1906, Box 45, CFATR.

225. W. G. Frost, Letter to A. Carnegie, May 2, 1912, Box 10, WGFP.

226. Frost, *For the Mountains*, 284; A. Flexner, Letter to W. G. Frost, January 13, 1916, Box 12, WGFP; H. S. Pritchett, Letter to W. G. Frost, July 30, 1906, Box 8, WGFP.

227. H. S. Pritchett, Letter to W. Buttrick, June 12, 1914, Box 45, CFATR.

228. Frost, *For the Mountains*, 292.

229. "Address of Frost and W.J. Hutchins, Inauguration," 1920, Box 15, WJHP, 26–27

230. Peck, *Berea's First 125 Years*, 96.

231. W. J. Hutchins, Letter to E. Embree, December 12, 1928, Box 41, WJHP.

232. W. G. Frost, Letter to W. J. Hutchins, June 30, 1931, Box 13, WGFP; W. G. Frost, Letter to Jesse Baird, January 8, 1926, Box 13, WGFP.

233. "The Case for Berea College," pamphlet, 1936, Box 116, WJHP.

234. Frost, *For the Mountains*, 301

235. Peck, *Berea's First 125 Years*, 157.

236. Digest of Education Statistics, "Table 333.90: Endowment funds of the 120 degree-granting postsecondary institutions with the largest endowments, by rank order: Fiscal year 2018," https://nces.ed.gov/programs/digest/d19/tables/dt19_333.90.asp, accessed on October 10, 2020. Long after Frost was dead, the GEB finally came around. In 1964, at the close of its spend-down period, the foundation gave its very last grant to Berea (J. Hampton, "$100,000 to Aid Berea Students," *Louisville Courier-Journal*, August 6, 1961.).

237. As part of their tuition remission, Berea students still participate in the mandatory Labor Program that Frost launched.

CHAPTER 6

1. "Protest Against 'Carnegieizing' State Universities," *Oakland Enquirer*, June 27, 1908.

2. "Massachusetts the First to Kneel," *Springfield Republican*, August 5, 1908.

3. "L.S.U. and the Carnegie Fund," *New Orleans Times Democrat*, July 4, 1908.

4. Quoted in "State Universities Refuse to Be Carnegie-$$$-Marked," *Los Angeles Herald*, July 23, 1908.

5. "Menace in an Educational Trust," *Baltimore Manufacturer's Record*, January 14, 1909.

6. H. S. Pritchett, "The Organization of Higher Education," *Atlantic Monthly* 102, 6 (1908): 783–89.

7. H. S. Pritchett, "Should the Carnegie Foundation Be Suppressed?" *North American Review* 201, 713 (1914): 554–66.

8. J. Rosen, *Louis D. Brandeis: American Prophet* (New Haven, CT: Yale University Press, 2016), 28–50.

9. L. D. Brandeis, *Other People's Money: And How the Bankers Use It* (New York: Frederick A. Stokes Co., 1914).

10. A. T. Mason, *Brandeis: A Free Man's Life* (New York: Viking, 1946), 419.

11. Rosen, *Louis D. Brandeis*, 13.

12. Rosen, 24.

13. Mason, *Brandeis*, 372–85.

14. Mason, 489.

15. M. J. Sklar, *The Corporate Reconstruction of American Capitalism, 1890–1916* (New York: Cambridge University Press, 1988), 183.

16. M. I. Urofsky, *Louis D. Brandeis: A Life* (New York: Schocken Books, 2009), 345–46.

17. Chernow, *Titan*, 565–65.

18. Chernow, *Titan*, 565–66.

19. "Iowan Keeps After Education Board," *Des Moines Register and Leader*, May 1, 1914.

20. "Says Oil King Hopes to Control Government; Senator Kenyon Gives Reasons for Desiring to Repeal General Education Board Charter," *Washington Evening Star*, May 2, 1914.

21. H. S. Pritchett, "The Relations of Christian Denominations.".

22. "Do Not Approve School Message from Pritchett," *Atlanta Constitution*, May 21, 1908.

23. W. A. Candler, *Dangerous Donations and Degrading Doles; or, A Vast Scheme for Capturing and Controlling the Colleges and Universities of the Country* (Atlanta, GA: n.p., 1909), 11.

24. H. S. Pritchett, "Is there a Place for a Profession of Commerce?" Speech typescript, Box 11, HSPP.

25. Candler, *Dangerous Donations*, 15–16.

26. Candler, 17–24.

27. Candler, 21–22.

28. Candler, 34–35. Bishop Candler, admittedly, had an ax to grind when it came to Northern philanthropy. Also in 1909, he argued for rejecting Rockefeller's gift of $1 million to fight the debilitating parasite hookworm, claiming that the donation was a form of "slander" ("Standard Oil and the Hookworm," *Charlotte News*, November 3, 1909.).

29. "'An Agnostic Steelmonger;' Carnegie So Termed by Bishop Candler," *Boston Globe*, June 19, 1913.

30. G. M. Marsden, *The Soul of the American University: From Protestant Establishment to Established Nonbelief* (New York: Oxford University Press, 1994), 278–79.

31. "Attacks Carnegie Work; His Educational Movement Fosters Agnosticism, Says Rev. D. T. Burrell," *New York Times*, February 12, 1910.

32. "No Carnegie War on Christianity," *Atlanta Constitution*, February 14, 1910.

33. P. Gleason, *Contending with Modernity: Catholic Higher Education in the Twentieth Century* (New York: Oxford University Press, 1995).

34. "Educational Trust a Menace to Religion," *The Irish Standard* (Minneapolis),

July 8, 1911. American Catholics in the early twentieth century were particularly alarmed by centralized educational authority, astutely believing that it might threaten their ability to run their own schools. In the 1920s, many Catholic leaders opposed the Sterling-Reed Bill, an unsuccessful attempt to create a cabinet-level Department of Education, including one who predicted that it would lead to "an army of bureaucrats, tens of thousands of inspectors, political interference in education" ("The Education Bill Advances," *Journal of the National Education Association* 13, 3: 112.). Some states passed laws that specifically sought to shut down Catholic schools, like Oregon's 1922 Compulsory Education Act, which banned private schooling and was struck down by the US Supreme Court in the landmark decision *Pierce v. Society of Sisters of the Holy Names of Jesus and Mary* (268 U.S. 510 [1925]).

35. Marsden, *The Soul of the American University*, 284.

36. J. R. Day, "The Carnegie Foundation and Syracuse University" (letter to the editor), *Syracuse Post-Standard*, April 8, 1910.

37. Candler, *Dangerous Donations*, 47.

38. Candler, 11-12.

39. H. S. Pritchett, "Mr. Carnegie's Gift to the Teachers," *The Outlook*, May 19, 1906, 120-25.

40. Cited in "The Carnegie Foundation and the Pritchett Bomb," *The Ohio Teacher* 30, 1 (1909): 7-13.

41. C. F. Kaestle, *Pillars of the Republic: Common Schools and American Society, 1780-1860* (New York: Hill and Wang, 1983), 147.

42. D. F. Labaree, "The Power of the Parochial in Shaping the American System of Higher Education," in *Educational Research: The Importance and Effects of Institutional Spaces*, ed. P. Smeyers, M. Depaepe, and E. Keiner (Dordrecht: Springer, 2013).

43. Pritchett, "Should the Carnegie Foundation Be Suppressed?" 6.

44. Carnegie Foundation for the Advancement of Teaching, *A Study of Education in Vermont* (Bulletin No. 7) (Boston: Merrymount Press, 1914), 3-4.

45. J. Royce, "The Carnegie Foundation for the Advancement of Teaching and the Case of Middlebury College," *School and Society* 1, 5 (1915): 145-50.

46. J. Royce, "A Plea for Provincial Independence in Education," pamphlet (Middlebury, VT: n.p., 1914), 8-9.

47. Royce, "A Plea for Provincial Independence," 11.

48. Royce, 12.

49. J. C. Scott, *Seeing Like a State: How Certain Schemes to Improve the Human Condition Have Failed* (New Haven: Yale University Press, 1999).

50. Royce, "The Carnegie Foundation," 146.

51. Royce, "A Plea for Provincial Independence," 18

52. *New State Ice Co. v. Liebmann*, 285 U.S. 262 (1932).

53. H. A. Buchtel, Letter to H. S. Pritchett, October 22, 1909, Box 50, CFATR.

54. H. Tiede, *University Reform: The Founding of the American Association of University Professors* (Baltimore: Johns Hopkins University Press, 2015), 48.

55. J. A. Karlin, "Conflict and Crisis in University Politics: The Firing of President E. B. Craighead, 1915," *Montana: The Magazine of Western History* 36, 3 (1986): 48–61.

56. A.E. Winship, "Why the Carnegie Resolutions?", *Journal of Education* 80 (October 8, 1914), 311–12.

57. Quoted in Ellen Condliffe Lagemann, *Private Power*, 185.

58. T. W. Churchill, "Carnegie Foundation," *The Journal of Education* 80 (September 3, 1914, 174–75.

59. "Foundation Born of Carnegie Evokes Varying Opinions from College Heads," *Cincinnati Enquirer*, June 18, 1914.

60. Royce, "The Carnegie Foundation," 146.

61. Tiede, *University Reform*, 87.

62. J. M. Cattell, "The Carnegie Foundation for the Advancement of Teaching," *Science* 29, 744 (1909): 532–39.

63. J. M. Cattell, "Academic and Industrial Efficiency," *Popular Science Monthly* 83, 1 (1911): 100–01, .

64. J. M. Cattell, "Correspondence in Regard to the Length of Service Pensions of the Carnegie Foundation," *Science* 32, 831 (1910): 797–800.

65. J. M. Cattell, *University Control* (New York: The Science Press, 1913).

66. Cattell, *University Control*, 31–35.

67. Cattell, 48.

68. Joseph Jastrow, "Academic Aspects of Administration," *Popular Science Monthly* 73 (October 1908): 326.

69. Jastrow, "Academic Aspects," 325–27

70. Tiede, *University Reform*, 153–55.

71. C. W. Barrow, "*Realpolitik* in the American University: Charles A. Beard and the Problem of Academic Repression," *New Political Science* 36, 4 (2014): 444.

72. C. A. Beard, "Professor Beard's Letter of Resignation from Columbia University," *School and Society* 6, 146 (1917): 446–47.

73. P. M. Rutkoff and W. B. Scott, *New School: A History of the New School for Social Research* (New York: The Free Press, 1986) 10–12.

74. Rutkoff and Scott, *New School*, 19.

75. R. F. Teichgraeber, "Introduction," in T. Veblen, *The Higher Learning in America: The Annotated Edition: A Memorandum on the Conduct of Universities by Business Men* (Baltimore: Johns Hopkins University Press, 2015), 5–7.

76. According to Teichgraeber, the book's original subtitle was *A Study in Depravity* (Veblen, *The Higher Learning*, 217 fn. 34).

77. Teichgraeber, "Introduction," 11.

78. Veblen, *The Higher Learning*, 80–85

79. Teichgraeber, "Introduction," 20.

80. Veblen, *The Higher Learning*, 204.

81. Veblen, 78.

82. Veblen, 168.

83. Veblen, 88–91.

84. Veblen, 223.

85. Veblen, 229–230.

86. Rutkoff and Scott, *New School*, 40.

87. Rutkoff and Scott, 22.

88. Z. Haberler, "The Role of Publicity in the Formation of the American Association of University Professors, 1913-1919," *Perspectives on the History of Higher Education* 31, 1 (2015): 49–78.

89. J. M. Wallace, *Liberal Journalism and American Education, 1914-1941* (New Brunswick, NJ: Rutgers University Press, 1991).

90. Wallace, *Liberal Journalism*, 33

91. U. Sinclair, *The Goose-Step: A Study of American Education* (Pasadena, CA: self-published, 1923), 163.

92. Sinclair, *The Goose-Step*, 23

93. Sinclair, 24

94. Sinclair, 115.

95. Sinclair, 134.

96. Sinclair, 407–12.

97. "The Carnegie Foundation Some More," *Charlotte News*, December 25, 1910.

98. Quoted in "The Carnegie Foundation Some More."

99. "The Carnegie Pension," (reprint from *The Springfield Republican*) *Journal of Education* 71, 17 (1910): 459.

100. "Foundations Menacing True Academic Freedom," *Burlington Free Press and Times*, July 16, 1914.

101. M. E. Curti, *The University of Wisconsin: A History* (Madison: University of Wisconsin Press, 1949), 57–58.

102. "The Efficiency Nostrum at Harvard," *New York Evening Post*, January 7, 1913.

103. "What Is at Stake at Wisconsin's University," *New York Evening Post*, April 10, 1915.

104. K. B. Zook, "Lost & Found: The AP Stylebook Turns 99?" *Columbia Journalism Review*, https://archives.cjr.org/behind_the_news/zook.php, accessed on February 1, 2020.

105. J. P. Gavit, *College* (New York: Harcourt, Brace & Co., 1925), ix.

106. Gavit, *College*, 102.

107. "The College and the Student," *Popular Science Monthly* 75, 1 (1909): 99.

108. Veblen, *The Higher Learning*, 120.

109. Gavit, *College*, 175–81. Also see Ris, "Hierarchy as a Theme," for how the extracurriculum helped prepare undergraduates for jobs in bureaucratic organizations.

110. A. M. Nickliss, "Phoebe Apperson Hearst's 'Gospel of Wealth,' 1883-1901," *Pacific Historical Review* 71, 4 (2002): 591-92.

111. Nickliss, "Phoebe Apperson Hearst's 'Gospel of Wealth,'" 600.

112. M. McClain, *Ellen Browning Scripps : New Money and American Philanthropy* (Lincoln, NE: University of Nebraska Press, 2017), 208.

113. E. E. Slosson, *Great American Universities* (New York: Macmillan, 1910), ix.

114. Slosson, *Great American Universities*, 515–17.

115. Slosson, 503.

116. Slosson, 504.

117. Slosson, 508.

118. Albert J. Nock, "The Vanished University," *The Freeman* 3, 68 (1921): 364.

119. D. K. Pearsons, Letter to A. Carnegie, February 16, 1906, Box 125, ACP.

120. D. K. Pearsons, *Daniel K. Pearsons: His Life and Works* (Elgin, IL: Brethren Publishing House, 1912), 394.

121. Pearsons, *Daniel K. Pearsons*, 5.

122. Pearsons, 48.

123. E. F. Williams, *The Life of Dr. D. K. Pearsons, Friend of the Small College and of Missions* (New York: The Pilgrim Press, 1911), 84.

124. Pearsons, *Daniel K. Pearsons*, 54.

125. H. S. Pritchett, "Address of Dr. Pritchett at Stevens Institute Alumni Dinner," typescript, 1910, Box 39, CFATR.

126. Du Bois, *The Education of Black People*,, 58.

127. Nock, "Vanished University."

128. A 1915 editorial in the *New Republic* argued that ministerial control of colleges had been tolerable and bemoaned the recent "passing of control from the ghostly to the moneyed element" (Wallace, *Liberal Journalism*, 33.).

129. S. Nearing, "Who's Who among College Trustees," *School and Society* 6 (September 8, 1917): 297–99.

130. Carnegie Foundation for the Advancement of Teaching, "The Support of Higher Education," *Third Annual Report of the President and Treasurer* (Boston: Merrymount Press, 1908), 148.

131. *Catalogue of the Officers and Students of Trinity College, 1889-1890* (Hartford, CT: Case, Lockwood & Brainard Co., 1889), 8–9.

132. *Trinity College Bulletin: Catalogue Number* (Boston: Merrymount Press, 1921), 9.

133. C. D. Bowen, *A History of Lehigh University* (Bethlehem, PA: Times Publishing Company, 1924), 92–93.

134. I. J. Lubbers, *College Organization and Administration: Current Practices in Independent Liberal Arts Colleges* (PhD diss., Northwestern University, 1931), 26.

135. Fisher, "The Role of Politics," 121.

136. R. S. Bourne, "Who Owns the Universities?" *New Republic* 3, July 17, 1915, 269–70.

137. A. D. White, Letter to A. Carnegie, February 16, 1906, Box 125, ACP.

138. F. Vanderlip, Letter to H. Pritchett, February 9, 1906, Box 31, CFATR.

139. Ris, "The Education of Andrew Carnegie," 420–22.

140. J. Bertram, Letter to H. Pritchett, June 6, 1908, Box 31, CFATR. Pritchett scolded Bertram in a letter the next year: "Your present method of giving almost surely prevents any recognition by Mr. Carnegie of college virtue. The moment a

college by good work and wise management of its resources comes into a place where it can do a better thing, you stop helping it and turn to assist some weak institution" (H. S. Pritchett, Letter to J. Bertram, March 24, 1909, Box 31, CFATR.).

141. H. S. Pritchett, "The Critics of the College," *Atlantic Monthly* 114 (September 1914): 332–41.

142. W. Clark, *Academic Charisma and the Origins of the Research University* (Chicago: University of Chicago Press, 2008).

143. S. E. Epler, *Honorary Degrees: A Survey of Their Use and Abuse* (Washington, DC: American Council on Public Affairs, 1941), 95.

144. Ris, "The Education of Andrew Carnegie," 422.

145. G. P. Benton, *The Real College* (Cincinnati: Jennings and Graham, 1909), 7.

146. I. Sharpless, *The Story of a Small College* (Philadelphia: John C. Winston Co., 1918), 224.

147. Sharpless, *The Story of a Small College*, 228–29.

148. B. I. Bell, "Why Do We Need Church Colleges?" *Living Church* 62 (December 6, 1919), 181.

149. *Report of the Commissioner of Education, Vol. 2* (Washington, DC: Government Printing Office, 1917), 291.

150. G. Johnson, "Education of the Negro," Letter to the Editor, *The Nation* 100, 2599 (1915), 443.

151. Anderson and Moss, *Dangerous Donations,* 93.

152. Leroy Davis, *A Clashing of the Soul: John Hope and the Dilemma of African American Leadership and Black Higher Education in the Early Twentieth Century* (Athens, GA: University of Georgia Press, 1998), 255–56.

153. Logan, *Howard University,* 154–55.

154. Harlan, *Booker T. Washington, ,* 98–101.

155. Mia Bay, *To Tell the Truth Freely: The Life of Ida B. Wells* (New York: Farrar, Straus, and Giroux, 2010), 232–74.

156. L. R. Harlan and R. W. Smock, "Introduction," in *BTW Papers*, vol. 13, 1984, xxii–xxiii. Villard sometimes alternatively referred to the organization as the Association of Negro Rural and Industrial Schools, and Harlan and Smock use that title, but this was not its actual name.

157. O. G. Villard, *Fighting Years: Memoirs of a Liberal Editor* (New York: Harcourt, Brace and Co., 1939), 236–41. The 1912 election presented a difficult choice for Black progressives, many of whom backed Wilson despite his obvious racism. The next year, amid the segregation scandal, Washington mocked Du Bois and Trotter in a New York newspaper for not following his lead in supporting Taft (Harlan, *Booker T. Washington,,* 411.).

158. Du Bois and Dill, *College-Bred Negro American.*

159. "The Persistent Onslaught," *The Crisis* 10, 3 (1915): 132.

160. "Philanthropy," *The Crisis* 16, 3 (1918): 113.

161. "Hampton," *The Crisis* 15, 1 (1917): 11.

162. W. E. B. Du Bois, Letter to N. A. White, July 24, 1924, WEBDBP; W. E. B. Du Bois, Letter to A. J. Allison, October 22, 1924, WEBDBP.

163. W. E. B. Du Bois, Letter to "Messrs. Wesley, Atkins, & Chandler," December 11, 1924, WEBDBP.

164. M. J. M. Washington, Letter to W. E. B. Du Bois, December 12, 1924, WEBDBP.

165. R. Wolters, *The New Negro on Campus: Black College Rebellions of the 1920s* (Princeton University Press, 1975), 40.

166. Wolters, *The New Negro on Campus*, 45.

167. Wolters, 48–49.

168. Wolters, 60–61.

169. P. D. Cravath, Letter to W. Buttrick, April 24, 1925, Box 52, CFATR.

170. M. D. Jones, "Student Unrest at Talladega College, 1887-1914," *The Journal of Negro History* 70, Summer-Fall 1985): 73–81.

171. Holland, *Nathan B. Young*, 76–79.

172. Holland, 81.

173. Holland, 83.

174. Holland, 98–101.

175. Wolters, *The New Negro on Campus*, 200–01.

176. Quoted in Wolters, 259.

177. Quoted in Wolters, 236.

178. Quoted in Wolters, 252.

179. Wolters, 245.

180. Wolters, 248.

181. Quoted in Wolters, 261.

182. Quoted in Wolters, 265.

183. Wolters, 271–74.

184. N. C. Crosby, *The First Half Century of Dartmouth College* (Hanover, NH: J. B. Parker, 1876), 53.

CHAPTER 7

1. S. Skowronek, *Building a New American State: The Expansion of National Administrative Capacities, 1877-1920* (New York: Cambridge University Press, 1982).

2. G. E. Fellows, "Address," *Association of American Colleges Bulletin* 1, 1 (1915): 49.

3. *Report of the Commissioner of Education, Vol. 2* (Washington, DC: Government Printing Office, 1900), 1913.

4. Association of American Universities, "The Call," in *Journal of Proceedings and Addresses of the First and Second Annual Conferences* (Chicago: University of Chicago Press, 1901), 11.

5. Association of American Universities *Journal of Proceedings and Addresses of the Eighth Annual Conference* (University of Chicago Press, 1907), 10; Hawkins, *Banding Together,* 108.

6. Carnegie Foundation for the Advancement of Teaching, "The Association of American Universities," in *Second Annual Report of the President and Treasurer,* 91.

7. Association of American Universities, *Journal of Proceedings and Addresses of the Ninth Annual Conference* (University of Chicago Press, 1908), 76.

8. Hawkins, *Banding Together*, 85.

9. W. K. Selden, *Accreditation: A Struggle over Standards in Higher Education* (New York: Harper, 1960), 47.

10. AAU, *Journal of Proceedings and Addresses of the Fourteenth Annual Conference* (University of Chicago Press, 1912), 58–59.

11. Hawkins, *Banding Together*, 85.

12. Hawkins, 38.

13. Hawkins, 15.

14. *Transactions and Proceedings of the National Association of State Universities, No. 5* (Bangor, ME: Bangor Co-Operative. Printing Co., 1907), 113. The NASU took a similar stance of complaint against the CFAT, accepting the foundation's authority as a standardizing agency but criticizing it for not including them (*Transactions and Proceedings*, 215–43.)

15. *Transactions and Proceedings*, 112–13.

16. "Finds New Trust to Bust; President MacLean of U. of I. out with Big Stick," *Sioux City Journal*, November 20, 1908.

17. "The Proposed Federal Department of Education," *Transactions and Proceedings of the National Association of State Universities, Vol. 16.* (Lexington, KY: Transylvania Printing Co., 1918), 162–68. The ACE representative who described the proposal for the cabinet-level department acknowledged that given the lessons of the war and the new spirit of Brandeis-style local control, the idea was up against the "fancied danger of Prussianizing our system of education" that might arise "in the minds of all Americans trained in the doctrine of local self-government."

18. S. P. Capen, "The Colleges in a Nationalized Educational Scheme," *School and Society* 9, 230 (1919): 613.

19. C. R. Mann, *A Study of Engineering Education* (CFAT Bulletin No. 11) (Boston: Merrymount Press, 1918), 107.

20. Hawkins, *Banding Together*, 65.

21. Noble, *America by Design,* 232–33.

22. Hawkins, *Banding Together*, 66–67.

23. "First Annual Meeting," *Association of American Colleges Bulletin* 1, 1 (1915): 59, 41.

24. "Second Conference, Held in the Offices of the Presbyterian College Board," *First Annual Report of the Council of Church Boards of Education* (New York: n.p., 1911), 7.

25. "First Annual Meeting," 43

26. "First Annual Meeting," 131.

27. *Proceedings of the Second Annual Meeting of the Association of American Colleges* (Dubuque, IA: Telegraph-Herald Print, 1916), 23.

28. "First Annual Meeting," 43.

29. "First Annual Meeting," 108.

30. *Proceedings*, 61.

31. "First Annual Meeting," 137.

32. "First Annual Meeting," 54.

33. "First Annual Meeting," 75; *Proceedings*, 115.

34. "First Annual Meeting," 12.

35. "First Annual Meeting," 49.

36. *Proceedings*, 23.

37. "First Annual Meeting," 5.

38. *Proceedings*, 5.

39. W. S. Learned, Letter to H. S. Pritchett, March 19, 1914, Box 38, CFATR.

40. *Proceedings*, 105–12.

41. "First Annual Meeting," 141–46.

42. "First Annual Meeting," 45.

43. "First Annual Meeting," 55.

44. *Proceedings*, 22.

45. *Proceedings*, 100.

46. Hawkins, *Banding Together*, 90.

47. Hawkins, 55.

48. Hawkins, 112.

49. G. Orwell, *Animal Farm* (New York: Harcourt, Brace, 1946), 118.

50. "First Annual Meeting," 49.

51. "First Annual Meeting," 74.

52. J. Dewey, "The American Association of University Professors Introductory Address," *Science* 41, 1048 (1915): 150.

53. Tiede, *University Reform*, 2, 58.

54. Quoted in T. R. Cain, *Establishing Academic Freedom: Politics, Principles, and the Development of Core Values* (New York: Palgrave Macmillan, 2012), 34.

55. H. S. Pritchett, Letter to G. S. Hall, January 28, 1914, Box 49, CFATR; Tiede, *University Reform*, 55.

56. A. O. Lovejoy, "The Retrospective Anticipation of the Carnegie Foundation," *Science* 31, 794 (1910): 414–15.

57. J. Jastrow, "The Academic Unrest," *The Nation* 108, 2796, (1919): 158.

58. Tiede, *University Reform*, 173.

59. Nearing, "Who's Who Among College Trustees?", 299.

60. Tiede, *University Reform*, 77.

61. Tiede, 80

62. Tiede, 92.

63. Tiede, 218.

64. Tiede, 104–10, passim.

65. Tiede, 104–10, passim.

66. Tiede, 126–29.

67. "General Report of the Committee on Academic Freedom and Tenure," *Bulletin of the American Association of University Professors* 1, 1 (1915): 39.

68. Quoted in "Recent Educational Discussion," *Bulletin of the American Association of University Professors* 6, 7 (1920): 23.

69. "Demands of the Professors' Union for Protection and Academic Freedom," *Current Opinion* 60, 3 (1916): 193.

70. Cain, *Establishing Academic Freedom*, 44–45.

71. J. H. Wigmore, "President's Report for 1916," *Bulletin of the American Association of University Professors* 2, 5 (1916): 42–43.

72. J. M. Cattell, *Carnegie Pensions* (New York: The Science Press, 1919), iii–v.

73. J. M. Cattell, "The Carnegie Foundation for the Advancement of Teaching," *Science* 29, 744 (1909): 533.

74. Tiede, *University Reform*, 203.

75. D. S. Jordan, Letter to H. S. Pritchett, January 13, 1916, Box 32, CFATR.

76. C. Van Hise, Letter to H. S. Pritchett, November 28, 1917, Box 32, CFATR.

77. J. Schurman, Letter to H. S. Pritchett, September 23, 1917, Box 32, CFATR.

78. Wigmore, "President's Report for 1916," 41–46.

79. Tiede, *University Reform*, 204–05.

80. Tiede, 172.

81. Fosdick, *Adventure in Giving*, 148

82. Tiede, *University Reform*, 213.

83. Tiede, 212.

84. Cain, *Establishing Academic Freedom*, 93–94.

85. C. A. Harper, *A Century of Public Teacher Education: The Story of the State Teachers Colleges as They Evolved from the Normal Schools* (Washington, DC: National Education Association, 1939), 138.

86. National Education Association, *Journal of Proceedings and Addresses of the Fifty-Second Annual Meeting* (Chicago: University of Chicago Press, 1914), 540.

87. "Won for Suffrage; Educators at St. Paul Session Laugh Down Opposition; Call Foundations Menace," *Washington Post*, July 10, 1914.

88. Winship, "Why the Carnegie Resolutions?", 311.

89. Lagemann, *Private Power*, 189.

90. H. S. Pritchett, Letter to W. S. Learned, July 14, 1914, Box 38, CFATR.

91. "Education Board to Answer Butler," *New York Times*, November 21, 1913. Peixotto led the fight to allow women to keep their teaching jobs when they became pregnant; her obituary in the *New York Times* credited her efforts as leading to the fact that in all fields of employment, "it is now a commonplace for a woman to be assured of her job if she leaves to have a baby" ("Mrs. Bridget Peixotto Dies; Teacher Won '15 Maternity Case," *New York Times*, April 12, 1972.).

92. H. S. Pritchett, Letter to W. S. Learned, July 14, 1914, Box 38, CFATR.

93. Winship, "Why the Carnegie Resolutions?" 312.

94. E. R. Ducharme and M. K. Ducharme, *The American Association of Colleges for Teacher Education: A History* (Washington, DC: AACTE Publications, 1998), 3–4.

95. Connerly, *The Effects of Isomorphism*, 119–27.

96. Winship, "Why the Carnegie Resolutions?" 312.

97. "Seerley Hits the Carnegie Fund 'Overlordship,'" *Des Moines Evening Tribune*, September 23, 1920.

98. H. H. Seerley, "Preliminary Statement," *Bulletin of the Iowa State Teachers College* 17, 4 (1917): 5.

99. "Iowa State Teachers College" *Educational Review* 56 (1918): 359–60.

100. Marion Talbot and L. K. M. Rosenberry, *The History of the American Association of University Women, 1881-1931* (Boston: Houghton Mifflin, 1931), 65-69.

101. Talbot and Rosenberry, *The History of the American Association*, 75-78.

102. Talbot and Rosenberry, 80-85

103. E. A. Colton, *The Various Types of Southern Colleges for Women* (Raleigh, NC: Edwards & Broughton Print. Co., 1916); J. M. Johnson, "'Standing Up for High Standards': The Southern Association of College Women," in *The Educational Work of Women's Organizations, 1890-1960*, ed. A. M. Knupfer and C. Woysnher (New York: Palgrave Macmillan, 2008), 30.

104. Johnson, "'Standing Up,'" 25-28.

105. Quoted in Brint and Karabel, *The Diverted Dream*, 33.

106. J. M. Wood, "The Function of the Junior College." In George F. Zook, ed., *National Conference of Junior Colleges, 1920* (Bureau of Education Bulletin No. 19) (Washington, DC: Government Printing Office, 1920), 3-5.

107. , D. MacKenzie, "Problems of the Public Junior College," In Zook, *National Conference*, 31-34.

108. P. P. Claxton, "The Better Organization of Higher Education in the United States," in Zook, *National Conference*, 24.

109. Robert Pedersen presents Claxton's role at the conference as more opposi-tional, demanding that the junior college serve as "the university's gatekeeper, re-sponsible for sorting out the less able, the poorly motivated, and the unprepared," while the assembled representatives pushed back and used the conference to claim "the junior college's freedom from the university" (R. Pedersen, "The St. Louis Conference: The Junior College Movement Reborn," *Community College Journal* 65, 5 [1995]: 26-30.).

110. Brint and Karabel, *The Diverted Dream*, 34.

111. T. R. Cain, "The First Attempts to Unionize the Faculty," *Teachers College Record* 112, 3 (2010): 876-913.

112. Du Bois, *The Education of Black People*, 18.

113. M. R. Dalton, *The Long Road to Recognition: A Historical Investigation of the Activities of the Association of Colleges for Negro Youth, 1913-1934* (PhD diss., Uni-versity of Tennessee, 1991), 61-65.

114. Dalton, *The Long Road*, 75.

115. Dalton, 78-81.

116. Dalton, 83-89.

117. Dalton, 93-106.

118. W. W. Brierley, Letter to W. E. B. Du Bois, June 16, 1930, WEBDBP.

119. Dalton, *The Long Road*, 106-09.

120. "List of Colleges and Universities Approved March 20, 1913," *Proceedings of the Eighteenth Annual Meeting of the North Central Association of Colleges and Secondary Schools* (Chicago: "The Association," 1913), 63.

121. L. E. Blauch, *Accreditation in Higher Education* (Washington, DC: Government Printing Office, 1959), 10-11.

122. *Proceedings of the Thirty-First Annual Convention of the Association of Colleges and Preparatory Schools of the Middle States and Maryland* (1917), 5.

123. Selden, *Accreditation*, 34–35.

124. Scott M. Gelber, *Grading the College: A History of Evaluating Teaching and Learning* (Baltimore: Johns Hopkins University Press, 2020), 110–11.

125. Gelber, *Grading the College*, 119–20.

126. W. A. Allen and C. G. Pearse, *Self-Surveys by Teacher-Training Schools* (Yonkers, NY: World Book Com., 1917), 15–28.

127. Seerley, "Preliminary Statement," 5–6.

128. Allen and Pearse, *Self-Surveys*, vii.

129. Samuel P. Capen, *Accredited Higher Institutions* (Bureau of Education Bulletin No. 17) (Washington, DC: Government Printing Office, 1917).

130. George F. Zook, *Accredited Higher Institutions* (Bureau of Education Bulletin No. 30) (Washington, DC: Government Printing Office, 1922).

131. E. B. Ratcliffe, *Accredited Higher Institutions* (Bureau of Education Bulletin, 1926, No. 10) (Washington, DC: Government Printing Office, 1926).

132. *Proceedings of the Thirty-Fifth Annual Convention of the Association of Colleges and Preparatory Schools of the Middle States and Maryland* (Swarthmore, PA: "The Association," 1919), 40–57.

133. Samuel P. Capen, "Seven Devils in Exchange for One," 1939, in *The Management of Universities: Samuel P. Capen*, ed. O. A. Silverman (Buffalo, NY: Foster & Stewart, 1953), 256–70.

134. Capen, "Seven Devils," 257.

135. Noble, *America by Design*, 210–14.

136. Samuel P. Capen, "American University Education," *School and Society* 16, 411 (1922): 540.

137. Capen, "American University Education," 541.

138. Samuel P. Capen, "The Preparation of College Teachers," 1938, in Silverman, *The Management of Universities*, 185.

139. Capen, "Seven Devils," 269. "Letters of marque and reprisal," mentioned in Article I of the US Constitution, were documents that conferred state power on private citizens to commit acts at sea that would otherwise be considered piracy.

CHAPTER 8

1. Hoover's ties to higher education did not mean that he would be its savior in times of need. David Levine specifically criticizes him for failing to offer a concrete plan for boosting the higher education sector during the Depression, despite acknowledging its importance (Levine, *The American College*, 195).

2. G. H. Nash, *Herbert Hoover and Stanford University* (Stanford, CA: Stanford University Press, 1988), passim.

3. W. E. Leuchtenberg, *Herbert Hoover* (New York: Times Books, 2009), 12.

4. "Text of Hoover Acceptance Speech Gives Broad Outline of Republican Nominee's Aims," *Los Angeles Times*, August 12, 1928.

5. Elliot A. Rosen, *Hoover, Roosevelt, and the Brains Trust: From Depression to New Deal* (New York: Columbia University Press, 1977).

6. Leuchtenberg, *Herbert Hoover*, 76–78.

7. Leuchtenberg, 114.

8. It is important to note that despite the widespread celebration of engineering during the time span of this book, some voices had been skeptical all along. One of those voices belonged to Mark Twain; the protagonist of his 1889 *A Connecticut Yankee in King Arthur's Court* was a time-traveling engineer who becomes "The Boss" of Camelot and ends up destroying the kingdom and perpetrating a holocaust using electrified weaponry.

9. W. A. Jessup, "The Integrity of the American College from the Standpoint of Administration," *Bulletin of the Association of American Colleges* 23, 1 (1936): 1–11.

10. George E. Vincent, "The Few and the Many in Education," *School and Society* 43, 1108 (1936): 386–91.

11. Franklin D. Roosevelt, "Address Delivered at the Harvard Tercentenary Celebration, September 18, 1936," in *Public Papers of the Presidents of the United States: Franklin D. Roosevelt, Vol. 5* (New York: Random House, 1938), 362.

12. Bacote, *The Story of Atlanta University*, 314–15.

13. "Opposition to Seth Low's End Spreads to Alumni, Residents," *Columbia Daily Spectator*, March 9, 1936.

14. S. V. Barnes, "A Lost Opportunity in American Education? The Proposal to Merge the University of Chicago and Northwestern University," *American Journal of Education* 107, 4 (1999): 289–320.

15. R. M. Hutchins, *The Higher Learning in America* (New Haven: Yale University Press, 1936), 22–23.

16. Hutchins, *The Higher Learning*, 119.

17. Rudolph, *The American College and University*, 480.

18. Hutchins, *The Higher Learning*, 6, 11.

19. M. A. Dzuback, *Robert M. Hutchins: Portrait of an Educator* (Chicago: University of Chicago Press, 1991), 128.

20. Hutchins, *The Higher Learning*, 4.

21. Hutchins, 26.

22. Hutchins, 39.

23. Hutchins, 13.

24. Frederick Rudolph also identifies Hutchins's 1936 book as an attack on "an American consensus," writing, "Hutchins was at war with the insidious combination of progress, evolution, and empiricism in jettisoning the past, in promoting adjustment as an ideal, and in substituting vocationalism for thought as the focus of the university" (Rudolph, *The American College*, 480.). Our assessments of the dialectical path to that consensus vary, however. Instead of the extramural power struggles I have described in this book, Rudolph describes it as an on-campus "quarrel with old gods," meaning a fight between defenders of old-fashioned intellectual ideals and progressives who wanted colleges to serve the needs of a democratic society.

25. Zook and Hutchins knew each other, although there isn't much correspondence between them in archives; Hutchins's father asked him to invite Zook to become a trustee of Berea College in 1936 (G. F. Zook, Letter to W. J. Hutchins, June 12, 1936, Box 45, WJHP.).

26. P. A. Hutcheson, "Zook, George Frederick (1885-1951)," *American National Biography*, 2000, https://doi.org/10.1093/anb/9780198606697.article.0900836.

27. Zook, *Accredited Higher Institutions*, 2.

28. H. Hawkins, *Banding Together: The Rise of National Associations in American Higher Education, 1887-1950* (Johns Hopkins University Press, 1992), 101.

29. G. F. Zook, "Who Should Control Our Higher Institutions?" in *Proceedings of the Association of Land-Grant Colleges and Universities* (New Haven, CT: Quinnipiack Press, 1938), 90–99.

30. Madsen, *The National University*, 75–78.

31. A. Flexner, "Adjusting the College to American Life," *Science* 29, 740 (1909): 361–72.

32. F. T. Gates, "Memo by Mr. Gates," February 28, 1910, Box 19, Group III 26, OMRO, 7.

33. Horowitz, *The Power and Passion*, 317–23.

34. A. Carnegie, Letter to H. S. Pritchett, June 15, 1909, Box 31, CFATR.

35. Diane Ravitch describes Eliot as a onetime defender of the liberal arts whose "defection" to vocationalism came around 1908. In reality, he was never firmly in either camp and always saw value in both (Ravitch, *Left Back*, 86-87).

36. J. G. Schurman, "Some Problems of Our Universities—State and Endowed," *Transactions and Proceedings of the National Association of State Universities, No. 7* (Bangor, ME: Bangor Co-Operative Printing Co., 1909), 30–31.

37. H. J. Savage, Letter to J. G. Bowman, March 16, 1950, Box 38, CFATR.

38. Dzuback, *Robert M. Hutchins*, 36–37.

39. Fosdick, *Adventure in Giving*, 164, 217.

40. E. S. Yellin, "The (White) Search for (Black) Order: The Phelps-Stokes Fund's First Twenty Years, 1911–1931." *The Historian* 65, 2 (2002): 349.

41. A. P. Stokes, Letter to W. H. Taft, October 15, 1917, Box 66, Group III 2G, OMRO.

42. L. W. Johnson, "The Need of the Day: A Correlated and Democratic Education," *University of Illinois Bulletin 3*, January 8, 1906, 335.

43. M. S. Herbers, "Progressive Era Roots of Highlander Folk School: Lilian Wyckoff Johnson's Legacy," in *Tennessee Women: Their Lives and Times, Vol. 2*, ed. B. G. Bond and S. W. Freeman (Athens, GA: University of Georgia Press, 2015), 337–359.

44. G. L. Imes, "To Tuskegee," in *Robert Russa Moton of Hampton and Tuskegee*, ed. W. H. Hughes and F. D. Patterson (Chapel Hill: University of North Carolina Press, 1956), 80–81.

45. The trustee was Thomas Jesse Jones, with whom Moton maintained Washington's alliance (R. R. Moton, Letter to T. J. Jones, November 3, 1917, Folder 21, Robert R. Moton Papers, Tuskegee University Archives.). Moton succeeded

in blocking this unnamed candidate, a Southerner. The Hampton board instead selected James Gregg, a Northern minister who would become a quiet advocate for racial equity and would turn Hampton into a legitimate college (J. E. Gregg, Letter to A. A. Rockefeller, Box 66, Group III 2G, OMRO; Wolters, *The New Negro on Campus*, 230–75.).

46. *A Brief Sketch of the Development of Tuskegee Institute* (Tuskegee, AL: Tuskegee Institute Press, 1940), 5–6.

47. James Gray, *The University of Minnesota, 1851–1951* (Minneapolis: University of Minnesota Press, 1951), 314.

48. A. B. Johnson, "From the Beginning: The History of Developmental Education and the Pre-1932 General College Idea," in *The General College Vision: Integrating Intellectual Growth, Multicultural Perspectives, and Student Development*, ed. Jeanne L. Higbee et al. (Minneapolis: University of Minnesota Press, 2005), 55.

49. Gray, *The University of Minnesota*, 308–22.

50. Lagemann, *Private Power*, 102–03.

51. Gray, *The University of Minnesota*, 318.

52. H. S. Pritchett, "Confidential Memorandum for the Executive Committee," November 7, 1933, Box 11, CFATR. Despite his efforts toward class-based egalitarianism through the General College, Coffman was also a bigot who discriminated against Black and Jewish students at Minnesota ("Report of the Task Force on Building Names and Institutional History" [University of Minnesota, 2019], 13–45, https://university-history.dl.umn.edu/.).

53. The Hampton board chose MacLean because of his "long and varied background of experience in the selection and guidance of the student, and in shaping the curriculum to meet current vocational opportunities" ("Dr. Malcolm S. MacLean to Become President of Hampton Institute on July 1," *Richmond Times-Dispatch*, May 8, 1940.).

54. Fosdick, *Adventure in Giving*, 131–136.

55. W. Buttrick, Letter to H. S. Pritchett, May 5, 1920, Box 52, CFATR.

56. Fosdick, *Adventure in Giving*, 226–38. In a strange twist, Flexner's partner in organizing the IAS was Oscar Veblen, a Princeton mathematician and Thorstein Veblen's nephew.

57. The Carnegie Foundation for the Advancement of Teaching, *A Statement to the Teachers in the Associated Colleges and Universities* (Boston: The Merrymount Press, 1918).

58. A. O. Lovejoy, "The Metamorphosis of the Carnegie Foundation," *Science* 37, 954 (1913): 546–52.

59. H. S. Pritchett, Letter to H. C. King, May 24, 1917, Box 32, CFATR.

60. "List of Carnegie Publications, 1906-2011," Carnegie Foundation Archive, http://archive.carnegiefoundation.org/publications/publications_list.html, accessed on May 1, 2020.

61. D. T. Williams, "Henry Suzzallo and the University of a Thousand Years," *History of Higher Education Annual* 5, 1 (1985): 57–82.

62. G. C. Earl, Letter to E. A. Dickson, October 3, 1919, Box 18, EADP.

63. H. S. Pritchett, "Confidential Memorandum for the Executive Committee," October 13, 1933, Box 11, CFATR.

64. F. C. Ferry, Letter to H. S. Pritchett, November 21, 1933, Box 11, CFATR.

65. W. A. Jessup, "Address by Walter A. Jessup at Inauguration of Eugene Gilmore as President of State Univ. of Iowa," 1934, Box 37, CFATR.

66. H. J. Savage, "Walter Albert Jessup," press release, 1944, Box 37, CFATR.

67. H. J. Savage, Letter to R. H. Palmer, August 20, 1935, Box 37, CFATR.

68. Jessup, "The Integrity of the American College," 5.

69. *Report of the Commissioner of Education* (1905), 537, 541, 755; *Biennial Survey of Education in the United States, 1936-1938* (US Office of Education Bulletin 1940, No. 2) (Washington, DC: Government Printing Office, 1942), 27.

70. Hawkins, *Banding Together*, 111.

71. J. R. Thelin, *The Rising Costs of Higher Education: A Reference Handbook* (Santa Barbara, CA: ABC-CLIO, 2013), 20–21.

72. S. M. Stoke, "What Price Tuition," *Journal of Higher Education* 8, 6 (1937): 297–303.

73. C. D. Goldin and L. F. Katz, *The Race between Education and Technology* (Cambridge, MA: Harvard University Press, 2009), 266–77.

74. W. J. Greenleaf, *Junior Colleges* (US Office of Education Bulletin 1936, No. 3) (Washington, DC: Government Printing Office, 1936), 16–21.

75. Greenleaf, *Junior Colleges*, 25.

76. Greenleaf, *Junior Colleges*, 25–28; M. W. Simpson, "National Emergency and Federal Junior Colleges in New Jersey." *American Educational History Journal* 34, 1/2: 173–87.

77. W. S. Learned, Letter to C. Furst, January 18, 1921, Box 38, CFATR.

78. "Faculties Welcome New Title for Schools; Fredericksburg Students Rejoice Over Action of General Assembly," *Richmond Times-Dispatch*, February 11, 1924.

79. Dunham, *Colleges of the Forgotten Americans*, 27–37.

80. Arthur W. Tarbell, *The Story of Carnegie Tech: Being a History of Carnegie Institute of Technology from 1900 to 1935* (Pittsburgh: Carnegie Institute Press, 1937), 51–76.

81. Tarbell, *The Story of Carnegie Tech*, 255.

82. R. Dilworth, and S. G. Knowles, "Timeline of Drexel History, 1889-Present," in *Building Drexel: The University and Its City 1891-2016* (Philadelphia: Temple University Press, 2016), xv–xxvii.

83. J. E. Brittain, and R. C. McMath Jr., "Engineers and the New South Creed: The Formation and Early Development of Georgia Tech," *Technology and Culture* 18, 2 (1977): 175–201.

84. R. B. Wallace, *Dress Her in White and Gold: A Biography of Georgia Tech* (Atlanta: Georgia Tech Foundation, 1963), 386–90; F. Litsky, "In 1916, a Blowout for the Ages," *New York Times*, October 7, 2006.

85. W. H. Robinson, *The History of Hampton Institute 1868-1949* (PhD diss., New York University, 1953), 161.

86. Holland, *Nathan B. Young*, 115–75.

87. Du Bois, "The General Education Board."

88. Dalton, *The Long Road to Recognition*, 116–34.

89. R. L. Kelly, "The Sphere and Possibilities of the Association," *Association of American Colleges Bulletin* 2, 3 (1916): 22.

90. D. Riesman, *Constraint and Variety in American Education* (Lincoln, NE: University of Nebraska Press, 1956), 31. See also G. Grant and D. Riesman, *The Perpetual Dream: Reform and Experiment in the American College* (Chicago: University of Chicago Press, 1978).

91. C. S. Boucher, "Current Changes and Experiments in Liberal-Arts Colleges," in *Changes and Experiments in Liberal-Arts Education*, ed. G. M. Whipple (Bloomington, IL: Public School Publishing Co., 1932), 9.

92. F. V. Speek, "One Hundred Twenty-Eight Outstanding Changes and Experiments," in Whipple, *Changes and Experiments*, 43–156.

93. A. Flexner, "Introduction," in R. C. Brooks, *Reading for Honors at Swarthmore: A Record of the First Five Years, 1922–1927* (New York: Oxford University Press, 1927).

94. "Reading for Honors at Swarthmore," *New York Times*, December 11, 1927.

95. Rudolph, *The American College and University*, 458.

96. Adam R. Nelson, *Education and Democracy: The Meaning of Alexander Meiklejohn, 1872–1964* (Madison: University of Wisconsin Press, 2001), 67–72.

97. Nelson, *Education and Democracy*, 99–102.

98. Nelson, 111–25.

99. E. D. Cronon and J. W. Jenkins, *The University of Wisconsin: A History, 1925–1945*, vol. 3 (Madison: University of Wisconsin Press, 1994), 125.

100. Nelson, *Education and Democracy*, 133–96; Cronon and Jenkins, *The University of Wisconsin*, 143–210.

101. H. T. Parlin, "The History of Plan II Honors," typescript from *Daily Texan*, reprinted by University of Texas College of Liberal Arts, https://liberalarts.utexas.edu/plan2/about/history.php, accessed on July 1, 2020.

102. G. Grant and D. Riesman, "St. John's and the Great Books," *Change: The Magazine of Higher Learning* 6, 4 (1974): 28–63.

103. W. F. Kuehl, *Hamilton Holt: Journalist, Internationalist, Educator* (Gainesville: University of Florida Press, 1960), 179–232.

104. Louis Adamic, "Education on a Mountain: The Story of Black Mountain College," *Harper's Magazine*, April 1936, 516–29. Experimenters often supported each other, despite their very different missions; Frank Aydellotte, who created Swarthmore's honors program, was one of Black Mountain's chief boosters. He urged Jessup to support it, writing, "They have no endowment or plant, but they do have ideas. . . . They are doing some things which no other institution could do. . . . It is a courageous little place, and you have only got to know it to want to help it" (F. Aydelotte, Letter to W. A. Jessup, March 25, 1936, Box 45, CFATR.).

105. Grant and Riesman (*The Perpetual Dream*, 21–24,) call Bennington and Black Mountain the leading exemplars of the "aesthetic-expressive" model of liberal arts education, which influenced not only scores of small colleges but also the

extensive arts programs of big universities like Northwestern, Boston University, and Brigham Young.

106. *Bennington College: A New College of Liberal Arts for Women*, self-published brochure, 1929, 18. For more on Finley, see M. E. Gettleman, *An Elusive Presence: The Discovery of John H. Finley and His America* (Chicago: University of Chicago Press, 1979).

107. L. W. Jones, "The Bennington Idea in Action," *The Journal of Higher Education* 18, 5 (1947): 238–43.

108. Rudolph, *The American College*, 476–77.

109. S. R. Herr, *Connected Thoughts: A Reinterpretation of the Reorganization of Antioch College in the 1920s* (Lanham, MD: University Press of America, 1996), 93–103.

110. Burton R. Clark, *The Distinctive College: Antioch, Reed and Swarthmore* (Chicago: Aldine, 1970), 30–31; Herr, *Connected Thoughts*, 59–71.

111. Herr, *Connected Thoughts*, 17–34.

112. Herr, 165.

113. Levine, *The American College*, 49.

114. Drexel initiated a co-operative model for its engineering program in 1919; today, it and Northeastern are the most famous "co-op" schools.

115. Fosdick, *Adventure in Giving*, 252.

116. Jessup, "Address by Walter A. Jessup."

117. W. S. Learned, Letter to W. A. Jessup, March 6, 1935, Box 38, CFATR.

118. Jessup, Walter A., "Improving the Quality of Training for Individuals" (typescript of speech before the Southern University Conference, December 4, 1936, Box 37, CFATR.

119. Ris, "Hierarchy as a Theme," 57-61.

120. Earle D. Ross, *Democracy's College: The Land-Grant Movement in the Formative Stage* (Ames, IA: Iowa State College Press, 1942), 70, 150.

121. J. M. Thomas, "The Present Trend of Education from the More Cultural to the More Practical: Does It Mean Loss or Gain?" Speech typescript, 1925, Box 36, CFATR.

122. B. I. Bell, "Statement of President Bell to Dr. Learned and Others," c. 1930, Box 45, CFATR.

123. Quoted in J. C. Brazzell, "Brick without Straw: Missionary-Sponsored Black Higher Education in the Post-Emancipation Era," *The Journal of Higher Education* 63, 1 (1992): 38.

124. "To Thoughtful Givers," *Berea Quarterly* 13, 3 (1909), 20, emphasis original.

125. "A Program for Mountain Uplift," *Berea Quarterly* 14, 3 (1910): 23.

126. "Trinity College: Bulletin of Important Facts," self-published brochure, 1909.

127. Ethan W. Ris, "God and Man at Yali College: The Short, Troubled History of an American College in China," *History of Education* 49, 2 (2020): 184–208.

128. "E. S. Harkness Gave $3,000,000 to Harvard," *Boston Globe*, December 27, 1928.

129. "E. S. Harkness Gave $3,000,000 to Harvard."

130. S. E. Morison, *Three Centuries of Harvard, 1636-1936* (Cambridge, MA: Harvard University Press, 1936), 476–77.

131. "Harvard House Plan Assailed at Yale," *Boston Globe*, October 7, 1931. The Yale publication, pointedly titled the *Harkness Hoot*, was closely aligned with Robert Hutchins's vision of higher education as a destination for intellectual elites. In 1931, its coeditor praised Hutchins's reforms at Chicago alongside Rollins College and Wisconsin's Experimental College, for working toward "making higher university training open only to exceptional men" and rejecting "attempts to hedge between the democratic ideal of mass education and the ideal of developing intellectual leaders"—in other words, rejecting the new consensus (quoted in "Consummate Intellect," *Harvard Crimson*, May 2, 1931.).

132. "E. S. Harkness Gave $3,000,000 to Harvard."

133. S. R. Jones and D. L. Stewart, "Evolution of Student Development Theory," *New Directions for Student Services* 154 (2016): 17–28.

134. "The Student Personnel Point of View," *American Council on Education Studies* 1, 3 (1937): 1.

135. Levine, *The American College*, 76. YMCA branches also established their own baccalaureate colleges: more than two dozen between 1916 and the 1930s, including, most notably, Northeastern University (D.E. Finnegan and B. Cullaty, "Origins of the YMCA Universities: Organizational Adaptations in Urban Education," *History of Higher Education Annual* 21, 1 (2001): 47–77.

136. L. B. Johnson, "Higher Education Act of 1965: The President's Remarks upon Signing the Bill at Southwest Texas State College," *Weekly Compilation of Presidential Documents* 1, 16 (1965): 478–81.

137. J. H. Finley, "The Ideal College," *Education* 35, 5 (1915): 320–328.

CONCLUSION

1. K. E. Weick, "Educational Organizations as Loosely Coupled Systems," *Administrative Science Quarterly* 21, 1 (1976): 1–19.

2. J. H. Holland, "Complex Adaptive Systems," *Daedalus* 121, 1 (1992): 17–30.

3. J. Ma and S. Baum, "Trends in Community Colleges: Enrollment, Prices, Student Debt, and Completion," College Board Research Brief, last modified April 2016, https://research.collegeboard.org/pdf/trends-community-colleges-research-brief.pdf. "Education deserts" exist in which there is no accessible broad-access college, but these areas are home to only a small percentage of the US population. (Nicholas W. Hillman, "Geography of College Opportunity: The Case of Education Deserts," *American Educational Research Journal* 53, 4 [2016]: 987–1021.)

4. E. J. James, "The Function of the State University," *University of Illinois Bulletin* 3, 1: 448–9.

5. Clark, *The Distinctive College*. As of 2018, four-year colleges that enrolled fewer than five thousand students and in which at least half of students lived on campus (a very generous definition of "liberal arts colleges") accounted for just 8.5 per-

cent of the overall US student body, including graduate students (Carnegie Classification of Institutions of Higher Education, "Classification Summary Table," http://carnegieclassifications.iu.edu/downloads/CCIHE2018-SummaryTables. xlsx, accessed on October 15, 2020.).

6. Levine, *The American College*, 21.

7. Clark, "The 'Cooling-Out' Function," 569–76.

INDEX

AAC (Association of American Colleges), 6, 232, 238–42; Committee on Academic Freedom, 245–46; as counter to AAU, 237; defense against the reformers, 238–40; rapprochement with the academic engineers, 240–42

AAJC (American Association of Junior Colleges), 253–54

AAU (Association of American Universities), 155–156; and academic engineers, 233; Committee on Classification, 233–34; criticism of, 234; membership, 233; relationship with CFAT, 61; role in establishing elite tier of universities, 61

AAUP (American Association of University Professors), 6, 209, 242–46; 1915 General Declaration of Principles, 245; as challenge to academic engineers, 243; conflict with AAC, 245–46; exclusivity, 244; rapprochement with AAC, 248; rapprochement with CFAT, 248

ACA (Association of Collegiate Alumnae), 252–53

"Academic and Industrial Efficiency" (Cooke Report), 20–21, 210

"academic charisma," 223–24

academic engineering (movement): antipathy toward liberal arts, 125; bigotry of, 149–61; on coeducation, 150–52; critics of, 195–221; ethos of, 15–16; focus on institutions, not individuals, 3–4, 22, 53, 60, 93, 124; against localism, 94, 206; positionality, 17–18; principles, 19; reverence for engineering, 19, 21–22; standardization and hierarchy, 35, 49, 89–90, 94, 109, 128, 149, 239

academic engineers (cohort), 4, 15–49; attenuation, 7, 118, 235–36, 263–64; German graduate education, 18, 117; how to identify, 16–19; interlocking directorate, 16, 40; outsider status, 18–19, 48–49. See also *individuals listed in Appendix*

academic freedom, 1, 210, 243, 244, 248, 317n10

accreditation, 256–61; Black colleges, 256; Catholic Educational Association, 256; process, 260–61; regional associations, 256–60; Samuel Capen rejects, 260–61. See also self-study

ACE (American Council on Education), 6, 233, 236–37, 260, 356n17; as lobbying group, 236; "the whole student" (1937), 289

ACNY (Association of Colleges for Negro Youth), 254–56, 280; as national accrediting agency for Black colleges, 256

Adams, Herbert Baxter, 81, 95, 142, 146

Addams, Jane, 126

administrative progressives (K12 education), 16–17, 92, 309n8

admissions, college, 58, 259, 273; certificate system, 92–93; discriminatory, 157–58, 296

Veblen, Thorstein: critique of academic engineers, 213; critique of vocational training, 213–14; *The Higher Learning in America: A Memorandum on the Conduct of Universities by Business Men*, 213–15, 266
Vermont, CFAT study, 133, 206–7
vertical integration, 91, 94, 198
Veysey, Lawrence, 32, 128, 313n83
Villard, Oswald Garrison, 178, 217, 226
Vincent, George E., 146–47, 265, 272–73
Virginia, higher education in, 334n49; faculty segregation, 229; normal schools, 278–79; women's colleges, 154
The Visible Hand (Chandler), 90–92

Washington, Booker T., 18, 46–48, 125–26; as academic engineer, 46, 162–63, 177; "Atlanta Compromise," 166, 341n87; Carnegie-funded pension, 47; code switching, 46; control of Black postsecondary education, 177–78; death of, 180–81; on Fisk and Howard boards, 168, 171; hostility to liberal arts, 160, 341n90; restrictionism, 48; sexism, 166–67; threatened by ANISS, 178–79; *Up from Slavery*, 46, 316n155. *See also* Tuskegee Institute, "Tuskegee Machine"
Washington College (Tennessee), 66, 68–69
Washington state, higher education in, 110–11; normal schools, 134
"Wealth" (Carnegie, 1889), 29
Weaver College, 71
Weber, Max, 84, 325n9
Webster, Daniel, 231
Wechsler, Harold, 92, 150, 155
Wellesley College, 144, 225
Wells, Ida B., 226

Wesleyan University, 285; denominational severance, 75; ending coeducation, 149–50
Western Reserve University. *See* Case Western Reserve University
Wheeler, Benjamin, 18; AAU involvement, 234; criticized by Upton Sinclair, 216; and junior colleges, 154; opposition to UCLA founding, 117–18, 295
White, Andrew D., 29–30, 82, 94–95; national university support, 99–101; support for Illinois College, 223
Whitewater Normal School, 131
"whole student," 289. *See also* student development
Wiebe, Robert, 89
Wilbur, Ray Lyman, 18, 141; on Yeshiva University, 158
Williams College, 67, 157
Wilson, Woodrow, 7, 218, 282; and Berea College, 189–90; at Bryn Mawr College, 153; as politician, 10, 198–99, 263; at Princeton University, 100, 127; racism of, 161, 226; sexism of, 150, 153
Winship, Albert, 249–50
Wisconsin, higher education in, 110, 130–31, 144; normal schools, 131, 259
"Wisconsin Idea." *See* University of Wisconsin
Wolters, Raymond, 173–74
women in higher education, 6, 149–54; group repulsion and segregation, 150–51; lack of graduate education, 154; and normal schools, 250; quotas on enrollment, 150. *See also individual women's colleges*
Women's College Coalition, 251
Wood, James M., 253
Woodson, Carter, obituary of Jones, 180